ENMITY

Remains Unresolved Until Christ Returns!

Past, Present, Future, Who Decides?

Gen 3: 15

Athanasius-John T. Nkomo

Athanasius-John T. Nkomo

Copyright © 2016. All rights reserved.

No part of this publication may be reproduced, stored in a retrieval system or transmitted in any way by any means, electronic, mechanical, photocopy, recording or otherwise, without the prior permission of the author except as provided by USA copyright law.

The opinions expressed by the author are not necessarily those of Revival Waves of Glory Books & Publishing.

Published by Revival Waves of Glory Books & Publishing

PO Box 5961 Litchfield, Illinois 62056 USA

www.revivalwavesofgloryministries.com

Revival Waves of Glory Books & Publishing is committed to excellence in the publishing industry.

Book design Copyright © 2016 by Revival Waves of Glory Books & Publishing. All rights reserved.

Published in the United States of America

Paperback: 978-1-68411-107-7

Athanasius-John T. Nkomo

**Jesus Christ is the way, life, and truth to
The Father in heaven [John 14: 6]**

Athanasius-John T. Nkomo

CONTENTS

Introduction 5
Chapter 1 10
Chapter 2 26
Chapter 3 134
Chapter 4 155
Chapter 6 197
Chapter 7 243
Chapter 8 323
Chapter 9 329
Chapter 10 380
Chapter 11 415
Chapter 12 425
Chapter 13 454
Unmatched Jesus Christ 478

Athanasius-John T. Nkomo

Introduction

I wrote this unmatched book for everyone to read and know that there is the living God forever! This book has no specific audience in mind, but it is for all people who care deeply seeking about God in the radiance of Jesus Christ the most highly commented perfect human being who came down from heaven lived on earthly life for 32 years and ascended to heaven. He is right now standing on the right hand of God Almighty in heaven!. I wrote this book for a number of reasons as a result of mass Enmity unreformed churches, denominations, and doctrines with a variety of interpretations and definitions that contradict God's truth. In other words, I wrote this book for people like me the person I was 50 years ago: Unmatched God's word in Christ compelled me to write!

I was born and raised in devastating poverty: My parents were illiterate: My grandfather practiced witchcraft, and he smoked me to cast out the evil spirits, according to Zulu's custom. Like every other child born into hopelessness of legalized apartheid, in South Africa, I learned to measure my life in Jesus Christ in days, weeks, months, and years! I educated myself because my parents who are illiterate, did not send me to school. I rose from the squalor and humiliation of days with no food to eat. Yet, I learned with Biblical knowledge that all men are created in the image of God and his likeness equally! This extra-ordinary faith is grounded in the belief that Jesus Christ is Lord and is the ultimate Judge of all mankind in the whole entire universe!. Also, I wrote this book for another audience those who have been struggling to persuade their relatives, friends, and neighbors, teachers, co-workers, or even politicians, religious, and others community representatives that something is eerily familiar about the way our modern world justice system operates, economic, social, but who have lacked the facts and data to back their claims about God. It is my hope and prayer that this book empowers you and allows you to fear God, speak your truth greater conviction, credibility, and courage to stand up like a house built on Christ a solid rocky stands unshaken forever!.

Last, but, definitely not least, I wrote this book for those trapped within world's latest vulnerable people like leper-caste system (Poverty, disease, and racism-apartheid): You may be locked up in or locked out of mainstream world's society, but you are not forgotten by God!

The Living Word of God Almighty in Christ is unmatched with all humankind's wisdom and intelligence. Unmatched God all is to look to Him and get saved all you ends of the earth! For God in Christ is unmatched eternal; indeed; he is unmatched there is no other God! [Is. 45: 22-23]

South Africa Children
(I am the smallest standing beside the lady)

"**Fleecy Lock and black complexion cannot forfeit nature's claim! Skin may differ, but affection dwells in black and white much the same! Were, I so tall to reach to the poll, or to grasp to the ocean-span; I must be measured by my soul! The mind is the standard of the man! "Let justice run down**

like water! And righteousness like mighty stream!" (Amos 5: 24): Glory to God Almighty! [M. L. King, Jr.

The fruit of Enmity is:

- **Feeling condition of: Ill-will hostility; hatred; conflict; crafting;**
- **Profligacy; grotesque; animosity, antagonism; disagreement; disobedience**
- **Bitterness springing up and defiling many nations! Long list, but**
- **Mention few.**

And I will put Enmity between you and the woman, between your seed (offspring) and her seed; will crush your head, and you will strike his heel!" (Gen 3: 14-19):

God places Enmity between the Serpent and the woman, between the seed (offspring) of both crushing each other: God proceeds with the sentencing, accepting full human being's responsibility and bringing all parties within the scope of the announcement. God, indeed, acts as Supreme Judge, calling each individual person of the participants before the [Throne Judgment Authority] (in the order of Genesis 3: 1-19) accordingly, and pronouncing sentence on each person "individually" in typical Supreme Judicial Courtroom Speech: "Because you have done this, God said: "Cursed are you above all livestock and above all beasts of the field, on your belly you shall crow and dust you shall eat all the days of your life." Which immediately takes effect) till this day! [Verse 14-15]: Yet, even in the sentencing, God remains in relationship with [creature] human beings involved, connected and concerned well enough to identify further what has just happened.

What are the effects of the sentencing? Enmity; God's prediction can and have the answers to our compelling questions. Most basically, the sentences pertain to their primary roles in life even more today modern' era; (in that of the past culture and present culture) roles of variety stature among the peoples and wild animals, roles of woman (wife) and mother, roles of tiller of soil and provider of food (the husband-father): Compared to the intense fury, the cries of excruciation pain, and the rivers of tears in the first three [Enmity] poems conveys a sense of exhaustion and remoteness, as strong man had brought sorrow and fury as far as they could go, so we are even more involved in enmity matters on daily basis until Christ returns. The major theme of enmity is the diminishment of life, the dimming of glory, the quite extinguishing of the future. Several of the enmity literary features works together with the theme to create what might be called a "people of diminishment." These include a less engaged speaker, a shortened acrostic form, and the absence of divine address. "God is not mocked:" Perhaps of equal importance to the reduced acrostic for the artful representation of diminishment of life is the bitterness springing up and defiling many on earth, omission of any speech addressed to God. During the wilderness, the people tested God's ability to lead them to the Promised Land, everyone else who deviated from God's path they perished. Unlike all the other persons during the exodus, never speaks to, indeed barely mentions, God: It is as emotions of the first three chapters have reached a pitch and are now spent, although nothing has changed: The Enmity evokes, suggests, and conveys with great clarity the sense of diminishment, dulling, and devastation that afflicts the nations and its populace. The Enmity divides nations into four thematic units:

1. **Dimming of Everything! Everything Grows Dully [e.g., Social Economic,**

2. **Sweating on faces for earning daily bread, but ever dissatisfied!**

3. **Retelling of the Attacked Ever Persists**
4. **Future Reversal God' Righteous Judgment (verses 21-22; 17-20; 11-16)**
5. **Unmatched God's word truth prevails. Jesus Christ is inevitable!**

Athanasius-John T. Nkomo

Chapter 1

ENMITY

Remain Unresolved Until

Christ Returns!

Past: Present: Future:

Who Decides? [Gen 3: 15]

"In the sweat of your face you shall eat bread:

Till you return to the ground: For out of it

You were taken: "For dust you are: And to

Dust you shall return!" God said to Adam.

[Gen 3: 19]

None can neglect or defer this work, but at the most fearful peril to our souls: It rests with us to cooperate with Christ Jesus who came down from heaven with the work of conforming/transforming characters to the divine perfect model. Enmity, it is what God most hats! Enmity is the most heinous sinful nature that mostly grieves God's heart since its existence in the beginning **[Bereshith]** in Eden Garden. The First man God had made disobeyed Him. Enmity is the highest treason crime that man ever commits on earth!. Breaking God's Perfect Law: It is an inexcusable crime! It constitutes the highest price to pay, resulting death: There was no death to begin with because God never dies. Now man chose death, so God allows it. As is written in the prophecy: "Do not seal up the words of the prophecy of this book, because the time is near:

- **Let him who does wrong continue to do wrong**
- **Let him who is vile continue to be vile**
- **Let him who does right continue to do right**
- **And let him who is holy continue to be holy!**
- **Let him who is righteous continue to be righteous!**
- **And merciful to continue merciful! [Rev. 22: 10-11]**
- **John's vision at Patmos Island**

God designed the human machine to run on himself. God is the fuel of our Spirits, were designed to burn continually no limit! Enmity creates unnecessarily limit to every God's fuel burning spirits. So God imposed Enmity allowing man's death as he deserves it. Still, God never dies for that reason God raised up Christ Jesus on the third day! It is the promise that stands for everyone who believes in the name of the Lord Jesus Christ, shall live forever! The teaching of Christ Jesus is practical! Living Christ' like draws all peoples to God! But Enmity causes people to separate from God unaware. Disobedient and hostility is instinct and tendency: It is so natural for many people to miss-behave in the sight of God because Enmity blinds them. Resistance; bitterness and disbelieving God's truth against God bring judgments to all nations on earth! A shining seraph, "son of the morning star;" how change, how degraded. From the council where once he was honored, he is forever excluded. Lucifer/Satan common known today seems paralyzed as he looks the glory and majesty of Christ. He who was once a covering cherub remembers when he has fallen:

Athanasius-John T. Nkomo

He has seen the crown placed upon the head of Christ by angel of lofty stature and majestic presence, and he knows that the exalted position of this angel might have been his at early years when he lived in heavenly paradise. Now he longs to be reinstated, which will never be from henceforth and forever. How sad will be the occasion for Lucifer. Enmity, which he brought upon himself on his neck it cannot be removed. Memory recalls the home of his innocence and purity, the peace and content that were his until he indulged in murmuring against God his maker, and envy of Christ. His accusations, his rebellion, his deceptions, to gain the sympathy and support of the angels, his stubborn persistence in making no effort for self-recovery or repentance when God would have granted him forgiveness all come vividly before him. It will also to all those who follow after him as they believe in him. He reviews his work among men and its results the Enmity of men toward his fellow men, the terrible destruction of life, the rise and fall of kingdoms, the overturning thrones, the long succession of tumults, conflicts, hostilities, resistance, disagreement, and grotesque profligate and revolutions, etc.: Lucifer recalls his constant efforts to oppose the perfect word of Christ and God's perfect Law: And to sink men lover and lower. Enmity, the highest treason crime now confronts him un-denied truth. He sees that his hellish plots have been powerless to destroy those who have put their trust in Christ Jesus. Like the day that the British Colonialism and South Africa apartheid rule that dominated African Indigenous for decades: They watched as their flags were slowing down, while the new African original flag rapidly rising up vividly showing their own restoring inheritance from God for good!

As Mahatma Gandhi predicted: "I want to teach your hearts: Only then will you change." Jesus Christ is inevitable!

As Lucifer/Satan looks upon his wicked kingdom, the fruit of his toil, he sees only total failure and ruin. He has led the multitudes to believe that the City of Mighty God would be an easy prey: He sowed the thistle seed and wild-thorns seed and so he reaps them as he sowed: But he knew that this is false: Like everyone who follows after him they know this false. Enmity; again and again, in the progress of the greatest grotesque profligate, has been defeated and compelled to yield!.

"Let him who is taught the word share in all good things with him who teaches: Do not be deceived: God is not mocked! For whatever a man sows, that he will reap!" [Gal 6: 6-9]. Enmity it is absolute self-destruction by choice like a farm that chose seeds. You ought to recognize its existence and acknowledge before the sight of the Sovereign Lord God the maker, and the Sustainer of all life. You and I well know that Satan knows too well the power and majesty of God's eternal powerful! God's Sovereignty, there's nothing is difficult for Him!. The aim of the a great rebel, hostility; hatred envy; crafting; disobedience; resistance; and disagreement has ever been to justify himself and to disapprove the divine authority-government responsibility for the rebellion! Lucifer's techniques and device is about crafting and cunning, deceitful for self-gain. Everyone else is practicing this crafting and cunning language everywhere on earth today! Particularly, those who are popular publishing houses, un-popular author meaningful books are despised by them through their crafting language. They reject the best-quality written Christian books by un-popular authors. So they stimulate reinforce for self-publishing houses who also screw un-popular authors. They re-sell the ebook to the author with large sums of money! At the end the vulnerable author gets nothing!. To this end he has bent all the power of his giant intellect!. He has worked deliberately and systematically, and with marvelous success, leading vast multitudes to accept his version of the great crafting-cunning language which has been so long in progress. The habits are deep! No easy way to radical eradicate such deep rooted habits at hearts. It works well for them. Truly, they are against God! All that surrounds them are God's providences. They own nothing! See Job. "You are born naked: You shall go to dust naked!" It is not faking fact: But truth!

For thousands of years, this chief-thief of conspiracy has palmed off falsehood-cheating for truth. But the time has now come when the rebellion, grotesque profligacy is to be finally defeated and the history and character of evil-Satan disclosed. Remember that God searches the heart of everyone's motives. The Bible has all evidence clear. Nothing can be hidden from the eyes of God. He knows well all your thoughts before you actually take the initiative - step forward. God is most genius: He makes it all for his glory. He is undefeated! All things are under His feet! It is well said:

"Heaven is my throne: The earth is my footstool!" [Isaiah 66: 1-3].

In his last (Satan) great effort to dethrone Christ, destroy his people, and Take possession of the city of Mighty God, the arch-deceiver has been fully unmasked! Those who have united with him see the total failure of his Cause. Jesus Christ' followers and the loyal angels behold the full extent of his machinations against the authority and government of the Mighty God!. He is the object of universal abhorrence!. The common phrase Satan sees that his voluntary rebellion, resistance, disagreement, hostiles, Enmity has unfitted him for heaven!. He has trained his feeble powers to war against God: The purity, peace, and harmony of heaven would be to him supreme torture! His accusations against the mercy and justice of God are now silenced: Mute!

The reproach which he has endeavored for years to cast the Christ rests wholly upon himself. And now Satan bows down and confesses the justice of his sentence. This is how Christ will ultimately radical eradicated Enmity once and for all! Jesus Christ is indeed, inevitable!

Read the Scriptures carefully. "And let us not grow weary while doing good, for in due season we shall reap if we do not lose hearts." But God forbid that I should boast except in the "Cross" of our Lord Christ Jesus, by whom the world has been crucified to me and me to the world." [Gal 6: 9; 14.] "Who shall not fear You, O Lord God: And glorify your name?" You only are holy: For all nations shall come and worship before you: For your judgments are made manifest." [V. 4]. Glory to God Almighty!

Every question of truth and untruth-error in the long standing grotesque profligacy has now been made plain-naked in the eyes of God as well as the wicked untruth. The results of every rebellion; profligacy; hostiles; disobedience; cheating; crafting-cunning, the fruits of setting aside the divine statutes, have all been laid down open to the view of all created human intelligences to fall-short in the eyes of God the maker of all perfect measure justice: The working out of Lucifer/Satan's rule in contrast with the perfect authority-Government of the Mighty God has been presented to the whole universe! No more contradicting Enmity dispute!. But silence-speechless only: Mute at last! Lucifer's own works have condemned him; including all who followed after him.

God's wisdom, His perfect justice, law, and His goodness stand fully vindicated!. The Lord Christ Jesus Crown triumph, victory! It is seen that all his dealings in the great persecution have been conducted with respect to the eternal good of all his people who followed after him and the good of the worlds shall be blessed!. The entire world that he has created shall be saved! "All your works shall praise you, o Lord God: And your Saints shall bless you!" [Psalm 145: 10].

The history of Enmity-Sin nature will stand to all eternity as a witness that with the existence of the Lord God's Perfect Law is bound up the happiness of all the human-beings that God has created!.

The beauty-sound music shall exceedingly boom around the whole entire world once and for all!. This prophecy is bound to take place at God's precise timing!. The Bible evidences are vividly clear to all believers! With all the facts of the great persecution; Enmity-Sinful in view, the whole universe, both current world affairs loyal and rebellious, with one accord declares! "Justice and truth are your ways Lord God Almighty! Thou King of Saints! Before the universe has been clearly presented or formed the great sacrifice made by the Father and the Son in man's behalf: The hour has come when Christ occupied his rightful position and is glorified above principalities and powers and every name that in name, Christ is above all!. All knees shall bow down before Him!. And Confess: "Jesus Christ is Lord!" Enmity, indeed, will cease! Who dares to believe this truth? Let him believe: Even deny: Jesus Christ is inevitable!.

It was the joy that was set before Him: That He might bring many people unto glory: That He endured the cross and despised the shameful-Enmity: And inconceivably great as was the sorrow and the shame: Yet greater is the joy and the glory! We need, and ought to remind ourselves beyond measure that Jesus Christ is Lord!. He looks upon the redeemed, renewed in His own image, every heart bearing the perfect impress of the divine; every face reflecting the likeness of their King. How magnificent; how marvelous; how wonderful and joy ever to stand! He beholds in them the result of the travail of His soul: And He is satisfied. The result of over-coming Enmity, is glorious End.

Then, in a voice that reaches the assembled multitudes of the righteous and the wicked: He declares: "Behold the purchase of My blood!" For these I suffered, for these I died: That they might dwell in My Presence throughout eternal ages!" How sweet is the name of Jesus' sound into the ears of a believer?" Very appropriate saying: And the song of praise ascends from the white-robed ones about the throne: "Worthy is the Lamb that was slain to receive power, and riches, and wisdom, and strength, and honor, and glory, and blessing." All that he deserves God granted: [Rev. 5: 12].

Notwithstanding that Satan has been constrained to acknowledge God's justice and to bow to the supremacy of Christ, his character remains unchanged. The spirit of rebellion-disobedient like a mighty torrent, again bursts forth. Filled with frenzy, he determines not to yield the great grotesque profligacy. Enmity stands against him. His shape remains unchanged. The time has come for a last desperate struggle against the King of heaven. He rushes into the midst of his subjects and endeavors to inspire them with crafting and cunning language with his own fury and arouse them to instant battle. He still has no rest, but ever-restless Enmity within himself knowing that it is his last minute for everlasting termination. He sees Christ, his final terminator-sword. He dares not to look. But all the countless millions whom he has allured into rebellion, there are none now to recognize and acknowledge his wicked supremacy. Like Pharaoh at Red Seas: He saw all his mighty horsemen floating on the seashore speechless while Israelites walked on dry land. Like the day of British colonialism: They saw their flags slowing down while new Africa flag rising up rapidly forever! The whole Africa continent was set free from their Enmity rebellion. God restores their inheritance for good!. Will man ever learn from past history? "I want to teach your hearts: Only then will you change." Who can change a man's heart? If not God the maker of all goodness: Enmity will persist until Christ returns. I repeat in saying this for your own understanding benefit. His power is an end. The wicked are filled with the same Enmity hostiles and hatred of God that inspires Satan: But they see that their case is hopeless: That they cannot prevail against the Mighty God their maker! Who is greater?

The clay or the potter! Their rage is kindled against Satan and those who have been his agents in deception, and with the fury of demons they turn upon them. This is the truth as we see it being practiced everywhere around the world. Past history is written to remind us about the past that it remains with us even today. History ought to change our shape, but it shall never change our shape until Christ returns. He is able to change our shapes. He creates a new world with new shape of hearts. God said: "Because you have set thine heart as the heart of God: Look, therefore I will bring strangers upon you, the terrible of the nations: And they shall draw their swords against the beauty of thy wisdom, and they shall defile thy brightness: They shall bring you down to the pit." [Ezek 28: 6-8, 16-19]. Enmity Lucifer, God imposed upon him. [Gen 3: 15]. God reminds ancient Israel about Lucifer's Enmity upon them. He judged them. So God will judge modern men same manner. Every battle of the warrior is with confused noise and garments rolled in blood, but this time shall be with burning and fuel of fire. The indignation of the Lord God is upon all nations on earth today: And His fury upon all their armies: He hath utterly destroyed them: He hath delivered them to the slaughter." Upon the wicked he shall rain quick burning coals, fire and brimstones and any horrible tempest: This shall be the portion of our cup; modern world current affairs! [Isaiah 9: 5; 34: 2]. Biblical prophecy is true! Will be fulfilled! [Psalm 11: 6]: Fire comes down from God out of heaven: The earth is broken up: The weapons concealed in its depths are drawn forth. Devouring flames burst from every yawning chasm. The very rocks are on fire! The day has come shall burn as an oven! The elements melt with fervent heat, the earth also, and the works that are therein are all burned up! [Mal 4: 1; &. 2 Pet 3: 10]. It is biblical truth! No fiction faking ebook! The earth's surface seems one molten mass! A vast seething lake of fire! It is about the time of the righteous judgment and perdition of ungodly Enmity men: The day of the Lord's vengeance and the year of recompenses for the Satan Enmity grotesque of Zion City. [See Is. 34: 8]. The wicked receive their recompense in the earth! Proverbs 11: 31].

They shall be stubble: And that day when it comes shall burn them up! Said the Lord God of hosts: [Mal 4: 1]. Some are destroyed as in a moment, while others suffer many days. The earthiest people will not appreciate to hear this truth. "Let the dead bury their own deaths." Jesus said. [Matt 8: 22].

All are punished according to their deeds. The Enmity sinful nature of the righteous having been transferred to Satan, he is made to suffer not only for his own rebellion, but for all the sinful which he has caused God's righteous people to commit Enmity.

His punishment is to be far greater than of those whom he has deceived. [See Gen 3: 14-15]. The old serpent, suppose had legs. Now he crawls on its belly: He eats dust: And cast out of heaven. Above all: God put Enmity upon him. After all have perished who fell by his deceptions: He is still to live and suffer on tormenting and torturing himself and everyone else crosses on his way. He has ever endeavored crafting and cunning, deceitful language for sympathy, support gain. Enmity it is his most heavy burden to carry on daily! So he sought help from those who follow Christ. "Be aware!" Christ warns his peoples. "You know them by their fruits."

In the cleansing flames the wicked are at last destroyed, root and branch: Satan the root, his followers the branches. The full penalty of the law has been visited: The demands of righteous justice have been met: And heaven and earth, beholding the righteousness declares: "The Lord God Almighty!" Satan's work of ruin is forever ended!" Four thousand years he has wrought his will, filling the earth with unceasing woes and causing grief throughout the whole entire world!. Now it is stopped! The whole creation has groaned enough and travailed together in pains for decades! Now God's creatures are forever delivered from his wicked presence and temptations no more! All true believers long for that day to come with eagerness. Enmity will persist, which they all know. In Christ, I shall overcome. He strengthens me.

The whole earth will be at rest and peaceful: They [the righteous] break forth into singing. [Isaiah 14: 7]. And a shout of praise and triumph ascends from the whole loyal universe. The voice of a great multitude, as the voice of many waters like that Zambezi River of Victoria Falls it possesses song sound when its waters fall powerful. It sounds like drums sending out messages. And as the voice of mighty thundering, is heard, saying: "Alleluia! For the Lord God omnipotent reigneth!" [Rev. 19: 6]. While the earth was wrapped in the fire of destruction, the righteous abode safely in the Holy City of God. Upon those that had part in the first resurrection, the second death has no power. While God is to the wicked a consuming fire: He is to His people both a sun and a shield. [Psalm 84: 11]. "I saw a new heaven and a new earth: For the first heaven and the first earth were passed away." John vision at Patmos Island claims what he saw [Rev. 21: 1] The fire that consumes the wicked purifies the earth. Every trace of the curse is swept away: No eternally burning hell will keep before the ransomed the fearful consequences of Enmity sinful.

One reminder alone remains: Our Redeemer will ever bear the marks of His crucifixion. Upon His wounded head, upon His side, His hands and His feet are the only traces of the cruel work that Enmity sinful has wrought! Prophecy says: "He had bright beams coming out of his side: And there was the hiding of his power:" Says the prophet [Habakkuk 3: 4]. Margin that pierced side whence flowed the crimson stream that reconciled man to God: There is the world's savior glory, there the hiding of his power. Mighty to save" through the sacrifice of redemption! He was therefore strong enough to execute justice upon them, that despised God's Merciful. And the tokens of his humiliation are his highest honor: Through the eternal ages the wounds of Calvary will show forth his praise and declare his power. "O Tower of the flock, the stronghold of the daughter of Zion, unto you shall it come, even the first dominion." [Micah 4: 8].

The time has come to which holy men have looked with longing since the flaming sword barred the first pair from Eden Garden, the time for the redemption of the purchased possession."

[Ephesians 1: 14]. The earth originally given to man as his kingdom, betrayed by him into the hands of Lucifer in the form of a serpent, and so long held by the mighty foe, has been brought back by the great plan of Christ' redemption. All that was lost by Enmity sinful has been restored. Thus said the Lord God: That formed the earth and made it: He has established it: He created it not in vain: He formed it to be inhabited: [Isaiah 45: 18]. God's original purpose in the creation of the earth is fulfilled as it is made the eternal abode of the redeemed. The righteous shall inherit the land!. And dwell therein forever!. [Psalm 37: 29]. A fearful of making the future inheritance seem too material has led many to spiritualize away the very truth which lead us to look upon it as our home: Christ Jesus assured his disciples that he goes to heaven to prepare mansions for them in the Father's house! Those who accept the teaching of God's word truth will not be wholly ignorant concerning the heavenly abode! And yet, eyes had not seen, nor ear heard, neither have entered into the heart of man, the things which God had prepared for them that love him. [1 Corinth 2: 9].

Human language is inadequate to describe the reward of the righteous. Good language and truth that matters. It will be known only to those who behold it and believe it. No finite mind can comprehend the glory of the Paradise of the Mighty God, power and wisdom. [See Isaiah 55: 8-9]. Who knows God's mind?

In the Scriptures-Bible the inheritance of the saved people is called a "country." [Heb 11: 14-16]. There the heavenly Shepherd leads his flock to fountains of living waters. The tree of life yields its fruit every month-season, and the leaves of the tree are for the service of the nations. There are ever-flowing streams, clear as crystal, and beside them waving trees cast their shadows upon the paths prepared for the ransomed of the Lord God. There the wide-spreading plains swell into hills of beauty, and the mountains of God rear their lofty summits. On those peaceful plains, beside those living streams, God's true-peoples, so long pilgrims and wandered, shall find a home upon it. No wickedness shall be admitted there! "My people shall dwell in a peaceable habitation and insure dwellings, and in quiet resting place." Violence, disagreement, and quarrels shall no more be heard or experienced in thy land wasting nor destruction within thy borders: But you shall call your walls "Salvation" and your gates "Praise!" They shall build houses and inhabit them: And they shall plant vineyards, and eat the fruit of them and fairness sharing with brothers, and neighborhood bound together. These are the words of the Lord God, he put in the mouth of prophet [Isaiah 32: 18; 60: 18; 65:21, 22]. There the wilderness and the solitary place shall be glad for them! And the desert shall rejoice, and blossom as the rose." Instead of the thorns shall come up the fir tree, and instead of the brier shall come up the myrtle tree." The wolf also shall dwell with the lamb peaceful and the leopard shall lie down with their kid: And a little child shall lead them." They shall not hurt nor destroy in all my holy mountains" God said:

Pain cannot exist in an atmosphere of heaven! There will be no more shading-tears, no funeral trains, and no badges of mourning what so-ever! It is the future "New Jerusalem" the heavenly metropolis of the glorified new earth! "A Crown of glory in the hand of the Lord Christ Jesus and a royal diadem in the hand of our Lord God Almighty the maker of all goodness!. It shall be established! Prophetic truth shall be fulfilled! [Isaiah 62: 3, Rev. 21: 11; &. Isaiah 65: 19; Rev. 21: 3]. In the City of God Almighty there shall be no more night or darkness. None will need or desire repose. There will be no weariness in doing the will of God and offering praise to his name. We shall ever feel the freshness-fuel of our spirits continually. The fuel of freshness shall ever feel fresh in the morning and shall ever be far from its close:

Truly, there will be no need of candles, neither light of the sun: For the Lord God gives them light continually. [Rev. 22: 5]. The light of the sun will be superseded by a radiance which is not painful dazzling: Yet which immeasurably surpasses the brightness of our noontide: The glory of God alone and the Lamb floods of the Holy City with unfading light. Nothing better than that, but perfectly well define: The redeemed walk in the sunless glory of perpetual day. It is no cheap place to dwell, but very costly purchased by the blood of the Lamb, Christ Jesus. Enmity is the greatest enemy of all God's goodness. Obviously, we behold the image of God reflected: As in a mirror, in the works of nature and in God's dealings with men: But then we shall see him face to face: Without a dimming veil between: We shall all stand in God's presence and behold the glory of God countenance! To be sure: Jesus Christ is inevitable! You ignore him at your own wicked Risky! There the redeemed shall know: Even as also they are known: The loves and sympathies which God Himself has planted in the soul shall there find truest and sweetest exercise: The pure communion with holy beings, the harmonious social life with the blessed angels and with the faithful ones of all ages who have washed their robes and made them whiter than snow in the blood of Christ Jesus the most perfect Lamb ever sacrificed: Pleasing God's heart forever. The sacred ties that bind together the whole large family in heaven and earth! [Eph. 3: 15]. These help to constitute the happiness of the redeemed!

The immortal minds will contemplate with never-failing delight the wonders of creative power: The mysteries of redeeming love: There will be no cruel, deceiving foe to tempt to forgetfulness-neglecting God: Every faculty will be well developed far perfected as ever before! Restoring Bereshith-Genesis: Every capacity well increased: The acquirement of knowledge will not weary the mind or exhaust the energies: Like Eagle will ever re-energies strengthened. God is the fuel of their spirits burning.

There the grandest enterprises may be carried forward the loftiest aspirations reached, the highest ambitions realized: And still there will arise new heights to surmount, new wonders to admire, new truths to comprehend, fresh objects to call forth the powers of mind and soul and body. No wonder why all true believers long to see such glorious magnificent truth prepared for them. Faith counts! All the treasures of the world will be open to the study of God's redeemed peoples. Unfettered by mortality, they wing their tireless flight to worlds after worlds that thrilled with sorrow at the spectacle of human woes and Enmity rang with songs of gladness at the tidings of a ransomed soul. With un-utter able delight the children of earth enter into the joy and the wisdom of unfilled beings: They share the treasures of knowledge and understanding full gained through ages upon ages in contemplation of God's handiwork!

With undimmed vision they gaze upon the glory of creation: Suns and stars and systems: All in their appointed order circling the throne of Deity. Upon all things, from the least to the greatest, the Creator's name is written: And in all are the riches of his power displayed. Who else to compare Him? None!

And the years of eternity, as they roll, will bring richer and still more glorious revelations of the Mighty God and of Christ Jesus! As knowledge is progressive, so will love, reverence, and happiness increase: The more men learn of God, the greater will be their admiration of God's character! As Christ Jesus opens before them the riches of redemption and the amazing achievements in the great Enmity-Sinful Satan, the hearts of the ransomed thrill with more fervent devotion, and with more rapturous joy they sweep the harps of gold: And ten thousand times ten thousand and thousands of voices unite to swell the mighty chorus of praise!

And all creatures which are in heaven, and on the earth, and under the earth-sea, and such as are in the air, and all that are in them: I heard saying: "Blessing, and honor, and glory, and power, be unto Him that sitteth upon the throne, and unto the Lamb forever and ever!" [See Rev. 5: 13]. The great Enmity Sinful is

Ended: Enmity and sinners are no more! The entire world is clean! One pulse of harmony and gladness beats through the vast creation: From Him who created all! Flow life and light and gladness" Throughout the realms of illimitable space: From the minutest atom to the greatest world: All things animate and inanimate, in their un-shadowed beauty and perfect joy: Declare that "God is Love!" This is the Big Picture all nations on earth ought to look. It stands for all! Jesus Christ is inevitable! If individual and humanity are to progress; Jesus Christ is inescapable! You ignore him at your own wicked Risky! [Isaiah 66: 1-3]. The work did not stand or established in the wisdom and learning of human beings, but it is in the power and wisdom of the Lord God Almighty! It was not the most talented or intelligent, but the most meekness; lowly and devoted who were first to hear the voice of the Lord God and obey the call such as Noah; Abraham; Moses; and finally the fishermen whom the Lord Christ called to follow him. Even farmers left their fields and crops standing in their fields, mechanics laid down their tools and with tears and rejoicing went out to give the warnings from their God who promised them to live forever! Those who had formerly led in the cause were among the last to join in this great movement! When God chose a man he knows exactly how he will guide and use adequately to accomplish his holy purpose. He never fails! The early century's churches in general closed their doors against it, and a large number of people or congregation who had the living testimony withdrew from their connection because they were not really chosen by God, so they closed their doors; like today's several man's made denominations; some are not truly connected to Christ Jesus; but are anti-Christ! In the providence of God, this cry united with the second call of God's message and gave the power to that work: God's truth always.

Chapter 2

Why Enmity Will Persist?
Past: Present: Future:
Who Decides?
[Gen 3: 15]

"I put Enmity between
You and the woman:"
"And between your seed and her seed:" [Zerah]

Biblical Prophecy: From the Crest of Olivet, Christ Jesus looked upon Jerusalem: He predicted: "For the day shall come upon you when your enemies will build an embankment around you, surround you and close you in on every side, and level you, and your children within you; to the ground; and they will not leave in you one stone upon another; because you did not know the time of your visitation!." [Luke 19: 43-44]. It is about future torturing experience until Christ returns: No resting from Satan harassments.

Nearly 40 years after Christ had predicted these events in [A.D. 66] the law maker experts [Israelites or Jewish] rebelled against the Roman Empire. Cestus withdrew his troops in [A.D. 67 to A.D. 70] Titus besieged the City of Jerusalem and in its fell. And that process still on its way until Christ returns. Enmity will persist no matter how the ancient and modern history overlook! For the word of God is living and active, it will not cease until it achieves its purpose uttered by the Mighty God' mouth!. What we learn from past church history and reformation? We repeat the same thing like a cycle-wheel!. Enmity causes all disagreement to filibuster politics in vain. Enmity entices all in the eyes of God. Fair and peaceful is the scene spread out before us, yet it never brings us peace and fairness. Why? We, like the ancient generations, do not recognize or know the visitation of Christ who came down from heaven to show us all the heavenly things. It is the same Big Picture we see from our forefathers: What change we have made since Christ Jesus ascended to heaven? Enmity surrounds us all still. In the midst of gardens and vineyards and green slopes studded with pilgrims tents, raise the terraced hills, the stately palaces, and massive bulwarks of modern men capital cities; it is same thing as the past with their emptiness of hearts!. No God's commitment deals!. The daughters of Zion seems in her pride to say: "I sit a queen, and shall see no sorrow; as lovely now, and deeming herself as secure in heaven's favor as when ages before the royal minstrel, misogyny sung. "I am beautiful!" We naturally deceive ourselves. Ecclesiastics proclaims: "Vanity!"

What the Israelites could gaze upon the scene without a thrill of joy and admiration! But far other thoughts occupy the mind of the Lord Christ Jesus: So it is the same thing for modern men today! Modern men like ancient Israel will not comply with Christ' deal neither! Also Jesus Christ is the same yesterday, today and ever! So who wins? When he [Christ] was come near, He beheld the city, and wept over it." [Luke 19: 41].

Amid the universal rejoicing of the triumphal entry, while palms branches wave while glad hosannas awake the echoes of the hills, and thousands of voices shouting-screaming powerful sound-voices [Him the King!] the world's redeemer is overwhelmed with a sudden and mysterious sorrow-heart of Christ like Bereshith [Gen 6: 6] grieves God's heart. He saw the perishing earth with its all inhabitants. The predicted Enmity was fulfilled!

So today **Enmity** will persist in our midst!

Jesus Christ is the Son of God Almighty. The promised one of Israel, whose power has conquered the sting death: And called its captives from the grave, **"Lazarus comes forth!"** And he who had died came out bound hand and foot with grave-clothes, and his face wrapped with a cloth: Jesus said to them; "Loose him, and let him go!" [John 11: 43-44]: The ancient Judaism Pharisees, Sanhedrin, Sadducees, Cynics, Stoics, and Hellenists like today they saw this magnificent powerful sign that Christ showed. He is now in tears, not of ordinary grief, but of intense, irrepressible agony. Was Christ weak being? Is He weak today? But he wept: He sees future destruction worse than the past Bereshith. Jesus Christ prediction will be fulfilled! Genesis grief is repeated. [Gen 6: 6]. Enmity God imposed it, so it will persist until Christ removes it.

His tears were not for Himself though he well knew whither his feet were tending. There before him lay Gethsemane: Not far distant was the place of crucifixion. Upon the path which he was soon to tread must fall the horror of great darkness as he should make his soul an offering for Enmity sinful. It remains with us even this day. Because we still resist: We refuse to repent! Yet it was not a contemplation of these scenes that cast the shadow upon him; in this hour of gladness. No foreboding spirit. He wept for the doomed of ancient and future modern Jerusalem temple. Because of the Enmity blindness and impenitence of those chosen Israel whom he came to save and bless. They rejected him and so modern men reject him same manner.

The ancient history and modern history years of privilege and God's blessing granted to all ages was, and is unfolded to the eye of the Lord Christ Jesus Second Advent as Crucial! The Scriptures stand today for our reminder! Modern men print out the Scriptures in order for making money in abundance rather than acknowledging God's powerful. The Scriptures today lost its valuable taste because modern men are lacking God's Ethic! There are no true committed leaders who can lead the world's nations to God! Their higher education based on high technology has unsealed their rolls and uttered their warnings. Like the past, their priests had waved their censers and daily offered the blood of slain lambs, pointing forward to the Lamb of God Christ Jesus. There had God dwelt in visible glory, in the Shekinah above the mercy-seat. There rested the base of that mystic ladder connecting earth with heaven: That ladder upon which angels of God descended and ascended, and which opened to the world the way into the holiest of all! Ancient Israel and modern men defiled it with deliberate intent. Enmity sinful nature blinds them to provoke God's righteous wrath!. They resist God rather than Enmity sinful. So modern men Enmity sinful blinds us to provoke God's righteous wrath! We resist God rather than Enmity sinful. We are no different or a better from the past because we are their offspring. Our forefathers' exposure remains in us. Modern men do not spend time discussing about Enmity sinful. But spend time discussing about how to make money; improve economic and business success. It is a major issue on the agenda! The world Governments or [GOP] attend conferences every fiscal year to discuss how to improve the world current affairs puzzling several world issues: They never come up with inclusive permanent resolutions. But their decisions ever fluctuates year after year while everything else remains stagnate!. They do not bring out world stability. Violence ever expanding!. They instill fear around the world and unsecured measure to every traveling person. Terrorist boasting every-where unresolved. Enmity will persist.

"They shall not leave in you one stone upon another." Jesus said. That is truth fact that we today experience. Everything else is falling apart none is left upon another. And there is outrage cries-weeping daily every-where around the world. Today' major Enmity sinful issue is Syria immigrants. Why the world current affairs are unable to resolve the issue? Is Syria' immigrants is it the only issue?   But there are many other unresolved issues which are being neglected. Yes! Enmity sinful will persist:

Had our forefathers as nation preserved their allegiance to heaven, ancient Jerusalem would have stood forever we too would stand still, the elect metropolis of God in Christ Jesus. But the history of that favored people of Israel was a record of backsliding, rebellion, grotesque profligacy, and so everyone else in modern world. They had resisted heaven's grace, abused their privileges; so we today are resisting heaven's grace, and abuse our privileges: It goes on to next generations. They slighted theirs and our opportunities. But God remains unshaken. He prolongs his patience for us to come to our senses for repentance: Do we repent? Who agrees with this teaching written in this book? Who will publish it? My name is un-popular. But truth stands compelling its Enmity sinful nature: I sense disagreement. But I am writing. I am obeying God's call to spread his word to the whole world. God knows!.

Amid forgetfulness and apostasy, God had dealt with ancient Israel as a loving Father dealing with a rebellious son: So, even today God deals with modern men the same way as before. No one on earth can dare or afford to deceive God: God ever wins evil man for good. How can I give you up? When remonstrance, entreaty, and rebuke had failed: God sent to his chosen people Israel the best gift of heaven: Nay, he poured out them all heaven in that one gift. Jesus Christ the precious name ever taught and heard. Jesus Christ came to his own in order to serve his own and give his own ever-lasting salvation. His own had been as a vine transplanted from Egypt into a genial soil. Jesus Christ healed the sick: Raised up the dead: Opened the blind eyes to see: Opened the mouth of mute to speak. Deaf could hear. What else he couldn't do? Physical handicap could walk. He did it all by his powerful mouth. And how on earth Israel could they reject such mysteries seen and experienced both mental and physical:

He was unwearied in his efforts to save his own creation. For three and half years on earth, Jesus Christ the Lord of law and world light and glory had gone in and out among his own peoples. He comforted the sorrowing souls: He spoke pardon and peace, meek and to repentance, lowly at heart: He gathered about him the weak and the weary: The helpless and the desponding; and extended to all without respect of age, wealth, poor, or character: The invitation of merciful extended to all: "Come to me all!" [Matt 11: 28-30]. Jesus Christ: Regardless of indifference and contempt: He had steadfastly pursued his ministry of love as a new commandment to all who follow after him. The perfect law of Exodus: "Love your neighbor as yourself." No frown upon his brow repelled the suppliant: He subjected himself to privation and reproach. He had lived to scatter blessings in his depth path, to plead with men to accept the gift of everlasting life. He still does even today! Jesus Christ is inevitable! The waves of merciful beaten back by the stubborn heart-resistance!. Returned in a tide of untiring love: Who is willing nowadays to fully understanding and accepting this truth? What is truth today anyway? Everyone else has his/hers own truth!. God's truth sanctifies many. His word is truth! [John 17: 17]. Enmity sinful nature, God hates!

The ancient Israel and modern men had turned away from the best giver and only helper ever exists. The pleading of his eternal love had been despised and it still being despised in modern era today! His counsels spurned: His warnings ridiculed: The hour of grace and reprieve was fast passing: The cup of God's long deferred wrath was almost full. The cloud of wrath that had been gathering through ages of apostasy and rebellion, resistance, hostilities, was about to burst upon a guilty wicked peoples: And he who alone could save them from their impending fate-consequences had been slighted, abused, rejected, and was soon to be crucified: Enmity theme; when Christ should hand on Calvary's cross, ancient Israel and modern men as a nation favored and blessed of God would be ended:

Athanasius-John T. Nkomo

The loss of even one soul is a calamity in comparison with which the gain of a world sinks into insignificance: But as Christ Jesus look upon ancient Jerusalem the doom of a whole city, a whole nation was before him: That ancient city: That ancient nation: Which had once been the chosen of God: His peculiar peoples-treasure: Priesthood: Prophets had wept over the apostasy of ancient Israeli. Jeremiah in particular had wished that his eyes were a fountain of tears: That he might weep day and night for the slain of the daughter of his people: "What, then, was the grief of him whose prophetic glance took in: Not years but ages? He beholds the destroying angel hovering over the ancient Israelites all of patriarchs and prophets: From the ridge of Olivet the very spot afterward occupied by Titus and army: He looks across the valley upon the sacred courts and porticoes, and with tears blinded eyes he saw in awful perspective, the walls surrounded by alien armies: Very unpleasant ancient Jewish history. Even today, it is very unpleasant history to experience: We are no better at all! We hear the tread of the hosts mustering for battle: We hear the voices of mothers:

Grandmothers: And children were crying for bread in the besieged city of Syrian immigrants: We see the awfully holy and beautiful houses; palaces; and towers; given to the flames: New York twin World Trade Towers exploded by notorious terrorists 2001. And where once they stood, only a heap of smoldering ruins today: No! We are no better at all! Filibuster politics no help at all! Jesus Christ has all answers when he returns. We have obligation to acknowledge to the world that Enmity will persist. Aware of its existence: We need meek, humbled Christian leader to lead us to God our maker who has all answers we need. We haven't one yet: No we shall not until Christ returns. Meanwhile we experience severe sufferings. So Christ warned: "Take heed that no one deceives you!" [Matt 24: 4-5]. Christ Jesus foresaw in the temporal retribution about to fall upon the earth. The ultimate judgment: Divine pity yearning love finds utterance in the mournful words:

See Matt 23.

Yes! Christ Jesus saw in ancient Jerusalem a symbol of the whole world hardened in unbelief and rebellion, resistance, hostilities, and rushing on to meet the retributive judgments of the Lord God! The woes of a fallen race: Ancient Israel and modern era are all on same online: Pressing upon his soul, forced from his lips that exceeding bitter outcry! Who is not out crying today? As the author: I am ever crying too. Christ Jesus saw the records of Enmity sinful in traced in human miseries, in tears and blood: His heart was moved in grief with infinite pity for the afflicted and suffering ones: Enmity sinful. Indeed, he yearned to relieve all: But they rejected! The same even today: We are rejecting: But he knew that even his hand might not turn back the incoming tide of human woes. See Matt 23. Few would seek their only source of help: He was ever willing to help and suffer and die to bring salvation for the whole world. But few would come to him that they might have eternal life: Why Enmity persist? The majesty of heaven in tears! The son of the infinite God troubled in Spirit: Bowed down with anguish! The scene filled all heaven with wonder-splendor. That scene reveals to us today the exceeding Enmity sinfulness. It shows us how hard a task it is even for infinite powerful: Christ felt it. To save the guilty from their consequences of transgressing the perfect law of God: Christ Jesus looking down to the last generation, he saw the world unclosed in a deception similar to that which caused Enmity sinful of ancient Jerusalem.

The great Enmity sinful nature of the ancient Jews and modern men was their rejection of Christ: Do we all accept Christ Jesus teachings in obedience? There aren't many!. The great sinful of Christian world today would be their rejection of the perfect law of God: The foundation of His earth and heaven: The precepts of God would be despised and set at naught! Millions in bondage to Enmity sinful, slaves of sinful of Lucifer Satan: Enmity which he carries makes him uncomfortable continually!

Doom to suffer the second death would refuse to listen to eternal word of truth in our day of visitation. Enmity terrible blindness! Strange infatuation! Two days before the Passover when Christ Jesus had last time departed from the temple, after he had denounced the hypocrisy of the Pharisees, Sanhedrin, Sadducees, and Hellenists traditionalists law maker like our modern men law maker, they are worse stiff-necks. Their law is unjust and unmerciful, and breaking their own laws as well as breaking God's perfect law. We all suffer! Christ again went out with his 12th disciples one of them is a betrayer! To the Mount of Olives, and seated there himself with them upon a grassy slopes overlooking the terrible Jerusalem city doom. He knew the outcome event! Once more Christ gazed upon its walls, its towers and palaces: Once more Christ beheld the temple in its dazzling splendor, a diadem of beauty crowing the sacred mount! It is to be destroyed once and for all! No stone upon another to be seen! 25 years to build the temple to its completion by the hand of King Solomon. A thousand years before had the psalmist magnified God's favoritism to Israel in making them holy house for God to dwell. He does not dwell in a place built by man's hand. "Heaven is my throne: "And the earth is my footstool: "Where is the house that you will build for Me?" "For all those things my hand has made: And all those things exist!" [Isaiah 66: 1-2].

He chose the tribe of Judah: The Mount Zion which God loved: And he built his sanctuary like high palaces: [Ps. 78: 68-69]. The first temple had been erected during the most prosperous period of Israel' history since King David supersedes Saul. Vast store of treasure for this purpose had been collected and gathered by King David and the plans for its construction were made by divine inspiration. God allowed Solomon, the wisest king of Israel' monarchs-emerge had completed the work: This temple, indeed, was the most magnificent building which the world ever saw! This is where the Ethiopian Eunuch came to worship: Yet the Lord Christ Jesus had denounced: Fulfilling prophet Haggai concerning the second temple: "The glory of this latter house shall be greater than of the former." [Haggai 2: 9, 7]. "I will shake all nations and the desire of all nations shall come, and I will fill this house." The prophecy results were fulfilled:

After the destruction of the temple by Nebuchadnezzar, king Babylon it was again rebuilt about 500 years before the Christ' birth by the people who came from a lifelong Babylon captivity had returned to exhausted, to a wasted, and almost deserted country!. There was absolute nothing had been left! There were then among them old-aged men who had seen the first glory of king Solomon's temple stand, and who wept at the foundation of the new building that it must so inferior to the former: Their past memories caused them to shade tears on their eyes for days! The feeling that prevailed is forcibly described by the prophet: "Who is left among you that saw this house in her first glory?" And who do you see it now? Is it not in your eyes in comparison of it as nothing?" [Haggai 2: 3]. Christ Jesus repeated his own words in the fulfillment of prophecy. Then was given the promise that the glory of this latter house should be greater than the former! Enmity will persist until Christ returns! For he spoke and it was done! Jesus Christ is inevitable! A thousand years is like yesterday! "Lord, You have been our dwelling place in all generations!" Before the mountains were brought forth: Or ever! You had formed the heaven and the world: Even from everlasting to everlasting: "You are God!" [Ps. 90: 1-2]. But the second temple had not equaled with the first in its magnificence: Nor was it hallowed by those visible tokens of the Divine presence which pertained to the first temple! No! There was neither manifestation of supernatural powerful to mark its dedication as the former. Solomon is dead he was not available to dedicate it. They are back to dust where they belong. Enmity compelling its call! "For dust you are: And to dust you shall return!" [Gen 3: 19]. No cloud of glory from above in heaven was seen to fill the newly built temple: No fire from heaven descended to consume the sacrifice upon its altar! The Shekinah no longer abode between the Cherubim in the most holy place: The ark, the mercy-seat, and the tables of the testimony were not be found around it therein: No voice sounded from heaven to make known to the inquiring priest the will of the Lord God! No more! Today, it looks like potsherds on ground.

For centuries the traditionalists Jewish had vainly endeavored to show where the promise of God, given by prophet Haggai; had been fulfilled: Yet pride and unbelief still blind their eyes and minds: So are the Gentiles who claim to be Christians. Enmity overwhelm blinds them. So much money emphasizes on agenda. No God's agenda under-what circumstance! Enmity persist!. What's matter with money? Those who monitor it: Are the cause for Enmity. Money possesses no mouth to speak: You speak on its behalf, that what's matter: You handle it reckless! Enmity sinful within you brings you troubles. Would you agree? If you are wrong [Really Wrong] would you want to know? So, why God should not judge you and me? Enmity, God imposed upon you because you and I deserve it:

Neither was the second temple honored by God! No sign was shown as the first temple God showed signs in his own appearance in the clouds. Fire descended to consume the sacrifice. This time in ages, till this day: God shows no more signs. Christ Jesus is the ultimate sign and Judge. But with the living presence of one in whom dwelt the fullness of the Godhead bodily, who was God himself manifest in the flesh: Jesus Christ lived in their midst: Even today he lives in our midst: The desire of all nations had indeed come to his temple when the Christ of Nazareth taught and healed in the sacred courts: Yes! Biblical evidences are obvious even today.

In the presence of Christ and in this only, did the second temple exceed the first in glory? But Israel or traditionalists Jewish had put from her the proffered gift of heaven: With the humble Teacher [Christ] who had that day passed out from its golden gate, the glory had forever departed from the temple as predicted by Christ Jesus. Already were fulfilled the saviour's words: "Your house is left to you desolate!" [Matt 23: 38] The 12th disciples had been filled with awe and wonder at Christ's prediction of the overthrow of the temple; and they desired to fully understand more about the meaning of his words. Wealth, hard labor, and architectural skill had for more than 40 years been freely expended to enhance its splendors.

Herod, great earthiest-heathen, no God fearing, had lavished upon it both Roman wealth and Jewish treasure, and even the emperor of the world had enriched it with his gifts. Massive blocks of white marble, of almost fabulous size, forwarded from Rome for this purpose, formed a part of its structure: And to these the disciples had called the attention of their Lord, saying "see what manner of stones and what buildings are here!" [Mark 13: 1.] To these words, the Lord Christ Jesus made the solemn prediction: And starting response: "Verily I say to you: "There shall not be left here one stone upon another!" All shall be thrown down!" [Matt. 24: 2]. Indeed, they are today's potsherds on ground. With the overthrow of Jerusalem the disciples associated the events of Christ' personal coming in temporal glory to take the throne of the whole universal empire! To punish the impenitent Enmity sinful traditionalists Jewish; Pharisees, Sanhedrin, Sadducees; and Hellenists including every modern scholasticism: And to break from off the nation the Roman yoke: The Lord Christ Jesus had told them that he would come back the second time! Yes! He will: You and I better believe it:

Hence at the mention of righteous judgments upon Jerusalem, their minds revert to that coming and as they are gathered about the saviour upon the Mount of Olives, they ask: "When shall these things take place? And what shall be the sign of your coming and of the end of the world? [Matt 24: 3]. Today's 1.2 billion Christian worlds do not take this notion serious consideration no more! They total ignore!. Enmity sinful blinds them!.

But Christ seriously meant it well what he had foretold. 1.2 billion Christian world is profoundly lacking authentic, intrinsically committed leader to guide and lead them to God! There is no true spiritual leader at all! If there is, then 1.2 billion Christians in the world: We would live in a perfect world. Then Christ should not come back!. It is the challenge facing all Christians today!. Enmity sinful persist because there aren't 1.2 billion good Christians on earth!. It is a faking figure to proclaim.

In the beginning, the future was merciful veiled from the disciples! Had they at that time fully comprehended the two awful facts the suffering Christ and death and the destruction of the temple and Jerusalem city; they would have been paralyzed with horror: Christ Jesus presented before them an outline of the prominent events to transpire before the close of time. This is very important point for us to consider to heartfelt seriously. Christ' sharp words were not then fully understood: But their meaning was to be unfolded as his people should need the instruction therein given. It also apply to us even today: Secular scholars and Christian scholars omit to this truth. They are both confined into the scholasticism.

Their agenda is about high education based on profound fundamental human perspective rather than God!. God never occupy their minds! They contend that they own their technology discovery. Nothing from God: They error! The prophecy which Christ fulfilled was twofold in its meaning: While foreshadowing the destruction of temple and Jerusalem it prefigured also the terrors of the last great day. The Lord Christ Jesus vividly affirmed these facts to his listening disciples the judgments that were to fall upon apostate Israel and modern world: And especially the retributive vengeance that would come upon them for their rejecting him and crucified him, the really anointed Messiah. It is the highest treason crime that they committed! It is also for us the highest treason crime that we are committing rejecting Christ. The dreadful hour would come suddenly and swiftly. Enmity sinful nature compels our destruction:

"When you therefore shall see the abomination of desolation," Jesus said: "Spoken by Daniel the prophet, stand in the holy place;" [Who reads this let him understand."] Matt 24: 15-16. When the awful idolatrous of the Romans as well as modern men should be set up in the holy ground, which extended some furlongs outside the city walls, then the followers of Christ were to find safety in flight. When the warning sign should be seen, judgment was to follow so quickly that those who would escape must make no delay. Jesus makes it clear: "He who can have a chance to be upon the housetop must not go down though his house into the street, but he must hesitate his way from roof to roof until he reach the city wall, and be saved, so as by fire." The same apply to those working in the fields or vineyards must not take time to return for the outer garment laid aside; etc. While they should be toiling in the heat of the day!" But secular world Christian today shift! They hesitate moments lest they get involved in the general secular world agenda in compromise. No stability! Filibuster politics implementation!. During the reign of Herod, Jerusalem had not only been greatly beautified city but by the erection of towers, walls, and fortresses added to the natural strength of its situation, it had been rendered apparently impregnable. Herod would at this time have foretold publicly its destruction; would, like Noah in his day, have been called a crazed alarmist. But the Lord Christ Jesus had said; "Heaven and earth shall pass away; but My words shall not pass away by any means." Will be proceed-forward!" [Matt 24: 35] Enmity sinful wrath had been denounced against Jerusalem and her profligate unbelief rendered her own doom certain. So it is also for our modern time. No escape! Christ had affirmed by Micah' prophecy: "Hear this I pray you, your heads of the house of Jacob, and princes of the house of Israel, that abhor judgment and pervert all equity." [Micah 3: 9-11].

How exactly did these words describe the corrupt and self-righteous inhabitants of Jerusalem! Like us today, self-righteous. While us false-claiming to rigidly observe the law of God with boasting figure of 1.2 billion Christians, while we fully transgress all its profound holy divine principles. They hated Christ, and so do we hate Christ far worse than ever! Who dares to live Christ' like purity and holiness? They hated him because his purity and holiness revealed their Enmity sinful nature, like today' priesthood lives like secular world's kings in palace. The Vatican palace, it is expensive to dwell and maintains. This sounds so offensive: Does it? This is why they hated Christ because he spoke truth. Their dirty garments and hypocrites were exposed to public. They were unveiled openly. They became offended. And they hated Christ for exposing out truth. The language is about Enmity sinful nature in our midst needs to be exposed out plainly. The phrase Enmity is explicitly well defined to be explicitly well understood.

And they maliciously accused Christ Jesus of being the cause of their instinct and tendency Enmity sinful and of all their troubles which had come upon them in consequence of their Enmity sinful. Although they knew Christ so well to be most holy and sinless, they had approved that his death was necessary to their safety as a nation. "If we let him thus alone," they shouted; they were Jewish law maker, Pharisees, Sadducees, and Sanhedrin, priest, and Hellenists leaders [Judaism] "all men will believe on him: And the Romans shall come and take away both our place and nation." Self-righteous justification is from their empty lips. Like us even today. [John 11: 48]. If Christ Jesus were sacrificed, they might once more become a strong united people. Thus they reasoned, and they concurred in the decision of their high priest, that it would be better for one man to die than for the whole nation to perish!" Thus had the Jewish leaders, as well as our modern leaders build up Zion with blood, and Jerusalem with Enmity sinful: And yet, while they slew their Messiah, the Christ because he reproved their

Enmity sinful, such was their self-righteousness that they regarded themselves as God's rightful favored people. It is the same picture we see in the Vatican Pope and Canterbury Archbishop. They are strong world Christian leaders. They are most prestigious Christian leaders on earth today in modern era. They are powerful to lead the weak to God. 1.2 billion Christians, would show great change around the world today. But who leads them? Indeed, no killings would take place on earth. No terrorism would emerge to threaten the world!. All public transport would be safe. No checking points necessary. Every passage is under suspect of terrorism when boarding into an international airplane. Fear instilled in every person's mind because of terror. They kill in the name of God! Who can stop them to practice such awful-shame in our modern civilized world? Enmity is sinful.

Therefore, continued the prophet to prophesy: "Shall Zion for your sake be plowed as a field and Jerusalem shall become heaps and the mountain of the house as the high palaces of the forest." Micah 3:12.

Yes! For 40 years after the destruction of temple and Jerusalem city had been predicted by Christ himself, the Lord God delayed His righteous judgment upon the city and the nation. Wonderful was the long-suffering persecution of God toward the rejecters of his true gospel proclaimed and murderers of Christ His Son. The parable of the unfruitful tree represented God's dealings with the traditionalist's Jewish nation and their leaders like our leaders today. The command had gone forth. "Cut it down!" Why cumbereth it the ground?" [Luke 13: 7] but divine merciful had spared it yet a little longer. There were still many among the Israelites who were ignorant of the character and the work of Christ. And the children had not enjoyed the opportunities or received the light which their parents had spurned. Through preaching of the disciples and apostles and their associates, God would cause light to shine upon them: They could see how prophecy had been fulfilled as predicted, not only in the birth and life of Christ, but in his death and resurrection.

The children were not condemned for the sinful of their parents, but when with a knowledge of all the light given to their parents, the children rejected the additional light granted to them they became partakers of their parents Enmity sinful, and filled up the measure of their parents guilty. How about the modern children are we partakers of our past parents awful Enmity sinful or accept God's teachings? After all, God spares our lives to show us his merciful.

The long-suffering-tolerance of God toward temple, Jerusalem, only confirmed the Israelites in their stubborn impenitence. In their Enmity hostile's hatred and cruelty toward disciples-persecution, they rejected the last offer of God's merciful. Then God withdrew his protection from them and removed His restraining power from Satan Enmity sinful and his angels and the nation was left desolate to the control of the leader she had chosen, like our modern leader we choose. They are no caring leaders. And indeed, their children and our children today had spurned the grace of Christ which would have enabled us to subdue our Enmity sinful-evil impulses. We are in a terrible trouble with God even today in our modern era. We suffer as the past on the same manner. Yes! We are suffering no matter how you overlook the issue. Enmity sinful is within in our midst. Seriously, consider the figure 1.2 billion Christians on earth today it is a very large number to consider that cannot show failure to influence the earthiest world to repentance from evil acts to goodness: But there is no show that there is 1.2 billion Christians who truly follow God fearful and fail to change the world!   Oh what a shameful challenge in the eyes of God? It is unresolved challenge because Enmity sinful overcomes all! No human resolution. If not Christ Jesus: Who else? So, all nations on earth are under God Almighty righteousness wrath judgment!. God possesses all ultimate rightful to claim for His own! Jesus Christ is indeed inevitable!

And now all these become the conquerors. Satan, Enmity sinful aroused the fiercest and most debased passions of the soul.

Men did not reason well enough: They were beyond reason till this day. Controlled by Enmity sinful impulse and blinds our outrage: Hostilities, disagreements; disobedience; hatred; bitterness; antagonism; animosity, grotesque profligate ever compelling at minds and hearts with unresolved issues. God long-suffering is now wearing off!. We have become satanic in our cruelty. In the family and in the nation, alike among the highest and the lowest classes, there was and still is suspicion, envy, hatred, strife, rebellion, and cold-blood-murder!. There was and still is no safety anywhere around the globe! We need to spell out all these awful activities-characters without fear or shame because the issues and situations affect all! We are fed up! So to speak: We have more than enough is enough of this Enmity sinful!. Therefore, all is contemporary required to repentance authentically: God is well faithful and justified to forgive sinners! Repent! Oh, sinner, repent! The ancient Israel had accepted false doctrines and false testimony to condemn the innocent Christ Jesus, the highest anointed Messiah, whom they eagerly expected. And so the modern men have accepted the false doctrines fiction ebook, and the false testimony to condemn the innocent young adults through their scholasticism a tool to shape the naïve young adults to believe to the things un-existence Christian fiction ebook theories: Now false accusations made their own lives uncertain and miserable! By their wicked actions and by our wicked actions we had long been saying: "Cause the Holy One of Israel to cease from before us!" [Is. 30: 11]. Now, and then our desire is granted like the ancient days The fear of God no longer disturbing us: Enmity sinful, Satan is at the head of all nation on earth today, and the highest civil and religious authorities are under his sway! Yes! We have big trouble with God our maker! Enmity, will you agree? How can you? As is written! "Let the dead bury their own dead!"

The leaders of the opposing factions at times united to plunder and torture their own wretched victims: And again they fell upon each other's forces: And slaughtered without mercy. Their own brothers and sisters weep without ceasing daily: Syria outcries they are their brothers and sisters in the name of Allah. Indeed, they are deceiving themselves. Enmity sinful nature blinds them forever! Even the sanctity of the temple could not restrain their horrible ferocity. The worshipers were stricken down before the altar, and the sanctuary was polluted with the bodies of the slain: There is so much to say about the atrocities of the past and of the present. Nothing new to speak about:

The past; present; and future: Yet in their blind as ours blind today; and blasphemous presumption the instigators of this hellish function publicly declared that they had no fear that Jerusalem would ever be destroyed because it is God's own city! "Wrong as always:" While they ignored and rejected Christ who came to protect the temple and Jerusalem city so that no Enmity sinful could fall upon it. They boast with their empty lips: To establish their power more firmly: They bribed false prophets to proclaim, even when Roman legions were besieging the temple that the people were to wait for deliverance from God. Yet, God stood in their midst un-noticed. To the last multitudes held fast to the belief that the Most High Messiah would interpose for the defeat of their adversaries. But Israel had spurned the divine protection and now they had no defense. Very unhappy Israel as well as modern era!. Rent by internal dissensions, the blood of their children slain by one another's hands, crimsoning their streets, while armies beat down their fortifications and slew their men/women of war! Very much alike today modern world current affairs!. All the predictions given by the Lord Christ Jesus concerning the destruction were fulfilled to the letter: And that includes us, Christ prediction will also be fulfilled:

Because we live in the midst of Enmity sinful nature today: And rejecting Christ as the past. There is no much difference! It must be made clear to all that we are the worst men who practice evil activities than ever before! We are the worse than past!. Everything, we take it easy: And that is the danger we face: We produce machines in order to kill vulnerable innocent children in the name of God: Enmity sinful rules the world today!. Nowadays with easy go communication: transportation: speed: even to land on the moon: We are great men ever to exist!. What else which is difficulty for us? Indeed, technology still on its way for advance!. Scientist claims to be a little god!. Power: Enmity sinful blinds:

"Talk no more so very proudly;" Scriptures teaches us: "Let no arrogance come from your mouth: For the Lord is the God of knowledge: And by Him actions are weighed!" The Lord kills and makes alive: He brings down to the grave and brings up: He raises the poor from the dust: And lifts the beggar from the ash heap!

For certain; man cannot restore life! All men face death as predicted. [Gen 3: 19]. Then what kind of power man possesses? God made the lowest man from dust: [1 Sam 2: 3, 6, 7, 8,]. Will you agree?

The ancient Israelites experienced God's truth words of warning after he had brought them out from Egypt slavery-bondage 450 years. "With what ye mete, shall be measured to you again." Signs and wonders appeared: Foreboding disaster and doom: A comet, resembling a flaming sword, for a year hung over the city. An unnatural light was seen hovering over the night and the clouds over the day guiding them the way. In their eyes was still not enough to see and believe in obedience. Upon the clouds were pictured of chariots mustering for Jericho battle. Mysterious voices in the mountain uttered the warning words: Among them were: Balaam's: [Numbers 22: 22-23], a donkey spoke. [Aaron molding a golden calf: [Exodus 32; and Aaron's two sons; Nabad &. Abihu profaned: [Num 3: 4]; Korah, Dathan, and Abiram, envy [Num 16: 1-3] and Achan took accursed garments; [Josh 7: 1]. Yes! Enmity sinful was intensified. God dealt with them effectively. This strange being was imprisoned and scourged: But no complaint escaped his lips. To insult and abuse Jesus Christ' response was: "Woe to you!" He still responding to modern men even today. "Woe to you hypocrites!" His warning ceased not until he was slain, he had foretold truth!

Not one true Christian perished in the destruction of temple and Jerusalem city, except the wicked perished. Christ had given his disciples warning, and all who believed his words watched for the promised sign. Like Noah's day. All other inhabitants on earth perished, but Noah with his household did not. After the Romans had surrounded the city, they unexpectedly withdrew their forces, at a time when everything seemed favorable for an immediate attack. In the providence of God the promised signal was thus given to the warning true-Christians, and without a moment's delay they fled to a place of safety. The refuge city of Pella, in the land of Perea beyond Jordan Rivers: Like Noah entered into the Ark. Will you agree? Enmity blinds. Their stores and our stores of provisions, if that would have been carefully preserved would have been sufficient to supply the world inhabitants forever! Fairness would not be lacking: Previously or Bereshith God had indeed, overwhelmed, abundantly supplied all to Adam, but through Lucifer, Enmity sinful envy, jealousy and revenge of the contending factions, sympathy, and support, and now all the horrors of spiritual starvation were since then experienced till our days in modern world era! A measure of wheat was sold for a talent. Great number of the people would steal out at night, like today to appease their hunger by devouring herbs and wild plants growing outside the city walls: Though they were often detected and punished with torture and death, like today unjust rules everywhere around the world. Some would gnaw the leather on their defense shields. The most inhuman tortures were inflicted by that in power like today, to force from the want-stricken people like vulnerable-homeless the last scanty supplies which they might have concealed. This kind of actions will go on and on until Christ returns! And these cruelties acts were not infrequently practiced by men who were themselves well fed, and who were merely desirous of laying up a store of provision for all and for the future.

As result, thousands men perished from famine and pestilence. Why? Was God's hand short in supply? Even today: Is God's hand short in supply? "Can a woman or a nursing mother forget her sucking child?" God asks: [Isaiah 49: 15]. God, the maker of all goodness never forgets feeding His creatures! But whose provisions which the unfair man squanders recklessly? Indeed, the man faces severe impending consequences in the eyes of God. Will you agree? "The hands of the pitiful woman have sodden their own children: They were their meat in the destruction of the daughter of My people." God said; [Lamentation 4: 10].

The Roman leaders, like our leaders today; endeavored to strike down terrorism and thus cause them to surrender: Like today' terror, they failed and they still fail even today. Terrorism reinforced by Enmity sinful persist. They shall not cease to exist and tearing nations until Christ returns! I have an interesting story to tell your readers: Christian publisher splits Conservative, progressive Imprints: Publishing by Lynde Langdon: Posted on Nov 5th, 2014: They are unaware about Enmity. A major Christian publisher recent announced changes to its organizational structure designed to satisfy criticisms it had not remained true to biblical teaching. The Crown Publishing Group announced yesterday it would separate the staff and operation of Water Brook Multnomah, which publishes books by evangelical authors, and Convergent, an imprint that allows for more liberal theology. This past spring, Convergent published God and the Gay Christian by Matthew Vines, which argues against the sinfulness of homosexuality. The book cost Water Brook Multnomah the trust of many in Christian publishing and membership in the National Religious Broadcasters [NRB]. Water Brook Multnomah and Convergent share staff and operate under the same corporate umbrella.

The NRB wanted Water Brook Multnomah to promise no one its staff would work on a Convergent book, which it could not do at the time. Both divisions and imprints, were under the leadership of President Steven Cobb, who told World in April 1St, "I want to believe that every book that publishes on my watch, whichever imprint in publishes in, is biblical based and developed credibly, which he said God and the Gay Christian was. We see you have' been enjoying the content on our exclusive member website. These materials can be found from: The International Christian Publishers website:] Ready to get unlimited access to all of world member content: Get your risk-free, 30-Day Free Trial Membership right now. How absurd? How sad? Christian publisher splits. Can you real see God to be involved?

Water Brook Multnomah, well known for its best-selling Christian titles, such as John Piper's Desiring God and books by evangelical authors David Jeremiah and Kay Arthur, began as the printing arm of Multnomah Bible College in Portland, Ore. Mainstream, secular publisher Penguin Random House, now owns the imprint and its parent company, Crown Publishing Group. They are Top Believers Publishers in the country. They block doors for true Christian books written by un-popular platform authors. They are killers!. But they will not last: Their days are numbered. To dust, they shall return. Mahatma Gandhi in India killed no one: He said this: "I want to teach your hearts: Only then, will you change." Dr. Martin Luther King, Jr. killed no one: He said this: "I have a dream." Nelson Mandela killed no one: He said this: "I long walk to freedom." Among one Christian: Dr. King. Christ Jesus who came to His own, said this: "I am the way, the truth, and the life: No one comes to the Father except through Me." [John 14: 6]. Among of these three prestigious men of our time;

cannot dare make the claim that Christ had claimed. And there shall never be an under the sun except Christ he is the way for all! You think about it:

Those prisoners, like Gandhi, King, Mandela, and finally the Lord Christ who strongly resisted against Enmity sinful when take, were scourged, tortured, and assassinated, and Christ was crucified before wall of the city, followed by his disciples and apostles, up to the day of church reformation. Hundreds were daily put to death. Yes! They were unbeatable.

The ancient Pharisees, Sadducees, and Sanhedrin as the lurid tide of their days rolled on, devouring everything before the eyes of God in heaven, the whole summit of the hill blazed like a volcano!. Enmity sinful it was their own self-destruction! Mingled with the roar of fire, the shouts of the Roman soldiers, and the crash of falling buildings were heard the frantic, heart-rending cries out of old and young, priests and rulers, same thing like today!. The very same mountains seemed to give back the echo! The awful glare of the conflagration lighted up the surrounding country like two New York World Trade highest towers illuminated the N.Y C and dust spread everywhere atmosphere causing overwhelming shouts were heard the frantic heart screams and the people gathered upon the hills, and gazed in terror upon the scene. The whole nation was mobilized to fill up churches to pray. The leaders of the ancient Jews forsook their impregnable towers, and Titus found them solitary. Titus gaze upon them with amazement, and he declared that the God of Israel had given them into his hands: For no engines, however, powerful, could have prevailed against those stupendous battlements. Both the city and the temple were razed to their foundations, and the ground upon which the holy house had stood was plowed like a field. So was the place which the World Trade stood was also plowed like a field. Will you agree? 3,000 innocent people perished. More than a million of ancient innocent people were slaughtered: The survivors were carried away as captivity into Babylon, others were sold as slaves, dragged to Rome to grace the pagan conqueror's triumph thrown to wild beast in the amphitheaters, or scattered as homeless vagabond-wanderers throughout the earth. Same thing even today until Christ returns.

The ancient Jews had forged their own fetters: They had loaded for themselves the clouds of vengeance: And so the modern men have forged their own fetters: Indeed, we have loaded our own clouds of vengeance as well: Will you agree? Enmity sinful is upon all. Past: Present: Future: All affected: If not so, why Enmity persist? The ancient sufferings are often represented as a punishment visited upon them by the direct decree of God. And so our sufferings are often represented as a punishment visited upon us by the direct decree of God in Christ Jesus' prediction, bound to be fulfilled. We reap what we sowed. This is a device by which the great deceiver seeks to conceal his own work in us as in the past. Stubborn rejection of divine love and merciful, the ancient Jews had caused the protection of God to be withdrawn from them, very much the same thing with us: And Enmity Satan is permitted as he was permitted in the ancient days. He snares everywhere among naïve minds and innocent as ever. He works tirelessly. Will you agree? You and I will never agree! So who is better in comparison, the past and the present? Why then, you dare to deceive yourself?

Disobedient, resistance, and unthankful to God your maker have great reason for gratitude for God's merciful and long-suffering in holding in check the Enmity cruel, malignant power of the evil one. You will not agree or admit to this truth! But when men of past the limit of divine forbearance that restraint is removed. God does not stand toward the evil-sinner as an executioner of the sentence against transgression: But God leaves the rejecters of His mercy to them, to reap that which they have sown themselves. Every ray of light rejected, every warning despised or unheeded-deaf, every passion indulged, every transgression of the law of God, is a seed sown on ground that grows which yields its unfailing harvest. Very truth, isn't it? The Spirit of God, persistently resisted, is at last withdrawn from the Enmity sinful-nature and then there is left no more power to control the evil mind act passions of the soul. Spells; "let the dead bury their own dead." Still, will you agree? How can you, you are dead seed planted. God knows all so well: Enmity God imposed. I wonder whether there is a better explanation than this: But God does not change easily. He is able to restore everything righteous accordingly. [See Gen 3: 14-19]. [See 2 Sam 11-12: David killed Uriah took his wife Bathsheba.]

The Spirit of God persistently resisting, is at last withdrawn from sinner and then there is left no power to control the evil passion of the soul, and no protection from the malice and Enmity of Lucifer Satan. You actually brought it yourself. Apparently, there is this consisting warning today: The Second Advent is foretold by lips which make no mistake: "There shall all nations of the earth mourn and they shall see Jesus Christ coming in the clouds of heavens, with great power and great glory. And Christ shall send his mighty angels with a great sound of a trumpet, and they shall gather together his elect from the four winds, from one end of heaven to the other!" [Matt 24: 30-31] Will you agree? It is truth! "Then shall they that obey not the gospel be consumed with the spirit of his mouth and destroyed with the brightness of his coming!" [2 Thess. 2: 8]. Will you agree? Stiff-necked and un-circumcised in hearts! God is able in Christ Jesus! This is the truth of the gospel proclaimed through all ages! Biblical truth! It lives in our midst today. Let men on earth beware lest they neglect the lesson conveyed to them in the words of Christ Jesus! He clearly affirmed that he will come back the second time to gather his faithful servants-ones to him and to take vengeance on them that reject his merciful. He warned: "Beware!" Jesus Christ is in inevitable! You ignore him at your own wicked risk. Nowadays; when life is going on in its unvarying round; when men and women are absorbed in great pleasure, in business, high education-careers, in traffic, in money-making; popularity; when religious leaders are magnifying the world's progress and enlightenment, and the nations are lulled in a false security; etc.; then as the midnight thief steals within the unguarded dwelling, so shall sudden destruction come far worse than Noah's day come upon them the careless and ungodly: "And they shall not escape not even one." Fair warning: Not threats! [Will you agree?]

In a few brief utterance of awful significance, Christ Jesus foretold the portion which the rulers of this modern world would mete out the church of the Lord God head Father! The followers of Christ Jesus must tread the same path of humiliation, reproach, and suffering which their Lord, Master trod: The Enmity sinful that burst forth against the world's creator, sustainer, and redeemer would be manifested against all who should believe on Christ Jesus' truth and his name.

The history of the early church testified to the fulfillment of the Lord Christ Jesus' true practical, powerful words! Even today his words at hearing pierces hearts of those are ungodly, and they feel uncomfortable and shameful. Yet they would not admit to this truth just as the early church history. The Enmity, the power of earth and hell arrayed them against Christ Jesus in the person of his followers! Earthiest, paganism as it is today, foresaw that should the gospel triumph, the temple and altars would be swept away: Therefore, they summoned her forces to destroy Christianity. As it is today, several trade publishers reject well written Christian biblical books, but they consider publishing Christian fiction ebook. This is another new form to destroy Christianity. Will you agree?

They use scripture to justify their ego' Enmity sinful. It is the work of Satan to tempt the young adults. He introduces scripture to attract his prey.

He did it to Christ. Satan, total failed to deceive Christ through his faking scripture, because Christ is the word and its author!. "It is written," Jesus insists: His own true word is written in Scriptures not to deceive God's righteous chosen people.

The fires of persecution were kindled. Christians were stripped of their possessions, and driven from their homes, approved by the Vatican' prelates and the pope. They endured a great fight of Enmity afflictions. They had trial of cruel-unjust-mocking and scourging, yea, moreover of bonds and imprisonment, final set them upon fire alive!. [Heb.11: 36]. Great numbers sealed their testimony with their blood. Noble and vulnerable men and slaves, rich and poor, learned and ignorant, were alike slain without merciful or pity. Oh how absurd picture to look! Will you agree?

Indeed, they were forced to seek concealment in desolate and solitary places: Destitute afflicted, tormented, of whom the world was not worthy, they wandered in deserts, and in mountains, and in dens and caves of the earth. [Heb. 11: 37-38] How about the Syrians immigrants who heap up to Europe and now to USA: How it can be difference from the past? The subterranean excavations connected with the city of Rome afforded shelter for thousand, like Germany has afforded to shelter the largest number of Syrian immigrants in Europe than another nation in Euro-continent [2015]. Filibuster politics [stagnate]. **Will you agree?**

Under the fiercest persecution, these true Christians witnesses for Christ Jesus kept their faith unsullied. Though severely deprived of every comfort provision, shut away from the light to darkness, from the light sun, making them their home in darkest but friendly bosom of the earth, they uttered no complaint to the authorities of the time. Who real would heed their cry? Like today who cares? Enmity persist. With words of faith, patience, and hope they encouraged one another among them, to endure privation and distress. Jesus Christ is their pillar to secure their feet as they stood firm in faith. The loss of every earthly blessing could not force them to renounce their belief in Christ Jesus. They were unshaken! They, on Christ the solid Rocky stand! All other ground is a sinking sand! Trials, and persecution were but steps bringing them nearer their rest and reward in Christ Jesus the ultimate righteous Judge. They vividly re-called to mind the powerful words of their Lord and Master, that "when persecuted for Christ's sake they were to be exceedingly glad! "For great would be their reward in heaven." The promise is bound to be fulfilled. His word is truth! So the ancient prophets were persecuted before them. Like God's servants of old, they were tortured, not accepting deliverance that they might obtain a better resurrection." [Heb 11: 35]. They rejoiced indeed. Nothing new to teach. Christ's word is powerful than mountains: Deeper than Ocean: So it's bound to tell out as we remind each other that Jesus Christ is Lord! Will you agree? [Rev. 2: 10].

In vain Satan Enmity efforts to destroy the church the body of the Lord Christ Jesus by malicious violence: The great Enmity sinful in which the disciples of the Lord yielded up their lives like their Master and Lord, did not cease when these faithful men standard-bearers fell at their post! Is Christ weak? By defeat they conquered. God's workmen were slain, but God's work went forth steadily forward un-defeated. Christ Jesus rose up from the dead, and so his disciples will rise. The true gospel continued and it will continue proclaimed until Christ returns! There's absolute [Nothing to hinder God's truth!] Jesus Christ is inevitable and inescapable! You ignore him at your own wicked Risky!.

In those days; the gospel continued to spread, and the number of its adherents to increase effectively and exponentially. It penetrated into deep regions that were inaccessible with the heathen's Roman rulers supported by Hellenists, Stoics, Cynics, Pharisees and Sanhedrin mentioning few, who were urging forward the persecution: So in our modern day, the gospel will continue to spread, and number of its adherents increase effectively and exponentially. God is Sovereign: Nothing is difficulty for Him. Said a faithful Christian, expostulating with the pagan earthiest rulers who were urging forward the persecution: "You may torment, afflict, and vex us: Your wickedness puts our weakness to the test, but your Enmity sinful, cruelty is no avail: It is but a stronger invitation to bring others to our persuasion. The more we are mowed down, the more we spring up again-undefeated." The blood of the Christians is seed planted which grows without ceasing. **Truth always prevails! What is truth today?** At Your name it. [John 17: 17].

If the true followers of the Lord Jesus Christ could be exclusively to be deceived by Enmity sinful, and led to displease the Living Mighty God in Christ Jesus, then their strength, fortitude, and firmness would fall, and they would all fall an easy prey! Compromise it is not God's nature! Now was the ancient Judaism and early modern Vatican church in fearful peril: Prison, torture, fire, and sword were blessings in comparison with this: "No compromise with Enmity sinful nature." Some of the Christians stood firm on Christ' solid rock stands! They firmly, intrinsically stood on solid rock proclaiming that they could make no compromise! Others reasoned that if they should yield or modify some features of their faith, and unite with those who had merely accepted a part of Christianity, it might be the means of their full conversion. That was a time of deep anguish to the faithful followers of the Lord Christ Jesus, up to this day!.

As an expostulating example: This past spring, Convergent published God and the Gay Christian by Matthew Vines, which argues-dispute against the sinfulness of homosexuality: No compromise with Gay-Lesbian act. Please see the whole brief story above. "Christian publisher splits." That was a time of deep anguish to the faithful followers of Christ. So it is even today, a time of deep anguish to the faithful followers of Christ. Homosexuals and abortionists: No compromise!

Under a cloak of pretended Christianity, Enmity Satan was insinuating into the church and he still insinuating into the church today, to corrupt their faith and turn away their minds-hearts, from the word of truth. Most of us know it so well the whole idea of mobilizing true-faithful church members to deviation. The same idea from Genesis chap. 3 crafting and cunning language in the ears of true believers: In the past a larger portion of the Christians Company lowered their standard, and a union was formed between Christianity and Paganism. Romans paganism and Judaism to compromise!. They extrinsically handed the Christ into the sinful hands of Romans. And shouted: "Crucify him!" Let his blood fall upon us!." Enmity sinful, resistance and hostility, they planted the seed of their own death! The same idea even today! We plant the seed for our own death! A time of deep anguish! We reap what we have sowed.

Although the worshipers of idols professed to be converted, and united with the true-church, they still clung to their idolatry, only changing the objects of their worship to images of Christ Jesus and even of Mary and the saints-images. The foul leaven of idolatry, thus introduced into the church, continued its baleful work till this day. What we see in practical sense, it is exactly about the past: We are on same online: Enmity sinful is not yet eliminated, not until Christ returns. Unsound-full doctrines, superstitious rites, and idolatrous ceremonies were incorporated in faith and worship. As the followers of Christ united with idolaters, the Christians became corrupted as it is even today. Compromise deal cannot work in the eyes of Christ. He never compromised with evil. How often Christ rebukes Peter? "Peter, Satan asked me to sift you like wheat."

Jesus said: Because Christ prayed for Peter to stand firm: He became a new creation. No more backsliding. There were some, however, who were not misled by these secular world delusions. They still maintained their fidelity to the Lord God the author of truth, and worshiped God alone.

In the past, there have ever been three classes: Conservatives: Liberals: Socialists: In our modern terms: Republicans: Democrats: Liberals: Stoics: Cynics: Pharisees: Sadducees: Sanhedrin: And Hellenists: You name it. But a long list of extreme classes exists today as in the past. Their behaviors are all alike. Factions and Fundamentalism: They are human beings: "But very stiff-neck." As God identifies them: [See Exodus Book]: They hold high prestigious status-quo: Law makers. Nothing new: Will you agree?

The Lord Jesus Christ taught that those who willfully indulge in Enmity sinful are not to be received into the church: Yet Christ connected with them himself who were in character and granted them the benefits of his teachings and example, that they might have an opportunity to see and correct their own wicked errors. Also, among the 12th disciples there was a traitor, Judas Iscariot: He was accepted, not because of his defects of character, but notwithstanding them. He too, was connected with the 11th disciples that through the instructions and example of Christ Jesus, he might learn what constitutes Christian character, and thus be led to see his wicked errors to repent and by the help of divine grace, to purity his heart-soul in obeying the truth. Enmity sinful caused him to resist in hostility toward his maker, the Christ to betray. Stiff-neck. Will you agree?

Judas Iscariot, self-indulgence in sinful, he invited the crafting temptations of Enmity Satan. The prophetic scripture was fulfilled. "Woe to him who quarrels with his maker! To him who is, but a potsherd among the potsherds on the ground!." Judas evil traits of character became predominant. Enmity sinful unresolved. So everyone else yields his/hers mind, heart, soul, to the control of the powers of darkness, both become angry when their faults are reproved and thus he/she will be led to commit the fearful crime. Enmity sinful constitutes everyone else characteristic. No escape!

In like manner do all who cherish Enmity evil under a profession of godliness hate those who disturb their peace by condemning their course of Enmity sinful nature. When a favorable opportunity is presented, they will; like Judas Iscariot, betray those who their good have sought to reprove them. Like Marilyn betrayed her husband John whose goodness had sought to reprove her. She sided with Kristin, Bekiwe, and Ivy [famish-friends] betray those who their good have sought to reprove them. They all divorced their husbands but Kristin remarried.

They were professional harlots. Extrinsically, they professed Christ. The early apostles encountered those in the church who professed godliness while they were secretly cherishing Enmity sinful. Well would it be for the church and the secular world if the principles that actuated those steadfast souls were revived in the hearts of God's professed people. There is an alarming indifference in regard to the doctrines which are the pillars of the Christian faith. The human crafting opinion is gaining great common ground that after all, these are not of vital importance.

This degeneracy is strengthening the hands of the agents of Enmity Satan, so that false theories and fatal delusions which the faithful in ages past, present imperiled their lives to resist and expose are now regarded with favor by hundreds of thousands who claim to be followers of Christ Jesus. They are symbol of empty joiners. Earlier chapter, we showed that there is 1.2 billion Christians in the world. But what kind of fruits they produce in order to change the world? The early Christians were indeed a peculiar people. Their blameless deportment unswerving faith was a continual reproof that disturbed the Enmity sinful nature's peace. They were unshaken. They firmly stood on Christ' solid Rocky. The catastrophe could not cause them to fall that was built on Christ' solid rocky!. All other ground is sinking sand: They were few in numbers, without wealth, prestigious position, or honorary titles, they were terror of evil-doers in the human eyes but in the eyes of God; they were pure in hearts: They could do all things in Christ who strengthened them. [John 15: 4-5] **"Abide in me,"** Jesus said: "And I in you: As the branch cannot bear fruit of itself unless it abides in the vine, neither can you, unless you abide in me." Powerful and meaningful words from the mouth of God the maker of all!. Therefore, they were hated by the Enmity wicked resistance: As it was in Genesis: Abel and Cain could not compromise to each other. Cain hated Abel his brother. Abel abides in God. Cain abides in Enmity Satan. Cain's hostilities resistance, envy, disagreement, disobedient, against God caused him to slaughter Abel!. "If you do well, will you not be accepted?" God said: "And if you do not do well, Enmity sinful lies at the door: And its desire is for you: But you must overcome it!" [Gen 4: 7]. Cain didn't overcome Enmity sinful. It was deeply rooted into his heart: Yet, God warned Cain with love-caring. "Am I my brother's keeper?" Many use this phrase with expostulating attitude. It spells self-destruction like Cain's Enmity.

It was for the reason that the ancient Israelites rejected Christ: And it is also for the same reason that modern nations reject Christ: And crucified the Messiah. Because the purity and holiness of Christ' Jesus character was constant rebuke to their awful selfishness corruption, disagreements, hostilities like Cain! From the days of Christ birth until now, Christ' faithful disciples and apostles have excited the Enmity hatred and opposition resistance of those who love and follow the ways of Enmity sinful nature. They were Judaism by faith. How then can the gospel be called a message of peace today? Prophet Isaiah foretold the birth of the coming Messiah: He ascribed to him the highest title: "Wonderful:

Counselor! Mighty God: Everlasting Father! Prince of Peace!" [Is. 9: 6-7] Isaiah's prophecy was fulfilled! Christ, indeed was born with all heavenly powers!. God himself walks on earth in flesh in the fulfillment on the Mount Sinai. "Before Abraham: "I AM!"

Jesus said: [John 8: 58] [See Exodus 3:14] "I AM." Yes! Biblical truth:

When the angels announced to the vulnerable shepherds that Christ is born: They sung overwhelming above the plains of Bethlehem: "Glory to God! In the highest! And on earth peace: Good will toward all men!" [Luke 2: 14]. How then, men on earth doubt? Enmity blinds them! There is a seeming contradiction between these prophetic truths: In other words: Christ did not bring peace on earth! **"Do not think that I came to bring peace on earth: I did not come to bring peace but sword!"** Jesus said: [Matt 10: 34]. Will you agree? Enmity sinful nature isn't eradicated yet, not until Christ returns! Scriptures evidences are obvious: Examine for yourself. No human perspective in interpretation. But truth from God's mouth: No addition. But rightly well understood: The two are in perfect harmony phrase from Christ's mouth.

Christianity is a system which received and obeyed God'' truth in Christ Jesus, would spread peace; and harmony; and happiness on the earth. This is future peace when Christ returns. They rejected him, how can there be peace on earth? It is obvious, isn't it? The really true born again Christian or Chris's followers will unite in close brotherhood all who will accept its teachings. It was the mission of Christ Jesus to reconcile all nations on earth to God and thus to his followers. True-followers. But there aren't many: Let me remind you again: 1.2 billion Christians on earth is a large number indeed to unite the whole world. But are they all true 1.2 billion Christians? Why then, no peace on earth today? No! It can't be until Christ returns. **"Do not think that I came to bring peace on earth?"**

Well said words from Christ Jesus. And well meant. They are fulfilled in action. Enmity persists! Furthermore; God predicted this to Abraham: "Know certainly that your descendants [children] will be strangers in a land that is not theirs; and will serve them;

and they will afflict those four hundred years! And also the nation whom they serve I will judge; afterward they shall come out with great possessions!" [Gen 15: 13-14]. By this time that God spoke to Abraham, God had not yet given Abraham any child because his wife Sarah was barren: He was 75 years old.

Enmity sinful nature; the world at large it is under the temporary control of Enmity Satan: Christ Jesus' bitterest foes: The true gospel presented to them principles of life which are wholly at variance with their habits and desires, and they rise in rebellion Enmity against it. They are resisting, and rebellion against God. They hate the purity holy life which reveals and condemns their Enmity sinful: And they persecute and destroy those who would urge upon them is merciful, justice, and truth, of holy claims. This is what Christ, the disciples had showed them in signs and wonders for them to see and believe. It is in this sense even today in our modern era, because the exalted truths it brings, occasion Enmity hatred, strive, hostilities and numerous divisions both denominations, that the gospel or a bible is called a sword. Man's grotesque profligate minstrel misogyny. They ever resist God with their stiff-neck un-circumcised hearts. The mysterious providence which permit's the righteousness to suffer persecution at the hand of the wicked, has been a cause of great Enmity sinful perplexity to many people who are weak and vulnerable in faith! We still have this kind of classes emerging from generation to generations. Some are even ready to cast away their confidence in God because he suffers the basest of men to prosper while the best and purest are afflicted and tormented by their Enmity sinful cruelty power. They ever grieve God's heart when visiting them. How is it asked, can one who is just and merciful, and who is also infinite in power, tolerate such injustice and oppression? This compelling question which we have nothing to do with it!. God in Christ Jesus has given us sufficient evidence of love: And we are not to doubt: His goodness because we cannot understand the working of God's providence. The Lord Christ Jesus foresaw the doubts that would press upon their souls and hearts in days of severe and deep anguish of trials, temptations, darkness, persecutions, and all malicious accusations upon them, said this: **"Remember the word that I said unto you:" "The servant is not greater than his master-lord. "If they have persecuted me, they too, will also persecute you." [John 15: 20.] "Do not think that I came to bring peace on earth." Jesus said.**

No peace: Jesus suffered far worse than any other of his disciples. He is Lord from heaven. Sinless and holy perfection is his nature. Yet, he suffered for us, Enmity sinful, more than all those who followed after him, can be made to suffer through the cruelty of wicked men. Those who are called to endure torture and martyrdom are but following in the steps of the Lord Christ Jesus the Son of God Most High.

"The Lord is not slack concerning his promise!" [2 Pet 3: 9]. He does not merely forget or neglect his children: He permit's the wicked to reveal their true characters that none who desire to do his will may be deceived concerning them. Again the righteous are placed in the furnace of Enmity affliction, that they themselves may be purified: That their example may convince others of the reality and unique of faith and godliness; and also that their consistent course may condemn the wicked ungodly and unbelieving. Yes! God permits the wicked to prosper and to reveal their Enmity sinful against him: That they shall have filled up the measure of their father's guilty: All may see his justice and merciful in their utter destruction. The set up altogether of his vengeance hastens when all the transgressors of his perfect law and the oppressors of his truths, and his people will meet the just recompense of their deeds: When every act of Enmity hostility, cruelty or oppressive toward God's faithful believers, will be punished as though done to Christ. This prophecy shall be fulfilled at precise time set up by God. Jesus Christ is indeed inevitable!

There is another important question that should engage attention of the men made churches of to-day! Saint Paul affirms this truth: "All that will live godly in Christ Jesus is bound to suffer-anguish and persecution." [2 Tim 3: 12]. Modern churches today do not suffer as the early church because to-day's modern church compromise with secular world. Why is it, then, that persecution seems in a great degree to slumber? The only reason is: That the church to-day has conformed to the secular world's standard, and therefore awakens no Enmity sinful opposition. The religion accept the Christian fiction ebook. They also approve homosexual same-sex marriage.

It is only the spirit of compromise with Enmity sinful nature: Because the great truths of the word of God in Christ are so indifferently regarded, because there is little vital godliness in man's made churches, that Christianity is apparently so popular platform with the secular world! Let there be revival as suggestion of the faith and power of the early church, and the spirit of persecution will be revived and the fires of persecution will be rekindled. Will you agree to this teaching? It is a mere book written by a mere un-popular author: But filled with passion spirit.

For three hundred years fierce persecution lashed at the early Christian Church: And in [A.D. 311] peace came, [not fully-peace] and things changed: Constantine the ruler of pagan Roman Empire decided for filibuster political reasons to become friends with the early Christian Church: And what it brought changed all history for all time to come: But only on temporary basis. Church Reformation was bound to emerge: Compromise, conformity, and persecution of former brethren began:

Gradually process the Church took all the steps down. It is same online even today. Probably there shall never be a major church reformation again. Compromise makes us to live comfortable! Not until Christ returns. The scriptures shows us: "Let no one deceive you by any means: For that Day will not come unless the falling away comes first, and the man of sin **[Enmity sinful-Satan]** is revealed, the son of perdition: Who opposes and exalts himself above all is called God or that is worshiped, so that he sits as God in the temple of God, showing himself that he is God!." [2 Thess. 2: 3-4]. It is more than enough warnings evidence for us to fully understand. Enmity will persist until Christ returns to reveal the Enmity sinful nature upon all nations on earth.

That gigantic system of false doctrines that each one of us see and experience it is a masterpiece device of Enmity sinful-Satan' dark power: A monument of his efforts to seat himself upon the throne to rule the earth according to his will illegally: Enmity Satan once endeavored to form a compromise with Christ: He came to the Son of God Most High in the wilderness to tempt: Christ Jesus 40 days no food to eat: No water to drink: He in human form hunger compelled upon him. Needs food to eat: Enmity Satan seized the opportunity. "If you are the Son of God," his crafting-cunning language, he said: "Command that these stones become bread!" Christ Jesus knowing all expostulated: "It is written, Man shall not live by bread alone, but by every word proceeds from the mouth of God:" Satan did his tempts three times: He failed! Christ success-victorious triumph. [Matt. 4: 3-4]. Satan dares to tempt Christ, why he should not tempt you and I? Jesus Christ would, but acknowledge the supremacy of the prince of darkness; Christ rebuked the presumptuous tempter and forced him to depart: "Away with you, Satan!" "For it is written: You shall worship the Lord God and Him only you shall serve!" Successful response uttered to Enmity Satan. No more tempts to Christ. "Away with you Satan!"

To secure secular worldly gains and honors, prestigious, the church was led to seek the favor and support of great men of secular world, and having thus rejected Christ and all his true followers therefore, the church was induced to yield allegiance to the representative of Enmity Satan; the bishop of Rome.

Compromise with secular world with God disapproval:

Like same sex-marriage. [Leviticus 20: 13]. Jesus Christ couldn't compromise with Enmity Satan; neither could his disciples! Why compromise with evil doers?

It is one of the leading doctrines of our modern world current affairs; churches, governments, that the Vatican Pope and the Archbishop of Canterbury is visible head of the whole universal church leaders of Christ in modern world current affairs!. They are world's power leaders. Their influences would bring great change to the world, if only they chose to live Christ like life style-meekness. Invested with supreme authority over bishops and ordinary priests and pastors in all parts of the world. More than this, the Vatican Pope and Archbishop of Canterbury has arrogated the very titles of Deity. They styled themselves "Lord God the Pope and Archbishop" assumes infallibility and demands that all men pay him honor and prestigious image around the world to-day! The word of God disapproves. Thus the same claim urged by Enmity Satan in the wilderness of temptation is still urged by him through the church of Vatican and Canterbury.

However, but who fear and reverence God meets this heaven daring assumption as Christ Jesus met the solicitations of the wily foe: **"You shall worship the Lord your God, and Him only shall serve!"** God has never given a hint in his powerful living word that he has appointed a man to be the head of the church. The doctrine of Vatican supremacy is directly opposed to the teachings of the Origin Scriptures. The Vatican Pope can have no power over Christ Jesus' Body Corner-Stone "Church" except by usurpation. There has so severe persisted in bringing against Protestant Churches the charge of heresy and willful separation from the true church. It is none their business but it is God's to determine the true church. But these accusations apply rather to themselves. They are the ones who laid down the banner of Christ, and departed from the true-faith once delivered to the saints. It is not human arguments, but it is true Biblical historical prophetic that Christ shall fulfills when he returns. Looking past; present; we see the same wheel cycle-moving. Christ prediction is ever fulfilled.

Enmity Satan, well knew and he still does that the Holy Scriptures would enable men to discern his deceptions and withstand his power. It was by the word that even the Christ Jesus of the world's savor has resisted his attacks. At every assault, Christ presented the Scriptures as his shield-defender insisting in saying: "It is written." To every suggestion of the adversary he opposed the Enmity sinful nature, the wisdom and power of the secular world invented by Satan.

In order for Satan-Enmity to maintain his sway over men on earth and establish the authority of the Vatican usurper, he must keep them in ignorance-arrogance of the Scriptures. The Holy Bible would exalt God and place finite men in their true position: Therefore its sacred truths must be concealed and suppressed. This logic was adopted by the Vatican Church. For many years the circulation of the Bible was prohibited. The people were forbidden to read it, or to have it in their homes. The Bible today is circulated around the world but with its grotesque doctrines written by secular world scholars. Young missionaries spread around the globe determined to translate the Bible to their indigenous language, so often in wrong translation because they do not fully know the language which they translate. Some of them do not even speak the language which they translate. I know few young missionaries who came to South Africa. They did not speak our Zulu language.

The director of the error having been removed, Satan worked according to his will. Prophecy had affirmed that the human beings were to think to change times and laws. [Dan 7: 25]. This work it was not slow to attempt. To afford converts from earthiest-heathenism, secular a surrogate for the worship of idols, and thus to promote their nominal acceptance of Christianity, the adoration of images and relics was gradually introduced into the Christian worship: The decree of a general council finally established this system of Vatican popish idolatry. To deep the anguish of individual believer: To complete the sacrilegious work, Vatican presumed to expunge from the law of God the second commandments forbidding images worship and to divide the tenth commandment, in order to preserve the numbers. The spirit of concession opened the way for a still further disregard of heaven's authority: Enmity sinful resisting, disagreement, and disobedient overwhelm overshadow upon him.

Enmity Satan tampered with the fourth commandments also and essayed to set aside the ancient law. This change was not at first attempted openly. In the first centuries the true Sabbath worship had been well kept by all Judaism and Christians' faith. They were obedient to honor both for God's glorious events; and believing that his law is perfect: They zealously guarded sacredness of its precepts. That was absolute excellent, and acceptable in the eyes of God. Saturday and Sunday both are to be honored according to God great establishments. [Creation and Resurrection] Greatest Events:

But with great subtlety, Enmity Satan worked through his evil agents to bring about his object. That the attention of the people might be called to the Sunday: It was made a festival in honor of resurrection of Christ. Religious services were held upon it: Yet it was regarded as a day of recreation: The Sabbath being still sacredly observed: Constantine, while still a pagan heathen issued a decree enjoining the general observance of Sunday as a public festival throughout all Rome empire regions: After his conversion, he remained a staunch advocate of Sunday: And his pagan edict was enforced by him in the interest of his new Orthodox faith. Mahatma Gandhi rejected when presented to him by mother Teresa in 1936. Gandhi is a Hindu by faith. But the honor shown this day was not yet sufficient to prevent Christians from regarding the true

Sabbath-Sunday as holy of the Lord God in Christ Jesus. Both are crucial events to honor God.

Another step must be taken: The false Sabbath must be exalted to an equality with the truth: Years later, after the issue of Constantine decree, the bishop of Vatican conferred on the Sunday the title of Lord's day: Thus the people were gradually led to regard it as possessing a degree of sacredness till this day. However, still Sabbath was kept even today with exception of few: There aren't many today.

Enmity sinful: The Arch-deceiver has not completed his work yet. As long as Christ still on his way to return, the Arch-deceiver will also continue. He is resolved to gather the Christian world under his banner! And to exercise his evil power Enmity through his vicegerent: The proud pontiff claimed to be the representative of Christ! Through half-converted secular world ambitious prelates and secular world loving compromise church-men: He accomplished his purpose! Vast councils were held from time to time till our modern era: In which the dignitaries of the church were convened from all over the world, still on same online till today! While the Scriptures is pronounced a relic of Judaism and its observers are denounced to be accursed. Moses obeyed God's perfect law. He did not endorse law. He maintained law. He was God's humbled servant.

The great apostate had succeeded in exalting himself above all that is called God: [Enmity Satan] the son of perdition is to be revealed when Christ Jesus returns. That is uniquely Biblical truth! Holy Scriptures reference is available showing all this truth! [2 Thess. 2: 3-6] also see Gal. 6] Satan or Lucifer, has dared to change the only precept of the divine perfect law that unmistakably points all mankind on earth to the true and living God. Enmity sinful dwells in our midst. Lucifer in evil spirit powerful upon all peoples on earth!. As we indicated earlier chapters: He tempted the Lord Christ Jesus in the flesh. Lucifer is a roaring lion and he devours all souls on earth!

And is thereby distinguished from all false gods: It was as a memorial of the work of creation that the seventh day was sanctified as a rest day for men. It was designed to keep the living God ever before the minds of men as the source of being and the object of reverence and worship. Enmity Satan in spirits strive to turn men from their allegiance to God their maker and from rendering obedience his perfect law: Therefore, he directs his efforts especially against that commandment which points to God as the Creator and Sustainer of all! Satan stands to oppose all that is called God! Satan, Hebrew word, translates: "Opposing: Resisting: Disagreements: Disobedience: Hatred: Bitterness: Hostility: Accusation: Malicious: Enmity: [Gen 3: 15]. Yes! It sums up all!

The Protestant Church now urges that the resurrection of Christ is on Sunday: No such honor was given to the day by Christ Jesus or his disciples after him. In the sixth century the Vatican papacy had become firmly established: Its seat of power was fixed in the imperial city of Rome. And the bishop of Rome was affirmed to be the head over the entire Vatican Church. [See Rev. 13: 2] Christ' prediction is fulfilled: See Heb. 12: 15]: The few faith builders upon the true foundation were now perplexed and hindered as the rubbish of false doctrines obstructed the work: Like the builders upon the wall of Jerusalem in Nehemiah's day, some were ready to say; "The strength of the bearers of burdens is decayed: And there is much rubbish: So that we are not able to re-build:" [Neh. 4: 10]. They got wearied with the constant struggle against persecution: Can you blame them? Fraud, Enmity; iniquity and every other obstacles that evil act devise to hinder their progress, some who had been faithful builders became disheartened and for the sake of peace and security for their property and their lives they turned away from the true foundation. Others undaunted by the opposition of their enemies fearlessly denounced; "Be not yea afraid of them:

Remember the Lord which is great and terrible." [Neh. 4: 14]. The same spirit of hatred Enmity and opposition to the truth has inspired the enemies of God in every age, and the same vigilance and fidelity have been required in Christ' servants till today modern era. The words of the Lord Christ Jesus to the first disciples and those followed after are applicable to his followers to the close of time. We shall not rest until Christ returns: "What I say unto you, I say unto all: "Watch!"   Jesus said, [Mark 13: 37].

There shall be no peace on earth, as Jesus had said: "I did not bring peace." The darkness seemed to grow denser even today. Images worship become more general: Candles were burned before images and prayers were offered to them. The most absurd and superstitious customs prevailed. Children nowadays are taught to celebrate Halloween. It is about witchcraft practice. In the early centuries church: The minds of men and women were completely controlled by superstition that reason itself seemed to have lost their sway: While the priests, prelates and bishops were themselves pleasure-loving sensual, and corrupt: It could only be expected that the people who looked to them for guidance would be sunken in ignorance and vice: One most step taken in Vatican pontiff' assumption was taken when in the 11th century: Pope Gregory VII proclaimed the perfection of the Vatican Church: Among the propositions which he put forth: Was one announcing that the church had never erred, nor would it ever error according to the Scriptures:

But the Scripture proofs did not agree or accompany the assertion: The human proud pontiff next claimed the power to depose emperors: And proclaimed that no sentence which he pronounced could be reversed by anyone, but that it was his prerogative to reverse the decisions of all others! In other words; he made himself as king and pope to rule the world. A well know striking example illustration of the tyrannical characteristic of the German king; Henry IV: For presuming to disregard the Vatican pope's authority: This Monarch was denounced to be excommunicated and dethroned: In order to make his appeasement for peace with Vatican, Henry IV crossed the Alps in mid-winter that he might show him his humble before pope Gregory VII. Upon reaching the castle where Gregory had withdrawn, he was conducted without his guards into an outer court, and there in the severe cold of winter with uncovered head and naked feet or no shoes on his feet, and in a miserable dress: He waited for the pope's permission to come into his presence for hours and days unnoticed! Not until he had continued three days fasting and making confession did the pontiff condescend to grant him pardon.

Even then it was only upon condition that the emperor Henry IV should await the sanction of the pope Gregory VII before resuming the insignia or exercising power for royalty: And Gregory elated with his triumph: Boasting that it was his duty "to pull down the pride of world kings to be under his feet." How profound, striking, the contrast between the over-bearing pride of this haughty pontiff and the meekness and gentleness of the Lord Christ Jesus: Who represents himself as pleading at the door of the heart for admission: That he may come in to bring eternal pardon and peace: Jesus Christ came to serve rather than to be served. "And whoever desires to be first among you, let him be your slave!" Just as the Son of Man did not come to be served: But to serve and to give His life a ransom for many:" Jesus said. [Matt 2: 27-28] The Holy Scriptures evidence obviously shows big picture contrast with Gregory VII behavior straining authority. It is un-biblical straining order. The advancing centuries witnessed a constant increase of corruption in the doctrines put forth from Vatican. They natural adopted Roman pagan straining authority rather than God.

Even before the establishment of the Vatican papacy, the teaching of earthiest secular world philosophers had received attention and exerted an influence in the church which were adopted from Greek Hellenists; Stoics; and Cynics: Many people who professed conversion still clung to the tenets of their human earthiest-pagan philosophy and not only continued its study them, but urged it upon others as a means of extending their influence among the heathens. They planted unfruitful seed. Like to-day scholasticism. Thus are teaching serious corruption among the young adults. Prominent among this belief in man's natural immortality and his consciousness in death!. Like modern medical scientific: Claim to prolong life while they themselves die like anyone else. They are not able to predict their own death: How then they dare to predict about other people's death? God determine each person's death: He is the maker of all life! He measures everyone else days and years: God is Sovereign! Enmity, will persist: Gregory VII is sleeping in dust grave among the potsherds for good!. All flesh end up into dust as predicted by God! In the early centuries church, the way was prepared for the introduction of still another invention of paganism: Which the Vatican named "Purgatory" and employed to terrify the credulous and superstitious multitudes: This heresy is affirmed the existence of a place of Enmity torment: In which the souls of such as have not merited eternal damnation are to suffer punishment for their Enmity sinful and from which, when freed from impurity, they are admitted to heaven if pardon take place upon their favor: God forgives sinners provided he/she intrinsically repents!

Still another fabrication was needed to enable Vatican pontiff profit the fears and the vices of their adherents. This was supplied by the doctrine of **"Indulgences:"** We have said this before: It's better to repeat the phrases. Full remission of Enmity sinful nature past: present: and future, and release from all the pains and penalties incurred were promised to all who would enlist in the pontiff's wars to extend his temporal dominion to punish his enemies, or to exterminate those who dared deny his spiritual supremacy! Above all; the people were also taught that by the payment of money to the Vatican church they would or might set free themselves from Enmity sinful nature: And also release the souls of their deceased friends, relatives who were confined in the tormenting flames of fire in hell. Many people were led to believe this teaching as heavenly truth! Like today medical scientific profession crafting to his vulnerable patient: "I will save you." We all end up into that dazzling hospital building which is extremely, extensive, expensive! Such means, luxury, and vice of pretended representatives as of Christ Jesus who had no a pillow where to lay his head: Slept under a tree-shade daily.

Jesus Christ! The scriptural ordinance of the Lord's supper had been supplanted by the idolatrous sacrifice of the mass pontiff, prelates, priests pretended by their senseless mummery to convert the vulnerable simple bread and wine into the actual body and blood of the Lord Christ Jesus: With blasphemous presumption: They openly claimed power to create their "Creator." And all Christians were required on pain of death to avow their faith in this horrible heavenly insulting heretic. How absurd in the eyes of the Mighty God: Enmity sinful nature: Those who refused were given to the flames of fire.

This is most sad and absurd part of early century's church history ever took place in Vatican. In the 13th century was established that most terrible of all the deep anguish the engines of the Vatican pontiff: The Inquisition: the prince of darkness wrought with the leaders of the pontiff-pope hierarchy. In their secret councils, Enmity Satan and his angel agents presided while unseen in the midst stood an angel of God taking the fearful record of their iniquitous decrees, and writing the history of deeds too horrible to appear to human eyes. "Babylon worse, the great was drunken with the blood of the saint's martyrdom. Today modern world reap sowed in the past: Yet, we refuse to agree to this truth! That it is within us because we are the seeds of the past: Our forefathers are dead, we took over from them. Without the past nothing would exist today. Neither we: This generation is passing away a new generation will take over!. We remain to be the same in characters. Therefore, we are no better than the past: Enmity remains in us all from past generations.

The mangled forms of millions of martyrs cried out to God for vengeance upon that apostate power! The Vatican popery had become the world's despot: Kings and emperors bowed down to the decrees of the Vatican pontiff. The destinies of men both for time and for eternity, seemed under pontiff control! For hundreds of years the doctrines of Vatican Rome had been extensively and implicitly received: Its rites reverently performed its festivals generally observed. Its clergy were profound honored and liberally sustained. Never since has the Vatican Rome Church attained to greater dignity, magnificence and powerful. Today, Vatican Church claims 1.2 billion Christian members world's dominates!. Are they all registered in the Book of Life in Heaven? God has the answer. In 13th century; the Vatican pontiff, the noontide of prelates was the world's moral midnight: The Holy Scriptures were almost unknown! Not only to the people but also to the pontiff, prelates, priest and papacy: Like ancient Pharisees, Sadducees, Sanhedrin; the Judaism the papist leaders hated the light which would reveal their Enmity Sinful: God's perfect law, the standard of righteousness having been removed, they exercised power without limit, and practiced vice without restraint! It is on same online even today modern world era! We cannot escape the terror of our forefathers.

Fraud avarice and profligacy prevailed. Men shrank from no crime by which they could gain wealth or position: The palaces of Vatican and prelates were scenes of the vilest debauchery: Some of the reigning pontiffs were guilty like priests who violated children in USA, of crime so revolting that secular world rulers endeavored to depose these dignitaries of the church as monsters too vile to be tolerated upon the throne. As an independent international evangelist and author; I write this, and preach this truth with no apology or compromise!. On Christ Jesus, the solid rocky! I stand! All other ground is sinking sand! I know for sure: For past centuries there was no progress in learning arts or civilization: A moral and intellectual paralysis had fallen upon secular Christendom. And so Enmity sinful nature has fallen upon all modern secular Christendom: In the condition of the world under the Vatican power as well as the modern world is presented a fearful and striking fulfillment of the words of prophet Hosea and the Lord Christ Jesus: "My people are destroyed for lack of knowledge:" "Because they have rejected Christ Jesus." I will also reject them." Will you truly agree? [Hosea 4: 1-2; Such is the results of banishing the word of God Almighty: Scriptures References: Psalm 2: 1-5; Isaiah 9: 6-7; 1 John 5:5-8; 2 Thess. 2: 3-5; Gal 6: 6-9: "Let no man deceive you by any means:"

Amid the gloom that settled upon the earth during the long [Bereshith-Genesis 3-4] period of Judaism and of early centuries papal Athanasius-John T. Nkomo supremacy: The word of truth from the mouth of the eternal God could not be wholly extinguished! It was, and still is absolutely impossible! In every age there were and still are witnesses for God: Men who cherished truth, strong faith in the Lord Christ Jesus as their only mediator between God and man who led the Holy true Scriptures as the only rule of life, and who hallowed the worship in Spirit and truth. [John 4: 24]. How much the world owes to these reformers men, posterity will never probably know but God does. They were branded as heretics, their motives impugned, their characters maligned, their writings suppressed, misrepresented, or mutilated, like today "Believers of Top Publishers" refuse good quality biblical Christian books, because unpopular author wrote. They build unbroken walls to protect their publishing industry from unpopular authors.

In the early centuries, they stood firm and from age to age till this day, maintained their faith in its purity, as a sacred heritage for the generations to come. Today, they are well known as we remind each other for their great achievement in their hard tasks. The history of God's faithful people for decades, and hundreds of years after Romans had attained world power, is known alone to heaven. Enmity sinful nature; they cannot be traced in human records, except as hints of their existence are found in the censures and accusations of their persecutors: It was their policy to obliterate every trace of dissent from their doctrines or decrees. Every heretical, whether persons or writings was totally destroyed to death. A single expression of doubt, a question or inquisitive mind after truth as to the authority of Vatican dogmas, was enough to cost the life of vulnerable people, rich or poor, high or low rank, Rome endeavored also to de destroy every record of their cruelty toward dissenters. It was indeed, an authoritarian dictatorship Rome!. Vatican councils decreed that books and writings containing such records should be committed to the flames-fire. Same idea with "Believers of Top Publishers" today. [See article by Edward Nawotka, July 25th, 2006 00: EDT]. Believers of Top Publishers hinder every book written by unpopular authors.

Before the invention of printing, books were few in number, and in a form not favorable for preservation, therefore there was too little to prevent the Romanists from carrying their purpose: So, there is too little to prevent Believers of Top Publishers from carrying out their purpose. They are powerful to protect their industry. They are secular world publishers.

No church within the limits of Vatican jurisdiction was long left undisturbed in the enjoyment of freedom of conscience. 1. 2 billion world Christians would make big difference in the world today!. Enmity sinful will not enable 1.2 billion world Christians to overcome such: They are secular world Christendom! Enmity causes them to disagree with this truth! "Let justice run down like waters! And righteousness like mighty stream!." [Amos 5: 24]. No sooner had the Rome obtained power than they stretched out their arms to crush all that refused to acknowledge their Enmity sway, and one after another, the church submitted to her own dominion. At the same time; in Great Britain a primitive Christianity had very early emerged: Faithful Christians men had preached the true gospel in that country with great zeal and success. Among the leading evangelists was an observer of the true Biblical teachings. And thus this truth found its way among the people for whom he labored. Toward the end of 16th century, missionaries were sent from Vatican Rome to England to spread and to convert the barbarian Saxons: They induced many thousands Saxons to profess the Vatican Rome faith, and as the work progressed, the Vatican pontiff leaders and their converts encountered the primitive Saxons Christians. Amazing and striking contrast gospel was presented to them. The latter were simple, meaningful gospel, humble and scriptural in true-character doctrine, and manners: While the former manifested the superstition, pomp and arrogance of pontiff rules. John Wycliffe emerged with great scripture knowledge and power to change the whole Great Britain face atmospheric. This time the people saw big differences.

Nowhere was the darkness deeper: Still there came rays of light to pierce the gloom and give promise of the coming day. The Lollards coming from England with the Bible and the teachings of John Wycliffe; did great, and much to preserve the knowledge of the true gospel and every century had its unique witnesses and martyrs. The emissary of Vatican pontiff demanded that these Christians church need acknowledge the supremacy of the sovereign Rome pontiff. The Britons at the time, meekly response that they desired to love all men created in the image of God equally, but that the Rome pontiff was not entitled to supremacy in the church, and they could render to him only that submission which was due to every follower of Christ. The "Believers of Top Publishers" are supporters of modern Vatican pope. They are probably one of 1.2 billion world Christians.

On Nov 5th 2014, Christian publisher splits conservative progressive imprints publishing. Among them, they dispute or argue this past spring, Convergent published God and the Gay Christian by "Matthew Vines" which argues against the sinfulness of homosexuality. Enmity sinful, resistance cause them to splits. Disagreement among them non-can yield in compromise. Neither could John Wycliffe yield. Indeed, the past lives in our midst even today. The spirit of Enmity will persist until Christ returns!

President Barak Obama in 2008 campaign proclaimed "Change!" What change we see in the White House Washington, D.C. today? Yes, the President has desire to change the face in the White House. Compromise is key issue that cause the change stagnate!. Will you agree? Enmity, disagrees: Who decides? [Gen 3: 15-19].

Repeated attempts were made in the early centuries to secure their allegiance to the pontiff: But these humble-meek Christians, amazed at the pride displayed by the apostles, steadfastly replied that they knew no other master than the Lord Christ Jesus! They refused to compromise. Now the true Enmity spirit of the Rome pontiff was vividly revealed: Said then the Rome pontiff leader: "If you will not receive brethren who bring you peace, you shall receive enemies who will bring you war." If you will not compromise and unite with us in showing the Saxons the way of life, you shall receive from then the stroke of death!" Obviously, God isn't inspiring them to suggest such. Enmity sinful is obvious.

These were no idle threats: War, intrigue and deception were employed against these true vulnerable God's witnesses for a truth: Bible truth, faithful until the church of Great Britain was destroyed or forced to submit to the pontiff authority. Still it was on temporary basis as the history reveals. In lands beyond the jurisdiction of Rome pontiff, there existed for many century bodies of Christians who remained almost wholly free from Rome pontiff papal corruption. John Wycliffe teachings was success and unshaken. Church Reformation wasn't yet at its peak targets. But it was its beginning.

They were surrounded by heathenism paganism from Rome, and in the lapse of ages were affected by its Enmity sinful nature, but they continued to regard the Bible as the only rule of faith, God's word truth, and adhered to many of its truths: This is what the "Believers of Top Publishers" today refuse to publish but accept publishing Christian fiction eBooks. They implement the same past procedures. Thomas Nelson: Harper Collins: Random House: Zondervan: Penguin: Mainstream secular publishers who claim Christians. Now, Crown Publishing Group: Fully financial secured: They consolidated. Early century they are British Publishing Companies sub-branches in USA. McMillan: Tyndale: John Knox: All British origin publishing companies came to USA. They were true Christian publishers.

These Christian publishers believed in the perpetuity of the law of God and observed the Scriptures. Churches had held to this faith and practice, existed in Central Africa and among the Armenians of Asia. In those days, like today; anyone who resisted the encroachment of the pontiff power, the true-faithful stood foremost. Like today unpopular platform authors, for centuries rise the churches of Piedmont maintained their independence: But the time came at last when Rome pontiff demanded their submission. After ineffectual struggles against the tyranny the leaders of these churches reluctantly acknowledge the supremacy of the Rome pontiff power to which the whole world seemingly bowed down to them. A considerable number, however, refused to compromise to yield to the pontiff authority or prelates. They were vigorous and determined to maintain their allegiance to Mighty God their maker, and to preserve the purity and simplicity-meek of their faith: A separation took place. No compromise! Some of the protesters crossed the Alps: And raised the standard of truth in foreign lands. Others retired into the more secluded valleys among the mountains, and there maintained their mutual freedom to worship the living God. 1.2 billion World' Christians among them; there aren't many who truly fear God. Perhaps none! "You will know them by their fruits." Jesus said. Do not get deceived. Large number does not count in the eyes of God. God wiped out the world by flood: Saved Noah only:

Many were invited: But few were accepted: God's way is mysterious. [Isaiah 55: 8-9] Who knows God? Jesus Christ His only Begotten Son knows God. [John 8: 19] Yes! It is truth!. But those herdsmen and vine-dressers in their obscure retreated, shut away from the world, had not themselves arrived at the truth in opposition to the dogmas and heresies of the apostate church. Theirs was not a faith newly received. Their religious belief was their inheritance from their forefathers. So is our religious, whatever, yours is whether Protestant or Catholic, Methodist, Congregationalist; Apostles; Hindu; Islam; it is your forefathers inheritance. So you and I live in the past because of our inheritances. And so is Enmity sinful nature. Will you agree?

In the past and present and future will contend for the faith of the apostolic church: The faith once delivered to the saints: You will keep your forefathers inheritance. It is yours! **Enmity sinful nature from our forefathers it remains with all generations, as a true instinct fact!**

Among the leading causes that had led to separation and not compromise the true church from pontiff Rome papacy, was to inveterate Enmity hatred, hostility of the latter toward the Bible: As prophesied and fulfilled by the Lord Christ Jesus, since from ancient Judaism up to early centuries pontiff: The papal power cast down the truth to the ground! The perfect law of the Mighty Lord God their maker was trampled under their feet to the ground, while the traditions and human' customs of men were profoundly exalted like today' science and technology is profoundly exalted! The churches were under the rule of the pontiff were early compelled to honor the Sunday as holy festival: The churches today that are under men made denominations and doctrines are compelled to honor scientists and every technology discoveries. Nothing wrong with science and technology; but the driving motives behind its existence matters! And so is money: Amid the prevailing Enmity sinful and superstition; many people even of the true believers of God; become so bewildered as the ancient times, that while they observed the truth of Christ's meekness-lowly in heart, they refrained from God's truth task. But this did not satisfy the Rome pontiff and prelates. They demanded not only that God's law be hallowed, but that Sabbath be profaned: And they denounced, in the strong language, those who dared to show its honor glorify its holiness. It was only by fleeing from the power of pontiff and prelates that any could obey God's perfect law in peace.

The early reformers were the first of all the peoples of Europe to obtain a translation of the Bible-Scriptures. Championed by John Wycliffe: It was still for hundreds of years before the real reformation had spread around Europe regions, they possessed the entire Bible in Manuscript in foreign languages such as: Hebrew; Greek; Latin; and Flemish to English; King James Version. They had the truth unadulterated; and this rendered them the special objects of Enmity hostile hatred, and resistance and persecution. These none-compromise deal, they profoundly denounced the pontiff Rome church to be the most appalling apostate as Babylon of the Apocalypse, and at the peril of their lives they stood firm on Christ solid rocky unshaken or shift as chaff blown by the windy! Authentically, intrinsically resisted against their corruptions. While under deep anguish, and pressure of long continued persecution-suffering; some merely attempt to compromise their weak-faith; little by little yielding to its distinctive principles, and others held fast-firm to their truth which is deeply rooted to their hearts. We see, and experience this kind of actions and motives in the modern men behaviors today. We behave on this manner according to our forefather's inheritances Enmity.

Throughout ages of darkness and apostasy, there were unique believers who denied the supremacy of Rome pontiff and prelates; who rejected image worship as idolatry and kept the true God's worship in Spirit. God is the fuel of our spirits, were designed to burn continually! Under the fiercest tempests of opposition they maintained their faith strong. Jesus Christ is their strength! Nothing could possibly hinder the work of true God!. "Abide in Me." Jesus promised. Though gashed by the Savoyard spear, fire, and deep pity under-darkest ground, and scorched by the cruel pontiff rules fagot, still they stood firm on Christ' solid rock unflinchingly for God's magnificent powerful word and God's profound holiness honor and glories!. "Yea! Though I walk through the valley of the shadow of death: I will fear no [Evil-Enmity] for you are with me: Your rod and Your staff, they comfort me." [Psalm 23: 4]. Will you agree? So much to suffer; they would not yield one iota of the truth: God's truth that sanctified them. His word is truth! [John 17: 17]. Yes! It is:

Behind the lofty bulwarks of the Mount Olive, Jesus Christ stood firm in agony prayer! In all ages the refuge of the persecuted and brutality of oppressive the early centuries reformers found a hiding place. Christ Jesus is their strong shield and defender! If not Christ, who else can be? "For me to live is Christ! And to die is gain." Will you agree to this truth?

Here the light of truth fueled by the Mighty God continued burning during the long deed anguish darkest night that descended upon the secular Christendom world! Here for centuries, they maintained ancient faith which also is inherited to those who still maintain this truth even today modern age. God had provided for those whom he chose a sanctuary of awful grandeur; befitting the mighty truths committed to their trustworthy. To those faithful of godly peoples, exiles, the mountains were an emblem of the immutable righteousness of the Lord mighty God! They pointed their children to the heights towering above them in unchanging majesty and spoke to them of about God almighty their maker with whom there is no variableness nor shadow of shifting chaff; whose word is as enduring as the everlasting hills. Good seed, God well planted forbearing good fruits.

You will know them by their fruits." God had set fast the mountains and girded them firm with strength; no arm but that infinite supreme power could move them out of their troubled place. Like Peter chained between two armed soldiers side by side, he had a mysterious escape!. The soldiers who guarded Peter, got their death execution penalty from Herod.

In like manner, during early ancient ages; three young men: Shadrach: Meshach: and Abed-Nego refused to worship idols of Nebuchadnezzar, king of Babylon: "But if not, let it be known to you o king, that we do not serve your idol gods, nor will we worship the gold image which you have set up!" [Dan 3: 18].

These three strong faithful young men stood up firm, with no fear before the sight of Nebuchadnezzar. But they only fear God their maker no one else. God had established law and the foundation of His high authority in heaven and on earth all to be under His feet! [Isaiah 66: 1-3].

The arm of feeble man might reach his fellow men and destroy their lives, but that arm could as readily uproot the mountain from their foundations, and hurl them into the sea, as it could change one precept of the law of God, or blot out one of his promises to those who do his will. In their fidelity to his law, God's chosen people should be as firm as the unchanging high hills as deep as ocean. The mountains that girded their lowly valleys were a constant witness of true living God's creative powerful, and a never failing assurance of his protecting care! It is from their forefathers' inheritance. So it remains in them continually, generations after generations until Christ Jesus returns!

Those pilgrims learned, and well-shaped to love the silent

symbols of the Lord God presence with great power! They indulged no repining because of the hardships of their lots; they were never lonely amid the mountain solitudes. They were truly deeply rooted-abiding in Christ. They ethically thanked God that he had provided for them an asylum from the wrath and cruelty of evil men on earth. Enmity sinful reinforced upon them, they rejoiced in their freedom to worship before the Lord God. What we learn from the past and present?

Often when pursued by their enemies, the strength of the hills proved a sure defense! From many a lofty cliff they chanted the praise of God, and the armies of pontiff Rome could not silence their songs of thanksgiving. Neither could the ancient Pharisees Judaism. So is today. Let justice run down like waters! And righteousness run like mighty stream!" Pure, simple, meekness and fervent was the piety of these followers of the Lord Christ Jesus! To whom we may compare the early centuries Christians from among our modern religious leaders? From 1.2 billion world Christians: Is there any among them? Well, let God answer this compelling-challenging question. Enmity sinful who else can/will radical eradicate it?

The principles of truth they valued above houses and lands, friends, relatives, kindred, even itself. These principles they earnestly sough to impress upon the hearts of the young adults in their scholasticism. From earliest childhood the youth were structure in the Scriptures, and taught to sacredly regard the claims of the law of God. Books and copies of the Bible were rare in those days; therefore its precious words were committed to memory. Many individual persons were able to repeat large portions of both the Old and New Testament to heart. Thoughts of God were associated alike with the sublime scenery of nature and with the humble blessings of daily life. Nowadays in modern age the picture has been modified; many young adults are committed to memory constituting of science textbooks. It is their well deep shape-task in mind and heart. Nothing else: Career and prestigious success is primary #1 crucial matters in general life. Both males and females: Their eagerness is to attain high rank-status. They ever endeavor to secure high status everywhere whether public or private sectors.

In the past, little children learned to look with gratitude to God as the giver of every favor and every comfort! Parents, tender and affectionate as they were; love their children too well wisely to accustom them to self-indulgence. But nowadays in modern age; children are taught to observe Halloween!. Witchcraft!. Before them was a life of trial and hardship, perhaps a martyr's death. You see them marching in big Malls wearing their black expensive fleecy-lock. Covering their faces with masks. Anything they choose to wear: Snake mask: Monkey mask: Puss-cat mask: Ape mask: Purchased by their parents. It is becoming popular festival event in every October month in USA nation-wide. That is the big picture we see every year toward the end of October.

In the past they were educated from childhood to endure hardness, to submit to control, and yet to think and act for themselves. Very early age, they were taught to bear responsibilities, to be guarded in wells speech, and to understand the wisdom of silence but seen in faces. One indiscreet word let fall in the hearing of their enemies, might imperil not the life of the speaker, but the lives of hundreds of his brethren for as wolves hunting their prey did the enemies of truth pursue those who dared to claim freedom of religious faith.

The early centuries reformers had sacrificed their worldly prosperity for the truth! And with persevering tolerance or patience they toiled for their bread. Every spot of tillable land among the mountains was carefully improved; the valleys and the less fertile hillsides were made to yield their increase. **"In the sweat of your face; you shall eat bread: Till you return to the ground: For out of it you were taken." God said. "For dust you are:**

And to dust you shall return!" [Gen 3: 19].

Will you agree to this Scriptures truth? **Enmity, God imposed: Why?** You may well ask: [Gen 3: 15]

In the past economy, like nowadays in modern age; severe-instability self-denial formed a part of the education that the children received as their only legacy: They were taught that God designed life to be an indispensable discipline and that their wants or desire could be supplied only by personal strength and hard work of physical laboring; by forethought care and faithful. In contrast today we use accelerating +machines to accelerate economy and stability security measure. Everyone else endeavors for his security achievement!. Yet, man is ever dissatisfied!. But how long: The process was physical laborious and wearisome but it was wholesome, just what man needs in his fallen state, the school which God has provided for his training and development.

While in the ancient days the youth were inured to toil and hardship, the culture of the intellect was not neglected. Lincoln was forced to be hired by his father, in order to bring bread home to eat. Lincoln hated his father for exposing him into that appalling nature. So he educated himself: Later years he became great President in America. They were taught that all their powers belonged to God and that all were to be improved and developed for God's service.

The church of the Alps in its purity and simplicity assembled the church in the first centuries. The people of God like sheep were led by true shepherds. The Bible was their textbook. They studied its meaning-purpose commitment to heart and memory the words from the mouth of the Lord Christ Jesus. The Scriptures, thus were brought forth the treasures of truth so long concealed by those who sought to exalt them above God. With patients untiring hard work, sometimes in the deep anguish, dark caverns of the Enmity earth, by the light of torches, were the sacred Bible written out, verse by verse gripping to their hearts, it was deep like tree planted by the waters: Its leaves never wither! But always green forever lasting! Thus the work went on, the revealed will of the Lord God is shining like pure gold or silver or diamond on a ring; how much brighter and clearer and more powerful. Pure gold, silver, diamond, well purified cannot be compatible with rust or stain. It remains pure and clear. When God purifies a human heart, mind, and soul cannot dare to live in Enmity sinful nature! All the wicked trials undergone for its sake, only those could realize who were engaged in the work. God sends angels from heaven surround these faithful saints in protection daily. **"Simon Peter, Satan asked to sift you like wheat: But I prayed for you to preserve your strength faith." Jesus said.**

Enmity Satan in the past and present urges ordinary Christians; pontiff; prelates; vulnerable-poor; rich; handicap; blind; and all wonderful human beings to bury the word of truth beneath the rubbish of crafting-cunning grotesque profligate words to be heresy like him. Currently, Satan seemingly wining; thus putting him in a position of increasing his forceful driving motives of Enmity sinful nature: Satan' capability is to destroy-kills but cannot rebuild or restores life. God's capabilities are able to kill and restore life: Destroys and rebuild. All things to God are possible! He is the Creator! Satan' power is very limited! His power does not last! While God's powerful is forever!

"Do not fear those who kill the body but cannot kill the soul," Jesus said: "But rather fear God who is able to destroy both soul and body in hell!" Therefore; "Fear God and keep His Commandments: For this is man's all! For God will bring every work into judgment: Including every secret thing; whether good or evil!" Enmity; see Eccles. 12: 13-14 &. Matt 10: 28].

It bore not the stamp of man: But the impress of the Mighty God! Men on earth have been unwearied in their Enmity efforts to totally obscure the perfect of God' plan; simples meaning of the Scriptures but very complex to maintain and to make them contradict their own testimonies: But like ancient the ark of Noah upon the billowy deep; the word of the Lord God out rides the storms that threatens it with destructions! As the mine has rich veins of gold; diamonds; and silver hidden beneath the surface-ground of South Africa; so that all must dig deep down who would discover its most precious stores: So the Holy Scriptures have the most great treasures of God's truth! That are unfolded only to the earnest; intrinsically; humble; prayerful seeker! It shows better picture of every other treasure than that man ever endeavors in pursuit for his ever dissatisfied soul! Fear God! Indeed, God invented and endorsed the Bible to be ever-classic Book containing his living true-word to all mankind in the whole entire universal: In childhood; youth; and adulthood; and to be studied through all times: Generations after generations until Christ returns.

The Lord God Almighty gave his word of truth from his holy mouth to men on earth in the fulfillment of Christ Jesus as a revelation of him: Every new truth discerned is direct fresh disclosure of the characteristic of the Mighty God Head Father its own Author fulfilled in Christ Jesus from Mount Sinai. **"I AM!"** [Exodus 3:14]

The Bible Study: The Scriptures is the means divinely ordained to bring men/women into closer connection with their indispensable Creator: And to give them a clearer knowledge and wisdom of his will like king Solomon. It is the best for modern world scholasticism to shape individual young adults to fear God and keep his commandment! Scholasticism that eradicate rough mountains and re-shape young adults for better and bring about wider unique 1.2 billion world Christians record of true God's fearing!

It is medium of communication between God and men on earth. When the early century reformers youth had spent some time in their schools in the mountains; some of them were sent to complete their education in the greater cities; where they could have a wider range for thought and observe than in their secluded homes. The youth were thus sent forth were exposed to temptation; they witnessed vice, they encountered Enmity Satan' wily agents who urged upon them the most subtle heresies; and most dangerous deceptions. But their education from childhood had been of a character to prepared them for all this concerning God. In schools whither they went; they were not to make confidants of any aspect. Their garments were well prepared as to conceal their greatest treasure, precious manuscript of true scriptures: Like Joseph's colorful coat designed by Jacob his father' favor distinguished or signal for power and authority above his 10th brothers: Caused jealous; envy; and hostility Enmity to his eventually sale of slavery to Egypt. [Gen 37: 28] read more the whole Genesis chapter 37 about Joseph' pilgrimage: Joseph ends up with greatest prestigious leadership in Egypt, because he fears God. These are the seeds and the fruits of Enmity took place from Bereshith for centuries of toil; our forefathers carried with them and whenever it could be done without exciting suspicion; they cautiously placed to receive it as the most Substantial inheritance gift for all generations after generations till this modern age generations; according to God's commands: **"I will put Enmity between you and the woman; and between your seed and her seed." [Gen 3: 15].**

From their mothers knee the first early centuries reformers youth had been well trained with this purpose in view; they well understood their work and faithful in God performed it: Converts to the truth of faith were won in these institutions of learning; and frequently its principles were found to be profoundly permeating the entire scholasticism: Yet the pontiff, prelates; and priest could not by the closest inquiry; trace the so-called "corrupting heresy" to its source: The reformers felt that God required more of them than merely to maintain the truth in their own mountains: That a solemn responsibility rested upon them with Christ' help to let the light shine forth to those who dwelt in darkness: It is the light of the Lord Jesus Christ that shines into the hearts of many!. **"I am the light of world!"** Jesus said: This truth ought to be proclaimed throughout the ages until Christ returns!

This is the talk ought to be uphold on daily basis: God's words of truth; they were to break the bondage of Enmity sinful which the pontiff Rome had imposed! It was a human law among them that all who entered the ministry should; before taking charge of a particular church at home; serve three years in the missionary field: As the hands of men of God were laid upon their heads; the youth saw before them; not the prospect of the earthly wealth material things or glory; but possibly a martyr's fate set up! The missionaries began their hard tasks in the plains and valleys at the foot of their own mountains going forth two and two as Christ sent out his disciples. These co-laborers were not always together; but often met for prayer-strength-courage and counsel; thus strengthening each other in the faith: It was necessary. To make known the nature of their mission would have insured its defeat; therefore they concealed their real character under the guise of some secular world profession; most commonly that of merchants or peddlers. They avoid Enmity. They offered for sale silks, jewelry, and other valuable articles and were received as merchants where they would have been repulsed as missionaries. All the while their hearts were uplifted to God for wisdom to present a treasure more precious than gold, diamond, or silver or gems.

They carried about with them portions of the Holy Scriptures; the Bible concealed in their clothing or merchandise and wherever they could do so with safety; they called the attention of the inmates of the dwelling to these manuscripts. When they saw that an interest was awakened; they left some portion with them as great gift. With their bare feet and in coarse garments; these missionaries passed through great cities, and traversed provinces far removed from their native valleys. These were true God committed missionaries, not like those who went to Africa later years to proclaim contradicting gospel. They were fugitives running away from their severe treason crimes. Africa new land of opportunity became their safety in missionary disguise. So much had happened in the past: And so much is happening in the present: The compelling question is: Who notice seriously about it? They saw under the guidance of the pontiff papacy and prelates; multitudes were vainly endeavoring to obtain pardon by afflicting their bodies for the Enmity sinful souls. Taught to trust their good works to save them; they were ever looking to them; their minds dwelling upon their Enmity sinful: No more talks about God! Like today modern age: Seeing them exposed to the wrath of God: Afflicting Enmity sinful souls and body: Yet finding no relief: Thus conscience souls bound by the doctrines of Enmity sinful nature: Thousands abandoned God: And spent their lives in Convent cells: Off-repeated fasts and cruel scourging by midnight vigils; by prostration for weary hours upon the cold damp stones of their dreary abode; by long pilgrimages; by humiliating penance and fearful torture; many vainly sought to obtain peace of conscience:

But where could they escape? Severely oppressed with a sense of Enmity sinful nature; and haunted the fear of God's avenging wrath; they suffered on until exhausted nature gave way and without one ray of like or hope; they sank into the tomb like us even today unnoticed:

The doctrine that good works can make satisfaction for transgression of God's law; they held as we do even today; to be based upon falsehood! Reliance upon human merits intercepts the view of the Lord Christ Jesus' infinite love: Christ died as men's sacrifice because they can do nothing to recommend them to God.

The merits of a crucified and risen Christ the world's savor are foundation of the Christian's faith! The union or reconciliation of the lost souls to Christ by faith is as real as close as that of a limb to the body or of a branch to the vine! "Without Me," Jesus said: "You can do nothing!" God is Original of our all images. So all ends up before God the Original:

The teachings of man contradicts has led many to look upon the character of God; and even of Christ Jesus; as stern gloomy; and forbidding: Jesus Christ the world's savor is represented as so far devoid of all sympathy with man in his fallen state that the mediation of pontiff and saints must be invoked. How then those whose minds had been enlightened by the word of God longed to point these souls to Christ Jesus their compassionate; loving savior; standing with-out of Enmity sinful nature; their care and weariness: They longed to clear away the obstructions which Enmity Satan had piled up that men might not receive the promises; and come directly to God: Confess their sinful and obtaining genuine pardon and peace: Eagerly did the Vaudois [Waldensian] missionaries unfold to the inquiring mind the precious truth of the gospel. Cautiously he produced the carefully written portions of the word of God.

It was indeed, his most great pleasure to give hope to the conscientious; Enmity sinful- stricken souls who could see only a God of vengeance: Waiting to execute justice: With quivering lips and tearful eyes did he, often on bended knees, open to brethren the precious promises from Christ that reveal the Enmity sinners' only hope. Thus the light of truth penetrated to many people who were in darkened minds-hearts; rolling back the cloud of gloom until the sun of righteousness shone into the hearts with healing in his beams. The sun of righteousness that shone in past is available even today to shine into the hearts with healing in our beams. Some portions of scriptures are read again and would assure himself that he heard right. Especially was the repetition of these words eagerly preferred: "As Moses lifted up the serpent in the Exodus wilderness, even so must the Son of Man be lifted up that whosoever believes in him should not perish, but have ever-lasting life." [John 3: 14-15]. In those days like today; there were many people deceived also un-deceived in regard to the claims of Judaism traditionalists; and early century pontiff Rome traditionalists. It is the inheritance seed of their forefathers which they repeat. Even though they saw how vain is the mediation of men or angels in behalf of the Enmity sinful nature. As the true light dawned upon their hearts and minds; they exclaimed with pleasing hearts; "Christ is my light; my priest; his blood is my sacrifice: His altar is my confession.

They saw this truth, acknowledged and repented. They cast out them wholly upon the merits of Christ Jesus: Repeating the words, "without faith it is impossible to please God!" [Heb 11: 6]. In other words: "Those who live in the flesh will not please God:" There is none other name under heaven given among men, whereby we must be saved: Only Christ Jesus is the name above all! [Acts 4: 12; &. Rom 8: 6-8] the assurance of the Lord Christ Jesus' love seemed too much for some of these vulnerable poor tempest-tossed souls to realize: So great was the relief which it brought, such a flood of light was shed upon them that they seemed transported to heaven. And so it is with us even today; their hands were laid confidingly in the hand of Christ Jesus; our feet were planted upon the solid Rock of Ages: All fear of death was banished! They could now covet the prison and the fagot if they might thereby honor the name of Christ their mighty redeemer. Jesus Christ is inevitable! You ignore him at your own wicked risk. In the secret places the word of God was thus brought forth and read like today; sometimes to a single soul, sometimes to a little company-group who were longing for the mighty word of God to heal their hearts. Often the entire night was spent in this manner; studying the Scriptures or preaching. So great would be the wonder-signs and admiration of the illuminating light as they heard in their listening ears and hearts keeping. That was the message of repentance, mercy was not infrequently compelled to cease his reading until well understood or could well grasp the tidings of salvation. This is what the modern world needs to hear. God's word of truth it is ever refreshing to the thirsty souls. Are you real thirsty for God's fuel to burn your spirit?

The compelling invitation from Christ, request for all! "Come to me, all you who labour and are heavy laden, and I will you rest!" [Matt 11: 28]. Will you agree? Often would words like these be uttered: "Will God indeed accept my offering? Will he real smile upon me? Yes! God in Christ would. You see; God has already promised. His word is truth: "Come to me." Jesus said. Faith grasps the promise and the glad response is heard: "No more long pilgrimages to make: No more painful Enmity. I may come to Christ Jesus just as I am." You ought to recognize your Enmity sinful nature and acknowledge it. God knows all your transgressions. Enmity resisting against God cannot take you that far. A tide of sacred pleasure would fill the heart, and the name of the Lord Jesus Christ would be magnified in praises and thanksgiving. Those happy lost souls returned to their homes to diffuse light, to repeat to others as well as they could, their new experiences that they had found the true and living way-life. You and I need that. Will you agree? [See Luke chapter 15]. The messenger of truth went on his way; but his experience of humility, his sincerity, his earnestness and deep fervor were subjects of frequent remark. In many instances his hearers had not asked him where he came from or whither he went: They had been so overwhelmed, at first with surprises and afterward with warmth gratitude and joyful, that they had not thought to question him. When they had urged him to accompany them to their homes, he had replied that he must visit the lost souls-sheep of the flock: They wondered among themselves: "Could he have been an angel from heaven? They queried.

Athanasius-John T. Nkomo

In many cases the messenger of truth was seen no more. He had made his way to another land he was wearing out his life in some unknown dungeon, or perhaps his bones were whitening on the spot where he had witnessed for the truth. But the words he had left behind could not be destroyed or forgotten. They were doing their work in the hearts of men and woman, the blessings results will be fully well known only in the judgment day. The early century missionaries were invading the kingdom of Lucifer Satan-Enmity; and the powers of darkness aroused to the greater vigilance. Every effort to advance the truth of God was well watched by the prince of Enmity evil, and he excited the fears of his agents. This kind of fears and evil agents, we see it in variety of activities today: Movie stars; Christian fiction ebook; Believers of Top Publishers rejecting true biblical Christian books; lacking strong religious leaders; Christians' compromise with secular world theories; and so forth:

The early century pontiff papal leaders saw a portent of danger of their cause from the hard work of those humble itinerants. If the words of truths were allowed to be spread or proclaimed to hearers unobstructed; it would sweep away the heavy clouds of their Enmity sinful that enveloped the people; it would direct the minds of men and women to God alone; and would eventually destroy or stop the supremacy of pontiff Rome. It was the same idea of ancient Judaism Pharisees; Sadducees; Sanhedrin; Priests; and Hellenists; so forth. It is also the same idea even today: There is no different:

The very existence of this people, holding the faith of the ancient church; present church; was and still is a constant testimony to ancient Judaism and early centuries pontiff Rome to present modern age. Their refusal and our refusal to surrender the Scriptures was and is also an offense that Rome could not tolerate: Neither modern world can tolerate!. This is not new thing! This is not arguments but true facts in our midst as it was in the past! It must be clear: That God is still the same as in the past! Nowadays; began the most terrible crusades against God our maker: Many people around the globe are in their awful mountain homes. Inquisitors were put upon their track, and the scene of innocent children before terrors is often repeated. It was also like that in the past: Innocent Abel was murdered by Cain: The first murder took place on earth since then no ceasing blood-sheds on ground till this day! God inquired: "What have you done?" And God still inquiring today, "What have you done?" [See Gen 3: 14-19 &. Gen 4: 10]. Will you agree?

Again and again were their fertile lands waste; their dwellings and chapels swept away, and the same procedures still with us; so that where once were flourishing fields and the homes of an innocent; industrious people; there remained only a desert; this kind of practice will not cease until Christ returns. Enmity as it was in past, will continue to persist. As the ravenous beast is rendered more furious by the taste of blood, so was the outrage of the Judaism and pontiff Rome kindled to greater intensity by the sufferings of their victims. If the Vatican Church and Canterbury Church are the light of the world: Why then the world still remains in its darkness? When 1.2 billion World Christians are shining around the world; would we not live in a better world? Many of these witnesses for a pure faith were pursued across the mountains and hunted down in the valley like hunting wild deer where they were hidden; shut in by mighty forest and pinnacles of rocks. No charge could be brought against the moral character of this proscribed class. Even their enemies praised them to be peaceable, quiet, pious people. When true born again Christian gather together; they will never disagree! The Holy Spirit makes them unanimous united. But there aren't many: We all know this evidence to be truth: [Acts 2]: Their great offense was that they would not worship God according to Judaism. For this crime, every humiliation insult and torture that men or devils could invent was heaped upon them. But this one particular day of Pentecost was different than all other occasion days; because the Holy Spirit from heaven was upon them.

The ancient Judaism Pharisees and the early centuries pontiff Rome at one time determined to exterminate the hated reformers [Enmity sinful sect,] a bull or decree was issued by the pontiff pope as the Pharisees did in the past condemning the work of Christ as heretics; and delivering them to the flames fire alive: The same idea as ancient Romans crucifying Christ on a tree!. They inherited the character of their forefathers; and so us even today modern age era we are on same online inheritance.

During the ancient days of Judaism; and during the early centuries pontiff prelates; they maliciously accused the disciples, as well as the reformers as idlers; dishonest; disorderly; because it was obviously seen that they had an appearance of earnest piety and zealous and sanctity seduced "many vulnerable souls as the sheep of the true fold. Therefore the pontiff ordered that the malicious and abominable sect of malignant, if they refused to abjure, "be crushed like venomous snakes." Did this haughty potentate expect to meet those words again? Did he know that they were registered in the Book of Life in Heaven to confront him at the righteousness judgment? **"Inasmuch as you have done it unto one the least of these my brethren; you did it unto me." [Matt 25: 40]. Jesus said:**

Nowadays the true-words of Christ are taken for granted as we ignore them. Yet, Christ meant it well with his words of truth. He will reclaim/fulfill his words when all nations will confront him at the righteousness judgment!. This decree or bull invites all to take up the cross against the heretics. In order to stimulate them in this cruel work, it absolved them from all Ecclesiastical pains and penalties; it released all who joined the crusade from any oaths they might have taken: It legalized their own conscience title to any property which they might have illegally acquired; and promised remission of all their Enmity sinful nature which they inherited from their fathers to such as should kill any heretic. Will you agree? But it is all about truth! We still practice this appalling Enmity sinful which we inherited from our forefathers! We are in their blood from generations to generations, it is unbroken chains!

It annulled all contracts in favor of Vaudois ordered their domestics to abandon them; forbade all persons to give possessions of their property. How clearly does this document reveal the master spirit behind the scenes! It is the roar of the lion-aggression to devour the vulnerable poor deer! It is every hungry! Human beings hunger for power; prestigious; proud; or puff! But for how long Enmity stands for your limit: You will not last long enough: For dust you are: And to dust you shall return!" God's commands firmly stand unshaken: Those who felt to be great leaders on earth; are all dead no more to be seen! But God lives forever! "I put Enmity between you and the woman!" God said: No change since then: Death prevails! Will you agree? Yes! You do! Truth is un-conquered! God's Truth! Medical scientific claims to prolong life: Yet he too dies! Can blind man guide another blind man? Both fall into a deep pit! It is also truth: The Lord Christ Jesus spoke the words of truth. "Hypocrites!" He denounced the ancient Pharisees. [See Matt 23.] His words live into many true saved souls unnoticed. Jesus Christ is inevitable! You ignore him at your own wicked risk:

The ancient and the modern world leaders would not conform their characters to the great standard of Christ Jesus' meekness, lowly in hearts; obeying God's perfect law; but erected their human corrupted Enmity sinful to suit them and determined to compel all to conform to this because they remain unresolved Enmity which they inherited from their forefathers! It is inescapable! The most horrible tragedies are enacted! Enmity corrupt and blasphemous world religious are compromising with secular world leaders! They take their false-sense of power and often leads them to false-sense of weakness in the eyes of God!

Justice and merciful has no place in their natures: The same spirit of their forefathers: Rejecting true Messiah, the Christ they crucified him! And slaughtered all those who followed after him! Today; we do not set Christians on flames fire alive as before: Methods differ: The idea of the gospel destruction is the same with different application to disguise past Enmity sinful: Numerous denominations development with numerous doctrines: Written Christian fiction ebooks: Believers of Top Publishers rejecting to publish true biblical Christian books that teach truth written by great emerging un-popular authors: Secular world scholars omitting teaching Scriptures into their scholasticism: Christians compromising with secular world: Bible translations: These are new modern methods which hinder the gospel of true-Christ Jesus growth. Well; highly designed device to oppose God's truth: Enmity. Who decides? The growth of Enmity increases exponentially on modern world era.

In the ancient day and in the early century's day, as well as the modern day; persecutions visited for many centuries upon the God's fearing people were endured by them with a patience and constancy that honored their great redeemer Christ Jesus.

Notwithstanding the crusades against them, and the inhuman butchery to which they were subjected; they continued to send out their young committed Christian missionaries around the world to scatter the precise true word of the Lord Jesus Christ: Still not all were committed to Christ who went around the world as missionaries: The righteous missionaries were hunted to the death while the unrighteous missionaries were not hunted to death because they sided and compromise with secular leaders. I am the living witness of Mt. Selinda Mission School from 1953-1959. Some missionaries; who came from westerns, were not born again Christians but wicked: Some were partial born again. One of them: John C. Heinrich. He was not a perfect man but he practiced God's truth than others. Heinrich one day damped me at Umtali country town stranded. He shows no pity: It was toward the end of British colony, in Southern Rhodesia now Zimbabwe.

Early century before Martin Luther was born. Scattered over many lands, they planted the seeds of the future to repeat reformation that began in the time of **John Wycliffe**: Grew broad and deep-deeds anguish the days of Martin Luther latter and is to be carried forward to the end of time by those who also are willing to suffer: All this for the word of Christ Jesus the world' savor: And God the Head Father and for the testimony of Christ Jesus.

Let us brief historical review: Romans Pagan Origins:

"Rites and Ceremonies" of which [Neither Christ; Peter; nor Paul] ever heard nor taught: Crept silently into use, and then claimed the rank of divine institutions: Officers for whom the primitive disciples could have found no place; and titles which to them would have been altogether unintelligible began to challenge attention; and to be named "Apostolic." See William D. Killen: [The Ancient Church] p xvi: The belief in miracle-working objects; talismans; amulets; and formulas was dear to Christianity, and they were received from pagans antiquity the vestments of the clergy and the papacy title of "Pontifix-maximus" were legacies from pagan Rome: The Church [Catholic] found that rural converts still revered certain springs; wells; trees; and stones; they thought it wiser to bless to Christian use: Pagan festivals, are dear to the peoples reappeared as Christian feasts; and pagan rites were transformed into Christian liturgy:

The Christian calendar of saints replaced the Roman [fasti-calendar of gods]; ancient divinities dear to the people were allowed to revive under the names of Christian saints: Gradually the tenderest features of "Astarte; Cybele; Diana; and Isis were gathered together in the worship of Virgin Mary." These images still exist even today. See Will Durant: [The Age of Faith; [1950, pp 745-746]. The Church [Catholic] the pagan Rome philosophy and made it the buckler of faith against the heathens: They took the Roman pagan Pantheon; temple of gods; and made it sacred to all the martyrs: So it stands to this day modern era: Like king Ahab who brought Baal idol from Tyre for his queen Jezebel to worship in true God's temple: Ahab built highways provoking God! [1 Kings 18: 24-26]. Elijah, God's true prophet challenged all Baal's pagan prophets; [500] slaughtered by Elijah's single sword. Both Ahab and Jezebel perished.

Early Church [Catholic] pontiff, prelates took the pagan festivals and made it the Christian Sunday: They took the pagan Easter [in honor of Ishtar] and made it the feast we cerebrate during this season [Halloween] witchcraft practice. Obviously it is all about past inheritance. Hence the church would seem to suggest "keep that ancient pagan system it is our inheritance" Indeed, it shall remain consecrated and sanctified;" human sanctification of course!.

Early Church [Catholic] dedicated to "Balder became the Christian sacred to Jesus Christ." 1.2 billion World' Christians believe as significant teaching Christ' approved. No wonder why the world still remains to its deepest darkness. 1.2 billion World' Christians show no different at all because they are anti-Christ living into the secular Christendom world. No matter how you overlook the issue: It makes sense. Our forefathers Enmity sinful inheritance dominates all! Jesus Christ will eventually bring the all answers we all eagerly long to see and hear. God will fulfill His holy word. "Let justice run down like waters! And righteousness like mighty stream!" [Amos 5: 24].

Therefore, bitter had been the war waged upon the Bible that at times there were very few copies in existence so that the word of God would be exponentially distributed around the world: But God had not suffered his word to be wholly destroyed! It is because the function of Enmity Satan still persisting until this day! Its truths were not to be forever hidden! God could as easily un-chain the words of life as he could open prison doors for Peter, Paul, and unbolt iron gates to set his saints merely free: Yet, God would allow some saints to suffer-death like Stephen; James; and others such as John Huss; Jerome; and John the Baptist: In the different countries and nations of tyranny Europe; men were moved by the Spirit of God to search for God's truth as hidden treasure. Providentially guided to the Holy true Scripture from God's mouth rather than the pontiff Rome' mouth: They studied the pure sacred pages with intense interests: They were willing to accept the true light shining direct from Christ, at any cost to them. The Scriptures shows us that God has never chosen a prominent human to make his purpose to be fulfilled: Never! He chose simple to prosper his purpose: His purpose never fails: That simple meek person in God's hand will burn like unquenched fire! He only obeys God; no one else no matter what cost! He will boldly go!

Though he does not see all things clearly, he will be enabled to perceive many long buried things of truth plainly as he trusts in his God. As heavens sent messenger he will boldly go forth; rending asunder the chains of Enmity sinful corruption and superstition; and calling upon those who had been long enslaved to rise and assert their true-liberty. Even if you trust in evil, you will still do it as you see it fitting. But death surprises you. Whatever you choose brings forth a reward. Who decides matters: Except among the [Waldenses] the word of God had for ages been locked up in languages known only to the highly educated; but the time had come for the Scriptures to be translated and given to the people of different languages in their native culture-tradition. And still on this day.

John Wycliffe was the herald-champion of reform, not only for England alone but for all secular world Christendom: Wycliffe was the progenitor of the Puritans; and his era was an oasis in the desert! Had no compromise mind with secular pontiff teachings: Wycliffe received a liberal education and with him the fear of the

Lord God was the beginning of his wisdom. He was early noted at college for his fervent piety as well as for his profound remarkable high potential talents and sound mind scholarship. His seed was highly selected before he was conceived into his mother's womb. God knew what quality of fruit he would produce.

John Wycliffe obtained his education from the civil and the Canon law, and he sought to become acquainted with every branch of knowledge. In his after tasks the value of his early discipline was apparent: While he could wield the sword of the Spirit, he was acquainted with the practice of the schools. This combination of accomplishments won for him the high respect of all parties of his peers. His followers saw with satisfaction that their teacher was foremost among the sages and doctors of his time. The Lord God saw him fit to in trust the work of reform to one whose intellectual ability would give character and dignity of his task-labour. This silenced the voice contempt and prevented the adversaries of truth from attempting to put discredit upon his cause by ridiculing the ignorance of the advocate. When John Wycliffe had mastered the necessary learning from the schools he then resumed the study of the Scriptures: **Brief historical review about John Wycliffe:**

All the events about John Wycliffe [1328-1415] occurred between [1328 A.D.] &. [1415]. He became Pastor of **Lutterworth in [1374]** and in [1377] papal bulls or decrees were hurled against him. Two rival popes were elected in [1378] and the Great Schism began. Their fighting lasted until in [1415]. Between [1382] &. [1384] John Wycliffe translated the Bible into English. It was not complete of both; Old and New Testament.

The events concerning John Wycliffe; John Huss; and Jerome happened between [1396] &. [1428]. He was appointed rector of the University Church; and the Bethlehem Chapel in [1402]. His denunciations of corruption began in [1405], and Prague was placed under interdict in [1412]. The Council of Constance [1414-1418] burned John Huss alive in [1415] and Jerome in

[1416]. The Hussite' wars lasted until [1434] in Bohemia. Martin Luther was not yet born in Germany: See John Wycliffe Biography.

Every subject to which Wycliffe turned his attention he was accustomed to exclusively investigate thoroughly, and he pursued the same course with the Bible. He would not miss-a single page. Heretofore he had felt a great want which neither his scholastic studies nor the teachings of the church could satisfy his eagerness of investigation. It was so natural for him for his own self-satisfaction. In the Scriptures he profoundly found that which he had before sought in vain: Here, Wycliffe saw the perfect plan of salvation revealed, and Christ Jesus set forth as the only advocate for man. John Wycliffe saw the pontiff Rome that has forsaken or omit the truth of the Scriptures or Biblical paths for human traditions. He gave himself to the service of Christ Jesus, and determined to proclaim this truth which he had discovered in the true Holy Bible that the pontiff Rome has omitted or disguise its truth. Therefore, he commenced with great prudence, but as he discerned more clearly the Enmity sinful of the pontiff papacy, he taught more earnestly; intrinsically the doctrine of true-faith in Christ! His knowledge-wisdom of the theology; his penetrating mind; the purity of his own personal life; and his unbending courage and integrity; won for him general confidence and self-esteem. Indeed, he was most able and earnest teacher and an eloquent-vibrate-preacher; and his daily life was a demonstration of this truth he proclaimed.

John Wycliffe; who could overcome him with all knowledge and wisdom? He was probably in the spirit of Stephen or Elijah or John the Baptist. Simple and lowly but powerful in spirit! "If Christ Jesus is on our side: Who can be against us?"

John Wycliffe; he expostulating and accused the pontiff clergy of having banished the holy scriptures and immediately demanded that the authority of the Bible should be re-established in the church! Many people in the church [Catholic] had become dissatisfied with their former faith!. Since they saw the Enmity sinful that prevailed in the pontiff Rome church, and they hailed with unconcealed pleasure of the truth brought to view in these discussions; but the pontiff leaders trembled with outrage-anger when they perceived that this John Wycliffe reformer was rapidly gaining the influence greater than their own corrupted influence. John Wycliffe was a clear thinker and filled with divine spirit and a keen detector of Enmity sinful nature; he struck the pontiff doctrines boldly against many of the human abuses sanctioned by the authority of the pontiff Rome. Thus Wycliffe brought upon him the Enmity sinful of the pontiff pope and his supporters. Repeated attempts were made to condemn and execute John Wycliffe for heretic; but God had given him favor as his best seed planted; protected him in the hand of princes who stood firm for his defense. Nothing could harm him if not authorized by high divine authority which is above all. While acting as Chaplain for the King, he had taken a bold/firm stand against the payment of the tribute claimed by the Vatican Pope from the British Monarch; and had forceful declared the pontiff pope assumption of authority over secular world rulers to be contrary to both reason and revelation. A few years later he ably defended the rights of British Crown against the encroachments of the Rome pontiff power.

The people of England as a whole sided with John Wycliffe including the princes, and his enemies could accomplish nothing against him. Upon one occasion, when he was brought to trial before a Synod of pontiff bishops, the multitudes of people surrounded the whole entire building where the Synod met, and rushing into it, stood firm-on hand chains between him and all harm. They awfully scarred them. About this time, strife was caused in the church by the Enmity conflicting claims of two rival pontiff popes. Each professed infallibility; and demanded obedience. Each called upon the faithful to assist him to make war upon the other enforcing his demands by terrible anathemas against his adversaries; and promises of rewards in heaven to his supporters. How dare could be? Putting themselves in a position of God: This occurrence greatly weakened the power of the pontiff papacy and saved John Wycliffe from further persecution. They couldn't put their dirty hands upon Wycliffe. God never authorized. God had preserved John Wycliffe with great favor for his cause to proceeds. For more important tasks ahead. John Wycliffe, like all other saints, preached the true gospel to the vulnerable poor in spirit. As a professor of theology, Wycliffe presented the truth to his students under his instruction, and received the title of "The Gospel Doctorate." In his parish he addressed the people as true friends and pastor. No distinction of superiority.

John Wycliffe greatest work in his life was to translate the Bible into English language. This was the first complete English ever made in England for New Testament. The printing industry being still unknown it was only by slow and wearing work that copies of the work could be multiplied; yet this was done and the people of England received the Bible in their mother language with great pleasure. Thus the light of God word began to shed its bright beams athwart the darkness. A divine hand was preparing the way for the great reformation. Yes! It was still a long walk to freedom of the Bible in the world: Enmity sinful world resisted intensively. But God strongest hand prevailed. Enmity took its place a long way back and it still going on a long way ahead. The appeal to men's reason aroused them from their passive submission to pontiff papal dogmas. The Scriptures were fully received with great favor by the higher classes who alone in that age possessed a knowledge of letters. John Wycliffe now taught the distinctive doctrines of Protestant salvation.

Through personally faith in Christ Jesus, and the sole infallibility of the scriptures!. Many of other priests joined in circulating the newly printed Bible and preaching the true gospel everywhere in England region: And great was the effect of these hard working new born again Christians depolarized from the pontiff tradition doctrine-teachings; because of John Wycliffe commitment writing influence that the new faith was fully accepted by nearly one-half of the nation-wide of England.

Far better great change in tiny island of England in [1328-1415] than 1.2 billion world Christians so claimed in the 20th century who make no different as that of John Wycliffe day. It is the challenge to the readers. Will you agree? The Enmity sinful nature, is the kingdom of deep anguish darkness trembled outrage-anger of the pontiff Rome in the early centuries church. Mendicant friars who swarmed in England, listened in anger and amazement to his bold eloquent vibrates utterances of words! Enmity, the hatred; hostiles; of the pontiff Rome was absolute kindled to greater intensity; and again they plotted to silence the John Wycliffe's great reforming voice! Like today's "Believers of the Top Publishers" industry forbid publishing good quality biblical Christian books written by those so called, "unpopular platform authors." They stimulate awful self-publishers who terribly screw unpopular platform authors: These self-publishers companies will never sale the books after they have been highly paid their packages. Suppose books sell by any means of fortunate-chance; still the author earns no royalty package which they promise to pay: They will not pay the unpopular platform author! His book becomes publisher' property.

In those days of John Wycliffe; the Lord Christ Jesus covered with his powerful-defense shield the messenger of truth! The efforts of his enemies to stop his perfect set up plan by the hand of the mighty God; and to destroy his life were alike unsuccessful; and in his 61 years old, John Wycliffe natural-death came to end rather than being tortured in flames fire by the Rome pontiff council: In the very service of the altar where Wycliffe died peacefully: The doctrines which had been taught by Wycliffe continued for decades to spread; but soon the pitiless storm of persecution burst upon those who had dared to carry on the Bible as their guide and standard of living. This Bible will never cease to be proclaimed it will continue until Christ returns! Jesus Christ is inevitable! Martyrdom succeeded martyrdom: The advocates of truth; proscribed and tortured; could only pour their suffering out-cries into the ear of the Lord.

The hunted reformers found asylum as best they could among the lower-lowly classes provided by the mighty God, like Elijah God sent him to a vulnerable widow at Sidon to feed him with her last drop of oil and bread. It never dried out for over three and half year drought-famine in the land. The preaching in secret places and hiding away even in dens and caves. Many bore fears witness to the truth in massive dungeons and Lollards towers. The Vatican pontiff had failed to work their will with John Wycliffe during his life; and their Enmity hatred could not be satisfied-but ever dissatisfied while his body peaceful rested quietly in the grave. Perhaps Wycliffe still sleeping this day, God knows, like all other saints still sleeping. When they wake up as God will eventually call them; they will not remember how long they have been sleeping. More that forty years after Wycliffe death; his death; his bones were disinterred and publicly burned; and the ashes were thrown into a neighboring brook. What a cruel act? "The brook," says an old famous writer: "Did convey his ashes into Avon: Avon into Severn into the narrow seas; and they into the main ocean; and thus the ashes of John Wycliffe are the emblem of his doctrine; while now is dispersed in the whole world over!"

Little did his enemies [the pontiff Rome] realize the significance of their malicious act: Enmity sinful; hatred; hostility; disagreement; opposition; envy; covet; still going on as we inherited these bitterness which defiles the world nations!. We cannot escape the righteousness wrath of the Lord God judgment! Yes! It was through the writings influence of John Wycliffe that John Huss of Bohemia was strongly led to renounce many of the

Enmity sinful hatred of Rome pontiff Pope, and for John Huss to enter upon the work of reform. Not only that; but to fulfill the prophecy fulfilled in the words of the Lord Jesus Christ: **"Not one stone shall be left here upon another; that shall not be thrown down!"** [Matt 24: 2].

Like John Wycliffe; John Huss was a noble Christian; a man of well highly educated and had answering devotion to the truth. His strength appealing the Scriptures and his fearless boldly denounced the awful scandalous and immoral lives of the clergy; prelates; priest; awakened wide-spread interest; and thousands gladly accepted-believing in a pure faith of the Lord Christ Jesus; taking path of John Wycliffe from England' inheritance. This excited the ire of pontiff pope and prelates and friars; and John Huss was brutal summoned to appear before the Council of Constance to answer to the charge of heresy! Enmity sinful they inherited is overwhelmed at hearts and minds excitedly evil. A safe-conduct was granted him by the German emperor and upon his arrival at Constance he was personally assured by the pontiff that no injustice should be done upon him: It was a malicious deceitful. In a short of time, however, he was placed under arrest by order of the pope and cardinals; and thrust into a loathsome dungeon for weeks with inadequate food/water supply. He was an ordinary monk: Why God could not save him? Yet, God saved John Wycliffe: Did God fail this time to save Huss?

Some of the nobles and ordinary people of Bohemia addressed the issue to the Constance Council earnest protests against this outrage anger. The emperor; who was loath to permit the violation of a safe-conduct; opposed the proceedings against him: But the enemies of the early reformers were malignant and determined. They were indeed hard with their stiff-necks. They appealed to the emperor's prejudices; to his fears; to his zeal for the church: They brought forward disagreements arguments of great length to prove that John Huss is well perfectly at liberty not to keep faith with a heretic; and that the council being above the emperor; could free his word. Thus they prevailed as evil they were Enmity sinful seemed to win at times. Even the cross for Christ could not be prevented:

After a long-range of trial in which he firmly maintained the truth; John Huss was required to choose whether he would recant his doctrines or suffer-consequence-death by flames-fire alive: Would he recant? John Huss chose martyrdom rather than to recant. **"Let this cup pass: "But nevertheless but not my will but your will not mine." Jesus prayed at Mount Olive. Christ chose the Cross. Prophecy fulfilled.**

John Huss like his high savior chose martyr's fate and after seeing his books given to the flames; he was himself burned to ashes at the stake. In the presence of the multitudes of the assembled dignitaries of church and state; the servant of the Lord Christ Jesus had uttered a solemn and truth faithful protest against the corruptions of the Rome pontiff pope hierarchy. Huss execution, in shameless violation of the most solemn and public promise of protection; exhibited to the whole world of the past; present; and future the perdifious cruelty; Enmity sinful hatred; malicious-deceitful nature man ever saw/heard on earth. Is God weak? Deaf, Blind? "I AM!" He proclaims: [Exodus 3: 14]. The enemies of truth; though they knew it not, were furthering the cause which they sought vainly to destroy. In truly; however; they repeated their own seed of their own destruction planted by their forefathers which now they reap. They inherited their forefather's evil seed. **"I put Enmity between you and between the woman; and between your seed and between her seed."** You and I are the seeds of the past which we inherited. See Gen 3: 15].

In the gloom of his dungeon; John Huss had foreseen the triumph of the true faith: Returning in his dreams to the humble parish where he had preached the gospel; he saw the pontiff pope and his bishops effacing the pictures of Christ Jesus which he painted on the walls of his Chapel. It was indeed a remarkable picture of Christ to look. The sight caused him great distress; but the next day was filled with pleasure as he beheld many artists busily engaged in replacing the figures in greater numbers and brighter colors. What is church history teaching us today? Also why historians records? When their work was completed; the painters exclaimed to the immense crowd surrounding them: "Now let the pope and bishops come! They shall never efface them more!" Said the reformer as he related his dream; "I am certain that the image of Christ will never be effaced! They have wished to destroy it but it shall be painted in all hearts by much better preachers than myself." The reformer said. Yes! It is better to paint the image of Christ into heart rather than paint it on walls.

Soon enough after the death of John Huss: Jerome his faithful friend; fearless but profound intelligent and a man of the same fervent piety character as Huss and of greater talent in Scriptures Education: He was also condemned and he met his fate in the same manner as John Huss. So perished God's true faithful servant with great light-bearers: But the light of the truths seed which they planted which they inherited the growth of their heroic example could not be extinguished. As well might men attempt to turn back the sun in its course; as to prevent the dawning of that day which was even then breaking upon the world: They couldn't turn back the sun that set apart for is triumphant-successfully. Neither today!

Notwithstanding the out-rage Enmity sinful nature of persecution; a calm; devout; earnest; intrinsically; patient protest against the prevailing Enmity sinful and corruptions of tradition human religious faith-meaningless continued to be uttered after the death John Wycliffe; John Huss; and now Jerome.

During the ancient Judaism Pharisees in Jerusalem: Like the believers of disciples; apostles; many saints freely sacrificed their worldly possessions for the cause of Christ Jesus: It is the same spirit was inherited by these mighty three men: Wycliffe; Huss;

and Jerome: The occurring event was close in neighborhood tiny islands of England and Bohemia. Those who were permitted to dwell in their homes gladly received their brethren who had been banished from home and kindled. When they too were driven forth; they accepted the lot of the out-cast and rejoiced that they were permitted to suffer for God's truths: "Rejoice and be exceedingly glad for great is your reward in heaven, for so they persecuted the prophets who were before you!" Jesus assured them the promise. [Matt 5: 12]: Furthermore; Jesus affirmed this fact: "Do not think that I came to destroy the Law or the Prophets: I did not come to destroy but to fulfill!" [v. 15].

Strenuous efforts were made to strengthen and extend the power of Enmity hatred; hostiles; resistance; and bitter of the Rome pontiff pope; but while the popes still claimed to be Christ's representatives, their lives were so corrupt as to disgust the godly people: Like ancient Judaism Pharisees in Jerusalem became their ancestors of early centuries religious leaders. By the aid of the invention of printing, the Scriptures were widely circulated, and many people were led to see that the pontiff papacy tradition teaching doctrines were not sustained by the word of the Lord God but man: Like today' Christian fiction ebook doctrines. It can't be true divine doctrines. When one witness was forced to let fall the torch of truth; another seized it from his hand and with undaunted courage held it aloft. The struggle had opened that was to result in the emancipation of slavery; not only of individuals and churches; but of nation-wide. This is how God mighty merciful operates No matter how you try. It will not work!. Why struggling; resisting; with God your maker? How far will you go? "For dust you are: And to dust you shall return!" When/how will you learn a lesson from God? Can't you see?

Across the gulf of a hundred years or more; men stretched their hands to grasp the hands of the Lollards of the time of John Wycliffe. Under Martin Luther began the radical reformation in

Germany: John Calvin preached the gospel in France: Zwingli preached the gospel in Switzerland: The world was awakened from the slumber of ages: As from land to land were sounded the magic words of truths: "Religious Liberty!" Whose religious liberty?

The Lord Jesus Christ repeated his words in the fulfillment of the all the prophecies; from Mount Sinai: Ancient Judaism: Early centuries church [Catholic]: Till this day modern age era: God and the testimony of Christ Jesus: "For I know this," Jesus said: "That after my departing shall all grievous wolves tribulations come upon you; not sparing the flock: Also of your own life shall men rise; speaking perverse things; to draw away all things that showed you and taught:" "Blessed are you when they revile and persecute you; and say all kinds of evil against you falsely or maliciously for my sake." Yes! It was well foretold: The phrase: "God knows:" We take it for granted: Indeed, God knows all things! Particularly our motives: God searches the heart' motives: What driving motive in your heart/mind that interests God. [Psalm 139: 1-4; 1 Sam 16: 7; Acts 20: 29-30; Matt 24: 9-12, 13, 20, 21, 22; &. 2 Thess. 2: 3-4; Rev. 12: 5; 14: 8] Biblical truth! Pierce the hearts. Will you agree?

Foremost among those who were chosen/called to lead the Church from the darkness of Judaism Pharisees in Jerusalem; Vatican popery; Canterbury Archbishop; Islam; into the light of a purer faith; stood: John Wycliffe; John Huss; &. Jerome: Latter, Martin Luther: Zealous as those with Enmity sinful nature: Ardent and devoted, knowing no fear but the fear of God, and acknowledging no foundation for religious faith but the Holy Scriptures: Among them young man named "Saul" zealous Judaism Pharisee. Both sides evil Enmity and goodness constitutes zealous: But who wins? **"Saul, Saul, why are you persecuting me?" "Who are you? "I AM Jesus! Who you are persecuting. It is hard for you to kick against the goads!"** Saul **trembling and astonished; said: "Lord, what do You want me**

to do? "Arise and go into the city, and you will be told what you must do." [Acts 9: 4-6]. From that moment Saul was transformed to true-zealous with new name, Paul was blinded and now he could see more clearly:

Martin Luther like Paul was the man for his time: Through him God accomplished a great work for the reformation of the church and the enlightenment of the world: Taking the steps of Saint Paul' zealous. Like the first heralds of the gospel, Martin Luther sprung from the ranks of poverty. From that poverty God uplifted him to high-top mountain' shining light. Luther's early years-childhood were spent in the humble home exposure/environment of a German peasant farm. When he saw those exposed into poverty environment; he fully understood with empathy-sympathy as his own nature. By daily toil as a miner, his father earned the means for his education. His father had desire for his son become a lawyer; but God designed seed for him to make him a builder of corner-stone in the great temple that was rising its foundation exponentially but sure through the early centuries until this day!. God's nature must fulfill its truths:

Inheritance from our forefathers is crucial: Martin Luther's father was a man of strong active mind and great force of character; honest; resolute; and straightforward!. Well balanced quality health to expose seed that Martin inherited from his early up bringing; poverty to be well shaped environment: It is well selected seed to plant for future growth to reap: His father and mother were true to his convictions of duty, let the consequences be what they might be: His sterling good sense led him to regard the monastic system with distrust. He was highly displeased when Luther enlisted without his father's consent entered a monastery, and it took two years before his father reconciled to him: Martin Luther had to obey God's calling rather than obey his father. After all who is the maker of Luther Senior? And even then his opinions remained the same. As good parents; Martin Luther parents bestowed great care upon the education and training of their children. They endeavored to teach/instruct them in the knowledge of God and the practice of Christian virtues. It was important for the whole Luther's family. The fear of the Lord God is the beginning of knowledge:

The father's prayer often ascended in the hearing of his son that the children might remember the name of the Lord God and one day aid in the advancement of his truth. Good seed planted for their inheritance is very significant: "You will know them by their fruits."

Their beginning efforts were earnest, intrinsically preserving to prepare their children for a health life of genuine piety and meaningful/purpose for God's glory. With their firmness faith and strength of character deeply rooted in Christ; they some-times exercised too great severity; but the reformer Martin himself consciously; that in some respect they had erred; and found in their discipline more to approve than to condemn: At elementary school which he was sent at very early age; Martin Luther was ill-treated with harshness and even physical-violence was practiced upon him. So great was the devastating poverty of his homely-parents, that for a time of decade he was obliged to obtain his food by public market-street singing from door to door; and he often suffered from empty stomach-hunger: I had same experience: I was born and raised up in devastating poverty in South Africa apartheid!. I would be obliged to pick up bread thrown into dust-bins. Yes! I ate it to satisfy my empty-stomach. I couldn't resist hunger!. Neither could the Lord. Enmity Satan took advantage to tempt the Lord because he too was hungry. The Lord had the righteous word for self-defense: "It is written." I had no knowledge of Scriptures.

The gloom; superstitious ideas of religion then prevailing filled with Luther and fear like I was in South Africa. He would lie down at night with a sorrowful heart/mind wondering; but looking forward with trembling to the dark unknown future: And of course; in constant terror at the thought of the Lord God as a stem; unrelenting Judge; a cruel tyrant rather than a king-loving heavenly perfect Father; the sustainer of all life. Yet under so many and so great devastating poverty; discouragements: Martin Luther, pressed on resolutely forward toward the high standard of moral good and intellectual excellence which God had planted, he had determined to achieve. No turning back! The Lord Christ Jesus is his shield.

Let's brief review Martin Luther historical-ground

The events of Martin Luther' life in this brief chapter covers the period of time: Between Nov 10th, 1483 and January 2nd, 1521 ; the first 37 years of Martin Luther's life: He was admitted at the [Erferth University in 1501]: Received his Master Degree in 1505]: He traveled to Vatican Rome in [1510]: Received his PhD in Theology in [1505] there he began preaching: Martin Luther wrote most compelling-appealing-astonishing piece of true Biblical challenging the pontiff Rome tradition teachings; 95 pages of his phenomenal "Theses" nailed it on the Castle Church door on October 31^{St}, [1517] where a multitudes could read it: Two years later: Tetzel died: Phillip Melannchthon arrived in [1518]:

Martin Luther's Trial at Augsburg took place in October [1518]: Two years later: Pope Leo X's bull/decree condemned Luther. Furthermore; Martin Luther eagerly thirsted for knowledge and the earnest intrinsically practical characteristic of his sober mind led him to desire further the solid and useful tasks rather than the showy minstrel-misogyny and superficial pontiff Rome.

When at the age of 18th years old, he entered the University of Erfurth his situation was more favorable and his prospects high-potentials-brighter than in his early elementary years. His vulnerable poor parents having/living by thrift but compelling industrial acquired a competence; they were able to render him all needed assistance. And the influence of judicious friends had some-what lessened the gloomy effects of his former training.

He now diligently applied himself to the study of the best scholar and author, enriching his understanding with their most weighty mature-thoughts and making the wisdom of the wise his own inheritance.

A well retentive memory, s vivid imagination, strong maturity-reasoning power, and energetic application to rightful studies; soon won for him the foremost right seed inherited rank among all other associates! As you may well see; God is very right: When He speaks about seed: "You will know them by their fruits!" Good seed: The fear of the Lord God dwelt in the heart of Martin Luther' father and mother enabling Martin to maintain his steadfastness of purpose and leading him to deep root-humility before the eyes of God his only maker. This is the truth: Inheritance: Martin Luther had an abiding sense of his forefathers of his dependence upon divine aid and he did not fail to begin each day with prayer; while his heart was continually breathing a petition for good/right guidance and support from God alone. It is something/powerful truth to grasp! To well pray with submission to God alone: He often said: "Is the better half of study." While one day examining the books in the liberty of the university; Martin Luther self-discovered a written Latin Bible: He had never seen/heard before translate-fragments of the Gospels and Epistles at public worship; it was absolute hidden to public eyes; and he thought that they were the whole of God's word truth! Like Saul, before was Paul: Ananias came to Saul to restore his sight: One word Ananias prayed: "Brother Saul, the Lord Jesus, who appeared to you on the road as you came; has sent me that you may receive your sight." Immediately there fell from his eyes like scales." [Acts 9: 17-18]

Martin Luther self-discovery like Saul self-discovery to eternal salvation first they need to open their eyes to see truth. It can't be if not Christ who is able to open the blindness of your eyes. Now for Martin Luther, for the first time like Saul; he looked upon the whole Bible written in Latin language at the time: Curious discovery: With mingled awe and wonder he turned the perfect sacred pages; with quickened pulse and throbbing heart-eagerness he read for hours at a quiet place himself the words of truth; life proclaimed; pursuing now and then to exclaim: "Oh, if God would give me such a book for my own inheritance!" Indeed; angels of heavens were by his side in support; and rays of light from the standing. Luther now, had ever feared to offend the living God; but now the deep root of self- conviction of his own condition as an Enmity sinful surrounding him; took hold upon him as never before and caused him throbbing heart.

"The fear of the Lord God is the beginning of knowledge: But fools despise wisdom and instruction." Non on earth can afford to object this teaching truth! [Prov. 1: 7]

An earnest desire to be free from Enmity sinful and to find peace with Christ Jesus his Lord, led him at last to enter a cloister; and devote himself to a monastic life. Here he was required to perform the lowest drudgery and to beg from house to house. Luther was at an age when respect and appreciation are most eagerly craved; and these mental offices were deeply mortifying to his natural feelings; but he patiently endured this humiliation believing that it was necessary because of his own Enmity sinful nature. Luther recognized this from early childhood. His foundation was well nurtured in devastating poverty. Every moment that could be spared from his daily-hash duties he employed in study robbing him of sleep; and grudging even the moments spent at his humble meals if there was any food available that God could provide. Above everything else he delighted in the study of God's word in Christ Jesus; this Latin Bible was his only source of life for him on daily basis. It was the secret disguise for big events to come. The mind of revolting against the pontiff Rome superstition wasn't yet present. He passively obeyed the pontiff rules. Like Joseph sold slavery in Egypt; did not know how/why/what God has prepared for him ahead. Neither Luther: The mysteries of God are high than mountains; deep than ocean. God has it all in His own authority-powerful.

Martin Luther had found a Bible chained to the convent wall and to this he often repaired the damages. As his own personal conviction of Enmity sinful deepened; he seriously sought by his own works to obtain pardon and peace. He led a most rigorous life; endeavoring to crucify the flesh of his own by daily fasting; praying; watching; and scourging etc.: He shrank from no sacrifice to become holy and gain heaven peace and happiness as promised by the pontiff Rome. He was zealous to his own faith. As the result of this physical painful discipline; he lost strength-weakened and suffered from fainting causing himself as he suffers from atrial-fibrillation heart rhythm; spasms; from the effect of which he never fully understood and not recovered; Enmity sinful deceit spiritual in the monastic life. But with all his efforts; his burdened soul found no relief at all! Did God bring this for him to suffer such agony? His obedience was to imitate eternal. The Scriptures which he read would bring him life. He needed more to be profound transformed like Saul whom Ananias restored his sight. God still has to deal with him more effectively. Martin Luther was at last driven to the verge of despair. Yet God had the true cure for him. When it appeared to Luther that all was lost; God raise up a faithful friend to help him.

The pious Staupitz opened the true word of God again to Luther's heart and mind; and bade him look away from himself; cease the contemplation of infinite punishment for the violation of God's law; and look to Christ Jesus for his Enmity sinful-to pardoning great world savior. Christ Jesus only can justify Enmity sinful nature! Instead of torturing yourself on account of you Enmity sinful; cast yourself into the arms of your savior Christ

Jesus only is able to justify. There is no human torturing justification; but only Christ Jesus can be justified. Put all your trust in Christ Jesus! Like Saul when Ananias came; restored his sight in the name of the Lord Christ Jesus! No one else!. Martin Luther was newly strengthened. Listened to his faithful friend true words from the mouth of Christ.

Trust in the Lord God: In the righteousness of his life in the atonement of his death. Listen to the Son of God Jesus Christ. He became man to give you the assurance of divine favor. Love; mercy; compassion; and justice: His words made a deep impression upon Martin Luther's mind. After many a struggle with long cherished human errors he was enabled to grasp the truth and peace came to his troubled soul.

Later; Martin Luther was ordained a priest and was called from the cloister to a professor-status in the University of Wittenberg. Here he applied well himself to the study of the Scriptures in the original language - Hebrew. He began to lecture upon the Bible; and the book of Psalms; the Gospels; and the Epistles-of Paul were opened to the understanding crowds of delighted listeners. Staupitz his faithful friend and superior-above him; urged him to ascend/stand on the pulpit and preach the word of God. Luther expostulating hesitated; feeling himself inadequate-unworthy to speak to the multitude of people in Christ's name-stead. It was only after a long struggle that Staupitz persuade him that he should yield to the solicitations of his faithful friend. Already he was mighty in the Scripture, and the grace of God is well rested upon him. Luther; with his eloquence-vibrating voice captivated his audience-hearers the clearness and power with which he presented the word of truth convinced their well understanding: His deep fervor touched their hearts. He was absolute highly talented to preach. This time, Luther was still a unique-true obedient to the pontiff, prelates Rome perhaps naïve at mind of the pontiff papal church; and had no thought that he would ever be anything else to resolve revolt. In the providence of God he decided to visit the Vatican Rome Church where pope dwells with all bishops; prelates; and priests. For him; it was like entering into heaven. Rome most prestigious city; ruler of the world at the time; it was indeed compelling place to visit and see it with open eyes how Rome paganism city looks like: Luther from devastating poverty lowly raised up; he did not know what Rome was like in the eyes of the mighty God: He expected a dazzling heaven illumination: Surprisingly; he saw most it as dark it can be: God initially give him an opportunity to see it.

Luther enthusiastically pursued his long mission to heaven Rome on foot, lodging at the nearby monasteries on the half-way. At a convent in Italy he was filled with splendor wonders as he saw the wonder splendor of the red-bricks apartment-buildings; the richness of the dresses; the luxury of the table-the extravagance everywhere on streets. With painful misgiving he contrasted this scene with self-denial and hardship of his own early childhood poverty life. His mind was becoming so perplexed: "Did I real expect to see things like this?" Finally; and at last he beheld in the distance the seven-hilled Vatican city. The real expected perfect heaven: With deep emotion he prostrated himself upon the earth: **Exclaiming: "Holy Rome," I salute thee!"** He entered the city; visited the churches; listened to the marvelous tales repeated by pontiff; priests; prelates and other ordinary monks of his own rank level; and performed all the ceremonies required.

Everywhere he enthusiastically looked upon scene that filled him with astonishment and horror: He saw that Enmity Sinful existed among all classes of the clergy. He heard indecent remarks-jokes from prelate's pontiff and was filled horror-hurts-hatred; at their awful profanity; even during mass-sermon. As Luther mingled with monks and citizens; he met dissipation; debauchery! He turns where he would in the place of sanctity he found profanation: Far worse than two Aaron's sons:

Nadab and Abihu.

God killed them both at spot for profaning God's holy Altar. Luther saw it.

"It is incredible!" He wrote: "What Enmity sinful nature and atrocities are committed in Vatican Rome!" If there be a hell; the Vatican Rome is built above it!" It is an abyss whence all Enmity sinful proceed!" He declared: Mistrust toward the Vatican; for Martin Luther depolarized. Like Saul; a zealous Pharisee after scales was removed from his eye blindness; denounced every form of Judaism teaching in Jerusalem! Paul a new name; was to confront a severe persecution as predicted by the Lord Christ Jesus. **"For I will show him how many things he must suffer for my name's sake!"** [Acts 9: 16]: Luther read a passage from Roman book "Justification." Paul wrote.

An indulgence had been promised by the Vatican pope to all who should ascend on their knees what was known as "Pilate's" "Staircase." A suspected step where Saint Peter walked Luther Martin was one day performing this act; when suddenly a voice like thunder boom seemed to say to him: "The just shall live by faith!" He sprung upon his feet in shameful and terrible horror; and fled from the scene of his folly: That text never lost or ceases its compelling power upon his lost-trembling soul. From that-moment he saw more clearly than ever before the fallacy of trusting to human works for salvation and the necessity of constant faith in the merits of Christ Jesus. His eyes now has been fully opened and were never again to be closed; to the satanic Enmity sinful: delusions of the Vatican papacy. Like Paul his eyes now has been full opened and were never again to be closed to the satanic Enmity sinful; delusion of the Judaism Pharisees in Jerusalem. Persecution he must confront: When Luther turned his face from Rome; he had turned away also in heart and from that time the separation grew wider until he severed all connection consequences with the Vatican papal church. No more compromise within the Vatican. After Luther had returned from Rome; he received at the University of Wittenberg the doctorate degree of divinity [PhD]. Now he was at more liberty to devote himself as never before to the Scriptures that he most loved. He had taken a solemn vow to study carefully and to preach with fidelity the word of God; not the sayings and doctrines of the Vatican popes; all the days of his life-long.

At this time; Martin Luther was no longer a mere monk-rank or a university professor; but fully the authorized herald of the Bible-true living God's word authority. He had been called to a zealous shepherd to feed the lost hunger flock of the living mighty God!. No matter what cost! Like Saint Paul: "For me to live is Christ! And to die is gain!" That were hungering and thirsting for truth. He firmly declared that Christians should receive no other doctrines that those which rest on the authority of God's Sacred Scriptures! These words struck very heavy upon the Vatican pontiff papal supremacy foundation. They contained the most vital essentially principle of the Church Reformation! John Wycliffe foundation was not that strong enough to change the Vatican Church teachings. But Wycliffe laid a foundation for future builders for its completion.

King David provided the materials for God's temple: But Solomon built the temple for its completion. Martin Luther saw the danger of exalting human theories above the word of God. He fearlessly attacked the speculative infidelity of human scholasticism and opposed the human philosophy and theology which had so long controlling influence upon many people in Europe. Even kings and emperors were under the feet of the Vatican Church. Even today; some are. Luther totally denounced: It was not Luther but God's Spirit in the form of Luther. He denounced such studies as not only worthless but pernicious and sought to turn the minds of his audience hearers from the sophistries of philosophers and theologians to the eternal truths set forth by prophets; Christ Jesus; disciples and apostles now to the early century church to present day. Christ Jesus triumph. The Lord God chose a man at a time to achieve his valuable purpose. It is too costly. Precious was the message which he bore to the eager multitudes that hung upon his words from the mouth of the living God. Never before had such teachings fallen upon their ears and hearts: The glad tidings of a savior's love; the assurance of true pardon and peace through Christ Jesus atoning blood; rejoiced their hearts; and inspired within them an immortal hope! It is like today; we preach true pardon and peace through Christ Jesus atoning blood. At Wittenberg community a light was kindled whose rays should extend to the uttermost parts of the earth; and which was to increase in brightness to the close of time. But light and darkness cannot harmonize. Between truth and untruth there is an irrepressible Enmity conflict. To uphold and defend the one is to attack and overthrow the other. Enmity sinful we attack in Christ Jesus to overthrow its evil authority on earth! There shall be no rest until this evil Enmity is radical eradicated! Christ only who can. He is our shield from the Bereshith. No! Church Reformation isn't complete yet; not until Christ returns. The compelling question is: Who will lead us? We constantly pray for God choose a leader like Luther to lead us. Perhaps this will never take place because Christ is coming back. But we all long for peace: Our Lord Christ Jesus said this vividly clear: "I came not to bring peace; but a sword." [Matt 10: 34]. Luther a few years after the opening the reformation said: "God does not conduct; but drives me forward. I am not master of my own actions. I would gladly live in repose; but I am thrown into the midst of tumults and revolutions."

Martin Luther was now about to be urged into the contest: The Roman Catholic Church had made merchandise of the grace of God. The tables of the money-changers like the day Jesus triumph entry into Jerusalem temple; he saw tables of the money changers; were set up beside the altar; and the air resounded with the shouts of buyers and sellers. The Pharisees; priests denied the Gentiles who truly sought to worship God in Spirit and truth. Christ' anger was out-rage; he turned upside down their tables of money changers! They were dishonest with their weighing scales-cheating the vulnerable poor widows. Luther saw these tables of money changers. Under the plea of raising funds for the erection of Saint Peter Basilica Church at Rome; indulgences for Enmity sinful were publicly offered for sale by the Vatican authority of the pope. Enmity sinful; made Luther to denounce against their evil actions. By the price of treason crime a temple was to be built up for God's true worshipers in Spirit. Today the Vatican boast to be world leader of 1.2 billion Christians. Yet, the world life is miserable!. The corner-stone laid with the wages of Enmity sinful. But the very means of pontiff aggrandizement provoked the deadliest blow to their power and greatness. Today the church is like chaff shifting as the wind blows to a direction. Yet, they are deaf to Christ' prediction: "I say to you; **not one stone shall be left here upon another; that shall not be thrown down!" Jesus said: [Matt 24: 2]. "On Christ solid rock will stand; but all other ground is sinking sand!."** Where is the Vatican Church built? But on potsherd among the potsherds on the ground: [Isaiah 45: 9]: "Woe to him who quarrels with his maker; to him who is but a potsherd among the potsherds on the ground!" God said. The prophecy will be fulfilled no matter how you overlook the issue. It was this that aroused the most determined and successful of the enemies of the Vatican and led the battle which shook the Vatican papal throne to its foundation; and jostled the triple-crown upon the pontiff's head.

The officials appointed to conduct the sales of indulgence in Germany: Tetzel by name had been convicted of the basest offenses against society and against the law of God: But having escaped the punishment due to his treason crimes; he was employed to further the mercenary and Athanasius-John T. Nkomo unscrupulous projects of the pontiff Rome Church. With great effrontery he repeated the most glaring falsehoods and related marvelous malicious tales to deceive an ignorant; credulous; and superstitious people. How could they deceive God? If not their own deceitful? It was to keep them under the control of the pontiff papacy; that they might swell the power and wealth of their ambitious leaders; that the Bible had been withheld from them.

As Tetzel entered a town; a messenger went before him announcing his arrival: "The grace of God and of the holy father is at your gates!" The multitudes of people welcomed the pontiff blasphemous malicious pretender as if he were God himself come down from heaven; a mere human who is also a great criminal in the community exalted him. The infamous traffic was set up in the pontiff church, and Tetzel ascending the pulpit; extolled indulgences as the most precious great gift of God. He declared that by virtue of his certificates of pardon, all the Enmity sinful which the purchaser should afterward desire to commit would be forgiven him; and that even repentance was not indispensable!

More than this he assured his audiences hearers that the indulgences had all power to save not only the living but even those who are dead sleeping in their graves shall rise; that the very moment the cash-money should clink against the bottom of his chest; the vulnerable distress soul in whose behalf it had been paid would immediately escape from purgatory and make its way to eternal heaven life. Many simple souls believed in his most pagan malicious pontiff crafting-cunning words in the ears of God whom they claimed to serve as holy vicarage. When Simon Magus "the magician" offered to purchase of the apostles the power to work miracles-signs:

Saint Peter answered him: "Let your money perish with you "Enmity Sinful-evil," because you thought that the gift of God could be purchased with money!" You have neither part nor portion in this matter; for your heart is not right in the sight of God!" "Repent!" Therefore of this your [Enmity sinful], wickedness, and pray God if perhaps the thought of

your heart may be forgiven you!" For I see that you are poisoned by [Enmity sinful] bitterness and bound by satanic!"

[Acts 8: 19-24]. The Bible shows us that Simon requested saying: "Pray to the Lord for me, that none of the things which you have spoken may come upon me." [See James 5: 16]

But Tetzel's offer was grasped with eagerness multitudes of people who believed his words from empty lips. Gold and silver flowed into his Vatican treasury. A salvation that could be bought with money manufactured by wicked human hands; far worse than idolatry worshiper-witchcraft!. Like today great multitudes spend money to watch the muscular sportsmen all day-long screaming; but ever dissatisfied in pleasure! They stimulate violence sport-watch.

Early centuries church; indulgence could be bought with money was more easily obtained than that which required repentance; faith; and diligent effort to resist Enmity sinful nature and overcome its deceitful crafting-cunning words!.

The doctrine of indulgences had been opposed by men of well learning and true-piety in the Vatican Rome Church; and there were many people who had no faith in pretensions like today; so contrary to both reasons and revelation. Yet no bishop dare lift his voice against the awful fraud and corruption of this Enmity sinful nature: Same alike 21st century priests who sexual malice young children more than 500 priests law-suit conviction; yet no bishop dare lift his voice against shameful-atrocities actions of corruption of this heinous Enmity sinful traffic. The minds of men were become and still becoming more disturbed even today and uneasy; and many eagerly inquired if God would not work through some instrumentality for the purification of God's temple. Nowadays there's this saying mutual "apology" on behalf of the Vatican Church. Miss-trust prevails among them.

Martin Luther thought still a pontiff of the straightest sort was filled with horror at the blasphemous assumptions of the indulgence-mongers! Many people of his own congregation had truly purchased certificates of pardon; and they soon began to come to their Pastor; confessing their various Enmity sinful; expecting absolution not because they were penitent and wished to reform; but on the ground of the indulgence. Martin Luther refused them absolution; and warned them that unless they should authentically repent and reform their lives; they must perish in their Enmity sinful nature. In great perplexity they sought out Tetzel and informed him that an Augustine monk had treated his letters with contempt; in reference to Luther refusal to their absolution. Tetzel; the friar was filled with out-rage anger-hostility; hatred against Luther. He uttered the most terrible curse causing fires to be lighted in the public square; and declared that he had orders from the Vatican Pope to burn the heretics-Martin Luther who dared oppose his most holy indulgences.

But Luther now vigorously entered boldly upon his work as a Champion of truth! He is standing on Christ solid Rock Foundation! His voice was boom-heard from the pulpit in earnest, intrinsically; solemn warning! He set up before the multitudes of people the offensive characteristic of Enmity sinful and taught them that it is impossible for a mere man; by his own works; to lesson' its guilty or evade its punishment! Nothing but repentance toward God and faithful in Christ Jesus can save the heinous sinner [Enmity sinful] no-one else!

The grace of Christ Jesus cannot be purchased! It is a free great gift from above in heaven!" Martin Luther counseled the people not to buy the indulgences no more! But to look in faith to a crucified the Lord Jesus Christ the world's savor! Luther related his own personal painful poverty -lowly experience in vainly seeking by humiliation and penance to secure salvation; it did not work; and assured his congregation audience that it was by looking away from him and believing in the Lord Jesus Christ that he found peace in personal-peace and joy. Through meekness-lowly humble in prayer. As Tetzel continued his traffic and his impious malicious pretensions; Luther further determined upon a more effectual protest against these awful crying abuses. The festival of all-saints was an important day for Wittenberg, like Halloween in USA in October. The costly relics of the church were then displayed and remission of Enmity sinful was granted to all who visited the church and made confession. Accordingly on this day the people in great large number as Halloween day in USA, resorted thither. On the day preceding the festival; Martin Luther went boldly and vigorous to the church to which crowds of worshipers were already repairing; and affixed to the door ninety-five [95] propositions against the doctrine of **indulgence:** Which Tetzel crafting propagating. Great excitement was created in the University community atmosphere including the whole Wittenberg city region. By these theses which Luther wrote; it showed that the power to grant the pardon of Enmity sinful nature and to remit its penalty; had never been committed to the Vatican pontiff pope or to any other man on earth! But through Christ Jesus only: No one else!

The whole scheme the 95 theses strongly urges: "Was a farce; an artifice to extort money by playing upon the superstitions of the people; a device of Lucifer Satan [Enmity sinful] to destroy the souls of all who should trust to its malicious lying pretensions." It was also clearly shown that the gospel of the Lord Jesus Christ is the most valuable-costly treasure of the Church; and that the grace of the Lord God in Christ Jesus, therein revealed is freely bestowed-given upon all who truly; earnestly; intrinsically seek it by faithful repentance and truth.

No human money can purchase God's perfect salvation!

Martin Luther's theses deeply challenged discussion: But no one dared accept the challenge: Like today 20th, century modern era dare accept the world current affairs challenges confronting them atmospheric! They contend to suggest that: "We are well secured-in every way of safety measure!" They are wrong! Without God's word' security measure: No human on earth dares to claim for such! The compelling questions which Luther proposed had in a few days spread throughout all Germany region; and in a few weeks they had sounded throughout world Christendom. Man devoted people who had seen and lamented the terrible Enmity sinful like today world's unceasing outcries prevailing in every form of man' invented denomination-churches; governments; but had not known how to arrest its progress; read the propositions with great joy and pleasure; recognizing in the true voice of the Mighty Living God!

They some felt that the Lord had graciously set up his hand to arrest the rapidly swelling tide of pontiff corruption that was issuing from the see of pontiff Rome. Princes, kings, emperors and court magistrates secretly rejoiced that a check was clearly put upon the arrogant power from which there was no human's appeal: Mind you; God enabled Balaam's donkey to speak: Because God put his powerful word into donkey's mouth to speak against Balaam' motives of corruptions: Balaam's motives displeased God; so God stopped him to compromise with Balak king of Moab. Num 22: 28-30]… So, God put the words into Luther's mouth to speak!

The Vatican papacy had to eventually bow down to knees and yield to God his maker!. But the Enmity sinful; and love of human superstitious multitudes were terrified as the sophistries that had soothed their fears were swept away! Crafting and cunning Ecclesiastics interrupted in the work of sanctioning crime and seeing their gains endangered; were enraged and rallied to uphold their pretensions. The modern man today is able to provide sophisticated crafting-cunning language for self-gain; it is pretty much the as the past!. See TV commercial advertising: They carry away your thoughts before you know.

The reformer [Luther] had bitter accusers to meet. Some charged him with acting hastily and from impulse. Others accused him of presumption; vividly denouncing/declaring that Luther is not direct ordained of God; but acting from selfish-pride and forwardness-for self-power above pope etc.: Who does not know." He responded, "That one can seldom advance a new idea without having some appearance of pride; and without being accused of acting quarrels?" Why were Christ and all the martyrs put to death?" Because they appeared proud despised of the wisdom of the times in which lived; and because they brought forward new truths without having first consulted the oracles of the old opinions." Furthermore; Martin Luther affirmed his faith: "What I am doing will not be effected by the prudence of man, but by the counsel of God. If the work of God who can stop? If it be not, who shall forward it? Not my will, not theirs, not ours, but "The will of the Holy Father who art in heaven!" In other words: "If God is on my side: "Who can be against me? " Do not be afraid; Abraham "I AM Your Shield!" God' promise. [Gen 15:1].

Although Martin Luther had been moved by the Spirit of God in Christ to begin his great task-work, he was not to carry it forward without severe Enmity hostility; conflicts. Like the ancient disciples and apostle before him went through all tribulations as foretold by the Lord Jesus Christ. He vividly knew what it takes to revolt against the Vatican. The reproaches of his enemies their malicious misrepresentations of his purposes and their unjust-unmerciful malicious reflections upon his character and conscience-motives, came in upon him like an overwhelming Tsunami earthquake flood; and they were not without effect. He had felt confident that the leaders in the church and the philosophers of the nations would gladly unite with him in efforts for reform. Words of encouragement and comfort-wisdom from those in high rank positions had inspired him with great joy and peace of mind given from above and hope. Already in anticipation he had seen a bright day dawning for the church.

The Body of Christ the corner-stone the builders rejected. He stood firm on Christ solid rock! All other ground sinking sand: But truth and encouragement had changed to reproach and condemnation. Many dignitaries both, of church and state were convicted of the truthfulness of his theses; but they soon saw that the acceptance of these truths would involve great changes: To enlighten and reform the stiff-neck people would be virtually to undermine the pontiff papal authority to stop-thousands of streams now flowing into their treasury and thus greatly to curtail the extravagance and luxury of the pontiff Rome-leaders. Furthermore; to teach the people's hearts to think and act as responsible beings, looking to Christ Jesus alone for their salvation they desperate need, would overthrow the pontiff' throne and eventually destroy their authority.

For this reason they refused the knowledge rendered them of God, and arrayed themselves against Christ Jesus and the truth by their opposition to the man whom he had sent to enlighten them in hearts. It was no easy task: Like the ancient days: Elijah; Daniel; Ezekiel; Babylon was tough to break. God had tougher word to break Babylon. Luther trembled as he looked upon himself, one man opposed to the mightiest power of earth-Vatican. He sometime doubted whether he had indeed been led of God to set himself against the pontiff authority of the church. "Who was I," he wrote: "To oppose the majesty of pontiff pope before whom the kings of the earth and the whole world trembled?" No one can know what I suffer in those first two years and into what dejection and even despair I was sunk. But Martin Luther like all who went before him; he was not left alone to become utterly disheartened. God mysterious rescued Peter on chains between two soldiers in jail.

When human support failed he fixed up his eyes upon Christ-looked to God alone and learned that he could lean in perfect safety upon that all human power reinforced by Enmity sinful Satanic arm.

To a faithful friend of the reformation: Martin Luther wrote: "We cannot attain to the understanding of Scriptures either by study or strength of intellect. Therefore your first duty must be to begin with prayer. Entreat the Lord to deign to grant you, in His rich mercy; rightly to understand his word. There is no other interpreter of the word but the Author of that word himself. Even as he has said; "they shall be all taught of God." Hope nothing from your study and strength of intellect but simply put your trust in God and in the guidance of His Spirit: Believe one who has made trial of this matter." Here is a lesson of vital importance to those who feel that God has called them to present to others the solemn truths for this time. These truths will stir the Enmity sinful of Satan, and of men who love the fables that he has devised. In the conflict; disagreement; disobedience; with the power of evil, there is need of something more than intellect and human wisdom.

Chapter 3

Wittenberg University's Guest House

In 1874, women were admitted to the college, and, the following year, blacks were admitted. The name of the school came from the historic Wittenberg University, in the town where then and theological professor Martin Luther [1483-1546] famously posted his 95' theses on the chapel church door on [October 31, 1517]:

Perlach market place in 1550] In 1530, the Augsburg Confession was presented to the holy Roman emperor at the Diet of Augsburg. Following the Peace of Augsburg in 1555, after which the rights of religious minorities in imperial cities were to be legally protected, a mixed Catholic and Protestant city council presided over a majority Protestant population; see Paritätische Reichsstadt.

Thirty Years' War

Religious peace in the city was largely maintained despite increasing Confessional tensions until the Thirty Years' War (1618-1648). In 1629, Holy Roman Emperor Ferdinand II issued the

Edict of Restitution, which restored the legal situation of 1552 which again curtailed the rights of the Protestant citizens. The inequality of the Edict of Restitution was rescinded when in April [1632] the Swedish army under Gustavus Adolphus captured Augsburg without resistance.

As Tetzel continued his traffic and his impious malicious pretensions; Luther further determined upon a more effectual protest against these awful crying abuses. The festival of all-saints was an important day for Wittenberg, like Halloween in USA in October. The costly relics of the church were then displayed and remission of Enmity sinful was granted to all who visited the church and made confession. Accordingly on this day the people in great large number as Halloween day in USA, resorted thither. On the day preceding the festival; Martin Luther went boldly and vigorous to the church to which crowds of worshipers were already repairing; and affixed to the door ninety-five [95] propositions against the doctrine of **indulgence** which Tetzel crafting propagating. Great excitement was created in the University community atmosphere including the whole Wittenberg city region. By these theses which Luther wrote; it showed that the power to grant the pardon of Enmity sinful nature and to remit its penalty; had never been committed to the Vatican pontiff pope or to any other man on earth! But through Christ Jesus only: No one else!

The whole scheme the 95 theses strongly urges: "Was a farce; an artifice to extort money by playing upon the superstitions of the people; a device of Lucifer Satan [Enmity sinful] to destroy the souls of all who should trust to its malicious lying pretensions." It was also clearly shown that the gospel of the Lord Jesus Christ is the most valuable-costly treasure of the Church; and that the grace of the Lord God in Christ Jesus, therein revealed is freely bestowed-given upon all who truly; earnestly; intrinsically seek it by faithful repentance and truth. No human money can purchase

God's perfect salvation! Martin Luther's theses deeply challenged discussion: But no one dared accept the challenge: Like today 20th, century modern era dare accept the world current affairs challenges confronting them atmospheric! They contend to suggest that: "We are well secured-in every way of safety measure!." They are wrong! Without God's word' secure measure: No human on earth dares to claim for such!

The compelling questions which Luther proposed had in a few days spread throughout all Germany region; and in a few weeks they had sounded throughout world Christendom. Man devoted people who had seen and lamented the terrible Enmity sinful like today world's unceasing outcries prevailing in every form of man' invented denomination-churches; governments; but had not known how to arrest its progress; read the propositions with great joy and pleasure; recognizing in the true voice of the Mighty Living God! They some felt that the Lord had graciously set up his hand to arrest the rapidly swelling tide of pontiff corruption that was issuing from the see of pontiff Rome. Princes, kings, emperors and court magistrates secretly rejoiced that a check was clearly put upon the arrogant power from which there was no human's appeal: Mind you; God enabled Balaam's donkey to speak: Because God put his powerful word into donkey's mouth to speak against Balaam' motives of corruptions: Balaam's motives displeased God; so God stopped him to compromise with Balak king of Moab. Num 22: 28-30]. So, God put the words into Luther's mouth to speak! The Vatican papacy had to eventually bow down to knees and yield to God his maker!. But the Enmity sinful; and love of human superstitious multitudes were terrified as the sophistries that had soothed their fears were swept away! Crafting and cunning Ecclesiastics interrupted in the work of sanctioning crime and seeing their gains endangered; were enraged and rallied to uphold their pretensions. The modern man today is able to provide sophisticated crafting-cunning language for self-gain; it is pretty much the as the past!. See TV commercial advertising: They carry away your thoughts before you know.

The reformer [Luther] had bitter accusers to meet. Some charged him with acting hastily and from impulse. Others accused him of presumption; vividly denouncing/ declaring that Luther is not directed/ordained of God; but is acting from selfish-pride and forwardness-for self-power above pope etc.: Who does not know." He responded, "That one can seldom advance a new idea without having some appearance of pride; and without being accused of acting quarrels?" Why were Christ and all the martyrs put to death?" Because they appeared proud despised of the wisdom of the times in which they lived; and because they brought forward new truths without having first consulted the oracles of the old opinions." Furthermore;

Martin Luther affirmed his faith: "What I am doing will not be effected by the prudence of man, but by the counsel of God. If the work of God who shall stop it? If it be not, who shall forward it? Not my will, not theirs, not ours, but "The will of the Holy Father who art in heaven!" In other words: "If God is on my side: "Who can be against me?" " Do not be afraid Abraham "I AM Your Shield!" God promise. [Gen 15:1].

Although Martin Luther had been moved by the Spirit of God in Christ to begin his great task-work, he was not to carry it forward without severe Enmity hostility; conflicts. Like the ancient disciples and apostle before him went through all tribulations as foretold by the Lord Jesus Christ. He vividly knew what it takes to revolt against the Vatican. The reproaches of his enemies their malicious misrepresentations of his purposes and their unjust-unmerciful malicious reflections upon his character and conscience-motives, came in upon him like an overwhelming Tsunami earthquake flood; and they were not without effect. He had felt confident that the leaders in the church and the philosophers of the nations would gladly unite with him in efforts for reform. Words of encouragement-comfort-wisdom from those in high rank positions had inspired him with great joy and peace of mind given from above and hope. Already in anticipation he had seen a bright day dawning for the church. The Body of Christ the corner-stone the builders rejected. He stood firm on Christ solid rock! All other ground sinking sand:

But truth and encouragement had changed to reproach and condemnation. Many dignitaries both, of church and state were convicted of the truthfulness of his theses; but they soon saw that the acceptance of these truths would involve great changes: To enlighten and reform the stiff-neck people would be virtually to undermine the pontiff papal authority to stop thousands of streams now flowing into their treasury and thus greatly to curtail the extravagance and luxury of the pontiff Rome-leaders. Furthermore; to teach the people's hearts to think and act as responsible beings, looking to Christ Jesus alone for their salvation they desperate need, would overthrow the pontiff' throne and eventually destroy their authority.

For this reason they refused the knowledge rendered them of God, and arrayed themselves against Christ Jesus and the truth by their opposition to the man whom he had sent to enlighten them in hearts. It was no easy task: Like the ancient days: Elijah; Daniel; Ezekiel; Babylon was tough to break. God had tougher word to break Babylon. Luther trembled as he looked upon himself, one man opposed to the mightiest power of earth-Vatican. He sometime doubted whether he had indeed been led of God to set himself against the pontiff authority of the church. "Who was I," he wrote: "To oppose the majesty of pontiff pope before whom the kings of the earth and the whole world trembled?" No one can know what I suffer in those first two years and into what dejection and even despair I was sunk. But Martin Luther as all who went before him; he was not left Athanasius-John T. Nkomo alone to become utterly disheartened. God mysterious rescued Peter on chains between two soldiers in jail.

When human support failed he fixed up his eyes upon Christ-looked to God alone and learned that he could lean in perfect safety upon that all human power reinforced by Enmity sinful Satanic arm. To a faithful friend of the reformation: Martin Luther wrote: "We cannot attain to the understanding of Scriptures either by study or strength of intellect. Therefore your first duty must be to begin with prayer. Entreat the Lord to deign to grant you, in His rich mercy; rightly to understand his word. There is no other interpreter of the word but the Author of that word himself. Even as he has said; "they shall be all taught of God." Hope nothing from your study and strength of intellect but simply put your trust in God and in the guidance of His Spirit: Believe one who has made trial of this matter." Here is a lesson of vital importance to those who feel that God has called them to present to others the solemn truths for this time. These truths will stir the Enmity sinful of Satan, and of men who love the fables that he has devised. In the conflict; disagreement; disobedience; with the power of evil, there is need of something more than intellect and human wisdom."

When indeed, enemies appealed to custom and tradition or to the assertions and authority of the Vatican pope, Luther Martin met them with the Bible in hand and the Bible alone was his strong weapon defender ever! "Do not be afraid Abraham; I am your shield!" [Gen 15: 1]: Here were intense arguments which they could not answer; therefore the slaves of formalism and superstition clamored for his blood, as the Israelites had clamored for the blood of their Lord, the Messiah; and savior of the world Jesus Christ. "He who is without sin," Jesus said: "Let him throw a stone at her first!" [John 8: 7] Scribes; Pharisees desired to justify their own self-righteous disguise their own conscience-guilty of Enmity sinful in hearts before Christ who searches motive-hearts. Jesus knew them all! "He is heretic," they expostulating malicious accusations upon Martin Luther crying on the face of innocent, the Vatican zealots; "it is a sinful to allow him to live an hour longer!" The vulnerable poor woman was saved from the Scribes and Pharisees wicked hands; Christ the righteous judge spared the woman' life and set her free. She was found committing adultery. While Luther is a champion-reformer. "Away with him at once to scaffold!" They shouted: Martin Luther did not fall a prey to their heinous Enmity sinful:

The Lord God had a great task ahead for him to do; build on the corner-stone Foundation which the pontiff rejected to build. The heaven opened its holy gates for the world to walk through the holy into holy place for earnest prayer which they block the way for decades. God protected Luther. Many people however, who had received from Luther the precious illuminating light, were made the objects of Enmity Satan's wrath and for the truth's sake fearlessly suffered torture and death! Martin Luther's teachings had already attracted the attention of thoughtful throughout all Germany regions. Even king and queen and emperor princes firmly stood with Luther! From his sermons and writings preaching and lecturing issued beams of great light could not be switched off but awakened and illuminated the whole nation of Germany. It was like fury unquenched burning flames breaking the rough high-ways of pontiff Rome! Elijah with a single sword slew 500 Baal's false prophets in a day [1Kings 18-19] Elijah first challenge to Ahab was successfully by the hand of God. Ahab was great, great grandson of King Solomon.

A living faith was taking the place of the dead formalism in which the church had so long been held. Like today modern age; there will be only a single sword to slaughter every false-malicious crafting-cunning Christian fiction ebook!

First early century Vatican; the people were daily losing confidence in the superstitions of Roman Catholic Church like today variety forms of denominations; religious statistics reports that USA Christianity is declining among the young adults. Much less church attending each Sunday. 89 percent. Very small number church attending on each Sunday in our time 21st, century era. The Second Advent; what the Lord Christ Jesus shall see? How dare the pontiff claims 1.2 billion world Christians leaders: In the past; the barriers of prejudice were giving way! The living God by which Martin Luther tested every doctrine and every claim, was like a two-edged sword sharper-piercing throats; cutting its way to internal hearts of multitude of peoples. Everywhere there was awakening in Germany a desire for new revival spiritual progress. Yes! It a spiritual revolutionary revival ever experienced; can we experience such a spiritual revolutionary revival today? Bill Graham is advanced in age who else? Who will replace Graham today?

In the past; everywhere was such a hungering and thirsting after spiritual righteousness as had not been known for decades; and ages! The eyes of the peoples, so long directed to human rights and human mediators were now turning in penitence and faithful to the Lord Christ Jesus; and Him only crucified! Yes! It pleased the Father-Head in Heaven: But Why? Enmity sinful nature: Will you agree? This wide-spread interest aroused still further stiff-neck the Vatican papal authorities: Martin Luther received a summons to appear at Rome to answer to the charge of heretic. The command filled his faithful friends with terror. They knew full well the danger that brutality expostulating threatening him in that corrupt Rome city, already drunk with human blood from John Huss; Jerome; of the martyrs of Christ Jesus. Luther's faith friends: They protested against his going to Rome and requested that he receives his examination in Germany his mother birth-land rather than to Rome foreign land! It was the greatest protest joined by young princes and nobles of Germany. As result of this great protest: The arrangement was finally effected and the pontiff Rome pope's legate was appointed to hear the case in Germany. The mighty hand of God prevailed: Did God allow Sarah to fall into the wicked hands of Pharaoh King of Egypt; and Abimelech king of Gerar? [Gen 12: 17-18 &. 20: 3-9]: "In the integrity of my heart,"

Abimelech said: "And innocence of my hands I have done this." Abimelech had already committed adultery in lust for Sarah Abraham's legitimate wife: **God saw that: "Yes! I know that!" God expostulating response; "you did this in the integrity of your heart: "For I also withheld you from sinning against Me; therefore, I did not allow you to touch her!"** [V. 6] Abimelech and Pharaoh could not dare to justify their conscience-guilty in the sight of God. "Now therefore, restore the man's wife; or else you shall surely die including all your-household!." God's righteous commands prevailed!.

In the instructions communicated by the pontiff to this official, it was stated that Martin Luther had already been denounced and declared a heretic! The pontiff legate was therefore charged to prosecute and reduce Luther to submission without any further delay. If Luther should remain steadfast; and the pontiff legate should fail to gain possession of his person, he was empowered to proscribe him in all places in Germany to put away curse and excommunicate all who were attached to him. And further the pontiff pope called upon his legate in order entirely to root out the pestilent heresy to excommunicate all, of whatever dignity in church or state, except the emperor who should neglect to seize Martin Luther and his adherents, and deliver them up to suffer the vengeance of pontiff Rome. Here then is displayed the true spirit of Vatican popery. Not a trace of Christian principle or ethic or even of common justice, is to be seen in the whole document. Luther then was at a great distance from the corrupt Rome city: He had, had no opportunity to explain or self-defend his position: Yet before his case had been investigated he was summarily pronounced a heretic; and in the same day exhorted; maliciously accused; unjust judged; and condemned; and all this by the self-styled holy pontiff father: The only supreme infallible authority in Catholic Church or State! Like Nelson Mandela facing malicious apartheid supreme court 1 in early in 1960's to 1994: Mandela was maliciously accused; unjust judged: 27 years unmerciful imprisonment: The only supreme infallible South Africa Apartheid rule: Dutch Reformed Church or State: So was Mahatma Gandhi in India: Early 1890's to 1948: And Dr. Martin Luther King, Jr. Early in 1955 Montgomery Bus Boycott to 1968: Rose Park revolts against bus segregation: They are our current modern world social; political; and economic reformers! Like early century Luther champion Church Reformer!

Now; Augsburg had been fixed upon as the place of trial for hero Luther the reformer set out on foot to perform the long journey thither: Obvious; serious fears were entertained on his behalf. Threats were severe; had been made openly that he would be away-land and murdered on the way and his close friends begged him not to venture or go. They even entreated him to leave-refugee Wittenberg for a time being; and find safe asylum with those who would gladly protect him from the hand of his enemies; the pontiff; prelates; and friars. But Martin Luther standing on Christ solid rock would dare not to shake his feet to shift either on right or left but boldly go to Augsburg and face his enemies. God is his strong shield in Christ Jesus: No one could craft his mind and soul fixed upon Christ Jesus the solid rock. "He is my chosen instrument to suffer for my name's sake." The Lord assured Ananias as he sent him to restore Saul's sight:

Neither Luther would leave the position where the Mighty God had placed him! He is well secured in the hand of the Mighty God. "His word my hope secures!" John Newton composed a magnificent Hymn. "Amazing grace!" He had a narrow escaped from wreckage ship in North Africa Seas. He ran away from African Chief who bought him slave. Newton traveled to Africa to trade slaves to England. God taught him a lesson: Instead he found himself being slaved: Yes! God's ways are mysteries:

As for Martin Luther must continue faithfully to maintain the Christ' truth; notwithstanding with the severe Tsunami storms that were beating upon him. His language was: "I am like Jeremiah and

Ezekiel; a man of strife and contention; but the more they increase their threatening; the more they multiply my joy-overflowing. They have already torn to pieces my honor and my good name: All I have left is my wretched body: let them have it; they will then shorten my life by a few hours:" But as to my soul; they shall not have that! He who resolves to bear the word of Christ Jesus to the world; must expect death at every hour!" Well spoken words from the mouth that truly trust in God. "Do not fear those who can kill only your body: But fear him who is able to kill both: Your body and your soul." Jesus said. Luther's confidence is deep.

The tidings of Martin Luther's arrival at Augsburg gave great satisfaction to the pontiff papal legate: Martin Luther like in the past; became the trouble-maker heretic because he was exciting-awakening the attention of the whole Europe regions and the world at large; seemed now in the enormous power of pontiff Rome; and the legate determined that Luther should not leave the city as he had entered. The Luther had failed to provide himself with safe-conduct. His faithful close friends urged Luther not to appear before the legate without a safe-conduct and they themselves undertook to procure it from the Germany emperor like John Huss and Jerome in Bohemia: They couldn't. It was a scandal safe-conduct of Bohemia emperor.

The pontiff legate intended to maliciously force Luther if possible to retract or failing in this, to cause him to be conveyed to pontiff Rome, to share the fate of John Huss and Jerome. Therefore through agents he endeavored to induce Martin Luther to appear without a safe-conduct; trusting himself to his God's merciful like Abraham, Isaac God did not permit Sarah and Rebekah to fall into the arms of the wicked kings who lusted for them to be in their bosoms. It was like that with Luther; the pontiff could not touch Luther. The champion Church Reformer, Martin Luther firmly declined to do so: Not until he had received the document pledging him the Germany emperor and prince's protection did he appear in the presence of the pontiff papal legate or ambassador. Luther resisted!

As a matter of policy and principle; the pontiff Rome had decided to attempt to win Luther-motives by an appearance of superficial-crafting-cunning words of gentleness. The legate when interviewed, with him professed great friendliness; but he demanded that Martin Luther submits implicitly to the pontiff Rome authority of the church, and yield every point without further argument or dispute dialogue or question. He had not rightly estimated the character of the man with whom he had to deal with. Luther had tougher God's word to break them all. It was for their own benefits. Like king Pharaoh; and Abimelech: Indeed; these wicked kings both restored Sarah to Abraham; then God saved them from His righteous wrath with fairness warning.

As for Martin Luther; in response; strongly expressed his regard for the church; his desire for the truth that would sanctify the whole Germany nation and Europe continent. His readiness to answer all objections to what he had taught and writing to submit his every written and proclaimed doctrine to the decision of certain leading Universities Institutions. But at the same time Luther expostulating he protested against the pontiff Cardinals' course in requiring him to retract without having proved him with Enmity sinful or of a human corruption as theirs!. Let God be the Judge between you and me. Luther insisted. The pontiff Rome legate response echo was: "Recant; recant!" It was supposed to be for their own recant in the sight of God: Like Pharaoh and Abimelech. They had no prove for Luther to recant or retract: Above all; it is about reforming the corrupted church. Today we see and experience about this awful doctrine, reforming the church. Who can if not Christ? He is the corner-stone!

Martin Luther showed that his position is sustained by the powerful word of God written in the Scriptures and he firmly denounced and declared that he could/will not renounce the truth written in the Scriptures from the mouth of the Mighty God! "It is written!" Christ Jesus insists! Yes! God's Word of truth is written! Jesus insists, and so is the Enmity sinful will persist until Christ returns! How is it that we ever live into darkness?

When the prelates saw that Martin Luther reasoning was unbeatable or unanswerable they lost all their self-control and in their Enmity sinful rage cried out again: "Retract! Or we will send you to Rome city to appear before the pontiff Papacy Supreme Judges Commissioned to take Cognizance of your treason case. We will excommunicate you and all your partisans and all who shall at any time countenance you, and we will cast them out of the church also." And the legate finally declared in a haughty and Enmity sinful hostiles-angry tone: "Retract! Or return no more!" The audiences into the court room were overwhelmed with silence fear that now Luther is reduced to ashes like John Huss and Jerome. What did they know behind the scene? God is in all controls: Martin Luther eventually retired with his faithful close friends; leaving the Cardinal and his supporters to look at one another in utter confusion at the unexpected result of the conference. It was unsuccessful efforts for the pontiff legate. Supposing, they knew that it is about time for their pontiff Cardinals Titanic-ship to sink into Deep Ocean irresistible: Martin Luther's efforts on this occasion were without good results. The large assembly-congregation present had opportunity to compare the two men and to make their judgment for them of the spirit manifested by them, as well as of the strength and truthfulness of their positions. How marked the contrast!

For certain they did not know God's mysteries of which are hidden in his own wisdom-powerful. Neither did Luther. Like Abraham and all the others after him did not know. Neither us even today: However; Martin Luther like John Huss and Jerome; firmly humble; stood on Christ' solid rock unshaken in the strength of the Mighty God's written Scriptures; having truth on his side;

the pontiff papacy representatives, self-important-prestigious; overbearing; haughty; and un-sober - unreasonable was without a single argument-dispute from the Scriptures; yet vehemently repeating their out-cries: "Retract, or be sent to Rome city for severe punishment!" Notwithstanding Luther had secured a safe-conduct from God's truth, the pontiff Rome were plotting more to seize and imprison Luther and final set him on flames-fire. They attracted multitudes; like Herod when he saw that the Scribes; Pharisees approval for executing John to death, Herod further arrested Peter and put him in prison. He too was to be executed to death on the next day. God mysteriously rescued Peter. They could not find him from his hiding!

As for Luther his close faithful friends urged that it was useless for him to prolong his stay; that he should return to Wittenberg without further delay and that the utmost caution should be observed in order to conceal his intentions! Martin Luther accordingly left Augsburg before day-break on horseback, accompanied only by a guard furnished him by the civil magistrate court. With many others forebodings secretly for his safe-guard made his way through the dark and silent streets of the city. Enemies vigilant and cruel; were plotting his destruction. Here is God's mysteries exercising as before during the ancient prophets; disciples; apostles; and now early century reformers. The same God still acting in forceful events.

Would actually Martin Luther escape the snares prepared for him by the pontiff Rome? Those were moments of anxiety and earnest prayer-resisting temptations; Enmity sinful Satanic would be obliged to seize the opportunity. Luther reached to a small gate in the wall of the city. It was opened for him, with his official guard he passed through without hindrance-obstacles. Once beyond the limits he soon left the city far behind. At this time Enmity Satan sinful and his emissaries were totally defeated! The man whom they had thought in their power was gone; escaped as a bird with wings flew away from the pontiff snare of the fowler.

At the news that Martin Luther departure the legate delegates were overwhelmed with surprise-fear and out-rage anger: They had expected to re receive great prestigious medals of honor for their wisdom and firmness in dealing with the disturber of the church; but their hopes were disappointed. They gave expression to their wrath in a letter to Emperor Frederick the Elector of Saxony; bitterly denouncing Martin Luther and demanding that emperor Frederick send Luther to Rome with immediate effect or banish him from Saxony. Threats that were not validated. In defense; Martin Luther urged the legate or the pontiff pope show him his errors from the Holy Scriptures and pledged himself in the most solemn manner to renounce his doctrines if they could be shown to contradict the true-Word of the Lord God! It is written! And he expressed his views-gratitude to the Lord Jesus Christ that he had been counted worthy to suffer in so holy a cause: These words made a deep impression upon the Elector Frederick and princess; and he resolved to stand as firm for Martin Luther safe-guard protection. Frederick no compromise with pontiff Rome Vatican refused to release Martin Luther to pontiff Rome city or to expel him from his Wittenberg city territories. Now the real Civil Government of Germany stood upon Luther's side what else could the Vatican pope do? The Elector Frederick stood in the position of God. Because God makes kings. Including the pope. They are all created in the image of God: Is it not so? When human obey Enmity Lucifer; they disobey God. That of course; it is high treason crime.

The Germany authority saw that there was a general breaking down of the moral restraints of society. Frederick stands on the strategic position to protect every civilian-citizen of Germany in the eyes of God his maker. King David and Solomon after him could not neglect God's Holy Temple to be defiled in the name of high Priest: David gave order to Levite Priest when the prophet Nathan communicate first to David as God utters his message through Nathan, David stood on God's side earnestly and so was Solomon. But there were other after them. Like Ahab and Balaam God judged them for their corruptions. The great task-work of Church Reformation was greatly necessary to be reformed! The complicated and expensive arrangements to restrain and punish criminals would be unnecessary if men in early century acknowledge and obeyed the necessary requirements of God in Christ Jesus, and the dedication-dictates of an enlightened conscience; like today God would still act as he did before in the past. Yes! Yesterday and today God is the same: So are the peoples! Enmity sinful nature remains with us today!

Martin Luther saw that he is laboring to secure this object and he secretly rejoiced that a better influence was making itself heart-felt in the reformed church. Martin Luther also saw that as a professor in the University of Wittenberg; Luther was absolutely eminently successful: From all parts of Germany regions; students; laymen; ordinary classes and nobles including the princes crowded to Wittenberg city to listen to his great teachings. Young adults in particular coming in sight of the city for the time; would raise their hands toward heaven; praising and thanksgiving to God that he had caused the illuminating-dazzling light of His truth overwhelming shining forth from that place throughout whole Germany community as in the ancient ages from Jerusalem Zion City is our God! Yes! Transformation has absolute arrived the people of Germany truly; authentically accepted. One singe man God chose to bring big differences as he mobilized the whole nation together. It was God true Holy Spirit discerned Luther in order to reflect it through all Germany regions.

Martin Luther was as yet; but partially converted from the Roman Catholic Church: But as he compared the holy oracles with the pontiff papal decrees and constitutions; he was filled with magnificence wonders: God's truth of splendor-wonders: It is unconquered: No matter how you would humanly try it won't work. But God is Sovereign all things are possible: Nothing is difficulty for Him! "I am reading," Luther wrote: "The decrials of the popes and I know not whether the pope is anti-Christ himself or whether he is apostle; so misrepresented and even crucified does Christ appear in them." He is indeed expostulating the pontiff to come to their sense to repentance like today; all are contemporary required to repentance: [Matt 11: 28-30]. Jesus Christ fully stretches his two arms welcomes all: "Come to Me, all you who labour and are heavy laden, and I will give you rest!" Familiar compelling words of truth:

Yet at this time Martin Luther was still a full supporter of Roman Catholic Church and had no slight thought that he would ever separate from the Catholic Church Communion. No! He didn't! He desired for its complete transformation and truly authentically teachings to the true written Scriptures. The Bible teaching principles was denied. Like Pharisees denied the Bible in all its application principles! So is today there are many who deny the Bible true teachings. So Jesus predicted: "Not all who call Me Lord, Lord will enter into heaven!"

Luther's writings and his doctrines were extending to every nation in the secular Christendom world. The work spread to Switzerland and Holland. Copies of his writings found their way to France; Spain and Portugal. In England his teachings were full received as the word of life. To Belgium and Italy also truth had extended. Almost everywhere in Europe continent thousands of peoples were awakening from their death-like stupor to the overwhelming joy and long-hopes of a life of faith. A radical change deeply took place among the western nations. The Roman Catholic Church now became more and more exasperated by the eventually attacks of Martin Luther newly found strong faith and it was secretly declared by some of his fanatical mobs opponents, that he who should take Luther's life would be without Enmity sinful nature. It was satanic device threat to stir hatred and hostilities or perhaps division among them. It was a malicious propaganda designed by the pontiff prelates to manipulate the weak minds of the young adults into violence.

One day a stranger with a pistol concealed under his cloak-or garment, and approached Luther; and inquired why he went thus alone? **"I am in the hands of God."** Martin Luther answered. "He is my help and my shield. What can men do unto me?" Upon hearing these faithful strong words, the stranger turned pale and fled away as from the presence of the angels of heaven. The pontiff Rome was bent upon the destruction of Martin Luther; but God in Christ was his real shield defense as God had promised Abraham: **"Do not be afraid Abraham, I am your shield."** [Gen 15: 1]. Martin Luther's doctrines were heard as extended everywhere in Europe continent: In convents; in cottages; in the castles of the nobles; in the universities-students; in the palaces of kings and princes; and noble men including every business were rising on every hand to sustain Luther's efforts. It was God almighty planted seed which exceedingly growth. You reap what you sowed. In a pontiff Rome to the emperor and nobility of Germany on behalf of the Church Reformation of Christianity; Luther wrote once again concerning the Vatican Pope: "It is monstrous to see him who is "called the **[Vicar of Christ;]** displaying a magnificence unrivaled by that of any emperor." Is this to represent the poor and lowly Christ Jesus or the humble of Saint Peter? The Pope, say they, is the lord of the world! But Christ, who's Vicar he boasts of being; "My kingdom is not of this world!" Can the dominions of a vicar extend beyond those of his superior?"

Martin Luther wrote thus of the Universities: "I fear much that the Universities will be found to be great gates leading down to hell; unless they take diligent care to explain the true "Holy Scriptures; and to engrave them in the hearts of youths: I advise no one to place his child where the Holy Scriptures are not regarded as the rule of life: Every institution where the word of God is not diligently studied, must become corrupt." As it is today in almost every [scholasticism] today do not regard the Holy Scriptures as the rule of life. They omit teaching Scriptures. Instead they allow Christian fiction ebook as religion textbook. This ebook accelerates its large sales everywhere in USA and Europe continent. This appeal was rapidly circulated throughout Germany; and exerted a powerful influence upon the all walks of life of peoples. The whole nation was roused to rally around the standard of reform. Many of Luther's opponents burning with a desire for revenge urged the pontiff pope to take decisive measures against Luther. It was decreed that his doctrines should be condemned immediately. Did they? Rather it was their own condemnation. Luther's doctrines prevailed. Sixty days [60] were granted to Martin Luther and his adherents after which if they did not recant, they were all to be excommunicated. That was a terrible crisis for the reformation. For centuries pontiff Rome sentence of excommunication had been swiftly followed by the stroke of death. Luther was not blind or deaf to the tempest about to burst upon him; but he stood firm all times trusting in Christ Jesus to be his support and shield. With a martyr's faith and courage he wrote again: "What is about to happen I well know not and I care not to know." Wherever the blow may reach me I fear not. Not so much as a leaf falls without the will of our Holy Father; how much rather will God care for us!" It is a little matter to die for the Word, since His Word that was made flesh for us, hath himself died. If we die with him we shall live with him and passing through that which he has passed through before us; we shall be where he is; and dwell with him forever." That is exactly what Paul said. "I am crucified with Christ my Lord."

When the pontiff bull reached to Luther; he said: "I despise it and resist it as impious and false. Christ himself who is condemned therein."

"I glory in the prospect of suffering for the best of causes. Already I feel greater liberty; for I know now that the pope is anti-Christ, and that his throne is that of Enmity Satan himself."

Yet the word of the pontiff of Rome still had power. Prison; torture; and sword were weapons potent to enforce submission. Everything seemed to indicate that Luther reformer' task-work was now about to come to an end. When Jonah was under deck of ship in his deep sleep; the weak sailors and superstitious trembled because the ship was about to sink. They did not know the cause. But the lots fell upon Jonah. "What have you done? Where do you come from? Who are you? With their eagerness they asked Jonah; he admits: "I am a Hebrew: I worship God the creator of the sea and dry land." The fear fell upon them all: Jonah volunteered: "Cast me into the water everything will be well with you." They tried hard to roll the ship to the sea-shore; they couldn't. Eventually they reluctantly threw Jonah into the wrath waters: Then the wind ceased its wrath waves at once!. [Jonah 1-2]. The weak/wicked and superstitious trembled before the decree of the pope and while there was general sympathy for Martin Luther; many people felt that life was too dear to be risked in the cause of church reform. But Luther like Jonah proceeded to publicly burn the pope's bull with the canon laws; the decrials and certain writings sustaining the papal power. By this action he boldly denounced and declared his final separation from the pontiff Roman Church. He accepted his excommunication and proclaimed to the Germany nation and Europe continent that between himself and the pope there must hereafter be war. God's war of course, upon human pontiff!. Who decides to win?

The great contest was now fully entered upon. Soon after, a new bull appeared and the excommunication which had before been threatened was finally pronounced against Luther and all who should receive his doctrines. Threats were indeed very severe and fearful. Opposition is the lot of all whom God employs to present his truth especially applicable to their time. There was a present truth; a truth at that time of special importance in the days of Martin Luther; there is a present truth for the church even today age! There aren't many who stand firm like Martin Luther today.

But truth is more desired by the majority of churches today than it was by the pontiff early century who opposed Luther. There is the same disposition to accept the theories and traditions of men for the word of God as in past ages. Those who present truth for this time should not expect to be received or accepted with greater favor heartfelt than were earlier century's reformers. The great Enmity sinful between truth and untruth; between Christ and Enmity Satan; is to increase in intensity to the end of this world current affairs and its history. Jesus Christ is inevitable! Ignore him at your own wicked risk. "Let justice run down like waters: And righteousness like mighty stream!" [Amos 5: 24].

Athanasius-John T. Nkomo

Chapter 4

Germany's throne wind of Change
brief historical review

Charles V [1500-1558] the youngest emperor in Germany history had ascended the throne was only 21 years when convened the Diet Council of Worms. Meeting in November [1520] Martin Luther appeared before it on April 17th, 1521, and gave his defense the next day. After being secretly taken to the Warburg Castle: He began translating the New Testament in December. It was published in September [1522].

A new emperor; Charles [V] the Fifth had ascended the throne of Germany, he was only 21 years old, and the emissaries of pontiff Rome hastened to present their congratulations; and induce the young monarch to employ his power against the reformation. On the other hand, the Elector of Saxony to whom Charles was in great degree indebted for his crown, entreated him to take no step against professor Martin Luther until he should have granted him a fair and just hearing. The young emperor was thus place in a position of great perplexity and embarrassment situation. The Rome pontiff papal would be profound satisfied with nothing short of an imperial edict sentencing Martin Luther to death as it was to John Huss and Jerome in Bohemia.

The Elector had early declared firmly that neither his imperial majesty nor anyone else had yet made it appear to him that Martin Luther's writings had been refuted; therefore he requested that professor Luther be furnished with a safe-conduct; so that he might answer or defense for himself before a pontiff legate tribunal of highly educated, pious, and impartial judges. The attention of all parties was now directed to the assembly of the Germany States which convened at Worms soon after the accession of Charles V to the empire of Germany. Frederick had early retired. There were important political aspiration questions and interests to be seriously considered by this national council; but these appeared of too little moment when contrasted with the cause of the monk of Wittenberg of the time.

The young Charles had previously directed the Elector to bring Martin Luther with him to the Diet, assuring him that the Luther should be well protected and secured from all hostilities violence; and should be allowed a free-and fair conference with one competent to discuss the disputed points. Martin Luther was rather anxious perhaps nervous to appear before the emperor. His health was at this time in bad shape, and much impaired; yet he wrote to the Elector: "If I cannot perform the journey to Worms in good health I will be carried there; sick as I am. For since the emperor has summoned me; I cannot doubt that it is the call of God Himself. If they intend to use vicious violence against me; as they probably do; for assuredly it is with no view of gaining information that they require me to appear before them; I place the matter in the Lord's hands: He still lives and reigns that preserved the three Israelites in the fiery furnace. If it be not God His will to save me; my life is of little consequence. Let us only take care that the gospel be not exposed to the scorn of the ungodly; and let us shed our blood in its defense rather than allow them to triumph. Who shall say whether my life or my death would contribute most to the salvation of my brethren?" Expect anything from me but flight or recantation. Fly I cannot; still less can I recant."

As the news was circulated at Worms that Martin Luther was to appear before the Diet; a general excitement was overwhelming creating atmosphere. Aleander; the pontiff papal legate to whom his case had been specially instructed, was alarmed and enraged: He saw that the result would be catastrophically-disastrous to the pontiff papacy cause: To institute inquiry into a case in which the Vatican pope had already pronounced sentence of condemnation, would be to cast contempt upon the authority of the sovereign pontiff: Furthermore; he saw apprehensive that the eloquent and powerful arguments; disagreements; resistance; hostility; well equipped-weapon with holy Scriptures of which Aleander himself was lacking; of this man Martin Luther; might turn away many of the princes from the cause of the pontiff pope. He therefore, in the most urgent manner; remonstrated with the young emperor Charles V against Martin Luther's appearance at Worms. He warned; entreated; and threatened; until the young emperor yielded; and wrote to the Elector that if Luther would not retract; he must remain at Wittenberg.

Had Goliath known that David is in the hand of God the mighty of Israel's arm; probably he would not dare to challenge the arm of the Lord: Even as David foretold him that his flesh will be given to the wild beasts and birds in the air," still Goliath didn't believe: Goliath; a Philistine giant was so much in his own self-confidence: [See 1 Sam. 17:45-47]: So David prevailed over the giant Philistine Goliath with a sling and a stone, and struck the Philistine giant and killed him." [Vs. 50-51] Luther like David, prevailed over the pontiff giant of Rome papacy because Luther was in the hand of **God Almighty!**

Aleander, the pontiff legate not content with this victory, he endeavored with all the pontiff power crafting and cunning at his own command to secure Martin Luther' condemnation. With his grotesque profligate persistence worthy of a better cause; he urged the matter upon the attention of princes, prelates and other noble members of the assembly; accusing professor Martin Luther of sedition; rebellion; impiety; and blasphemy etc.: But the vehemence and passion manifested by the legate plainly revealed that he was actually by Enmity hatred and revenge rather than by zeal for religion. It was the prevailing sentiment of the assembly that Martin Luther is innocent.

Aleander with redoubled Enmity zeal, he urged upon the newly emperor Charles V the duty of executing the pontiff papal edicts. Overcome at last by this importunity; Charles bade the legate present his case to the Diet.

The Vatican Rome had few advocates better fitted by tradition nature and well educated to defend their cause. Like today modern scholasticism institutions possess their adequate advocates better fitted by tradition nature and well highly educated to defend their cause of scientific and technology. The close friends of Professor Martin Luther looked forward with some profound anxious and anxiety to the result of Aleander's speech. Aleander eagerness speech is to secure Luther's condemnation to death:

There was not so much or little excitement when the legate Aleander, with great pontiff dignity and pomp, appeared before the national assembly. Many people called to mind the scene of the Lord Christ Jesus trial; when Annas and Caiaphas falsely presented evidence before the judgment seat of Pilate-Roman; demanded the death of the most high anointed Messiah, the Christ 'that perverted the people at large." The pontiff legate Aleander; with all human tradition power of learning and vibrate-eloquence he set up himself to overthrow the truth from God' holy mouth. Charge after charge Aleander hurled against Luther as an enemy of the Catholic Church and the State; the living and the dead; clergy and laity; councils and all private Christians, etc.: "There is more than enough!" The pontiff grotesque poignancy expressed tone. "In the error of Luther:" He insisted: "To warrant the burning of a hundreds heretics."

In conclusion; Aleander vigorously endeavored to cast contempt upon the adherents of the reformed true faith: "What are all these and who are all these Lutherans?" A motley rabble of insolent grammarians; corrupt priests; dissolute monks; ignorant lawyers; and degraded nobles; with the common people whom they have misled and perverted! How greatly superior is the Catholic Party in numbers; intelligence; and power! A unanimous decree from this illustrious assembly will open the eyes of the simple; show the minstrels-misogyny unwary their danger; determine the wavering; and strengthen the weak hearted." Crafting-cunning words from Aleander's mouth sound like he is judging himself. His contradicting speech it is what Luther is showing them to transform for better through Scriptures which they were lacking to implement and teaching. Their hearts supposed to be depolarized for better. With such weapons have the advocates of truth in every age been attacked. The same arguments are still urged even today against all who dare to present; in opposition; disagreement; resistance to established Enmity sinful-errors the plain and direct teachings of God's true word. Who are these preachers and teachers of new doctrines? Exclaimed those who desire a popular platform religion; like today modern world Believers Top Christian Publishers would only publish Christian fiction ebook written by those with popular platform. They will not publish good quality true Christian book written by those without popular platform.

"They are unlearned," argued Aleander: "Few in numbers; and of the vulnerable poor class." Yet they claim to have the truth; and to be the chosen people of God!" They are ignorant and deceived." Aleander repeated his malicious cunning poignant tone. "How greatly superior in numbers and influence are our denominations! How many great and learned men are in our churches! How much more power is on our side!" **Whose power? Human tradition or God?** These are the arguments that have a telling influence upon the world till today: But they are no more conclusive now than in the days of Martin Luther; John Huss; Jerome; and John Wycliffe. Furthermore: Mahatma Gandhi; Dr. Martin Luther King Jr. and Nelson Mandela.

The Church Reformation did not; as many suppose has ended with Martin Luther. Neither! But it is a process needs to continue until Christ returns: Enmity sinful still with its persistence-existence: It is to be continued to the end of this modern world current affairs greatest history. Martin Luther; John Huss; Jerome; and John Wycliffe had done great work in reflecting to others this great illuminating light which God had permitted to shine upon the earth it shall not be quenched or switched out by human hands: Yet these past reformers did not receive all the light which was to be given to the world, but it will be complete given when Christ returns the ultimate righteous Judge; once and for all!

From that time to our present day; new light has been continually shining upon the Scriptures; and new truths have been constantly unfolding:

The compelling question is: Who notice this shining light today? There aren't many! We need to focus seriously to this phrase: Enmity God imposed! The pontiff legate's address made a deep impression upon the Diet. Martin Luther was not present when Aleander delivered his speech to the assembly. With the clear convincing truths of God's word, to vanquish the pontiff papal champion!. No attempt was made to defend Martin Luther. There was manifest a general impulse to root out the Lutheran heretic from the empire. The Vatican Church had enjoyed the most favorable opportunity to defend their cause. The greatest of their orators had been well spoken. All that they could say in their own vindication had been well crafted said. But the apparent victory was the signal of their really-self defeat or fall. Henceforth the contrast between truth and untruth would be more clearly seen; as they should take the field in open warfare! God had already set it up for them to have their big fall like a house built on sand, is sinking. Slowly but sure: Like Titanic ship could no longer resist the deep ocean but to slowly sink until the ocean completely swallow it up! Never from that day would the pontiff Rome stand as secure as they had been before for decades. The majority of the noble assembly were ready to sacrifice Luther to the demands of the pontiff Rome pope; but many of them saw and deplored the existing depravity in the early century Catholic Church; and desired a suppression of the abuses suffered by the German people in consequence of the Vatican corruption and greed of self-gain. The legate Aleander had presented the papal rule in the most favorable rites: Now this is moved upon a member of the Diet to give a true delineation of the effects of Vatican papal tyranny. With noble firmness; Duke George of Saxony stood up in that princely assembly; and specified with terrible exactness the deceptions and abominations of pontiff popery; and their dire results. In closing his words he said: "These are but a few of the abuses which cry out against Vatican Rome for redress. All shameful is laid aside; and one object alone incessantly pursued: "Money!" Evermore money!" So that the very men whose duty it is to teach the truth; utters nothing but falsehoods; and are not only tolerated but rewarded; because the greater their malicious lies; the greater are their gains: Said the Duke George of Saxony. "This is the foul source from which so many corrupt streams flow out like waters on every side. Profligacy and avarice go hand in hand: "Alas! It is the scandal caused by the clergy that plunges so many vulnerable poor souls into everlasting perdition. A thorough reform must be effected!." Argued the Duke George of Saxony: God put his word into the Duke George of Saxony to speak loud. A more able and forcible denunciation of the Vatican papal abuses could not have been made by Martin Luther himself; and the fact that the speaker was a determined enemy of Luther gave greater influence to his words from God's mouth. Had the eyes and ears of the assembly been well open; they would have beheld angels of God in the midst of them; shedding beams of light athwart the darkness of Enmity sinful; and opening minds and hearts to the reception of God's truth. Indeed; it was the power of God and truth and wisdom that controlled even the adversaries of the Church Reformation:

And thus prepared the way for the great work about to be done and accomplished.

Martin Luther and all others went before him had not been present; but the voice of One greater than Luther had been heard in that great noble assembly. Therefore the council now demanded for Luther to appear before the pontiff legates. Notwithstanding the entreaties protests and threats of Aleander's speech; the newly young emperor Charles V at last consented; and Luther was summoned to appear before the Diet. With summons was issued a safe-conduct; insuring his return safety to Wittenberg a place of security. These were borne to him to Worms. This time again; the close faithful friends of the professor Luther were terrified and well distressed: Knowing the pontiff prejudice and Enmity sinful against Luther; they feared that even his safe-conduct would not be respected like John Huss and Jerome; and they entreated him not to imperil or even to jeopardize his life: But Martin Luther response to his faithful friends was: "The papist have little desire to see me at Worms; but they long for my condemnation and death. It matters not: Pray not for me; but the word of God." Christ will give me his Spirit to overcome these ministers of Satan. I despise them while I live: I will triumph over them by my death!" They are busy at Worms about compelling me to recant: My recantation shall be this: "I said formerly that the pope was Christ's vicar; now I say that he is the adversary of the Lord and the apostle of the devil!"

Luther said: Martin Luther was not to make his perilous journey alone. Beside the imperial messenger; three of his firmest faithful friends determined to accompany him. A multitude of student's fare citizens to whom the gospel was precious; bade him fare-well with weeping eyes as he departed. Thus Professor Luther and his all companions set out from Wittenberg to Worms. He was well secured. Both with spiritual and men support; which comforted him with hope in the Lord his God. During the long journey they saw that the minds of the people were oppressed by gloomy forebodings. At some towns no honors were proffered them. As they stopped for the night; a friendly priest expressed his fears by holding up before Luther the portrait of an Italian reformer who had suffered martyrdom for truth' sake!. On the next day as they journeyed; they heard that Luther's writings had been condemned or banned at Worms. The imperial messengers were proclaiming the emperor's decree and urging all citizens to bring the proscribed works to the magistrates. The herald in alarm asked Luther if he still wished to go forward. Luther answered; "I will go on though I should be put under interdicts in every town."

At Erfurth, Luther was received with honor. Surrounded with many admiring crowds; he entered the city where in his earlier youth years; where he had often begged a morsel of bread. They sincere requested him to preach. This he had been forbidden to do; but the herald gave his consent and the monk whose duty it once was to unclose the gates and swept the aisles; now ascended the pulpit while the people listened to his words as if spell-bound. The bread of life was broken to those starving souls like today there are many starving souls.

Christ Jesus was lifted up before them as above pope's legates; emperors; and kings. Luther made no reference to his own perilous position. He did not seek to make himself the object of thought or sympathy. In the contemplation of Christ he had lost sight of self. He hid behind of Christ on Calvary Mount seeking only to present Christ Jesus as the Enmity-sinful redeemer. Luther as the reformer proceeded on his long journey he was everywhere regarded with great interest. Every multitude eagerness thronged about him and friendly voices warned him of the purpose of pontiff Enmity hatred. "You will burned on fire alive," they, "and your body reduced to ashes like was that of John Huss and Jerome:" Luther answered: "Though they should kindle a fire all the way from Worms to Wittenberg; whose flames of the rise up to heaven, I would go through it in the name of the Lord God and stand before them; I would enter the jaws of this behemoth and break his teeth; confessing the Lord Christ Jesus."

The tidings news of his approach to Worms greatly spread commotion. His close faithful friends fearful/trembled and concerned for his safety: But his enemies the pontiff feared for the success of their cause. Strenuous efforts were made to dissuade him from entering the main city. The pontiff legates urged him to Dottier to the Castle of a friendly Knight where they thus inevitably avoid all difficulties could be amicably adjusted. The advocates of truth endeavored to excite his fears by describing the dangers that threatened him. All their efforts failed. However, the faithful Luther still unshaken stated: "Though there should be as many devils at Worms as there are tiles on its roofs; I would enter!" Upon Luther's arrival at Worms; the crowd that flocked to the gates to welcome him was even greater than expected at the public entry of the emperor himself. The excitement was intense and from the midst of the throng a shrill and plaintive voice chanted a funeral dirge as a warning to Luther for the fate-death that awaited for him. "God will be my defense," said Luther; as he alighted from his horse carriage. The newly young emperor Charles V, immediately convoked his council to consider what course should be pursued toward Martin Luther; theological professor of Wittenberg University. One of the pontiff bishops, a rigid papist announced: "We have long consulted on this matter. Let your majesty get rid of this man at once!" Did not Sigismund bring John Huss to the stake?" We are under no obligation either to give or to observe the safe-conduct of a heretic!."

No! The newly your emperor Charles replied: "Not so!" We must keep our promise!" Charles V strongly in nobility refuted: It was therefore decided that Martin Luther should now be heard in person before the Diet. The eagerness Worms city multitudes were fully fixed up to see this profound remarkable man he had enjoyed but a few hours' rest when noblemen Knights; priests ;and citizens gathered together about him. Even his enemies marked his firm determination; and eagerness; courageous bearing; the kindly and joyous expression upon his countenance and the solemn elevation and deep-anguish earnestness that gave to his words an irresistible power: It was given to him from above. Some were convinced that a divine influence attended him; others suggested him as had the Pharisees concerning Christ, "He had a devil!." Indeed; on the following day Luther was finally summoned to attend the Diet. An imperial officer was appointed to conduct him to the hall of audience: Yet it was with difficulty that he could reach the place. Every place of avenue was crowded with large number of spectators; eager to see the hero and champion reformer from very ordinary up bring rising to the top and change the face of Vatican; Luther with God divine strength had dare to resist the authority of the pontiff Rome pope. He is a human being: But God who is above all creatures ought to be worshiped in Spirit and truth.

As Luther is about to enter to the presence of the pontiff judges; an old general the hero of many battles, said to Luther kindly words: "Poor monk! Poor monk! You are now going to make a nobler stand than I, or any other battle captains have ever made in our most blood battles. But if your cause is just, and thou art sure of it; go forward in God's name and fear nothing! He will not forsake you." For a bit longer Luther stood before the Diet council. Then the newly Emperor Charles V fully occupied the throne. He was surrounded by the most illustrious personages in the Germany Empire. Never had a man appeared in the presence of a more imposing noble's assembly than that before which Martin Luther stood to answer for his unique divine faith. The very fact of that appearance was a divine signal victory for the truth. That a man whom the Vatican pope had condemned should be judged by another tribunal; it was virtually a denial of the pontiff Rome supreme authority. If it is not the high divine behind the whole process who else could be? Professor Martin Luther placed himself under ban and denounced from human fellowship by the Vatican pope; had been assured protection and he was granted a hearing; by the highest dignitaries of civil nation of his day. While the Vatican Rome had commanded him to be silent: But Luther was about to speak in the presence of thousands of multitudes from all parts of secular Christendom world.

In the presence of that powerful and title assembly the lowly born upon devastating poverty up bringing now seemed awed and embarrassed all nobles because he stood for God's truth! Several of the princes observing his emotion, approached him and one of them whispered: "Fear not them which kill the body, but fear that kills both; the body and the soul." Another said: "When you shall be brought before governors and kings for My sake, it shall be given you, by the Spirit of your Father; what you shall say." Thus the words quoted from Christ' mouth were brought to Luther by these great German princes to strengthen Luther speak well and courage in their hearing in the hour of his severe trial. These young princes saw truth of Luther's writings and teachings.

Therefore, Martin Luther was conducted to a position directly in front of the young emperor Charles V throne. A deep silence fell upon the noble crowded assembly. The Germany Imperial Officer arose and pointed to a Collection of Martin Luther's writings; demanded that Luther to answer two imposed questions: "Whether he acknowledges the writings as his:" Whether he proposed to retract the opinions which he had therein advanced:" Martin Luther replied that as to the first question; he acknowledged the books to be his.

As to the second, he said: "Seeing it is a question which concerns faith; the salvation of souls and the word of God; which is the greatest and most precious treasure either in heaven or earth; it would be rash and perilous for me to reply without reflection: I might affirm less than the circumstances demand; or more than truth requires; in either case I should fall under the sentence of Christ: "Whoever shall deny Me before men; him will I also deny before the Father which is in heaven." For this reason I entreat your imperial majesty, with all humility; to allow me time that I may answer without offending against the word of God."

In making this request; Luther moved wisely. His course convinced the assembly that he did not act from passion or impulse. Such calmness and self-command; unexpected in one who had shown himself bold and un-compromising added to his power; and enabled him afterward to answer with a prudence; decision; wisdom; and dignity; that surprised and pride. Again on the next day Luther is to appear to answer his second question. For a time his heart sunk within him as he contemplated the forces that were combined against the truth.

Luther' faith seems faltered as his enemies seemed to multiply before him and the powers of Enmity-darkness to prevail. Dark clouds gathered about him and he seemed to separate him from God. Enmity sinful Satan tempts him. "As the deer pants for the water: So pants my soul for You O God!" So Luther's soul longed for the assurance that the Lord God of hosts would be with him: In deep anguish of spirit he threw himself with his face upon the earth; and poured out those broken heart-rending cries which none but God can fully understand. [Psalm 42: 2].

In his helplessness his soul fastened upon the Lord Christ Jesus the mighty deliver. It was not for his own safety but for the success of the church; that he wrestled with God like Jacob: And he prevailed! He was renewed and strengthened with the assurance that he would not appear alone before the Diet council. Peace returned to his soul, and he rejoiced that he was permitted to uphold and defend the word of God to whom put his trust before the world' rulers of the nation in Germany. An all wise providence had permitted Luther to realize his peril that he might not trust to his own strength and wisdom and rush presumptuously into danger. God was preparing him for great work-task before him.

As the time was drawing near for him to appear before the pontiff: Luther approached to a table where laid the Holy Scriptures; placed on his left hand upon the sacred volume and raising his right hand up to heaven; he solemn vowed to adhere constantly to the gospel; and to confess his faith freely even though he should be called to seal his testimony with his own blood. When he was again ushered into the presence of the Diet, this countenance bore no trace of fear or embarrassment. Calm and peaceful: Yet grandly brave and noble manner: The imperial officer now demanded his decision as to whether he desired to retract his doctrines: Luther made his answer in a subdued and humble tone; without violence or passion. His demeanor was diffident and respectful: Yet he manifested a confidence and joy that surprised the noble assembly and spectator audiences.

He naturally stated that his published works were not all of the same character. In some he had treated of faith and good works; and even his enemies plainly acknowledged them not only harmless but profitable. To retract these would be to condemn truths which all parties confessed.

The second class consisted of writing exposing the corruptions and abuses of the pontiff papacy. To revoke these works would strengthen the tyranny of the Vatican Rome, and open a wider door to many and great impieties'.

In the third class of his books he had attacked individuals who had defended existing evils. Concerning these he freely confessed that he had been more violence than was becoming. He did not claim to be free from fault: But even these books he could revoke for such a course would embolden the enemies of truth; and they would then take occasion or opportunity to crush God's people with still greater cruelty. "But as I am a mere man; and not God," he continued; "I will defend myself as did Christ who said: "If I have spoken evil; bear witness of the evil." By the mercy of God, I implore your imperial majesty, or anyone else who can, whoever he may be to prove to me from the writings of the prophets that I am in error. As soon as I shall be convinced; I will instantly retract all my errors and be the first to cast my books into the fire to be burned. What I have just said will show that I have considered and weighed the dangers to which I am exposing myself; but far from being dismayed by them; I rejoice exceedingly to see the gospel this day as of old and a cause of trouble and dissension. This is the character the destiny of God's word. Said Christ Jesus, "I came not to send peace, but sword." God is wonderful and terrible in his counsels. Let us have a care lest in our endeavors to arrest discords we be found to fight against the holy word of God, and bring down upon our heads a frightful deluge of inextricable dangers; present disaster, and everlasting desolation.

I might cite examples drawn from the oracles of God. I might speak of Pharaohs or king of Babylon Nebuchadnezzar; or of Israel; who were never more contributing to their own ruin than when; by measures in appearance most prudent; they thought to establish their authority. "God removed the mountains, and they know not." Martin Luther first delivered his speech in German language: But he is now requested to repeat the speech in same words in Latin language. Although exhausted by the previous effort; he complied with pontiff Diet; and again delivered his speech with the same clearness and energy as at the first in Latin language.

God's providence directed in this matter. The minds of many of the princes were so blinded by pontiff corruption-error and superstition that at the first delivered they did not see the force of Luther's reasoning: But the repetition enabled them clearly to perceive the points plainly presented to them. Those who stubbornly closed their ears and eyes to the light; and determined not to be convinced of the truth were enraged at the power of Martin Luther's strong words. As he ceased speaking the spokesman of the pontiff Diet said angrily tone: "You have not answered the question adequate!" A clear and express reply is demanded: "Will you or will you not retract?" Luther answered: "Since your most serene majesty and the princes require a simple answer; I will give it thus: Unless I shall be convinced by proofs from Scriptures or by evident reason [for I believe neither in pontiff popes nor in councils; since they have frequently erred; corrupted and contradicted truth themselves], I cannot choose but adhere to the word of God alone which has possession of my conscience! Nor can I possibly nor will I ever make any recantation; since it is neither safe nor honest to act contrary to conscience." Furthermore Luther said: "Here I take my stand! I cannot do otherwise: God be my help! Amen." Thus stood this righteous man upon the sure foundation of the word of God: The true light of heaven illuminated his countenance: His greatness and purity of character; his peace and joy of heart were manifest to all as he testified against the power of Enmity and witnessed to the superiority of that faith that overcomes the world. The whole assembly were for a time speechless with amazement. The emperor himself and many of the princes were deeply struck with admiration. The partisans of pontiff Rome had been worsted their cause appeared in a most unfavorable light. They sought to maintain their power, not by appealing to the Scriptures but by a resort of threats; Rome unfailing argument. Said the spokesman of the Diet: "If you do not retract, the emperor and the State of empire will proceed to consider how to deal with an obstinate heretic:"

Martin Luther's good close friends who had with great joy listened to his noble defense; trembled at these words: But the professor of theology himself said calmly: "My God be my **helper!" For I can retract nothing!"** The theological professor; Martin Luther in Christ; firm as a solid rock he stood; while the fiercest billows of worldly fable power beat harmlessly against him: The simple energy of his words; his fearless bearing; his calm; speaking eyes; uncompromised; and the unalterable determination expressed in every single word and act; made a deep impression upon the princes; emperor; and noble assembly: It was absolute evident that Luther could not be merely induced; either by promise or threats; to yield to the pontiff mandate Diet of the Vatican Rome: The pontiff papist bishop leaders were chagrined that their power which had cause kings and most prestigious nobles to tremble should be thus despised by a humble monk; a son of a peasant farm: They longed to make him feel their wrath by torturing his life away: But Martin Luther understanding and awareness of his danger; had spoken to all with Christian dignity and calmness. He shows no apprehension; emotions; or perturbed at mind; like king Herod; when he was told by three wise men from the East that a king is born: He was awfully perturbed and all Jerusalem nobles with him.

Herod in command killing every infant from zero to 5 years [Matt 2: 3] [v.16.]

Martin Luther; lost no sight of himself and of great men surrounding him; and felt only that he was in the presence of Christ Jesus the solid rock where he stood on infinitely most high superior than popes; prelates; kings; emperors; queens; or noble; or prestigious: Christ had indeed spoken through Luther's testimony with great power and grandeur that for the time inspired both friends; relatives; Christians; and all supporters; and foes with awe and wonder. The wind of change prevailed! Do we see the wind of change today? The Spirit of the Lord God has been present in the past in that pontiff council; impressing the hearts of the chiefs of the empire: Several of the princes openly acknowledged the justice of Martin Luther's cause. Many other people were well convinced of this truth; but with some the impressions received were not lasting. It is the same today! The wind of change impresses others but others are not impressed. In the past there was another class like today there are many other classes who did not at the time express their convictions; but who having searched the Scriptures for themselves; at a future time appreciated with great boldness for the reformation. Earlier, the Elector emperor Frederick had look forward with anxiety for Martin Luther appearing before the pontiff Diet; and with deep emotion he listened to Luther' speech. He then, eventually rejoiced in delight at Luther's firmness and courage; and self-dignified possession; and he was proud of being his safe-conduct protector. Frederick contrasted the parties in contest; and saw that the wisdom of popes; kings; and prelates had been brought to naught by the power of God's truth: The Vatican papacy had sustained a defeat which would be felt among all nations and in all ages on earth. And so everybody is aware about the early century pope's failures. Are we better than the early century popes? Enmity stands still until Christ returns. We are ever dissatisfied!

As the early legates perceived the effect produced by Martin Luther's powerful speech; he feared as never before; for the security of the pontiff Rome-power and resolved to employ every means at his command to effect the Luther' overthrow. Did he? Or could he? Luther stands on Christ' solid rock: Who can be against him? With all his natural vibrate eloquence and diplomatic skill for which he was so eminently distinguished; he represented himself to the youthful newly emperor Charles V the folly and danger of sacrificing; in the cause of an insignificant monk; the friendship and mutual support of the powerful see of pontiff Rome. How arrogant; how tough fell upon the pontiff Vatican? Martin Luther' words were not without effect.

On the day following Luther's answer; Charles V caused a message to be presented to the Diet: Announcing his determination to carry out the policy of his predecessors to maintain and protect the Catholic religion. Since Luther had refuted to renounce his doctrine errors; the most vigorous measures should be employed against him and the heresies he taught.

Nevertheless; the safe-conduct granted him must be respected; and before proceeding against him could be instituted; he must be allowed to return home in well safety. "I am firmly resolved to tread," said Charles V: "In the footsteps of my ancestors," vigorously wrote the young newly monarch: He had naturally decided that he would not step out of the path of the custom; even to walk in the ways of truth and righteousness. Because his fathers did; he would uphold the papacy; with all its cruelty and corruption. Thus Charles took his position refuting to accept any light in advance of what his father had received or to perform any duty that they had not performed.

Charles V seemed to feel that a change of religious view would be inconsistent with the dignity of a king. There are many at the present day thus clinging to the customs and traditions of their fathers' Enmity. When the Lord Christ sent them with additional light they refused to accept it because not having been granted to their fathers; it was not received by them. We are not place where our forefathers were; but consequently our duties and responsibilities differ as theirs. We still remain to be their seeds. And reap what we sowed. Therefore; we shall not be approved of God in looking to the example or implement of our forefathers duties to determine our duties instead of searching the word of God' truth for ourselves:

But if we don't search for God's truth we are doomed as our forefathers were. Therefore; today our responsibilities are greater than was that of our ancestors. We need to focus better before the eyes of God our maker. Otherwise; we are all accountable for the light which they received; and they handed it down as an inheritance for us today; and we are accountable also for additional light which is now illuminating-shining upon us all from the truth word of God our maker. Will you agree?

"If I had not come and spoken to them," Jesus said: "They would have no Enmity sinful nature!" But now they have No Excuse for their Enmity sinful nature!" He who hates Me hates My Father also!" [John 15: 22-25]

It is the very same divine great power that Luther had delivered to Diet; emperor; prelates; princes; and to all Germany nobles and ordinary walks of life. It is also the very same divine great power that the reformer Luther deliver to the modern world religious leaders; presidents; prelates; bishops; GOP; and to all 1.2 billion secular world Christendom! And as the light shone forth from the Mighty God' Word His Spirit pleaded for the last time with many nations in that assembly. Like Pilate; as Roman early centuries before; permitted selfish-pride with prestigious for self-popularity to close his heart against the most high anointed Messiah the Christ the Savior of the world!

As the trembling Felix bade Paul the messenger of truth, "go your way for this time; when I have a convenient season I will call for you:" As the proud Agrippa superficial confessed: "Almost you persuaded me to be a Christian?" Yet he turned away from the true heaven sent message; so had Charles V yielding to the dictates of worldly selfish-pride and policy; decided to refute the light of truth followed his ancestors. Enmity sinful will persist until Christ returns! We have a major obligation to establish this Great Commission Commanded By the Lord Jesus Christ: [Matt 28: 18-20]. Church Reformation is still on it's a long way to go.

Several of early century pope's adherents demanded that Luther safe-conduct or protection should not be respected. "The Rhine," plainly said that they should or must receive Luther's ashes as it received those of John Huss and Jerome earlier before Luther. Rumors of the designs against Luther were widely circulated; accusing stimulating great excitement throughout the cities of Wittenberg; Augsburg; and Worms. The theological professor Luther; had made great; faithful many friends; who were well aware about the treacherous cruelty of pontiff Rome toward all that dare to expose or oppose their corruptions; resolved that Luther should/will not be sacrificed: Hundreds of high prestigious German nobles pledged themselves to well protect the theological professor, Martin Luther. Not a few openly denounced the royal message as evincing a weak submission to the controlling power of pontiff Vatican. On the gates of houses and in public places; placards were overwhelming posted; some condemning and others sustaining Luther' safety. On one of them were written merely expostulating the significant words of the wise man: "Woe to thee O land; when thy king is a child!"

The popular enthusiasm in Luther's favor throughout all Germany region convinced both the emperor and the Diet that any injustice shown upon Luther would endanger the peace for whole Germany Community including the empire and even the stability of the monarch throne.

The old Frederic emperor of Saxony maintained a studied reserve; carefully concealing his really feelings toward the theological professor and reformer Luther; while at the same time he guarded him with tireless vigilance: Watching diligently all his movements and all those of his enemies: But there were many people who made no attempt to conceal their sincere-genuine sympathy and empathy: Princes; Knights; Gentlemen; Ecclesiastics; and Common People surrounded Martin Luther' lodgings entering and gazing upon him as though he were more than human. Even those who believed him to be in error could not but to admire that nobility of soul which led him to imperil his own life rather than violate his conscience. The pontiff eagerness earnest efforts were made to obtain Luther's consent to a compromise or retract with Rome total failed. Some German nobles and princes represented to Luther that if he persist in setting up his own judgment against that of the church and the councils; he would soon be banished from the empire and then would have no defense from any. To this appeal the theological professor response was: **"It is impossible to preach the gospel of Christ without offense: Why then, should the fear of danger separate me from the Lord and that divine word which alone is truth? No! I**

would rather give up my body; my blood; and my life."

Again Luther was urged to submit to the judgment of the emperor and then he would have nothing to fear.

"I consent," said Luther in response: "With all my heart that the emperor the princes; and even the humblest noble Christian should examine and judge my writings; but on one condition; that they take God's word for their guide: Men have nothing to do but render obedience to that. My conscience is in dependence upon that word; and I am the subject of its authority." Luther said:

Again to another appeal: "I consent to forego my safe-conduct and resign my person life to the emperor's disposal; but as to the word of God: "Never!" Luther actually stated his willingness to submit to the decision of a general council but only on condition that the council be required to decide according to the Holy Scriptures the [Bible-Sacred Word.] Martin Luther strongly convinced all his friends-inquisitive for his safety; both friend's relatives and foes were all at last unanimous convinced that further effort for reconciliation would be worthless-useless:

Enmity sinful crafting-cunning in the form of his faithful-trustworthy friends engaged tempting dialogue. Like Eve with Serpent. Luther defended his cause through Scriptures: "The word of God."   Such as that of Christ; "It is written!" was Christ' defense:

Had the theological professor yielded a single point that his friends had imposed; Lucifer-Enmity-Satan sinful would dominate or blind Luther; and Satan with his evil hosts would have gained the victory: Didn't Lucifer in the Serpent form gain victory over Eve? [Gen 3: 16] See v. 4-5:]

Yes! He did: The Bible is the best weapon for self-defense from Satan temptations. Often times; Satan appeals in the form of your close friend; wife; girl-friend; husband in order to break down harmony/mutual relationships.

Yes! He does: Will you agree?

As for the theological professor Luther; his unwavering firmness was the means of emancipating the church and beginning a new and better era for us today and future. The influence of this one single man who dared to think and act for himself in religious; not man's made religious but true God's made; matters: Was to affect the church and the world: Not only in his own time: But in all future generations which is us today and to come: Can you see this good picture? Will you agree? Martin Luther; his firmness and fidelity would strengthen all to the end of time; who should pass through a similar experience. The power and majesty of God Almighty in Christ Jesus stood forth above all the noble counsel of men; above the mighty power of Lucifer Enmity Satan. Is there any easy way?

Martin Luther was soon commanded by the authority of the emperor Charles V to return home in Wittenberg; and he knew that this notice would be speedily followed by his condemnation. Threatening deep dark clouds overhung his path: But as he departed from Worms to Wittenberg; his heart was filled with exceeding joy and praises. "Satan himself; said: "He kept the pontiff pope's citadel; but Christ has made a wide breach in it; and the devil has been compelled to confess that Christ is mightier than him."

On this time journey to Wittenberg; the theological professor Luther received the most flattering attentions from all walks of life nobles; poor; rich; businessmen; young and elder people all uplifted him with great attentions. Dignitaries of the church welcomed the professor of Wittenberg University upon who the Vatican pope's curse rested; and secular world officers honored the monk who was under the ban of the Germany Empire. Luther had not been that long absent from Worms when the pontiff prelate's papist prevailed upon the young Charles V emperor to issue an edict against him.

In this decree Luther was denounced as "Satan under the semblance of a man in a monk's hood." It was commanded that as soon as his safe-conduct should expire; measures be taken to stop his work:

All people were forbidden to harbor him or associate with him, to give him food or drink, or by word or act, in public or private; to aid or abet him for anything. He was to be seized wherever he might be; and delivered to the authorities. His adherents also were to be imprisoned; and their property forceful confiscated. His writings were to be all destroyed; and finally; all who should dare to act contrary to this Vatican high divine authority decree were all included in its condemnation. That was the decree or law manifested from the Vatican Catholic Church in Early Century imitating the ancient Judaism Pharisees; Roman pagan arena: The young Charles V had spoken and the Diet had given its sanction to the decree: The Vatican Romanists Head Quarter; Prelates; Friars; Clergy; Bishops; as well as the Papal were jubilant: Now they considered the fate of the theological professor and reformer Martin Luther sealed. God's way not Pope's way! The Vatican Pope was very unaware! The Living God: Who is Above All!

Had provided a magnificent a way for the theological professor to escape for his faithful messenger in this hour of peril: A great vigilant eye had been following/watching the theological professor Luther' all movements; and a true honorable noble heartfelt had resolved upon his personal rescue: It was well plain that Vatican Rome would be satisfied with nothing short of his death; only by concealment could he be preserved from the jaws of the cruel-hunger lion:

Elijah; God's true prophet: King Ahab profoundly hated Elijah for proclaiming God's truth: Drought would take place for three and half years: There would be a severe famine upon the whole nation from Jerusalem to Judea and everywhere. Ahab didn't believe: But Ahab vigorously endeavored to kill Elijah: He couldn't! God preserved Elijah!. He sent him to Sidon: Where Ahab could not find him. Famine remained squeezing all until three and years expired: Then rain God poured on earth. Afterward; Elijah slaughtered 500 false prophets: [1 Kings 17-19] full story is told:

Frederick of Saxony: God gave wisdom to Frederic of Saxony to devise God's perfect plan for the theological professor preservation. With the cooperation of true faithful friends; the Elector's purpose was carried out and Martin Luther was effectually hidden from friends and foes: No one knew where about Luther is safely confined: Upon his homeward journey; he was seized; separated from his attendants and hurried conveyed through the forests to the Castle of Wartburg: An isolated mountain fortress:

Far better than Sidon where Elijah escaped into a vulnerable poor widow' household. Both his seizure and his concealment were so involved in God's mystery that even old Frederic himself for a long year time knew not whither he had been conducted. Probably God disguise it in the human eyes for this purpose. Elijah hides in caves for years unknown to Ahab: Who knows? This ignorance was not without design: So long as the Elector knew nothing of Luther's whereabouts; he could reveal nothing! He satisfied that the theological professor was well safe; and with this knowledge he was content in his heart. Yes! It is God's unrevealed secret:

Spring: Summer: and autumn passed: Winter came and Luther still unknown whereabouts confined. The pontiff Aleander and his partisans were at their well rejoicing pleasure that the light of the gospel which Luther had truly spread; seemed about to be extinguished forever: But instead of this; the theological professor is in absolute filling his whole lamp from the store-house of God's truth to fully shine forth in due season-time with much more brighter radiance: Like Elijah; the rain God has to pour and fill the earth with new crops growth.

In the friendly security of the Wartburg; Luther for a time rejoiced in his release from the heat and turmoil of battle: But he could not long find satisfaction in quiet and repose. Accustomed to a life of daily activity and stern conflict; he could ill endure to remain inactive: In those solitary days; the condition of the church rose up before him; and he cried in despair: "Alas! There is no one in this later day of his anger to stand like a wall before the Lord God; and save Israel!" Again his thoughts returned to himself; and he feared being charged with cowardice in withdrawing from the contest. Then he reproached himself for his indolence and self-indulgence: Yet at the same time he was daily accomplishing more than it seemed possible for one man to do. His writing pen was never idle. While his enemies flattered themselves that he was silenced; they were astonished and confused by tangible proof that he was still in well active. A host of tracts issuing from his writing pen circulated throughout all Germany regions: He also performed a most important service for his countrymen by translating the New Testament into Germany language. As John who prominently confined at Patmos Island: Martin Luther continued for nearly a whole year to proclaim the gospel and rebuke the Enmity sinful and all the Vatican corruptions of the times. But it was not merely to preserve Martin Luther from the wrath of his enemies; nor even to afford him a season of quiet for these important tasks; that God had withdrawn him from the stage of public life:

There were great results more precious than these to be secured: In the solitude and obscurity of his dark mountain retreat; Martin Luther was removed from earthly supports and shut out from human praise: He was thus saved from the human selfish-pride and self-righteous and confidence that are so often caused by successfully: Prestigious: Popularity: Publicity: Power: Knowledge: Wisdom: Material wealth: Money: The theological professor; by suffering and humiliation he was well prepared again to walk safely upon the dizzy heights to which he had been so suddenly exalted: As in his early youth life; Luther had never lived luxury life but he was born and raised in devastating poverty: God had well prepared him since then. But God filled him with Holy Spirit. Like all others in the past: As men rejoice in the freedom which the truth brings them they are inclined to extol those whom God had carefully chosen as his useful instrument to break all the chains of Enmity sinful nature and traditions. Enmity Satan seeks to divert men's thoughts and affections from God and fix them upon human agencies; to honor the mere instrument; and to ignore the powerful hand of God that directs all the events of providences: We all fail to full grasp this truth and practice daily. Enmity sinful is our main enemies:

Too often; religious leaders who are thus well-highly praised and reverenced lose sight of their dependence upon God; and they are led to trust in them: Jesus Christ never received any the praise from men: Neither did his disciples: But they often time were scourged and mocked and given bad labels at their backs. Their lives was basically uncomfortable like their Master the Lord and Savior of the world Christ Jesus whom they truly served and severely persecuted to their death. Today; we all fall-short in the fulfillment of the disciples life-style: As a result for today' religious leaders; they seek to control the minds and conscience of the people; who are disposed to look to them for guidance instead of looking to the word of God the sustainer of their lives. Our religious leaders today live very comfortable. The work of reform is often retarded because of this spirit indulged by its supporters: From this danger; God would guard the cause of the Church Reformation. Martin Luther desired that work to receive; not the impress of man; but of God his maker and Lord. He took the path of true discipleship: The eyes of men had been turned to Luther as the expounder of the truth; he was removed from the public so that all eyes might be directed to the eternal author of truth Jesus Christ the world savor.

The newly young emperor Charles V in Germany the pontiff royal supporter denounced Martin Luther and summoned him to condemnation-death following the Vatican papal' curse: And Luther miraculously disappeared: As it were from the face of the earth. Who had taken him away? His friends or his enemies? Had the great theological professor which he had begun, come to sudden stop? God's mysterious act is invisible!. And so His greatness is unsearchable! [Psalm 145: 3]

The theological professor: Martin Luther mysterious: Miraculously disappearance excited consternation throughout all Germany regions: Inquiries investigations concerning him were overwhelmed heard everywhere around tiny Europe continent. Even his enemies were more agitated by his sudden disappearance than they could have been by his presence: The wildest rumors were circulated; and many people believed that he had been cold blood-murdered: There was great lamentation in all Germany; not only by his avowed friends; but by thousands hundreds who had not openly taken their stand with the Church Reformation: Many people bound themselves by a solemn oath to avenge for his death: [Psalm 2: 1] "Why do nations rage? And the people plot a vain thing?" "The kings of the earth set themselves: And the rulers take counsel together: Against the Lord and against His Anointed: Saying: "Let us break their bonds in pieces!" [v. 2-3]. "He who sits in the heavens shall laugh:" The Lord shall hold them in derision: Then shall speak to them in His wrath: **And distress them in His deep displeasure!" Will you agree? [v. 5]**

The Roman Catholic Church leaders saw Luther disappearance with terror to what a pitch had risen the feeling against them. Although at first exultant at the supposed death of Martin Luther; they now are ashamed desiring to hide the really wrath of the people whom they maliciously entrusted their solemn confidence and trust. Those who were enraged against him when he was at large; were filled with fear and horror now that he was in captivity: "The only way of extricating ourselves," one of the pontiff said: "Is to light our torches and go searching through the entire earth for professor Luther; till we can restore him to a nation that will have him: The edict of the emperor Charles V seemed to fall powerless: The Vatican papal legates; Aleander; prelates; and all other bishops were filled with indignation as they saw that it commanded far less attention than did the fate of the theological professor Martin Luther. Feeling condition of Enmity is: Ill-will: Hatred: Hostility: Envy: Covets: Bitterness springing up and defiling many:

The tidings that Luther is safe; although he is secretly confined to a place like a prisoner; calmed; isolated; the fears of the people; while it still further aroused their enthusiasm in his favor: His writings were read with greater eagerness than ever before. Like Jonah into a big fish's belly for three days and three nights earnestly praying for his great event to proclaim God's great message into Nineveh city. The powerful word of God needs to be proclaimed to all earth! The crew of the ship feared what could happen to Jonah as they threw him into the deep wrath ocean. Neither did the crew know what God had prepared for Jonah. But Jonah was very safe in the hand of God Almighty: So, was Luther:

The increasing numbers actually joined more the cause of the accused heretic man. Martin Luther who had at such fearful odds; defended the word of God. The theological professor was constantly gaining in strength. The seed which Luther had planted sprung up everywhere around Europe continent. His unknown hiding place into an old Castle accomplished a great work which his public presence would probably have failed to do. God knew how the work could be well done: Also other hard workers felt a new responsibility; now that their great leader was removed from their presence. Like South Africa architect of apartheid Dr. H. Verwoerd sentenced Mandela to life imprisonment to an isolated island: Later on his own guard assassinated him in 1960. Then God raised up Tutu to carry on Mandela great work till 1994. With new faith and earnestness they pressed on forward to do all in their power; that the work so nobly begun might not be hindered: One female said: "We shall not cease to fight for our cause till the last drop of our blood!" Enmity; Lucifer Satan: But is not idle: He now attempted what he has attempted in every other reformatory from the beginning Genesis movement; to deceive crafting-cunning and destroy the people by palming off upon them a counterfeit in place of the unique-true work: As there were false-Christ or anti-Christ in the first early ancient century of the secular world Christendom church like today; so there arose false-full prophets in the 16th century: A few-hand-full men; deeply affected by the excitement in the religious world; imagined themselves to have truly received special revelation from above in heaven; and they claimed to have been divinely commissioned to carry on forward to its fully completion Church Reformation but feebly begun by the theological professor Martin Luther. Well; very appealing and convincing inspiring truth: Remember Eve; how she was deceived. "Surely! You shall not die!" Said Lucifer in the form of Serpent: In truth, they were undoing the very work which Luther had accomplished.

They rejected the fundamental principle of the reformation; the word of God as the all-sufficient rule of faith and practice: And for that unerring guide they substituted the changeable; uncertain standard of their own feelings and impressions. By this act of setting aside the great detector of Enmity-crafting and malicious-falsehood; the way was opened for Enmity-Lucifer to control minds as best pleased himself like he did to Eve: Envy! One of these prophets claimed to have been instructed by the Angel Gabriel: A student who united with him abandoned his studies; claiming that he had received from God himself the ability to explain the Scriptures: Others who were naturally inclined to fanaticism united with them. The proceedings of these enthusiasts created no little excitement. But big: The writings and preaching of Luther had aroused great number of people everywhere to feel the necessity of reform; and now some really honest peoples were misled by the pretensions of the new prophets. Jesus early warned the disciples. "Be-aware of the false prophets!" They shall come in my name." So is today there are many: Everyone else will tell you all these good things in the name concerning Jesus. "You will know them by their fruits." Jesus said:

The leaders of the movement proceeded to Wittenberg; and urged their claims upon Melancthon and his Co-la-borers: Said they: "We are sent by God to teach the people. We have received special revelation from God direct, and therefore know what is coming to pass: We are apostles and prophets; and appeal to the theological professor Martin Luther to the truth of what we say." They were very serious in saying like Lucifer: "Surely! You shall not die!" Eve believed. What we hear and what we see today? Same stories of deceiving each other everywhere! Watch their steps and their productive-action. "You will know them by their fruits." Jesus said:

Many of the reformers were astonished and perplexed: This was such an element as they had never before encountered; and they knew not what course to pursue. "There are indeed spirits of no ordinary kind in these men: But what spirits?" Melancthon said: On the one hand; let us be-aware of quenching the Spirit of God; and on the other; of being seduced by the spirit of Enmity-Lucifer Satan." The Lord Jesus Christ knew Satan so well and recognized him all his evil motive steps. Satan never approaches his prey in evil manner. But in excellence manner to trap his prey: How you ketch a fish? You provide special trap to attract the fish to bite a sharp hooky: We exact know so well what a fish loves to eat: Don't we? So, is the clever monkey: We trap it easily: He loves to eat peanuts! Yes! We do: Enmity it is the greatest device that traps all nations on earth! It is old seed that persist its growths. [Gen 3].

In the days of Martin Luther; John Huss; Jerome; and John Wycliffe: The fruit of the new teaching soon became apparent: The minds of many people were diverted from the word of God like today; or even decided prejudiced against it. The secular scholasticism were thrown into confusion: Students like today; sprung all restraint; abandoned their studies: The men who thought themselves competent revive and control the work of the reformation; succeeded only in bringing it to the very brink of ruin! The Vatican again; now regained their confidence; and exclaimed exultingly; "One more effort; and all will be ours." Martin Luther at the Wartburg; hearing of what had occurred or took place; said with deep concern; "I always expected that Satan would send us this plague." He perceived the true character of those pretended prophets; and saw the danger that threatened the cause of God's truth. The opposition of the pontiff pope and the emperor had not caused him so great perplexity and distress as he now experienced. From the professed friends of the reformation had risen its worst enemies! The very truth which had brought peace to his troubled heart had been made the cause of **dissension in the church:**

During the work of church reformation; Martin Luther in the Spirit of God was very eager and vigorous to carry on forward in the Spirit of Christ; disciples; and apostles as God had commissioned him to carry on this truth beyond the earth. He had not purposed to take such position as he did or to make it so radical changes. No! It was not so for him to do. God's true- is universally. All need to be saved provided all peoples on earth believe. Martin Luther; like Paul and all other before him had been but the God's instruments in the hands of infinite-divine power: As Christ indicated; "Without Me; you can' can do nothing!" Abide in Me as branch abides in the vine." [John 15: 5] "You are my friends if you do whatever I command you." Jesus said: [v. 14]. Martin Luther; throughout most of the church reformation became a venerated figure: His writings; preaching; lecturing together with the gospel; became the foundation of the Reformation Church Movement: He had Christ on his way to Wittenberg University to be persecuted for Christ. [See Phil. 1: 21-22]. "For me to live," said Paul: "Is Christ! To die is gain!" [v. 21]. Yet, others trembled for the results of his great powerful work. For Luther has once said himself: "If I knew that my writing-doctrines had injured one human being; however poor and unknown; which it could not; for it is the very gospel; I would rather face death ten times [10 X] over than retract it!"

And now a whole city and that city of Wittenberg itself were now fast sinking into a manipulative of confusion with dilemmas. The doctrines taught by Martin Luther had not caused this Enmity evil thing; but throughout Germany his Vatican pontiff; prelates were charging it upon Luther to disgrace his integrity. In Enmity-bitterness for soul, Luther sometimes asked: "Can such be the end of this great work of the reformation?" Again as he personally wrestled with God's truth in earnest prayer-peace meditations flowed into his heart. "The work is not mine; but it is the work of the Lord God in Christ Jesus own." Luther said: Like Paul: "I live for Christ; I press on till to the crown." For I am hard-pressed between the two; having a desire to depart and to be with Christ; which is far better." Paul said: He is a former zealous Pharisee; now he suffers for Christ his Lord who met him on his way to Damascus to persecute the Church of Christ!. Who am I, writing this compelling-challenging Christian book? I am not the Vatican Pope: I am not the Canterbury Archbishop neither! I am the least of the most unpopular platform vulnerable poor author: To tell the world this great tidings Word of the Lord Jesus Christ whom I most cherish. Will you agree? This work is not mine: But it is the work of the Lord my God and your God: He even cares for a falling sparrow on ground.

Athanasius-John T. Nkomo

You shall not suffer it to be corrupted by the tradition malicious superstition or fanaticism. But the thought of remaining longer from the Enmity sinful-conflict in such a crisis becomes insupportable: Like Martin Luther; and Paul: Luther determined to return to Wittenberg with no slight psychological subconscious objection of fearful at mind: Without further delay he set out on his perilous journey. He was under the ban of the Germany Empire and the Vatican pope authorities: The Vatican authority was unanimous at liberty to take Luther's life on flames of fire alive! Friends; relatives were all forbidden to aid to his needs or even to shelter him to every public and private sector. The imperial government under Charles V adopted the most stringent measures against his adherents or associates. But Luther saw that the work of God's great gospel was more imperiled; and in the name of the Lord Christ Jesus he went forth once more to most fierce-battle for truth beyond human scope!.

With great caution and humility: Yet with great divine decision and rock firmness; he entered upon his work as usually: By the mighty word," said Luther; "we must refute and expel what has gained a place and influence by violence. I would not resort to force against the superstitious and unbelieving." Let there be no compulsion. I have been working hard for liberty of conscience. Liberty is the very essence of true faith." Ascending the pulpit Luther with God's excellence-great wisdom; meek gentleness instructed; exhorted; and reproved; and by the power of God's gospel brought back the misguided of multitude peoples into the way of truth. He plainly showed up himself. The theological professor had no specific desire to encounter the fanatics whose course had been productive of so great Enmity evil at Wittenberg city and at University environment atmospheric. He knew them so well to be men of Enmity-hasty and vicious-violent tempter; who, while claiming to be especially illuminated prophets from heaven; would not endure the slight psychological phenomenal contradiction; or even the kindest admonition! Like today's

Christian fiction ebook written by popular platform authors:

Arrogating; grotesque; profligacy; Enmity sinful to themselves supreme authority; they required everyone else without a question; to acknowledge their malicious falsehood claims! So is today' young adults confined into secular world scholasticism; they require everyone else without a question to acknowledge their malicious falsehood Christian fiction ebook claims!. The young adults read their ebooks. They are being manipulated unaware!.

But as they demand an interview with him, he consented to meet them; and so successfully did he expose their pretensions; that the impostors at once departed from Wittenberg. "Then there arose some from what is called the Synagogue of the Freedmen [Cyrenians; Alexandrians; and those from Cilician and Asia] disputing with Stephen: And they were not able to resist the wisdom and the Spirit by which Stephen spoke." In other words: Stephen totally defeated them all: They did not like their defeat.

Enmity sinful overwhelms to harden their hearts. Like today; they do not like to be defeated through Scriptures; [See Acts 6: 9-13] Reason with them through sciences. They will never have the right answer neither! Never! Wrong questions: Wrong answers: That is a fact! God has all the answers: Will you agree?

The fanaticism prophets were checked for a time; but several years later it broke out with greater violence and more terrible results occurred. Martin Luther said concerning the leaders in this movement: "To them the Holy Scriptures were but a dead-deaf letter and they all began to cry; "the Spirit!" But most assuredly I will not follow where their spirit leads them. May God in his mercy preserve me from a church in which there are none but saints? I wish to be in fellowship with the humble; the feeble; the sick; who know and feel their sins and who sigh and cry continually to God from the bottom of their hearts to obtain his consolation and support."

Thomas Munzer one of the most active fanatics; was a man of considerable ability of his time which rightly directed; would have enabled him to do good; but he had not learned the first principles of true religion. He imagined himself ordained of God for reform the world; forgetting; like many other enthusiasts; that the reform should begin with himself. He was very self-ambitious to obtain prestigious position and influence; and unwilling to be second; even to Martin Luther. So he charged the theological professor Martin Luther with establishing by their adherence to the Bible alone; a species of popery. He considered himself called of God to remedy the evil; and held that manifestations of the Spirit were the means by which this was to be accomplished; and that he who had the Spirit possessed the true faith; though he might never see the written word. Munzer with all other fanatical teachers eventually gave themselves up to be governed by impressions calling every thought of the mind voice of God; consequently they went to great extremes: Some even burned the Bibles; exclaiming: "The letter killeth; but the Spirit giveth life. Men naturally love the marvelous and wonder whatever flatters their pride; and many were ready to accept Thomas Munzer's teachings. He soon denounced all order in public worship and declared that to obey princes was to attempt to serve both God and Belial.

The minds of the peoples already beginning to throw of the yoke of the pontiff papacy; were also becoming impatient under the restraints of the civil authority of Charles V. Munzer's Enmity evil revolutionary proclaiming divine sanctions; led them to break away from all control: And given the rein to their prejudices and passions: The most terrible scenes of sedition and strive followed; and the fields of Germany were all drenched with human blood. The deep agony of soul which Luther once had so long solved before experience in his unknown Castle at Erfurth; now pressed upon him with redoubled evil power as he saw the results of fanaticism charged upon him. The Vatican papist prince's declaration force; and many believed that Luther's doctrine now had been the cause of the rebellion. Like Nero who set up fire upon the whole Rome city he Christians escape-goat who truly proclaimed Christ Jesus; as Rome rebellion. Nero wanted a ground to slaughter every Jew Christian residing in Rome. This was the time that Saint Peter and Paul were executed to death. Although this charge imposed upon Luther was without the slightest foundation like Christians escape-goat; it could not but cause the Luther great distress. That the work of heaven should be thus degraded by being classed with the basest fanaticism; seemed more than he could humanly endures!. On the other hand; the leaders in the revolt Enmity hated Luther because he had not only opposed the Vatican their doctrines and denied their claims to divine inspiration; but had pronounced them rebels against the civil authority. So much in saying but also very divine confirmed. They believed. In retaliation they denounced him as a base of escape-goat like Nero pretender: Nero however; afterward subdued by his x-wife and Nero committed an awful suicidal. The Roman Empire ceased to exist. And then, Constantine ascended to Rome imperialism:

He seemed to have brought upon himself the Enmity sinful nature of both princes and common people who are their subjects. The Vatican Rome this time exulted expecting to witness the speedy down fall of Martin Luther' hardest work; and they blamed Luther even for the cause which he had been most earnestly endeavoring to correct the Vatican teachings. The fanatical party; By false claiming to have been treated with great injustice Succeeded in gaining the sympathy of a large class of the people Than Luther at this time; and as is usually the case with those who Take the wrong side; they came to be regarded as martyrs: Thus The ones who were exerting every energy in opposition of Martin Luther were more pitted and lauded as the victims of cruelty and Oppression!. This was the work of Enmity Lucifer-Satan prompted By the same spirit of rebellion which was first manifested in the Heavenly Eden Garden for Eve and Adam: Lucifer in the form

These sophisticated abilities for easily depolarizing everyone who Were first for Luther's support; now they are all in the form of Enmity-Lucifer: He is most capable to depolarize and opposing All that is called of God!. [2 Thess. 2: 3-5]. His envy continually Burns upon godly people!. But Enmity Lucifer is rather weak in the eyes of God Almighty see book of Job:

Satan is constantly seeking to deceive and depolarize men and Women and lead them to call Enmity sinful righteousness; and Righteousness is Enmity sinful: **"Woe to those who call Evil good! And good Evil!"** [Isaiah 5: 20-21]: How successful has been his Work! How often are censure and reproach cast upon God's Faithful peoples because they will stand fearlessly in defense of God! Men who are but agents of Satan are praised and flattered and even looked upon as martyrs; while those who should be well respected and sustained for their fidelity to God are left to' stand alone or even denied, under suspicious and distrust. So, in often times the guilty is acquitted; while the innocent is guilty in our judicial tradition courts. Counterfeit holiness; spurious sanctification; is still doing its work of deception. Under various forms it exhibit's the same spirit as in the day of Martin Luther and our day; diverting minds from the Scriptures, And leading men to follow their own feelings and impressions Rather than to yield obedience to the perfect law of God. They contend that they are creative with new ideas. As a matter of fact there's aren't new ideas that they claim to be creative. But a Constant repeated cycle. This is one of Satan's most successful Devices to depolarize; to cast reproach upon purity and truth. He is skilled in doing it?

Fearlessly did Martin Luther defend the gospel so well from the attacks which came from every quarter of Enmity sinful. The word of God proved itself a mighty weapon in every Enmity conflict. With that powerful word he warred against the usurped authority of the Vatican, and the rationalistic human philosophy of the scholasticism while he stood firm as a solid Christ rock against the fanaticism that sought to allay itself with the true reformation. Each of these opposing elements was in its own way setting aside the Holy Scriptures; and exhausting human wisdom as the source of religious truth and knowledge. Rationalism idolize faking reason and makes this criterion for religion. The Vatican Rome church, claiming for their sovereign pontiff an divine inspiration descended in unbroken line from the apostles, and unchanging able through all time; gives ample opportunity for every species of extravagance and corruption to be concealed under the sanctity of the apostolic commission the inspiration claimed by Munzer and his associates proceeded from no higher source than the vagaries of imagination and its influence was subversive of all authority, human or divine. True Christianity received the word of God as the great treasure house of true divine inspired truth; and the test of all divine Inspiration.

Upon his return from Wartburg Castle, Luther completed his translation of New Testament; and the gospel was soon after given to the people of all Germany in their own language. This translation was unanimously received with great joy by all who loved to read the truth about God true-living word; but it was scornfully rejected by those who chose human tradition and the commandments of men in Vatican Rome. The Vatican priests were alarmed at the thought that the common people would now be able to discuss with them the precepts of God's Word and that their own ignorance would thus be exposed. The really weapon for self-defense of their carnal reasoning were powerless Against the sharp sword of the Spirit: The Vatican Rome summoned all their authority power to prevent the circulation of the New Testament translation in Germany language; but decrees; anathemas; and tortures were alike in vain. The more they condemned and prohibited the Bible the greater was the eagerness of the people to know what it really taught. All who could read were eager to earnestly study the word of God for themselves. They carried it about with them everywhere they go and read and read; and could not be stopped as they were not satisfied for it seemed to quench their thirsty soul from drinking the real living water that springs up on its own fountain. **"If you knew the gift of God; and who it is who says to you; "Give Me a drink; you would have asked Him; and He would have given you living water." Jesus said.** [John 4: 10]. Yes! They could not be satisfied until they had committed large portions to memory and filling their thirsty till feel no more thirsty. Seeing the great favor with which the New Testament was received, Martin Luther immediately began the translation of the Old Testament and published it in parts as fast as completed.

Martin Luther's writings were welcome alike in city and in hamlet. At night the teachers of the village schools read them aloud to small groups gathered at the fireside during winter time. With every effort, some souls would be convicted of the truth, and receiving the word with gladness, would in their turn tell the good news to others.

"[Psalm 119: 130] "The entrance of your words gives light: It gives understanding to the simple."

The truth of inspiring God's words were truly verified! Because God's word gives full understanding to the simple soul which pants for God; like deer pants for water! As deer pants for water; so pants my soul for you, O God! [Psalm 42:] The study of the Scriptures was working a mighty change in minds and hearts of the multitudes of people in Germany. The Vatican papal rule had placed upon its subjects an iron yoke which held them in ignorance and degradation. Human tradition; a superstitious observance of forms had been scrupulously maintained; but in all their service the heart and intellect had, had so much less part: The preaching of Martin Luther and writings, setting the plain truths of God's word; and the word itself; placed in the hands of the vulnerable people; and aroused their dormant powers not only purifying and ennobling the spiritual nature but imparting new strength and vigorous to the intellectually. Today there isn't a leader for reformer of church like Luther to lead a nation to church reformation. All walks of life in Germany were to be seen with the Bible like their daily national newspapers in their hands; defending the Luther's doctrines and church reformation. The early century Vatican church its leaders who had left the study of the Scriptures to the prelates; Priests and monks; now called upon them to come forward and refute the new Luther's teachings. But ignorant alike of the Scriptures and of the power of God; priest and friars were totally defeated by those whom they had denounced as unlearned common and heretical. One of the pontiff, unhappily expressed his feelings: "Luther has persuaded his that their faith ought only to be founded on the oracles of Holy Writ." Crowds would gather to hear the truth advocated by men of much less educated; and even discussed by them with those well-educated and eloquent theologians. The shameful ignorance of these great men was made apparent as their arguments were met by the simple teachings of God's word. Women and children; artisans and soldiers; had a better knowledge of the Scriptures than had well educated professional-doctors of surplice priest.

As the Vatican clergy saw their congregations diminishing, they invoked the aid of the magistrates; and by every means in their power endeavored to bring back their hearers. The people had found in the new teachings that which adequately supplies the needs of their souls and they turned away from the pontiff Rome church that had so long with the worthless husks of human paganism rites and human traditions. When persecution was kindled against the teachers of the true word of Christ Jesus, they gave heed to the words; when they persecute you in this city; you will flee into another." This true light penetrated everywhere unstoppable. The fugitives would find somewhere a genuine hospitable door wide-opened to them and there abiding they would preach Christ Jesus; sometimes in the church, or if denied that privilege; in private houses or in the open air. Wherever they could obtain a hearing was consecrated temple. The truth proclaimed with such enormous energy and assurance; spread with irresistible power. In vain were both Ecclesiastical and civil authority invoked to crush the heresy. In vain they resorted to imprisonment; torture; fire threats; and sword. They could not stop the powerful divine authority from above in heaven no matter what manner they tried. Thousands of believers sealed their faith with their last drop of their blood and yet the work we on as usually according to Christ's commands. The extensive of Vatican persecution served only to further extend the truth; and the fanatics prophets which Satan endeavored to unite with it; resulted in making more clear the contrast between the work of Lucifer Satan and the work of God Almighty! But with no compromise with evil doers!.

"Hear O, Israel: The Lord our God, the Lord is one! You shall love the Lord your God with all your heart; with all your soul and with all your strength." [Deut. 6: 4-6] See [Matt 22: 37-40] On these two Commandments hang all the Law and the prophets:" Jesus said: "Love your neighbor as yourself." [v 40]. Enmity; Jesus Christ is inevitable! Ignore him at your own wicked risk:

Athanasius-John T. Nkomo

Chapter 6

Protest of the Noble Princes

Spires in 1529

The noblest witnesses ever proclaimed for the Church Reformation is the protest submitted by Christian Noble Princes at Diet Council of Spires in 1529: The entire future course of the Reformation depended on the decision they there made: The combined forces of Europe continent were gathered together to crush out the newly emerging reformation. But noble Christian men protested and refuted to deny their faith or yours!. Their honesty zeal protest at the Diet Council of Spires that year 1529 has given us the name; "Protestant." Here you will discover of the unique and reality of our early century spiritual forefathers; the first Protestants and of the fundamental principles of Protestantism that they have bequeathed to all!

Their fearless courage; faith; and firmness zealous of these men of God, gained for phenomenal succeeding ages liberty of thought and Conscience: Their protest gave to the reformed church the name of Protestant; its high spiritual principles are the very essence of Protestantism today and ever! A dark and threatening days had come for the Church Reformation. For a season religious toleration had prevailed in the human empire; God's providence had held opposing elements in check; that the gospel might obtain a more firm foothold; but the Vatican Rome had now summoned their wicked forces to crush this truths: At Spires the pontiff papists openly manifested their Enmity-hostility toward Martin Luther and all who followed him in his favor, Melancthon: "We are the execration and the sweepings of the earth; but Christ will look down on his poor people; and will preserve them." The evangelical princes in attendance at the Diet were forbidden even to have the gospel preached in their dwellings:

But the people of Spires desperate thirsted for the word of God; and notwithstanding the prohibition; thousands flocked to the morning and evening worship still held in the chapel of the Elector of Saxony. This hastened the crisis! An imperial message announced to the Diet that given rise to great disorders; the young emperor declared it to be annulled. This arbitrary act excited the indignation and alarm of the evangelical Christians. "Christ has again fallen into the hands of Caiaphas and Pilate:" One faith Christian said: The pontiff Vatican papacy became more violent. A bigoted papist declared: "The Turks are better than the Lutherans: For the Turks observe fast days; and the Lutherans violate them. If we must choose between the Holy Scriptures of God and the old corruption of the church; we should reject the former." Melancthon said: "Every day, in full assembly, Faber casts some new stones against the Gospellers."

Religious toleration had been legally established, and the evangelical States were resolved to oppose the infringement of their rights. Luther, being still under the ban imposed by the edict of Worms; was Not permitted to be present at Spires; but his place was represented By his co-laborers and the noble princes whom God had raised up to defend his cause in this emergency. The old noble Frederick of Saxony Luther's former protector at this time was natural dead But the Duke John his brother, who succeeded to the throne had joyfully welcomed the reformation and while a friend of peace, he displayed great energy and courage in all matters relating to the interests of the faith.

The pontiff priests demanded that the States which had accepted the Reformation submit implicitly to pontiff Rome jurisdiction which had previously been granted. They could not consent that pontiff Rome should again bring under the word of those nations that had with so great joy received the word of God.

Athanasius-John T. Nkomo

The Diet finally decreed that where the reformation had not become established; the edict of Worms should be rigorously enforced; and that in the evangelical States; where there would be danger of revolt; no new reform should be introduced; there should be no preaching upon disputed points; the celebration of the mass should not be opposed; and no Roman Catholic Church member should be permitted to embrace the Lutheranism: If this decree became a validated law; the reformation could neither be extended where as yet it had not reached; nor be established on a solid firm foundation where it already existed: Liberty of speech would be prohibited! No conversions would be allowed! And to these restrictions and prohibitions the faithful followers of the Reformations were required at once to submit. The hopes of the world seemed about to be extinguished! The re-establishment of the Vatican Rome hierarchy would inevitably cause a revival of the early ancient century abuses; and an occasion would readily be found for completing the destruction of work that had already been shaken by those first steering stranger's fanaticism and dissension. The wise God could not permit such Enmity sinful to occur.

As the evangelical party met for consultation; one looked to another in blank dismay. From one another passed the inquiry; "What is to be done?" Mighty issues for the world were at stake. Had these men been controlled by vigorous ambition or selfishness; they might have accepted the decree. They themselves were apparently left free to maintain their faith. Ought they not to be satisfied with this? Should they throw themselves into the Enmity conflict to wrestle for liberty of conscience in all the world. Should they expose themselves to the vengeance of pontiff Rome?

Never were these men placed in a more trying position; but they came forth from the test with principles unsullied. As the mist that had hovered over their minds cleared away, they saw what would be the result of this decree. Should they lend their influence to restore? The stake and the torture? Should they oppose the advancement of truth; oppose the Spirit of God in its work of calling men to Christ? Could real refute obedience to the Lord Christ Jesus' Command: **"Go into all the world and preach the gospel to every creature! [Mark 16: 15].** Ought they to consent that those who might desire to renounce Enmity sinful should be denied the privilege?

Having entered the kingdom of heaven themselves; should they bar the way so that other could not enter? Rather would they sacrifice their dominions; their status; and their own lives: So they exclusively resolved to refute the unjust decree: "Let us reject this decree," the noble princes said: In matters of conscience the majority had no power!." The deputies declared that Germany was indebted to the Decree of toleration for the peace and harmony which the Germany nation enjoyed; and that its abolition would fill the Germany Empire with enormous amount of troubles and divisions:

"The pontiff Diet Council is incompetent;" said the noble Princes: "To do more than preserve religious liberty until a council meets." To protect liberty of conscience is the duty of the State; and this is the limit of its civil authority in matters of religion." Every secular world government that attempts to regulate or enforce religious observances by civil authority is sacrificing the very principle for which the evangelical Christians so nobly struggled! The Vatican papists; prelates determined to put down what they termed daring obstinacy: They began with so much endeavoring to cause more divisions among the supporters of the reformation; and to severe intimidate all who had not openly accepted in its favor or obligation. The noble princes were at last summoned before the Diet Council to stand for their nobly obligation for the whole Germany Nation to attain religious liberty and conscience!. These noble princes pleaded for mutual delay; but their plea was in vain. Those who still refuse to sacrifice liberty of conscience and the right of individual judgment well knew that their position marked them for future criticism; condemnation; and persecution.

One of the strongest reformer supporters said: "We must either deny the word of God or be burned!" King Ferdinand; the despotic emperor's representative at the Diet Council, saw that the pontiff decree would cause more serious divisions unless the noble princes could be induced to accept and sustain it. He therefore tried the Crafting-cunning technique language of persuasion; well knowing that to employ force with such evil men would only render them more determined. He natural; malicious begged the young noble princes to accept the decree; maliciously assuring them that such an act would be highly gratifying to the newly young ascended emperor Charles V. But these faithful young noble princes nobly acknowledged a unique Authority above that of earthly rulers; and they well-wisely answered calmly: **"We will obey the emperor in everything that may contribute to maintain peace; harmony; and the honor of God."** But Peter and John answered and said to them: **"Whether it is right in the sight of God to listen to you more than to God; you judge: "For we cannot but speak the things which we have seen and heard!"** [Acts 4: 19-20]. Also see Acts 1: 8; 2: 32 &. 1 John 1: 1, 3]. The German noble princes had this in minds the compelling words of Saint Peter and John before the sight of Caiaphas; Scribes; Pharisees; and Sadducees; in the midst of early ancient Jewish Enmity sinful Church Reformation which the Vatican inherited. In the presence of the pontiff Diet Council; the king Ferdinand at last announced to the elector and his friends that their only remaining course was to submit to the majority: Having thus spoken; he withdrew from the despotic assembly; giving the Lutherans no opportunity for deliberation or response. In vain they sent messengers entreating him to return. To their remonstrance's he answered only; "It is a settled affairs; submission in all that remains." The Germany imperial party were convinced that the Christian young noble princes would adhere to the Holy Scriptures as superior to Human doctrines and requirements; and they knew that an Acceptance of this principle would eventually overthrow the Vatican pontiff papacy. But they flattered themselves that weakness was on the side of the reformation; while strength was with the emperor and the Vatican pontiff pope. Had the reformers made flesh their arm; they would have been as powerless as the pontiff papacy supposed. Good enough the reformers stood on Christ' solid rock firm!.

Although the reformers were seemingly weak in numbers; and at variance with Vatican Rome; they had their strength! They appealed from the decision of the pontiff despotic Diet to the word of God; and from the emperor of Germany to the king and Lord of lords Jesus Christ for their fixed hope and faith. As Ferdinand had refused to regard their conscientious convictions; the young noble princes decided to heed his absence; but to bring their protest before the national council without a further delay. A solemn declaration was therefore drawn up, and presented to the despotic Diet Council; and wrote document:

"We protest by these presents; before God; our only Creator; Preserver; Redeemer; and Saviour; and who will one day be our Judge; as well as before all men and all creatures; that we; for us and our nation; neither consent nor adhere in any manner whatever to the proposed decree in anything that is contrary to God; to His Word; to our right conscience; or to the salvation of our souls: We cannot assert that when Almighty God calls a man to his knowledge he dares not embrace that divine knowledge: There is no true doctrine but which conforms to the word of God: The Lord forbids the teaching of any other faith: The Holy Scriptures; with one text explained by other and plainly texts; are; in all things necessary for the Christian; easy to be well understood; and adapted to enlighten: We are therefore resolved by divine grace to maintain the pure preaching of God's only Word; as it

is contained in the Holy Scriptures of the Old and New Testament; without anything added thereto: This Word is the only truth! It is the sure of all doctrine and life; and can never fail or deceive us! He who builds on this foundations shall stand against all the powers of hell-Enmity; whilst all the vanities that are set up against it shall fall before the face of God." We therefore reject the yoke that is imposed upon us!"

A very anguish impression was deeply heartfelt upon the pontiff Diet Council in Vatican Rome. The majority were filled with enormous amount of amazements and alarms at the boldness-courage of the young noble Princes Protesting: They now appeared to them stormy and very uncertain! The highest Divine Authority from above has ultimately spoken and it cannot be changed or stopped by any means of human beings inadequate formation: Dissension; strife; and bloodshed seemed inevitable: But the Lutherans were now to be seen with clear assurance of the justice of their cause; and relying upon the arm of Omnipotence God; were full of courage and solid rock firmness. The Princes protest unanimously denied the right of civil rulers to legislate in matters between the soul and God; and declared with prophets and apostles; Peter; John; Paul: "We ought to obey God rather than men!" It rejected also the arbitrary power of the Vatican Catholic Church; and set forth the unerring principle that all human being tradition teachings should be in subjection to the oracles of God Almighty the Creator of all resources in heaven and in earth! No! One-Else! The princes protesters had profoundly unanimously thrown off the yoke of human tradition supremacy; and had exalted the most high world Saviour the Lord Jesus Christ; the corner-stone which the early Jews and the early pontiff Rome builders rejected to build: The Lutherans in Germany truly had exalted Christ as supreme in the church; and his solid word in the pulpit. The powerful of conscience was set above the State; and the civil authority of the Holy Scriptures above the visible church.

The unbeatable or undefeated Crown of the Lord Jesus Christ once again is uplifted above the human pontiff pope's tiara and the mere human emperor's diadem! For the Lord spoke and it was done! The three young noble princes protesting had moreover affirmed their divine right to freely utter their convictions of divine' truth: They would not only subconscious believe and obey what the word of God presents; and they denied the right of pontiff or magistrate to interfere. The prince's protest at Spires was a solemn witness against human tradition religious intolerance and an assertion of the right of all men created in the image of God to truly worship according to the dictates of their own human consciences. This kind of Enmity sinful it what God most hates!

The Declaration of Spires had been made in 1529: And the Declaration of Slavery Emancipation had be made in 1863: It was written in the unique and reality of thousands; and registered in the most unique and truth in the Divine Books of Heaven where no effort of a mere man could erase or alter it! All evangelical Germany adopted the protest as the expression of its faith from henceforth:

Everywhere men and women beheld in this most compelling declaration the promise of a profound new and better era! The compelling question to ask is: Who dares to remember this most profound unique of God's true providence in our midst today?

One of the young Prince said to the Protestants of Spires: "May the Almighty who has given you grace to confess energetically; freely; and fearlessly; preserve you in that Christian firmness until the day of eternity!" Who dares to receive this truth today? Had the Lutherans, after attaining a profound degree of success; consented to temporize to secure favor or sympathy; or compromise; with the world; it would have been untrue to God and to itself; and would thus have insured its own destruction as it is for many failing found upon every other emerging diversity denominations today! They contend to compromise in order to gain favor and sympathy from men rather than from God the sustainer of all sources: The experience of those early century reformers contains a serious danger-lesson for all succeeding generations: This serious danger is Enmity sinful which all generations have ever experiences till today' modern era; no escape!

Enmity sinful; Satan's full skill manner of working against God and opposing all that is called God's word has not; and is not resolved or changed; he is still as much opposed to the Scriptures being made the genuine guide of life as since Genesis 3: 14-19; as in the 16th century till today!. In our time there is a wide departure from its doctrines and precepts; and there is desperate need of a profound return to the great Protestant principle; the Bible and the Bible only as the rule of all faith and all duties of: Scientist; religious; government; and all other walks of life on earth! All are contemporary called upon to fully obey the only One God the Creator of all! Enmity sinful Lucifer is still working hard through every means which he can control to destroy true-God's liberty: The anti-Christ or Christian power which the prince's protest of Spires repudiated; is now with renewed vigor seeking to re-establish its lost supremacy. Modern scientist boast like a little god in medic skill. Some are unaware that one day death will fall upon them:

For example: Atrial Fibrillation [AF] is an abnormal heart rhythm: Currently they have successful invented what they call "Pacemaker." It is a sophisticated small machine, runs by a battery to stimulate electric into heart. Its use has been for 50 years. I am not sure who or how many on earth possess a pacemaker into their bodies. For certain, pacemaker does not work well for all persons who got it into their body system. It might work well for others but it can't be for all to prevent or prolongs death: Moreover; pacemaker constitutes of several high potential risks: A physician dies like anyone else. A Physician can be contaminated with a disease: He can't prevents all diseases occurring around the world;

neither can he prevents his own life: A physician cannot prolong a life at all! God can! His skill is limited: He does not have all the answers in his medical field: God has it all! And is able to maintain; sustains all living life on earth! God is the Creator of all living things! It is not argument but truth! Will you agree? Enmity sinful is our enemy:

The same unswerving adherence to the word of God manifested at that crisis of the Church Reformation; is the only hope of reform of heart for every individual person today! There appeared token of dangers to the Protestants. There were tokens; also; that the divine hand was stretched out to protect the faithful believers. It was about this time that Melancthon hurried his faithful friend Grynaeus through the streets of Spires to the Rhine; and urged him to cross the river without further delay: Grynaeus; in astonishment; desired to know the reason for this sudden flight. Melancthon said: "An old man of grave and solemn aspect; but who is unknown to me appeared before me; and said; "In a minute the officers of justice will be sent by Ferdinand to arrest Grynaeus." On the banks of the Rhine River, Melancthon waited until the waters of that stream interposed between his beloved friend and those who sought for his life: When he saw him on the other side at last; he said: "He is torn from the cruel jaw of those who thirsty for innocent blood." Grynaeus had been on intimate terms with a leading pontiff papist doctor; but having been shocked at one of his sermons; he went to him; and entreated that he would no longer war against the truth: The pontiff papist concealed his anger; but immediately rushed to the king; and obtained from him a warrant authorizing to apprehend the Lutherans protester: When Melancthon returned to his house; he was informed that after his departure officers in pursuit of Grynaeus had searched it from top to bottom. He ever believed that the Lord had saved his friend by sending a holy angel to give him warning.

The Church Reformation was to be brought into greater

prominence before the mighty ones of the earth. The evangelical princes had been denied a hearing by King Ferdinand; but they were to be granted an opportunity to present their cause in the presence of the emperor and the assembled dignitaries of Church and State. To quiet the dissensions which disturbed the empire; Charles V convoked a Diet at Augsburg city, over which he announced his intention to preside in person. Thither the Protestant leaders were summoned to appear: Great dangers threatened the reformation; but its advocates still trusted their cause with the mighty God; and pledged themselves to be solid firm like rock to the gospel of Christ. They determined to prepare a statement of their views in systematic form with the evidence from the written Scriptures to present before the pontiff Diet; and the task were committed to Martin Luther; Melancthon and their faithful associates-supporters. The Confession thus prepared was well accepted by the whole newly Protestants as an exposition of their faith; and they assembled to affix their names to the important document. It was a solemn and trying time. The reformer members were solicitous that their cause should not be confounded with political questions; they felt that the reformation should exercise no other influence than that which proceeds from the word of the mighty God. As the Christian young noble princes advanced to the Confession; Melancthon interposed; saying "it is for the theologians and ministers to propose these things; while the authority of the mighty ones of earth. Is to be reserved for other matters. "God forbid," John of Saxony response; "that you should exclude me. I am resolved to do my duty without being troubled about my crown:

"I desire to confess the Lord my electoral hat and robes are not so precious to me as the cross of Jesus Christ." Having thus spoken; he wrote down his name: Said another of the princes as he took the pen; "If the honor of my Lord Jesus Christ requires it; I am ready to leave my goods and life behind me." Rather would I renounce my subjects and my State; rather would I quit the country of my fathers; staff in hand he continued; "than to receive my other doctrine than is contained in this Confession." Such was the faith and daring of those men of true God. The precise appointed time came to appear before the Germany newly young emperor: Charles V, seated upon his throne, surrounded by the Germans despotic Electors and the Princes; gave audience to the Protestant Lutherans reformers of their strong faith were read. In that August 10th, 1529 assembly the truths of the gospel were clearly set forth; and the Enmity sinful of the pontiff papal church were pointed out: Well done have that day been pronounced; "the greatest day of the Church Reformation and one of the most glorious in the history of Christianity and of the world ever told.

But few years had passed since the theological professor of Wittenberg; Martin Luther solid firmly stood at Worms before the Pontiff [Despotic Diet National Council]. Now in his stead the noblest and most powerful princes of the empire. Luther had been forbidden to appear at Augsburg; but he had been present by his written words and earnest prayers. "I am overjoyed," Luther wrote: "that I have lived until this hour, in which Christ has been publicly exalted by such illustrious confessors, and in so glorious an assembly Herein is fulfilled what the Scriptures said; "I will plainly testify thy testimony in the presence of kings!" Like in the days of Saint Paul, early ancient Judaism zealous Pharisee; transformed to the truth of gospel for which he is now often times put in prisons and brought him before the princes and nobles of the Rome imperial city. So on this occasion, that which emperor Charles V had forbidden to be preached from the holy pulpit; is now plainly proclaimed in the very emperor's palace; what many had regarded unfit even for the emperor's servants to listen to such; it is now well listened and heard with their ears and hearts with great splendor and wonders by the masters and despotic or lords of the empire. For God spoke and it was done! God is Sovereign: With God; all things are possible and nothing is difficulty with him!

Kings and great men of earth were the auditory crowned princes were the preachers and the sermon was the royal truth of God. Since the apostolic age, says a writer; "there has never been a greater work or a more magnificent confession of Christ Jesus." All that the Lutherans' have said is true, and we cannot deny it," acknowledge a pontiff bishop. Can you by sound reasons refute the Confession made by the elector and his allies?" asked another of Dr. Eck. Not with the writings of the apostles and prophets; was the reply" "I understand, then," responded the one who questioned, "that the Lutherans are entrenched in the Scriptures and we are only outside." Truth, always prevails! What is truth today in our day era? Will you agree? Some of the princes of Germany were won to the reformed faith. The emperor Charles V himself finally recognized the reformers and firmly acknowledged that the "Protestant articles were but the truth!" The Confession was translate into many languages and circulated through all Europe continent; and it has been unanimously accepted by a multitudes in millions of people in succeeding generations as the expression of their faith till this day: Christ' truth triumph! All prophets; disciples; apostles; and early 16th, century are fulfilled. Jesus Christ had foretold all the events to take place in the life time of the disciples and in the life time of this day also fulfilled.

God's faithful corner-stone builders were not toiling alone: While Principalities; and powers and Enmity-wicked spirits in high places were leagued against them, the Lord God did not forsake them. He is their strong shield which protected them all-long from the beginning Genesis and wilderness Exodus up to Luther: Now it is to us, he is the same God shielding to his peoples. "Surely every man walks about like a shadow: He heaps up riches; and does not know who will gather them." [Ps. 39: 6; see Luke 12: 18-21]

Could their eyes/ears have been opened; they would have seen as marked evidence of divine presence and aid as was granted to ancient Prophets of the beginning [Genesis] and wilderness

Exodus: When Elijah's pointed his servant Elisha to the hostile army surrounding them and cutting off all opportunities for escape, the prophet Elijah prayed; "Lord, I pray thee, open his eyes that he may see." [2 Kings 6: 17]:

And lo he saw, the mountain was filled with chariots and horses of fire heavenly army stationed to protect the one man Elijah who truly feared God. Thus did angels guard the workers in cause of the reformation. So was for Mahatma Gandhi in India 1896-1948: Dr. Martin Luther King, Jr. in U.S.A. 1929-1968: And Nelson Mandela in South Africa, 1907-2013:

God indeed had commanded them to build; and no Enmity hostility opposing forces could drive them from the walls profound founded on Christ' solid rock foundation! From the secret place of prayer came the invisible divine powerful that shook the world in the Great Church Reformation; Colonialism in India; Africa; and Segregation in U.S. A. and Apartheid in South Africa: There with holy calmness, the faithful men of the Lord God set their feet upon the Christ's solid rocky stood firm unshaken for the divine guarantee promises! They overwhelmed prevailed! God's way it is not man's way! Will you agree? God shows his invisible divine attribution power to be visibly in-full practical actions! Therefore no excuse! [Rom 1: 20-21].

During the reformation Enmity-struggle at Augsburg; Martin Luther did not fail him to devote three hours each day to earnest prayer and these were taken from that portion of the day most favorable to study: In the privacy of his chamber he was heard to pour out his soul before the eyes of God in words full of adoration; fear; and hope; as if speaking to a friend. "I know that you are our Father and our God; he said; "and that you will scatter the persecutors of your children; You are Thyself endangered with us: All this matter is yours and it is only by your constraint that we have put our hands to it. Defend us then 0 Father!"

To Melancthon who was crushed under the burden of anxiety and fearful he wrote; "Grace and peace in Christ! In Christ, I say and not in the world; Amen!" I hate with exceeding hatred those extreme cares which consume you. If the cause is unjust, abandon it; if the cause is just; why should we belie the promise of him who commands us to sleep without fear?" Christ will not be wanting to the work of justice and truth. He reigns what fear, then, can we have?"

God did with full alert ear/eye listen to the cries of his faithful peoples. He gave princes and ministers grace and courage to maintain the truth against the wicked rulers of the darkness of this world. God said: "Behold I lay in Zion a chief corner-stone, elect; precious; and he that believe on him shall not be confounded." [1 Pet 2: 6]. The Protestant reformation had built on Christ, and the gates of hell could not prevail against them. While Martin Luther was opening the closed Bible to the people of Germany Tyndale was impelled by the Spirit of the Mighty God to do the same for England: John Wycliffe did not complete the task-work. But he only cultivated unfinished path. Tyndale took over following in obedience to God's compelling divine call. Tyndale was a diligent students of the Scriptures and fearlessly preached his personal convictions of truth, urging that all doctrines be brought to the test of God's word! His zeal could not but excite opposition from the pontiff papist. Well educated Catholic doctor who engaged in dispute with him exclaimed; "It were better for us to be without God's law than without the pope's." Tyndale response was; "I defy the pope and all his laws; and if God spare my life; ere many years I will cause a boy who drives the plow to know more of the Scriptures than you do." The purpose which he had begun to cherish of giving to the people the New Testament Scriptures in their own language; was now Confirms and he immediately applied himself to the work:

Athanasius-John T. Nkomo

Confession Augustana Augsburg 1530

Theological disputes within the expanding sphere of Lutheranism to other territories in the latter half of the 16th century led to the compilation of a definitive set of Martin Lutheran Confessions in the Book of Concord in 1580. The Book of Concord includes the Augsburg Confession and the Apology of the Augsburg Confession as the foundational confessions of the Martin Lutheran faith.

Martin Luther statue in Worms, Germany

'Martin, said he, "there is no one of the heresies which have torn the bosom of the church, which has not derived its origin from the various interpretations of the Scripture. The Bible itself is the arsenal whence each innovator has drawn his deceptive arguments. It was with biblical texts that Pelagius and Arius maintained their doctrines. Arius, for instance, found the negation of the eternity of the Word-an eternity which you admit, in this verse of the New Testament-Joseph knew not his wife till she had brought forth her first-born son; and he said, in the same way that you say, that this passage enchained him. When the fathers of the council of Constance condemned this proposition of John Huss: The church of Jesus Christ is only the community of the elect, they condemned an error; for the church, like a good mother, embraces within her arms all who bear the name of Christian, all who are called to enjoy the celestial beatitude.'" Martin Luther died on Feb 18th, 1546: He was 62 years old. [1483-1546] D0B: Nov 10th 1483.

Aleander, the pontiff legate not content with this victory, he endeavored with all the pontiff power crafting and cunning at his own command to secure Martin Luther' condemnation. With his grotesque profligates persistence worthy of a better cause; he urged the matter upon the attention of princes, prelates and other noble members of the assembly; accusing professor Martin Luther of sedition; rebellion; impiety; and blasphemy etc.: But the vehemence and passion manifested by the legate plainly revealed that he was actually by Enmity hatred and revenge rather than by zeal for religion. It was the prevailing sentiment of the assembly that Martin Luther is innocent.

Aleander with redoubled Enmity zeal, he urged upon the newly emperor Charles V the duty of executing the pontiff papal edicts. Overcome at last by this importunity; Charles V bade the legate present his case to the Diet. The Vatican Rome had few advocates better fitted by tradition nature and well educated to defend their cause. Like today modern scholasticism institutions possess their adequate advocates better fitted by tradition nature and well highly educated to defend their cause of scientific and technology. The close friends of Professor Martin Luther looked forward with some profound anxious and anxiety to the result of Aleander's speech. Aleander eagerness speech is to secure Luther's condemnation of death:

There was not so much or little excitement when the legate Aleander, with great pontiff dignity and pomp, appeared before the national assembly. Many people called to mind the scene of the Lord Christ Jesus trial; when Annas and Caiaphas falsely presented evidence before the judgment seat of Pilate-Roman; demanded the death of the most high anointed Messiah, the Christ 'that perverted the people at large." The pontiff legate Aleander; with all human tradition power of learning and vibrate-eloquence speech he set up himself to overthrow the truth from God' holy mouth. Charge after charge Aleander hurled against Luther as an enemy of the Catholic

Church and the State; the living and the dead; clergy and laity; councils and all private Christians, etc.: "There is more than enough!" The pontiff grotesque poignancy expressed tone. "In the error of Luther." He insisted: "To warrant the burning of a hundreds heretics."

In conclusion; Aleander vigorously endeavored to cast contempt upon the adherents of the reformed true faith: "What are all these and who are all these Lutherans?" A motley rabble of insolent grammarians; corrupt priests; dissolute monks; ignorant lawyers; and degraded nobles; with the common people whom they have misled and perverted! How greatly superior is the Catholic Party in numbers; intelligence; and power! A unanimous decree from this illustrious assembly will open the eyes of the simple; show the minstrels-misogyny unwary their danger; determine the wavering; and strengthen the weak hearted." Crafting-cunning words from Aleander's mouth sound like he is judging himself. His contradicting speech it is what Luther is showing them to transform for better through Scriptures which they were lacking to implement and teaching. Their hearts supposed e to be depolarized for better. With such weapons have the advocates of truth in every age been attacked. The same arguments are still urged even today against all who dare to present; in opposition; disagreement; resistance to established Enmity sinful-errors the plain and direct teachings of God's true word. Who are these preachers and teachers of new doctrines? Exclaimed those who desire a popular platform religion; like today modern world Believers Top Christian Publishers would only publish Christian fiction ebook written by those with popular platform. They will not publish good quality true Christian book written by those without popular platform.

"They are unlearned," argued Aleander: "Few in numbers; and of the vulnerable poor class." Yet they claim to have the truth; and to be the chosen people of God!" They are ignorant and deceived." Aleander repeated his malicious cunning poignant tone. "How greatly superior in numbers and influence are our denominations! How many great and learned men are in our churches! How much more power is on our side!" **Whose power? Human tradition or God?** These are the arguments that have a telling influence upon the world till this day: But they are no more conclusive now than in the days of early ancient Greeks, Hellenists; Romans; Prophets; Judaism Priest Caiaphas; Pharisees; Sadducees; Sanhedrin; through 13th century, John Wycliffe; John Huss; Jerome; Martin Luther: Furthermore; 20th, century, Mahatma Gandhi; Dr. Martin Luther King, Jr. and Nelson Mandela in South Africa:

The Church Reformation or social politics and economic did not; as many suppose has ended with Martin Luther. Neither! It is a process needs to be continued until Christ returns: Enmity sinful still with its persistence-existence: It is to be continued to the end of this modern world current affairs greatest history. John Wycliffe; John Huss; Jerome; Martin Luther; these great men had done great work in the world in reflecting to others this great illuminating light which God had permitted to shine upon the earth it shall not be quenched or switched out by human hands! Yet these past reformers did not receive all the light which was to be given to the world, but it will be complete given when Christ returns the ultimate righteous illuminating light and Judge; once and for all! He is inevitable!

From that time to our present day; new light has been continually shining upon the Scriptures; and new truths have been constantly unfolding: The compelling question is: Who takes notice this shining light today? Like in the past; there aren't many! We need to focus seriously to this phrase:

Enmity God imposed! The pontiff legate's address made a deep impression upon the Diet. Martin Luther was not present when Aleander delivered his speech to the assembly. With the clear convincing truths of God's word, to vanquish the pontiff papal champion. No attempts was made to defend Martin Luther. There was manifest a general impulse to root out the Lutheran heretic from the empire. The Vatican Church had enjoyed the most favorable opportunity to defend their cause. The greatest of their orators had been well spoken. All that they could say in their own vindication had been well crafted said. But the apparent victory was the signal of their really-self defeat or their complete fall!. Henceforth the contrast between truth and untruth would be more clearly seen; as they should take the field in open warfare! God had already set it up for them to have their big fall like a house built on sand; its fall sinking it is big!. Slowly but sure: Like Titanic ship could no longer resist against the deep powerful ocean but to slowly sink until the ocean completely swallows it up all! Never again from that day would the pontiff Rome stand as secure as they had been before for decades deceitful crafting!. The majority of the noble assembly were readily to sacrifice Martin Luther to the demands of the pontiff Rome pope; but many of them saw and deplored the existing depravity in the early 14th, century Catholic Church; and desired a suppression of the abuses suffered by the German people in consequence of the Vatican corruption and greed for self-gain!. The legate Aleander had presented the papal rule in the most favorable rites. Now the Lord God moved upon a member of the Diet to give a true delineation of the effects of Vatican papal tyranny. Like he did to Balaam's donkey; God opened its mouth to vigorously speak to Balaam: "What have I done to you that you have struck me these three times? "Because you have abused me!" with his hostiles anger; Balaam replied: Why did Balaam not get astonished hearing his donkey speaks for the first time? After all, he is a prophet: Enmity hostiles blinded him: "What have I done to you?" God asks Balaam in the form of his donkey: It was his own abuse, so to speak. Yet, he is unaware: Not until God shows him. [Numb 22: 28-31]. Like Balaam; the pontiff Aleander did not see the angel stood against him. Neither Caiaphas nor Pilate saw Christ Jesus as the most illuminating light into their eyes: Enmity hostiles blinded them like Balaam; and Aleander. It is the same with today's modern men neither they see Christ Jesus as their most illuminating light. A bigoted pontiff papist expostulating his own Enmity hostiles abuse like Balaam, Aleander, declared; "The Turk are better that the Lutherans; for the Turk observe fast-days, and the Lutherans violate them: We must choose between the Holy Scriptures of God and the old errors of the church, we should reject the former!"

Tyndale: Driven from his England home by persecution; he went to London, and there for a time being pursued his task hard work undisturbed for a while: But again the pontiff violence forced him to flee from the pontiff presence. All England seemed almost closed once again against him; and Tyndale eventually resolved to seek for asylum in Germany. Here again; he began the printing of the English New Testament. Twice as much the work was stopped; but when forbidden to print in one city; he went to another city! His divine eagerness caused him to persist tirelessly. At last he made his way to Worms where a few years before Martin Luther had profoundly defended the gospel before the pontiff Diet Council which Aleander had monitored as the pontiff high rank. In that ancient city were many great faithful friends of the church reformation; and Tyndale there prosecuted his remarkable work without further hindrance from pontiff Rome. Three thousand copies [3,000] of the New Testament were soon finished and another edition followed in the same year 1538. With great earnestness-zealous and perseverance he persisted- continued his hard tasks. Notwithstanding the English authorities had guarded their ports with the strictest vigilance, the word of God was again in various ways secretly conveyed to London city, capital of England, and thence circulated throughout the whole country.

The Vatican Rome once more attempted to suppress the truth; but still in vain! The Archbishop of Durham at one time bought a large amount of a bookseller-store who was a faithful friend of Tyndale; his whole stock of Bibles; for the purpose of destroying them all; supposing that this would greatly hinder or paralyze the whole business that God has set up for his purposes. But, on the contrary; the money thus furnished; purchased more abundant material for a new better edition; which; but for this, could not have been published! Another God's perfect mysterious is attained. When Tyndale was afterward made a prisoner for his successful; his liberty was offered him on condition that he would reveal the names of those who had helped him meet the expenses of printing his large amount of Bibles: He replied that the honorable-noble Archbishop of Durham had done more than any other pontiff person; for by paying a large price for the Bibles left on hand; he had enabled him to go on with good courage and faith.

Tyndale then, was betrayed into the wicked hands of his enemies; and at one time suffered several imprisonment for many months or years. He finally witnessed for his faith by a martyr's death like those who had gone before him: But the powerful weapons which he prepared have enabled many other soldiers to wage the holy battle-field through all the centuries even to our time today's era. Our next topic: In Scotland Enmity.

Edinburgh, Scotland Enmity:

In Edinburgh, Scotland the gospel found profound an uncompromising champion in the person of John Knox: This true-faithful hearted church reformation feared not the face of a man threats. The fire flames of martyrdom blazing around Europe continent served only to quicken Knox's eagerness and zealous to greater intensity! With the Scottish tyrant's queen ax held menacing over his all head; and Knox stood firm on the Christ's solid rocky unshaken! Left to demolish Scottish idolatry!. Thus he kept to his purpose praying and faithful fighting the good fight the battle of the Lord until the whole Scottish land is merely free! John Knox would neither dare to yield to the queen of Scotland.

Thus John Knox kept to God's purpose; fighting the Megiddo Battle-Field of the Lord God until Scotland was free! In England; Latimer maintained from the pulpit that the Bible ought to be read in the language of the English indigenous people! And the Author of the Holy Scriptures," he insists: "Is God Himself!" and this Scripture partakes of the mighty and eternity of its Author: There is neither king nor emperor nor archbishop that is not bound to obey it! Let us beware of those by-paths of human tradition, full of stones, trembles and uprooted trees! Let us follow the straight road of the word: It does not concern us what the Fathers have done, but rather what they ought to have done!

The faithful friends of Tyndale; Barnes and Frith, arose to defend this truth. Then the Ridleys and Cranmer followed him. These strong faithful leaders in England were men of well-educated and well respected, and most of them had been highly esteemed for their personal zeal or piety in the pontiff communion. But they found something far better to satisfy their egos and prestigious despotic of their time. But neither shall they last forever: Only God last forever and sustains all source of lives; he is the one whom they need to consider serious account and live. In England like Bohemia; and Germany, Scotland and all other European nations need God as their creator. Their opposition to the pontiff Rome papacy was the result of their knowledge of the Enmity sinful nature of corruption of the holy see. Their acquaintance with the mysteries of ancient; Babylon and Jerusalem Judaism Pharisees gave greater power to their testimonies against their own destruction! So it is same thing like today: Our continuing living in corruptions and errors are the imitations inheritance of our forefathers!

"**Do you know,**" said Latimer: "Who is most diligent bishop in England? I see you listening and hearing that I should name him. I will tell you: It is the really **"Devil!"** He is never out of his Diocese: You shall never find him idle! Call for him when you will; he is ever at home; he is ever at the plow: You shall never find him remiss; I warrant you:"

Where Enmity-Lucifer the devil is resident, there away with books and up with candle-lights; away with Bibles; and up with beads; away with the light of the gospel and up with the light of wax tapers; yea, at noonday; with Christ's cross, up with the purgatory pick-purse; away with clothing the naked; the vulnerable poor; the impotent; up with the decking of images and the gay garnishing of stones and stocks; down with God and his most holy words; up with traditions; human council; and a blinded pope:"

Oh that our prelates; priests; and clergy would be as diligent to sow the corn of good/wheat doctrine as Satan is sow cocked and darnel!" What you sow? Will you agree?

God greatest high principle maintained by Tyndale; Frith; Latimer; and the Ridleys was the divine authority with well sufficiency of their Sacred Word; the Scriptures. It is bread of life and well satisfying to eat: Like ancient Babylon; Judaism; and now early century Vatican pontiff rejecting the assumed authority of popes councils; fathers and kings human to rule the conscience in matters of religious faith man's made. There is absolute living God! "I AM!" [Exodus 3: 14].

The Bible was their daily living standard, and to this day, they brought all doctrines and all claims: Faithful in God and all his words from his holy mouth; sustains these holy men as they yielded up their lives at the stake: "It is written," Jesus said: "Man shall not live by bread alone; but by every word that proceeds from the mouth of God!" [Matt 4: 4].

Be of good comfort," exclaimed Latimer to his fellow martyr as the fire flames were about to silence their voices, "we shall this day light such a candle in England as I trust, by God's grace shall never be put out." The Church of England following the steps of Vatican Rome persecuted dissenters from the established true-faith of God. In the 17th century thousands of godly fearing pastors were expelled from their ministry positions. The people were forbidden on pain of very heavy fines, imprisonments; and banishment to attend a Protestant faith meetings except such as were sanctioned by the

Athanasius-John T. Nkomo

Vatican Rome church.

Those who were faithful to worship God, were compelled to meet in dark alleys, in obscure garrets and at some seasons in the woods at midnight. In the asylum depths of the wild forest, a natural temple of the Lord God's own building, those scattered and persecuted faithful godly people; the Lord God assembled them to pour out their thirsty souls like deer pants for water; so pants their souls for the Lord God their maker! They earnestly fast in prayer and praises! God heard them in His Mighty Temple in Heaven.

But despite all their precautions many people suffered for their faith: The jails or dungeons were all over-crowded: Families were torn-apart! Many others were banished to foreign lands as fugitives for no cause. Yet God was with them and persecution could not prevail to silence their deeply rooted cause to spread truth that God has entrusted into their hearts. Like bread, the word of God needs to be shared to all! Jesus Christ is inevitable! He is the fuel of our spirits that continually burns unquenched. Even many were forced driven across the ocean to America; Africa; and Asia unknown existing lands; and here and there they laid the foundations of civil and Christianity liberty which have been the bulwark and glory of our time today's era! Still Enmity persist unresolved! I repeat; unresolved! Till Christ returns! As the early ancient centuries prophets Babylonian; Judaism Pharisees disciples; and apostle's persecution turned out rather to the furtherance of the gospel.

In a loathsome dungeon crowded with profligates and grotesque felons; John Bunyan breathed the very dazzling atmosphere of heavenly and there he wrote magnificent compelling his wonderful allegory of the most despicable or un-denial psychological phenomenal of the [Pilgrim-Progress] long journey from the horrible land of destruction to the most atmospheric "Celestial City!." For over two hundred years [200] that compelling vibrating voice from Bedford jail has been profoundly spoken with great thrilling power to the hearts of many peoples' hearts till this day.

John Bunyan; a classic book "Pilgrim's Progress" un-perishable book, and "Grace Abounding to the Chief of Enmity sinful" have guided many fealty-dirty feet into the path of new transformed life. Baxter, Flavel, Alleine, and other men of talent; well-educated and deep Christian experience; stood up in valiant defense of the faith once delivered to the saints. The work accomplished by these men proscribed and outlawed by the rulers of this world Enmity-Lucifer; can never perish! Flavel's "Fountain of Life" and "Method of Grace" have taught thousands men and women how to commit the keeping of their souls to Christ Jesus. Baxter's "Reformed Pastor" has proved a blessing to many who desire a revival of the work of God, and his Saints' Everlasting Rest" has done its work in leading souls to the rest that remained for the people of God."

Many years later in days of great spiritual darkness; Whitefield and Wesley appeared as light illumination for God. Under the rule of the established church; the people of England and Scotland had lapsed into s state of religious declension hardly to be distinguished from heathenism, or paganism. Natural religion was the favorite study of the clergy and included most of their theology. The higher class sneered at piety and prided themselves on being above what they called its fanaticism. The lower class or working vulnerable persons were spontaneously or grossly ignorant, and abandoned to vice which the church had no courage or faith to any longer support the downfallen cause of this truth that existing in their presence time. The same thing even today, vulnerable population still live in sneering circumstances with grossly ignorant; devastating poverty still remains unresolved. John Booth the founder of Salvation Arms Church prepared for their work by long and sharp personal convictions of their own lost condition; and that they might be able to endure hardness as good soldiers marching for Christ; they were subjected to the fiery ordeal of scorn, derision, and persecution both in the university and they were entering the ministry: Today Salvation Arms Church no more marching as the Christ soldiers. Why?

Athanasius-John T. Nkomo

They were members of the Church of England; and were strongly attached to their forms of worship, but the Lord had presented before them in his word a higher standard. The Holy Scriptures urged them to preach Christ and him crucified. The power of the highest attended their hard works: Many thousands were earnest convicted and truly converted. It was necessary that these lost sheep souls be well protected from Enmity sinful ravening wolves. What we learn from these faithful committed men? Or who remembers them? Like all other past generations forgot; so we forget!. Mysterious and trying was the opposition which these faithful preachers encountered from the established church; yet God in his powerful wisdom, had overruled events to cause the reform to begin where it did: Had it come wholly from without it would not have penetrated where it was so much needed:

"And this is eternal life that they may know you," Jesus prayed: "The only true God, and Jesus Christ whom you have sent." [John 17: 3.] See also John 10: 38; 17: 11, 23; Gal. 3: 28]

England-Scotland: Brief historical review

William Tyndale' English language translation of the New Testament began to be printed in 1526; and the complete Bible was printed in about 1536; the year he was fire flamed-burned at the stake. The King James Version Bible [1611] was 90 % unaltered: Tyndale translation. The martyrdoms in England of faithful Protestants continued through the years 1530's to 1560's and beyond; even though Henry VIII repudiated or refuted the Vatican papal supremacy in January 1531. Persecution of Christians continued on through the 17th century. Between 1660 and 1675: John Bunyan wrote his books in prison; [Pilgrim-Progress]. John and Charles Wesley; and George Whitfield brought a major revival to England: George was converted in 1735, John and Charles in 1738: All three spent the rest of their lives preaching Christ's gospel. Charles Wesley wrote 6,000 hymns and John Wesley traveled 250,000 miles on horseback from one speaking appointment to the next. John Wycliffe [1328-1415] natural death: John Huss burned in **1415, and Jerome in 1416 was also burned in Bohemia.**

As the revival preachers were churchmen and workers within the pale of the church where they could find opportunity, the truth had an entrance where the doors would otherwise have remained closed. Some of the clergy were roused from their moral stupor; and became zealous preachers in their own parishes: The churches that had been petrified by formalism were quickened into life. Men of different gifts or talents performed their appointed work. They did not harmonize upon every point of doctrine; but all were moved by the Spirit of God; and united in the absorbing aim to win lost souls to Christ Jesus.

The differences between Whitefield and Wesley threatened at one time to create alienation; but as they learned meekness in school of Christ, mutual forbearing and charity reconciled them into Christ's brotherhood oneness. They had no time to dispute; while Enmity Lucifer cunning and sinful were teeming everywhere, and ungodly-sinners were going down to ruin. They worked hard and prayed together in oneness and their mutual friendship was restored and strengthened in spirit; they sowed the gospel seed in the same fields. Here Enmity Lucifer retreats.

These faithful of God's instruments trod a rugged path. Men of influence and well educated of their time engaged their powers against them. After time many of the clergy manifested determined Enmity hostility, and the doors of the churches were closed against a pure faith and those who proclaimed it. The course of the clergy in denouncing them from the pulpit, aroused the elements of darkness, ignorance; and Enmity sinful. Again and again did John Wesley escape death by miracle of God's mercy. When the outrage of the Enmity hostiles mob was aggressive hateful excited against him and there seemed no way of escape; an heavenly angel in human form came to his side the angry mob fell back, and the faithful-fearful of

Christ: Wesley passed in safely from the place of great danger like Peter who was rescued by the heavenly angel from Herod's wicked hands. As in the past; and present: Men and women fail of eternal salvation only through their own self-willful refusal to accept the free eternal life from God their Creator. The Spirit of God is freely bestowed to enable every man to lay holy upon the means of eternal life. Thus Christ Jesus, the true way, life; light; lighted every man that comes into the world." [John 1: 9].

In answering to the claim that at the death of Christ the precepts of the Decalogue had been abolished with the ceremonial law: Wesley said: "The moral law, contained in the [Ten Commandments] and enforced by the prophets: Jesus Christ fulfilled all prophecies on earth. Christ did not take away anything: It was not the design of his coming to revoke any part of this: This is a law which never can be broken; which stands fast as the faithful witness in Heaven:

All powers and authority are given to Christ as the ultimate righteousness Judge: No one else! This was from the Bereshith; the beginning of the world being written not on tables of stones; but on the hearts of all creation of men when they came out of the hands of the Mighty Creator: And however the letters once written by the finger of God are now in a great measure of defaced by Enmity sinful nature: Yet can they not wholly be blotted out; while we have any consciousness of good and evil-Enmity. The law written in hearts it is what God searches: All men' secret motives are found in the hearts/minds and conscience: No secretes hidden in the eyes of God: Psalm 139: 2-4]: See 2 Kings 19: 27: Job 14: 16: 31: 4: Matt 9: 4: &. Heb 4: 13]. Every part inch of this perfect law must remain in great force upon all nations whether secular world, or Christian world, and in all age of generations past; present; or future: As not depending either on time or place, or any other aspects of life and circumstances liable to change; but on the nature of God in Christ Jesus, and the nature of all human kind on earth; and their unchangeable relation to each other all-long until Christ returns. As Christ Jesus earlier indicated: "I am not come to destroy the law but to fulfill all prophets written in the Scriptures." Without any human' inquisitive; his meaning in this place is consistently with all that goes before and follows thereafter;   "I am come to establish it in its fullness, in spite of all the glosses of men; I am come to place in a full and clear view whatsoever!" Dark and obscure therein; I am come to show the world the wholly practical truth and fully important of every part of this unbroken perfect law all of it!" To show the length and breadth; the entire extent of every commandment contained therein at Mount Sinai and the height and depth; the inconceivable purity and spirituality of it in all its full branches!" Jesus Christ is inevitable! There is; therefore; the close connection that can be conceived; between the law and the gospel. On the one hand, the perfect law of God continually makes way for and points us to the gospel; on the other, the gospel continually leads us to a more exact fulfilling of the perfect law of God. The perfect law of God; particularly demands us to love God with all heart; strength soul; and love your neighbor; to be meek; humble; or holy: We feel that we are not sufficient for these things: **Yet, that with man this is impossible!** Enmity resistance blinds all! Naturally; we see true promise of God to give us that love, and to make us humble; meek; and holy; we lay hold of this truth; gospel of these glad tidings; it is done to us according to our true-faith; and the righteousness of the law is fulfilled in, through faithful which is in Christ Jesus! No one else!. This is the truth that sanctify all: God's word is truth!. It truly guarantees: No deceit: [John 17: 17: See Rom 8: 6-8] Enmity will persist until Christ returns! Will you agree? Enmity blinds multitudes:

In the lightest rank of the enemies [Enmity-Satan] of the true gospel of our Lord Christ Jesus; are they who openly and explicitly judge the law itself, speak evil of the law; who teach men to break; to dissolve, to loose, to unite the obligation of not one only; whether of the least or of the greatest; but all the commandments of God at a stroke. Man on earth has lost sense of fear or even to reach out to God his maker: He is naturally dead! As it is written: "Let the dead bury their own dead!" You follow me and live!" Matt 8: 22. The most surprising of all the circumstances that this strong human Enmity-delusion is that they who are given up to it, really believe that they honor Christ by overthrowing his perfect law, and that they are magnifying his righteousness and glory; while they are destroying his true doctrine that sanctify their souls. Yea; they real honor Christ just like Judas Iscariot did: When he said; "Hail, Master, and kissed him." Yet it is a kiss of a betrayer deceitful. So Jesus said; "Not all who call me "Lord, Lord, will enter into the kingdom of God." And Christ, may as justify say to every one of them; betrayed thou the Son of Man with a kiss?" Judas had no response.

It is not other than betraying Him with a kiss; to talk of his blood and take away his crown; garment to set light by any part of his perfect law under pretense of advancing his gospel. Like Christian fiction ebook. It is one of the current secular world betrayer being applied as a kiss. Nor indeed can anyone escape this charge who preaches faith in any such a manner as either directly or indirectly tends to set aside any branch of obedience; who preaches Christ so as to disannul; or weaken in any wise; the least of the commandments of God: In the eyes of God; we have big trouble. How you and I will face God? It is a matter of personally consciences and motives which interests God in searching to all men on earth. Will you agree?

To those who urged that the preaching of the gospel answers all the ends of the law: This we utterly deny! It does not answer the very first end of the law; namely, the convincing men of Enmity sinful nature; the awakening those who are still in deep asleep on the brink of hell. Paul; once upon a time a Judaism zealous Pharisee replied: "By the law is the knowledge of Enmity sinful and not until man is convicted of Enmity sinful, will he truly feel his need; and not until man is convicted of Enmity sinful, will he truly feel his need of atoning blood of Christ Jesus."

They that be whole, as our Lord Christ himself observes; need not a physician; but they that are sick need a physician." Referring to himself as the perfect physician who possesses all answers of sickness-cure. It is absolute absurd, therefore, to offer a physician to them like Christ that are whole, or that at least imagine themselves so to be: You are first to convince them that they are very ill! Christ is able to guarantee cure: Otherwise they will not thank you for your hard work. It is equally absurd to offer Christ to them whose heart is whole having never yet been broken. See the prodigal son [Luke 15: 11-22].

But the multitudes that through his honesty hard work and pure life, and the number who by this teaching had attained to a deeper and richer experience will never be known till the whole family of the redeemed shall be gathered into the kingdom of God.

Among the early century reformers of the church an honorable place should be given to those who stood in vindication of a truth generally ignored; even by the Protestants; those who maintained the validity of the true God's commandments and the obligation of the true holy Bible. When the church reformation swept back the pontiff darkness that had rested down on all secular world Christendom! Were brought to light in many lands and nations. No class of Christians have been treated with greater injustice by popular historians than have those who honored them. They are easily forgotten in hearts and souls. But many recall Hitler Enmity sinful nature for his systematically exterminating six million Jews. People today imitate Hitler's hostilities; hatred; aggression; and wearing the symbol of Hitler Red-shirt-flag. They have been stigmatized as semi-Judaizers, or denounced as superstitious and fanatical. The arguments which they presented from the Scriptures in support of their faith were met as such arguments are still met with the out-cry: The fathers, the fathers! Ancient tradition the authority of the church! Martin Luther with his faithful associates accomplished a most high noble work for the Lord God in Germany according to God's precise timing. But coming as they did from the pontiff Rome church, having themselves strong faith; believed and advocated their doctrines it was not to be expected that they would discern all these appalling Enmity sinful of pontiff corruptions. It was God's work to break the fetters of Rome, and to give the Bible to the world today. David did not break Goliath; God did through the hand of David. I presume; they knew that God was behind of the scene otherwise without God, they couldn't. Yes they did.

God indeed; has in his abundant providence preserved the history a few of those who suffered for their obedience to the true God's commandments; but there were many other who endured the world knows nothing; who for the same truth endured severe persecution and martyrdom. There are many unknown. But God knows them all. Those who oppressed the followers of Christ called themselves Protestants; but they abjured the fundamental principle of Protestantism, the Bible, and the Bible only as the rule of faith and practice. The testimony of the Scriptures they thrust from them with disdain. This spirit still lives even this day, and it will increase more and more as we near the close of Second Advent; Christ' returns!

Enmity will persist. Today's Enmity is worse than the past or ever! Will you agree? If professed Christians would but carefully and earnest prayerfully compare their views with true Scriptures; laying aside all selfish-pride of opinion and desire for the supremacy a flood of light would be shed upon the churches now wandering in the darkness of Enmity sinful nature. As the first past; the people can hear it, the Lord God reveals to them their Enmity sinful-corruptions in their doctrines and their defects of characteristics. From age to age God has raised up men and well qualified-nurture them to do a special work needed in their time: But to none of these did God commit all the light which was to be given to the world. Wisdom does not die with them. It is not the will of God that the work of reform should cease with the going out of Martin Luther's life; it was not God's will that at the death of every other reformers, the Christian faith should become stereotyped.

The work of reform is progressive until Christ returns: Go forward is the command of our great Saviour and Leader; Jesus Christ; "forward unto all world's victory!" [Matt 28: 18-20]. We shall not be accepted and honored of God in doing the same work that our early century fathers did. We do not occupy the position which they occupied in the unfolding of truth. In order to be accepted and honored as they were; we must improve the illuminating light which shines upon us, as they improved that which shone upon them: We must do as they would have done, had they lived in our day. Martin Luther and others were reformers in their time. It is our duty to continue the work of reform. If we neglect to heed the light, it will become darkness; and the degree of darkness will be proportionate to the light rejected.

The prophet of God declared that in the last days knowledge shall be increased: There are many truths to be revealed to the humble seeker: The teachings of God's word are to be freed from the human's errors and superstition with which they have been encumbered. Doctrines that are not sanctioned by the Scriptures have been widely taught and many have honestly accepted like Christian fiction ebook; but when the truth is revealed; it becomes the duty of every one to accept it. Those who allow worldly interests, desire for popularity or prestigious, or pride of opinion; to separate them from the truth, must render an account to God for their deliberate intent neglect. [Deut 5:33]. Also see Phil 4:19]

Enmity: The terrible French Revolution of 1790 is long since gone; but it is the direct grotesque result of 200 years struggle over the Bible! History has many lessons for us to learn! If we will not learn from them; we may have to repeat them as we remind ourselves! This history took place 2nd centuries ago; but it is full of truth meaning to us today: We are the most terrible experiment of a nation that began with religious persecution and ended in vilest atheism and death to many! I am the trouble maker consistently intent disobeying God! I am my own crime treason deserving death. "Woe to the world for offenses! For the offenses must come; but woe to that man by whom the offense comes!" Jesus said: Enmity hatred; disobedient; resistance upon God. The suppression of the Scriptures under the dominion of pontiff Rome, the terrible results of that suppression, and the final exaltation of the word of God, are vividly portrayed by the prophetic truth!

To John the exile on lonely Patmos Island was given a clear view of the 1260 years which the pontiff Rome papacy Enmity-hatred power was permitted to trample upon godly fearing people truth word of God and oppress true godly people! History it is obviously teaching and purging our hearts. But we will not allow our hearts to be purged!. I am the trouble maker in the sight of God. It is my own treason crime! "But leave out the court which is outside the temple, and do not measure it, for it has been given to the Gentiles: And they will tread the holy city underfoot for two-months. And I will give power to my two witnesses, and they will prophesy one thousand two hundred and sixty days [1260] clothed in sackcloth." [Rev. 11: 2-3]. Also see Ezek 40: 3-42:20] the angel of the Lord God told John who is isolated at Patmos Island prison. It is Greek Island under the Rome rule. Christians were then severely persecuted.

The period here mentioned are the same alike representing the time in which God's faithful witnesses remained in a state of obscurity. The Holy Bible contains God's Sacred Word spoken on Mount Sinai: In the fulfillment of Christ Jesus who spoke the living word to all. No one can quench it out. Old and New Testaments both are truly inspiration written as spoken from the mouth of the most holy God to purify the defiled human beings who were defiled by Enmity sinful nature. Both books are witnesses also to the perfect plan of everlasting salvation. Jesus Christ came down from heaven to fulfill all the prophecies. The Holy Scriptures tell of a great saviour of the world who has come in the exact manner foretold by type and prophecy!

These are the two olive trees and the two candlesticks standing before the God of the earth. [Rev 11: 4] "Thy word is a lamp on my feet and on my path." [Psalm 119: 105]… The Rome pontiff a mere human power sought to hide or even destroy from the people the word of truth and set before them malicious false witnesses to contradict its truth testimony! When the true Bible was proscribed by religious and secular world authority; when its testimony was perverted and every effort made that men and demons could invent to turn the minds of the people from it; yet all men are created in the image of God and likeness; when those who dared to proclaim its sacred truths were hunted, betrayed, tortured, buried in dungeon cells; set on fire flames alive, martyred for their faith or compelled to flee to mountain fastness's and to dens and caves of the earth! Then indeed did the faithful witnesses prophesy in sackcloth! They were indeed filled with the Holy Ghost from heaven!.

But men cannot with impunity trample upon the word of God! God specifically warned in advance; concerning his faithful witnesses; "If a man will hurt them; fire proceeded out of their mouth; and devoured their enemies; and if a man will hurt them; he must in this manner be killed!" [Rev 11: 5]. The meaning of this fearful denunciation is set forth in the closing book of Revelation: "I testify unto every man that hearth the words of the prophecy of this book. If a man shall add unto these things; God shall add unto him the plagues that written in this book. And if a man shall take away from the words of the book of this prophecy, God shall take away his part out of the book of life; and out of the holy city and from the things which are written in this book." [Rev 22: 18-19]… Jesus

Christ is inevitable! If individuals and humanity are to progress; Jesus Christ is inescapable! You ignore him at your own wicked risk: "Let justice run down like waters! And righteousness like mighty stream!. [Amos 5: 24].

Such are the warnings which God has given to guard men against changing in any manner that which God has revealed or commanded: These solemn denunciations apply to all who by their influence lead men to lightly regard the perfect law of God.

They should cause those to fear and tremble-throbbing hearts who flippantly declare it a matter of little consequence whether we obey God's perfect law or not! No time-to squander!. All who exalt their own opinions-self-confidence above the written God's word; all who would change the plain meaningful of Scripture to suit their own ego convenience; or for the sake of conformity to the secular world; are taking upon themselves awful-terrible fearful responsibility! Their own death! God is not mocked! The written word; the perfect law of God; will measure the character of every man on earth, and condemns all whom this unerring test shall declare wanting: Notwithstanding the Lord God Almighty witnesses were clothed in sackcloth; they continued to prophesy God's truths throughout the entire period of 1260 years! This God's unique message is powerful it is still ongoing until Christ Jesus returns! Noah did not cease to appeal to the multitudes and building the ark until God poured the awful flood to wipe out all inhabitants on earth.

In the darkest times like our modern era, there were faithful men who loved God's word and were jealous-envious for God's honor: To these loyal servants were given wisdom, power, knowledge; and authority to proclaim God's truth during the whole of this time, like today' era! Enmity sinful it is the substance of death that all men will face before the sight of God! Today; multitudes are carried away by the secular world attraction while they deliberately intent ignoring the provider. God is the provider of all resources we benefit on daily basis. At the same time we ignore God with deliberate intent. We are the trouble maker before our Creator.

Enmity sinful nature subsequently creates our own deaths: Will you agree? And when they shall have finished their testimony, the beast [Enmity] that ascended out of the bottomless pit shall make bitter-war against them, and shall overcome them, and kill them. And their dead bodies shall lie in the street of the great city which spiritually is called "Sodom and Egypt" where also our Lord Christ was crucified." [Rev 11: 7-8]. According to Rev 13: 1, 3-5] The Holy Bible vividly predicted that the terrible little horn power of [Daniel 7 and 8 was indeed to rule the world for 1260 years: It has been well-known for centuries that this little horn of Daniel 7, and the first beast of Rev 13 symbolize the early century Vatican pontiff papacy cruelty. Also called the "man of sin" [2 Thess. 2: 3-4], affirmed or repeated in fulfillment by the Lord Christ Jesus [John 8: 44-45]: "He was a murderer from the beginning and does not stand in the truth!" Jesus said: Enmity Satan [Gen 3: 15] and the architect of anti-Christ" [1 John 4: 3] the early century Vatican papacy was definitely prophesied to have this power for 1260 years from the ascended of early centuries Judaism high priest Caiaphas who advised the Jews that it was expedient that one man should die for the people." [John 18: 14] unaware he prophesied his own:

When did this predicted time span begin and when did it end? No! Still ongoing. Enmity remains unresolved. I must make it clear; that it is not my opinion but true-written Scriptures supported by scripture references.

These events were to take place near the close of the period in which the witnesses testified in sackcloth. Through the medium of the early century pontiff papacy, Enmity Satanic had long controlled the powers that ruled in Church and State like today; they compromise with secular world Christendom. The most fearful results were especially apparent in those countries that rejected the light of reformation like today rejected truths; man opinions matters.

There was a state of moral debasement and corruption similar to the condition of Sodom and Egypt just prior to its destruction, and to the idolatry and spiritual darkness that prevailed in Egypt in the days of Moses: It is very much alike today darkness in the days of Mahatma Gandhi; Dr. Martin Luther King, Jr. and Nelson Mandela.

In no land had the spirit of Enmity sinful against Christ Jesus and the truth been more strikingly displayed than in giddy and godless French in France Revolution 1790. Nowhere had the gospel encountered more bitter and cruelty opposition-disobedient in the sight of God direct far worse than the Philistine giant uncircumcised Goliath. In the streets of Paris; Christ Jesus had indeed been crucified in the person of his saints. The world at large still recalls with shuddering horror the scenes of that most cowardly and cruel onslaught; the Massacre of Saint Bartholomew. The king of France; urged on by the pontiff; prelates priests and pope; lent his sanction to the dreadful work. The palace bell tolling at midnight, gave the signal for the Massacre slaughter to begin! Protestants by hundred thousand; sleeping quietly in their homes; trusting to the plighted honor of their king; were dragged forth without a warning; and brutal murdered in cold blood: Like Cain murdering Abel his brother in cold blood. God direct spoke to Cain; "Where is Abel your brother? What have you done?" am I my brother's keeper!" Rude tone upon God; Cain replied. [Gen 4: 9-11]. Enmity, it penetrates into Cain's heart; conscience and motive, inherited from his father Adam. [Gen 3: 19]. Environment exposure defiled by parent extends to offspring continually.

Enmity; Satan or Lucifer, in the person of the past; present pontiff Rome zealots, led the van. As Jesus Christ was the invisible leader of his people from Egypt bondage; so was Lucifer the unseen-invisible leader of his subjects in this horrible work of multiplying Enmity- hatred leading to martyrs of innocent blood. For three full days of cold butchery went on; more than thirty thousand men and women perished: The result caused great joy to the hosts of darkness. The Roman pontiff, sharing in diabolical rejoicing, proclaimed a Jubilee to be observed throughout his dominions; to celebrate the great event. The same master spirit that urged in the Massacre of Saint Bartholomew, led also in the scene of the French Revolution 1790. Enmity Lucifer seemed to triumph. Notwithstanding the tasks of the reformers; he had succeeded in holding vast multitudes in ignorance concerning God and God's word truth. Now he appeared in a new guise. In France arose an atheistically-barbarians power that authentically openly declared war against the authority of heaven where God dwells. Mew threw off all restraint! The perfect law of God was trampled under dirty foot!. Those who could engage in the most heaven-daring blasphemy and the most abominable wickedness were most highly exalted in France! Fornication; harlotry was sanctioned by law: profanity and corruption seemed deluging the earth.

In all this, supreme homage was paid to Lucifer-Satan; while Christ Jesus, in his characteristics of truth, purity and unselfish love was crucified.

The Bible was publicly burned in France: The Sabbath was blotted out: The pontiff Rome had enjoined image worship; now divine honors were paid to the vilest objects worship. The work which the papacy had begun, atheism completed. The one withheld from the people the truths of the Bible; the other taught them to reject both the Bible and its author the seed sowed by priests and prelates was indeed yielding its evil Enmity hatred hostile's fruit. Terrible indeed was the condition of infidel France: The word of truth lay dead in her streets and those who hated the restrictions and requirements of God's perfect law were jubilant. But transgression and rebellion were followed by the sure result. Doom-unhappy France reaped in blood the harvest they had sowed to reap. And they reaped.

The war against the Holy Bible and the perfect law of God banished peace and happiness from the hearts and homes of men.

No one was secure: He who triumphed today was suspected, condemned, to-morrow. Violence and terror reigned supreme. The land was filled with treason crimes too horrible for pen to trace. God's faithful witnesses were not long to remain silent. The spirit of life from God entered into them, and they stood upon their feet; and great fear fell upon them which saw them. [Rev 11:11]. The world stood aghast at the enormity of conscience guilty which had resulted from a rejection of the Sacred Word, and men were glad to return once more to faith in God and his word. Concerning the two witnesses the prophet proclaimed further; "And they heard a great voice from heaven saying unto them; "come up hither! And they ascended up to heaven in a cloud; and their enemies beheld them." Rev. 11: 12]. Since the French Revolution the word of God has been honored as never before: The Bible has been translated into nearly every language spoken by men, and scattered over every part of globe till this day still on its ongoing. After being, as it were, thrust down to hell it has, in truth, been exalted to heaven. [Phil 4: 19].We are very nearly the end of time, who knows: Thinking men everywhere recognize it so well: Yet how few are getting ready for what is coming so rapidly upon the earth. It vital essential that we daily surrender our lives into God's hands, so he may guide us: We dare not fall away into apostasy. We all need Christ Jesus perfect model to imitate.

Those who received the great blessings of the reformation did not go forward in the path so nobly entered upon Martin Luther. A few faithful men arose from time to time to proclaim new truth, and expose long-cherished error but the majority, like the ancient Jews in Christ' day, or the early pontiff papist in the time of Luther; were content to believe as their forefathers believed; and to live as they lived:

Therefore religion again degenerated into formalism; and corruptions and superstitions which would have been cast aside had the church continued to walk in the light of God's true word; were retained and cherished. Thus the spirit inspired by reformation gradually died out; until there was almost as great need of reform in the Protestant churches as in the Roman Catholic Church in the time of Martin Luther. There was the same spiritual stupor, the same respect for the opinions of men like today, the same spirit of secular world-lines, the same substitution of human theories for the teachings of God's word; Christian fiction ebook: Pride and extravagance were fostered under the guise of religion even today still alike in path.

The churches become corrupted by allying themselves with the secular world. Thus were degraded the great principles for which Martin Luther and his fellow associates labored had done and suffered so much. Enmity satanic saw that he had failed to crush out the God's truth by persecution, he again resorted to the same plan compromise which had led to the great apostasy and the formation of the Church of Rome. Lucifer once more induced Christians to ally themselves, not now with pagans, but with those who, by their worship of the little god of this world, as truly proved themselves idolaters. Enmity Satan could no longer keep the Bible from the people; it had been placed within the reach of all. But he led thousands to accept false interpretations-definitions and unsound theories without searching the Scriptures to learn the truth for themselves. Truth: What is truth today by definition and interpretation? Everyone else has his/hers definition and interpretation: "My opinion: My right: My appropriates. My experience: The list is long enough so forth.

Lucifer Enmity; had long corrupted the doctrines of the Bible, and traditions which were to ruin millions were taking deep root. The church was upholding and defending these traditions, instead of content ending for the faith once delivered to the saints of God. [John 17: 17]. Truth:

And while wholly unconscious of their condition and their peril, the church and the world were rapidly approaching the most solemn and momentous period of earth's history; the period of the revelation of the Son of Man: Already had the signs which Christ Jesus himself had promised; the sun clothed in darkness by day and the moon by night; proclaimed his coming near!

When Jesus pointed his disciples to these signs; he foretold also the existing state of worldliness and backsliding, and gave warning of the result to those who refused to arouse from their careless security measure. Thou hast shalt not watch, I will come on thee as a thief, and thou shalt not know what hour I will come upon thee." [Rev 3: 1-3]...

He who knows the end from the Bereshith-beginning, and who inspired prophets and disciples-apostles-saints to write the future history of churches and of nations, was about to accomplish another reform similar to that of the days of Luther. The Lord God raised up men to investigate his true word, to examine the foundation upon which the Christian world were building; and to raise up the solemn inquiry: What is truth? Are we today building upon the Christ' solid rock or upon shifting sand? A house built on sinking sand; its fall is big falls. A house built on Christ' solid rock stands firm!

God saw that many of his professed people were not building for eternity; and in his care and love he was about to send a message of warning to arouse them from their stupor, and prepare them for the coming of their Lord. The warning was not to be entrusted to learned doctors of divinity or popular ministers of the gospels. Had there been faithful watchmen, diligently and prayerfully searching the Scriptures, they would have known the time of night; the prophecies of Daniel and John would have revealed to them the great events about to take place. If they had faithfully followed the light already given, some star of heavenly radiance would have been sent to guide them into all truth like the three wise-men from East they followed the star guiding them where Christ was born in a manger.

At the time of Christ's first advent, the priests and scribes of the holy city Jerusalem to whom were entrusted the oracles of God, should have discerned the signs of the times, and proclaimed the coming of promised Messiah One. They didn't! Three Eastern wise-men saw the star. Micah prophesied well Christ's birthplace. [Micah 5: 2 &. Dan 9: 25] profoundly specified the time of Christ where to be born. God had committed these prophecies to the Jewish leaders; therefore they were without excuse if they did not know and proclaim to the people that the Messiah was at hand. Their ignorance was the result of Enmity sinful neglect like today modern age.

God did not send his messengers to the palaces of kings to the assemblies of philosophers; Hellenists; or to the school of the Judaism Rabbis; to make known the wonderful tidings news fact that the true redeemer of the world was about to appear at Bethlehem upon the earth. The Jews were building monuments for the slain prophets of God, while by their difference to the great men of the earth they were paying homage to the servants of Lucifer-Satan. Absorbed in their ambitious for place and power among men, they lost sight of the divine honors proffered them by the king of heaven, the Lord God the Creator of all life!.

With what profound and reverent interest should the Elders of Judaism Israel since God had rescued them from Egypt they have been studying the place, the time, the circumstances, of the greatest event of their forefathers whom God rescued in the world history; the coming of the Son of God to accomplish the Messiah' redemption of all nations on earth! Oh, why were not the people watching and waiting that they might be among the first to welcome the Saviour of the world! Oh, why we are not the people watching and waiting that we might be among the first to welcome the Saviour of the world Jesus Christ' Second Advent!

"But you, Bethlehem Ephrathah: Though you are little among thousands of Judah: Yet out of you shall come forth to Me: The One to be Ruler in Israel: Whose goings forth are from of Old: From Everlasting!" Micah 5: 2] they knew nothing because Enmity sinful blinds them like us today: These words from prophet Micah were fulfilled: Indeed, Christ Jesus was born at Bethlehem where also David was born. Christ the Bereshith "I AM" now in full flesh form.

God blinded them in a manner of meekness. He was not born into a king palace but into a manger where animals resides. But lo, at Bethlehem three weary traveling men from East saw guiding star led them to the great Ruler where he lays into a manger. From a mere man and mere woman, Joseph and Mary of Nazareth. God chose them to nurse Christ; the Messiah; most highly anointed!. He shall not cease but he is for-everlasting!. Jesus Christ is inevitable! Jesus Christ indeed, is the one we all ought to be fearful in adoration: Examine carefully his lifestyle on earth: Yet, he came to his own: And his own did not receive him: [John 1: 11]. Why? We may well ask:

Heavenly angels had seen the glory which the Son of God shared with the Father in heaven before the earth was founded; and they had looked forward with intense interest of Christ's appearance on the face of earth as an event fraught with the greatest joy-thrills to all nations on earth! Angels were appointed to carry on that glad tiding to those who were well prepared to receive it; and who would joyfully make it known to the inhabitants of the earth. Jesus Christ has stooped to take upon himself man's nature; he is to bear an infinite weight of woes as he shall make his soul an offering for Enmity sinful nature among nations; yet angels desire that even in his humiliation, the Son of the highest may appear before men with a dignity and glory befitting his character.

While the great men of earth assemble at Israel's capital to greet his coming? Will legions of angels present him to the expectant company? An angel visit's the earth to see who are prepared to welcome Christ Jesus: But he can discern no tokens of expectancy. He hears no voice of praise and triumph that the period of the

Messiah's coming is at hand! The angel hovers for a time over the chosen city and the temple where the divine presence was manifested for ages; but even here is the same indifference. The priests, in their pomp and pride, are offering polluted sacrifices in the holy temple of God. Pharisees; Sadducees; Sanhedrin; Hellenist; Cynics; and Stoics are all with loud voices addressing or crafting-cunning malicious gospel to the people, or making boastful-show-long public prayers at the corners of the streets to be seen by passing by people.

There is no evidence that Christ Jesus is expected; and no preparation for the noble prince of life neither!. In amazement the celestial messenger proclaims Christ is born to eternal heaven with the shameful tidings, when he discovers a group of extra-ordinary shepherds who are watching their sheep by night; and; as they gaze into the starry heavens; are contemplating the prophecy of a Messiah to come to earth; and longing for the advent of the world's saviour. Here is a company that can be trusted with the heavenly message. And suddenly the angel of the Lord God appeared proclaiming the good tidings of great-thrills-joy flooded all the plain; an innumerable company of angels were revealed and as if the thrills-joy were too great for one messenger to bring from heaven; a multitude of voices broke forth in the anthem which all the nations on earth of the saved shall one day sing; "Glory to God in the highest; and on earth peace; good will toward men!"

Chapter 7

Nothing New But Old Generational!

Oh, what a lesson is this wonderful story of Bethlehem! How it rebukes our unbelief; our selfish-pride and self-sufficiency today? How it warns us all to beware; lest by our own treason criminal indifference we also maliciously fail to discern the signs of the times; and therefore know not the day of our precise visitation: It is "unto them that look for Christ;" that Christ is to "Appear the second time without Enmity sinful unto salvation." [Heb. 9: 28]. Who else dares to-day to heed? So much man's opinions: Yes! Everyone else opinion appropriation: Is it working? But never last: God lasts for-ever! Jesus Christ sends his disciples a message of warning to prepare them for second coming. To the prophet John at Patmos Island was made known the closing work in the great perfect plan of man's redemption: John at Patmos Island, isolated; beheld an angel flying in the midst of heaven having the everlasting gospel the word; to preach unto them that dwell on the earth; and to every nation; and kindled; and tongues on earth; and to every nation and people saying with a loud voice; "Fear God; and give glory to Him! For the hour of His Judgment is come and worship Him that made heaven and earth; and the ocean; and the fountains of waters!" [Rev 14: 6-7].

The angel represented in prophecy as delivering this message; symbolizes a class of faithful men who obedient to the promptings of God's Spirit and teachings of His word proclaim this warning to the inhabitants of the earth today' age. This message is ongoing from the Bereshith: This message was not to be committed to the religious leaders of the people. They had failed to preserve their connection with God! And had refused to accept this truth, the light from heaven; therefore, they were not of the number described by the apostles Paul; like some of our religious leaders today: God knows them: "But you; brethren, are not in darkness, so that this day should overtake you as a thief." [1 Thess. 5: 4-5]. "You are all sons of light and sons of the day: We are not of the night or of darkness:" Paul said: [v. 5].

The watchmen upon the walls of Zion should be the first to catch the tidings of the salvation's advent, the first to lift their voices to proclaim Christ's near the first to warn the nations to get well prepared for his coming. But the priest; Pharisees; they were at easy dreaming their night-mere Enmity sinful dreams of peace and safety; while the Israel people were asleep in their sinful nature: Jesus Christ saw his church, his body, like the barren fig-tree covered with pretentious leaves; yet destitute of precious fruit: Christ rebuked. "You shall no more bear a from henceforth." Its leaves immediately withered for good. There was a boastful observance of the forms of religion; while the spirit of true humility, penitence and faith which alone could render the service acceptable to God; was lacking. It is the same thing like today!. No much difference!. We are on same judgment!

Instead of the grace of the Spirit; there were manifested pride formalism; vainglory; selfishness oppression. Same thing even this day age!. The process is ongoing until Christ returns. Backsliding compromising church closed their eyes-ears to signs of the times; the same thing as it is to-day age! Perhaps we could be worse: God did not depart from Christ; but they separated themselves from Christ's love that came in the form of human to communicate with them equally. As they refused him to comply with the conditions; his promises were not fulfilled to them; neither it is fulfilled with us even to-day! God is the same! No change! The choice we have made to reject Christ; we have also made the choice to condemn ourselves to death: Not many modern Christians will agree with this: But it is exactly the same as the past; they did not agree with

Christ; the disciples; apostles; early centuries Judaism up to early century pontiff papacy the days of Martin Luther until today remain to be the kind of people who are anti-Christ! For this reason; the nations are divided! Enmity negative Lucifer; Christ Jesus positive; cannot coordinate! Hat cannot drive out hate: Darkness cannot drive out darkness!. Only light can do that: Hat cannot drive out hat: Only love can do that. Only through Christ Jesus: He is able to do that. He is inevitable!

Love for Christ Jesus and faithful his coming waxed cold: Such is the sure result of neglect to appreciate and improve the light and privileges with God bestows. Unless the church will follow on Christ' opening providence, accepting every ray of light, performing every duty which may be revealed, religion will inevitably degenerate into the observance of forms, and the spirit of vital godliness will eventually disappear! This truth teaching nothing new; it has been repeatedly illustrated in the history of the church. God requires on His own peoples works of authentic faith and obedience corresponding to the blessings and privileges bestowed: God possesses all power to re-create according to His own sovereign authority: Nothing is difficulty for God! Obedience requires or demands a sacrifice and involves a severe cross to carry on; and this is why so many people of the past; and present profess followers of Christ Jesus refused to receive the ever-lasting light which Christ brought direct from heaven illuminated the whole world and, like the ancient Israel knew at Mount Sinai not the time of their visitation: Because of their selfish-pride and stiff-neck unbelief, the Lord God passed them by and revealed His truth to men in meek-humble hearts who had given heed to all the light they had received! [Luke 19: 44]… Therefore, we cannot afford to ignore intentional or unintentional intent about the past; because we all from the past seeds of our forefathers!

A tiger cannot be a lion: Or a lion can be a tiger: Neither a thistle can be a fig tree. Or a fig tree can be a thistle: By characteristics they differs both color and their productive. Therefore, Enmity we inherited remains within regenerating upon each generation progressively. No escape we duplicate the character as we are exposed. Our nurture-nature ecosystem chain never cease, but it is continually ongoing!. Enmity will persist.

"The name of Lord God is a strong tower! The righteous runneth into it, and is very safe for-ever!" [Proverbs 18: 10]. Human beings consistently-ever deceiving while God's truth evidence ever compelling with its appealing.

What happens when people dedicate their lives to God and then open the Bible and begin studying it carefully for years! There is enormous amount of strength in the Word of God! And there is a wealth of knowledge and wisdom in its prophecies: The open Bible is the basis of most powerful weapon; revivals and revivals that authentically intrinsically change men's lives! No more shifting-chaff blown by the windy!

An upright; honest-hearted farmer, who had been led to doubt the divine authority of the Scriptures, yet who sincerely desired to know the truth; was the man chosen of God to proclaim the nearness of Christ Jesus' second coming. Like many other reformers; William Miller had in early life battled with devastating poverty like Luther early youth life; and had thus learned the great lessons of energy and self-denial. His mind was active and well-developed and he had an eagerness-thirsty for knowledge. Though he had not enjoyed the advantages of a collegiate education or career his love of study and a habit of careful thought and close criticism rendered him a man of profound sound judgment and comprehensive views:

He possessed an irreproachable moral character and an enviable reputation, being generally self-esteemed for his integrity, thrift, and benevolence. During his childhood, William Miller had been subject to religious impressions; but in early manhood, being thrown almost exclusively into the society of deists, he was led to adopt their sentiments which he continued to hold for about 12 years.

At the age of 34 years, however, Holy Spirit inspired into his heart with a sense of his condition as a sinner Enmity. He found in his former belief no assurance of happiness beyond the grave. The future was dark and gloomy. Referring afterward to his own feelings at this time; he said to himself: "Annihilation was a cold and chilling thought; and accountability was sure destruction to all. The heavens were as brass over my head, and the earth as iron under my feet. Eternity what was it? And death why was it? The more I thought and reasoned; the further I was from demonstration: The more I thought, the more scattered were my conclusions: I tried to stop thinking: But my thoughts would not be controlled: I was truly wretched: But did not understand the cause: I murmured and complained, but knew not of whom: I knew that there was a wrong; but knew not where or how to find the right: I mourned, but without hope." Truth confession from honesty man before the sight of God: Really truth; the prodigal son!. Hope Faith works together!.

In this state William Miller continued for some month's search-truth for his own hope: Suddenly he says to himself: "The character of a Saviour was vividly impressed upon my mind. It seemed that there might be a being as good and compassionate as to himself atone for our transgressions, and thereby save us from suffering the penalty of sin-Enmity. I immediately felt how lovely such a being must be, and imagined that I could cast myself into the arms of, and trust in the mercy of such a one: But the question arose:

"How can it be proved that such a being does exist?"

Aside from the Bible, I found that I could get no evidence of the existence of such a Saviour, or even of a future state."

"I saw that the Bible did bring to view just such a Saviour as I needed; and I was perplexed to find how an uninspired book should develop principles so perfectly adapted to the wants of a fallen world. I was constrained to admit that the Scriptures must be a revelation from God. They became my delight: And in Christ Jesus I found a friend: The Saviour became to me the chiefest among ten thousand: And the Scriptures, which before were dark and contradictory, now become a lamp to my feet and a light to my path. My mind became settled and well satisfied: I found the Lord God to be a Rock in the mind of the Ocean of life: The Bible now became my chief study, and I can truly say, I searched it with great delight! I found the half was never told me. Oh, I wondered why I had not seen its beauty and glory before, and marveled that I could ever have rejected it. I found everything revealed that my heart could desire, and a remedy for every disease of the soul. I lost all taste for other reading, and applied my heart to get wisdom from God." How now publicly professed his faith in the religion which he had despised? But his infidel associates were not slow to bring forward all those arguments which he himself had often urged against the divine authority of the Scriptures: He was not then prepared to answer them, but he reasoned, and searching that if the Bible is a revelation from God; it must be consistent with itself; and that as it was given for man's instruction; it must be adapted to his understanding. He determined to study the Scriptures for himself, and ascertain if every apparent contradiction could not be harmonized. Yes! He searched with great determination interest to find his own truth in God through the Bible. God's written Word: Compelling truth sharper than two-doubled-edged sword. It charges; corrects; discerns: judges; and illuminating light heart from darkness.

Endeavoring to lay aside all preconceived opinions, and dispensing with commentaries, he compared scriptures with scriptures by the aid of the marginal references and the concordance. He pursued his study in regular and methodical manner: Beginning with Bereshith Genesis, and reading verse by verse, he proceeded no faster than the meaning of the several passages so unfolded as to leave him free from all embarrassment when he found anything obscure; it was his custom to compare it with every other text which seemed to have any reference to the matter under consideration. Every single word was permitted to have its proper bearing upon the subject of the text, and if his view of it harmonized with every collateral passage, it ceased to be a difficulty.

Thus whenever he met with a passage hard to be well understood, he found an explanation in some other portion of the Scriptures etc.: He would not yield or ignore but boldly searching till he finds truth. It is a great testimony to share and cherish its truth to heart.

William Miller; as he intensively studied with earnest prayer for divine enlightenment that which had before appeared dark to his own understanding was made clear. He experiences the truth from psalm words which says: "The entrance of Thy words giveth light; it giveth understanding unto the simple." [Psalm 119: 130]. Self-discovery makes you better than being told by someone else. When you engage argument and disagreement with someone you sometimes not away that the argument and disagreement you engage with someone it is about Enmity and your own death. There are many people who do not recognize this. Arguments and disagreements spontaneously cause anger; emotions; hatred; hostiles; eventually physical fight. Which results killing? You do not have any idea how to discover for yourself like Miller did. Because you possess no sense to search for truth within yourself!. All about you is self-righteous based on negative unaware of your own death. You never wish to consider that you are your own trouble maker which result your own death. For example; when you kill, when you steal; when you cheat; when you maliciously lie; or fornicate; or anything contradicting truth: You well know that it is wrong! Otherwise you would not hide; would you? You are ever on run for the rest of your life until one day you get apprehended by the police man. It is your death isn't it? Yes! It is! So why you should deceive yourself!

All men die because everyone else brings his/hers own death! I need to make sure that I am the trouble maker: The trouble that I cause will bring back my own death!

I reap what I sowed: Anything I sow; good or bad I reap on same manner!. After many years of careful researching I was fully satisfied that the Bible is its own interpreter; that it is a system of revealed truths so clearly and simply given that the wayfaring man, though a fool, need not err therein; that all scripture is given by inspiration of God alone, and is profitable for doctrine, for reproof; for correction; for instruction; for judgment; for every righteousness! See 2 Tim 3: 16] that prophecy came not in old time by the will of man; but holy men of God spoke as they were moved by the Holy Ghost: [2 Pet 1: 21]. That it was written for our learning; that we through patience and comfort of the Scriptures might have hope and faithful. [Rom 15: 4]… And that is the precise truth!

With intense interest I eagerly studied the Books of Genesis: Exodus: Leviticus: Numbers: Deuteronomy; Samuel; Ezekiel; Jeremiah: Daniel: Amos: Micah: and all New Testament and others up to the book of Revelation: Employing the same principles of interpretation-definitions as in the other scriptures, and found to my great thrills-joy-peace that the prophetic symbols, and opening to my understanding prophecies which had ever been dark to God's true-faithful people. I know this to be sure that God is the same of the past; present; and future: The Bible it is a miller shows my daily dirty face.

Like after link of the chain of truth rewarded my efforts. Like an infant growth; step by step tracing self-growth error and trial down the great lines of prophecy until I reach the solemn conclusion that in many years growth the Son of God would become the Second Advent: Jesus Christ is inevitable! If individuals and humanity are to progress; Jesus Christ is inescapable!. You ignore him at your own wicked risk.

Athanasius-John T. Nkomo

Deeply moved-impressed by these great momentous I felt that it was my own duty to give the warning to the world, and now I'm writing the books. I expect no encounter opposition as it was in the days of John Wycliffe; John Huss; Jerome; and Martin Luther in Germany; from the uncircumcised ungodly people; but I am confident that all true Christians born again would rejoice in the hope of meeting the Lord Jesus Christ the World Saviour! I only fear that in their great joy at the prospect of glorious deliverance; so soon to be consummated; many would receive the doctrine without sufficiently examining the Scriptures in demonstration of its truth.

I therefore, hesitate to present it, lest I should be in awful error, and be the means of misleading others: I'm thus led to review the evidence in support of the conclusions at which I have arrived; and to consider carefully every difficulty obstacle which presented itself to my mind. I found that objections vanished before the light of God's word as mist before the rays of the sun. Eight years spent thus, left me fully convinced of the correctness of my position: I was born and raised in most devastating poverty; and exposed unto appalling apartheid rule in South Africa, and lived without hope for what tomorrow might bring for more obscurity. And now the duty of making known to others what I believed to be so clearly taught in the Scriptures; urged itself with new force upon my shoulder. When I was about my business, I said to myself; it was continually ringing in my ears: "Go and tell the world of their danger-Enmity: This theme was constantly occurring to me like an iron harmer breaking through. I couldn't resist no more: When I say unto Enmity, the wicked; Oh wicked man like me a trouble maker in the sight of God my creator; my heart throbs. Thou shalt die; if thou dost not speak to warn the wicked from his way; that wicked man shall surely die in his Enmity sinful nature; but his blood will I require at thine hand. Nevertheless, if thou warn the wicked of his way to turn from it; if he do not turn from his way; he shall die in his Enmity sinful; but thou has delivered thy soul." See Ezek. 33: 8-9].

I then felt that if the wicked could be effectually warned, multitudes of them would repent; and that if they were not warned; their blood might be required at my hand." God is right to urge Ezekiel that he ought to warn Israel -exiled in Babylon for their repentance. I am doing just that: that some minister might feel their force and devote themselves for their promulgation. But I cannot banish the conviction that I have a personal duty to perform in giving the warning. Enmity will persist until Christ returns. The words are ever recurring to my mind. "Go and tell it to the world!."

The Lord God, in his great merciful, does not bring judgments upon the earth without ample giving warning to its inhabitants by the mouth of his prophets: "Surely the Lord God will nothing, but he revealed his secret unto his servants the prophets." [Amos 3: 7]… When the Enmity sinful of the antediluvians moved God to bring a flood of waters upon the earth, God first made known to all his purpose through Noah; that they might have opportunity to turn away from their evil ways: But the people didn't heed! For decades and decades was sounded in their ears the warning to repent, lest the wrath of God be manifested in their destruction. The city of Nineveh God spared the people because they repented; when Jonah proclaimed to them concerning the upcoming wrath of God's judgment. Noah's day the people refused to repent: Sodom and Gomorrah refused to repent: Egypt king refused to repent: So God's wrath judged them to death.

But the message seemed to them an idle tale, and they believed it not. From the unbelief they proceeded to scorn and contempt ridiculing the warning as highly improbable, and unworthy of their notice. Like today modern era. Emboldened in their wickedness; they mocked the messenger of God; made light of his entreaties, and even accused him of presumption. How dare one man stand up against all the great men of the earth? If Noah's message were true; why did not all the world see it and believe it? While the people of Nineveh city believed it. One man's assertion against the wisdom of secular world thousands! They would not credit the warning, nor would they seek asylum in the ark for their safety with Noah. But only Noah with animals entered into the ark.

Scoffers pointed to the things of nature: To the unvarying succession of the seasons; to the blue skies that had never poured out heavy rains; to the green fields refreshed by the soft dews of night: Like today modern weather cast unpredictable God's nature they claim to know. "Doth he not speak parables?" In contempt they declared the preacher of righteousness to be a wild enthusiastic; and they went on, more eager in their pursuit of human pleasure, more intent upon their evil ways, than ever before. But their unbelief did not hinder the predicted event. God bore long with their Enmity-wickedness, giving them ample opportunity for repentance; but at the appointed time God's judgments were visited upon the rejecters of his merciful. Will you agree? Jesus Christ vividly declares that there will exist similar unbelief concerning his Second Advent Great coming: Where is your conscience and motives drives you to?

As the people of Noah's day knew not until the flood came and wiped them all away by surprise: "So shall also the coming of the Son of Man be." Jesus said: [Matt 24: 39]. When the so called Christians of God are uniting with the world, living as they live in compromise and joining with them in forbidden secular world pleasure; when the luxury of the world becomes the luxury of the church; when the marriage bells are same-sex marriage chinning, and all are looking forward to many years of worldly prosperity; then suddenly as the illuminating lighting flashes from heavens, will come the final end of their temporary bright visions and psychological delusion hopes. As God sent His servants to warn the corrupted world of the coming awful flood, so God sent chosen messengers to make known the nearness of **the greatest day of final judgment:**

Why then, this profound wide spread ignorance concerning an revelation of the Lord Jesus Christ; which God gave unto him to show to all nations on earth the things which must shortly come to pass; and God sent and signified it by truth; and angels unto His faithful servant John at Patmos Island isolation; who bare record of the word of God; and of the testimony of the Lord Jesus Christ the world's saviour; and of all things that he saw. "Blessed is he that reads; and they that hear the words of this truth; and keep those things which are written therein; for the time is right at hand!" Jesus said: "Repent!" [Rev 1: 1-3]. There are some who will not read; the blessing is not for them: And they that hear" there are some also who will refuse to hear this truth. They are not the right chosen seed! On the other hand; they are not Abraham's seed. See John 8: 44]. "You are of your father the devil!" Jesus declared: And they are the seed that refuse to believe in Jesus Christ the most High Son of God:

They are totally unable to keep those things that are written in the Bible; they truly refuse to read and hear the truth. Their truth is sinking sand. But death it is absolute! None of these can dare to claim the blessing promised! All who ridicule the subjects of the prophecy and mock at the symbols here solemnly given; all who refuse to reform their own lives; and prepare for the coming of the Christ Jesus will be humblest.

Why this modern world generation general reluctance to investigate its teachings? It is the result of a studied effort of Enmity Lucifer-darkness to conceal from men that which reveals his deceptions: For this reason; Christ the revelator foreseeing the warfare that would be severely waged at Megiddo Battle-Field against the final Enmity sinful eradication. The Revelation pronounced a blessing upon all who should read, and hear; and observe the truth words of the prophecy: Jesus Christ finalized the words no more to be repeated. Those who believed and those who still believe that the Second Advent movement was of God; went forth as did Martin Luther and his associates with their Bible in their hands; and with fearless firmness met the Enmity sinful opposition of secular world's great teachers like to today unto modern scholasticism. They never considered a compromise within the secular world theories. There are many people today have looked for instruction in divine things were proved to be ignorant both of the Scriptures and of the power of God. Yet their very ignorance rendered them more determined; they could not maintain their positions by the Scriptures; and they were driven to rational-resort to the saying and doctrines of men's made to the traditions of their forefathers: So Jesus charged the Jews that their father is the devil, rather than Abraham. John 8: 44-45. Still they would not yield to Christ the very expected Son of God in their midst. Why they could not yield to Christ Jesus? It is the same compelling question: Why modern men do not yield to Christ Jesus? There aren't many. Yet they too claim to follow Jesus; like ancient Jews who claimed to be Abraham's descendants. Jesus totally condemned them: "Your father is the devil!" Not Abraham at all!. If God is your Father; as you claim; then you would love me." Jesus said: "I come God and He sent me to come to you." Why my language is not clear to you?" Jesus asked them: It is the same language that Jesus utters this day:

But the word of God was and is the only pure testimony accepted by the advocates of truth: The Bible and the Bible only was and is our watchword: "It is written!" The weakness of all arguments brought against them, revealed to Adventists the strength of the profound foundation upon which they stood: On Christ' solid rocky they stood firm unshaken!. It is on the same Christ' solid rocky all ought to stand firm even today! Yes! Jesus Christ; yesterday; today, and ever he is the same! [Heb 13: 8].

At the same time Enmity it angered their opponents who, for want of stronger weapons, resorted to personal abuse: Grave doctors of divine sneered at Martin Luther as an unlearned and feeble adversary. They used these phrases to expostulate Mahatma Gandhi; Dr. Martin Luther King, Jr. and Nelson Mandela. In the end they saw themselves that they were the most ignorant; unlearned; feeble adversary at their own society-community, led many people to astray. Shamefully overshadow their own' death.

Because these committed reformers stood firm on Christ' solid rock!. They saw it but they didn't yield: Daniel and John were denounced as men of fanciful ideas who made visions and dreams his hobby. The plainest statements of the Bible facts-truths which could not be controverter were met with the cry of heresy, ignorance; stupidity, insolence. So God stood in their midst charged them to zero! As is written in Psalm 2: 4-5]: "Then He shall speak to them in His wrath: And distress them in His deep displeasure!" [v. 5.] Will you agree?

Many churches were thrown open to the enemies of the Advent faith; while they were closed against its friends-associates. The sentiments expressed by Dr. Eck concerning Martin Luther were the same that inspired every other ministers and people to refuse Second Advent a hearing. "I am surprised at the humility and modesty with which the Rev. Dr. Luther undertakes to oppose alone, so many illustrious Fathers, thus affirming that he knows more of these things than the sovereign pontiffs, the councils, the doctors, and the universities." Said the pontiff papal champion: He couldn't afford to ill-filibuster before the sight of God his maker: As result he found out himself to be the least among the pontiffs. The first shall be the last: And the last shall be the first: It would be surprising, no doubt if God had hidden the truth from so many saints and martyrs until the advent of the reverend father. Thus thought great and wise men in the days of Noah; Abraham; Moses; followed by Christ' disciples up to John Wycliffe; John Huss; Jerome; and Martin Luther early centuries past up to this day. There are many others who had gone before them and us for the sake of truth: Later years; William Miller and thus still argue those who oppose the proclamation of the Second Advent faith and the commandments of the Lord God: They accused Martin Luther for preaching novelties: Luther defended: "These are not novelties that I preach!" But I affirm that the doctrines of Christianity have been lost sight by those whose special duty it was to preserve them! By the learned; by the bishops: I doubt not indeed that the truth has still found and abode in some few hearts! " Poor husband men and simple children in these days understand more of Jesus Christ than the pope, the bishops, or the doctors!." Luther said: His passion was like burning bush but unconsumed! For God designed a human machine to run on himself! God is the fuel of our spirits designed to burn continually! And so when William Miller was charged with showing contempt for the doctors of divinity; he pointed out to the word of the living God as the standard by which all doctrines and theories on earth must be tested; and knowing that these doctrines have God's truth on his side; Miller went forward in his task work undismayed:

In every age, God has called the best of his servants yet they were exposed in the least environment on earth; God would lift them up high their voices against the prevailing human Enmity-corruption upon the multitudes of evil doers: Noah was called to walk with God to stand firm to warn the ante-diluvia world And so Abraham was called to walk with God: And so Moses and Aaron were called to walk with God and voice high against kings of Canaan and all Israel his chosen people. And there are many others who followed their steps up to this day.

The majority of people are usually to be profound found on the side of Enmity sinful corruption and falsehood teachings unto their scholasticism- tool to shape others. The fact that doctorate of divinity have the secular world on their side does not prove them to be on the side of God's truth neither! The wide gate and the broad road attract more the multitudes of people; while the strait narrow gate way are difficulty to find but found only by few-handful of people. That led to eternal salvation; while the wide gate with multitudes leads to eternal destruction. Jesus said. Compare the multitudes of the football game and the multitude of the church: Which is larger? Church or football? Sports gates are ever over parked with large number of people than anything else activity taking place today. It was also like that in the past: Arena fight. Attracted large gathering in the past!.

If church ministers, laymen, and people had really desired to know the truth of God, and had given to the Second Advent doctrine the earnest, authentically, intrinsically, zealous than anything else to occupy minds, prayerful attention which its importance demands, they would have seen that it was in harmony with the Scriptures. The Divine Spirit would stand in their midst daily as it was before: That is the basic truth of church history. We also well know that the church history has also been of a backsliding history. Had they been united with its advocates in their hard work, there would have a resulted such a revival of the work of God as the secular world has never witnessed. Today whose religious leader would dare to lead? We hear and see about Enmity sinful leadership everywhere around the globe. Today, we live into most great danger world than ever before!. Suspicious; fearful; miss-trustful; we have developed checkpoint everywhere men traveling destination which never had existed before. Airway's in particular and sea checkpoint surrounds the suspected poor traveler. At some checkpoints, the traveler is likely to be striped searching for atomic exposure. Enmity will persist.

If we are wrong; earnest prayer show us wherein it consists our doing wrong: Show us from the word of God who searches the heart; conscience; and motives that we are in error; we have had ridicule far-enough that can never convince us that we are in the wrong; the word of God alone can change each one of us, views; opinion, or even appropriation-operational.

I am very aware that this kind of teachings as good as it sound;

it is the most difficulty thing to practice. First to fear God: And keep God's commandments: It is the hardest thing man experience on earth since God had imposed Enmity. Gen 3: 15. Since then man has ever lived in a failing life. As it is written; "All men fall-short in the sight of God." There is no one is good, none!" Enmity will persist. Jesus Christ is inevitable! He has all the answers when he returns. [Rom 3: 10-11] see v. 9]. "What then, are we better than they?" Not at all!" See Ps. 14: 1-3]. Will you agree? Scripture evidences are obviously compelling as we search for truths:

My conclusions have been formed deliberately and prayerfully, as I have seen the evidence of the Scriptures: I now realize that I am the trouble maker of my won destruction. So, I earnestly, authentically, intrinsically pleads before God's feet for mercy. I am under His feet: Where else can I go? God is everywhere! "Heaven is my throne; and the earth is my footstool!" God declares: [Is. 66: 1-3].

Jesus Christ is inevitable! If individuals and humanity are to progress; Jesus Christ is inescapable! You ignore him at your own wicked risk: [Rev. 22: 12-13]. "I am coming back quickly; and My reward in with Me, to give to every one according to his/hers work." Jesus assured. He is inevitable!. This writing is not a threat! But warnings from the Lord Jesus Christ to whom we all need to take serious accounts!. Will you agree?   Yes! You ought to!. It is good news to all!

It is true but not wonderful, when we become acquainted with the state and corruption of the present age: That I have met with great opposition from the colonialism; apartheid; and professed religious press; and I have been instrumental, through the preaching and writing making it quite manifest that not a few of our theological teachers are infidels in disguise. I stand for Christ Jesus alone nothing else! As apostle Paul said: "As for me to live is Christ! And to die is gain!" I press on until I reach to the end of my destination race.! I cannot for a moment believe that denying the resurrection of the body or the return of Christ to this earth, or a judgment day yet future is any the less infidelity now that it was in the days of infidel colonialism and apartheid; or segregation, and yet who does not know that these things are as common as church pulpits and presses are? And which of these questions are not publicly denied in our church pulpits, hospitals, scientist, and by the writers and editors, publishers of the public papers? Enmity stands in between, and among all race because God imposed it for his purpose. None of us can remove or eradicate Enmity sinful nature within all persons on earth! God only, with all his powerful is able:

Surely, we have fallen on extra-ordinary strange times! I expected of course the doctrine of Christ Jesus' speedy coming would be opposed by infidels, blasphemers, drunkards, gamblers; grotesque; profligates, and the like; but I did not expect that church ministers of the gospel and professors of religion or theologians would unite or compromise with character of the above description, at stores and public places, in ridiculing the solemn doctrine of the Second Advent. Great event ever to be seen by all whether in the grave or alive!. Jesus Christ is indeed, inevitable!

There are many people whether Christians or secular-heathens who were not professors of religion have affirmed to me these truths and say they have seen them and have felt their blood chilled at the sight. These are some of the effects which are produced by preaching, teaching, and writing this solemn and soul-stirring doctrine among our current modern world Pharisees; Stoics; Cynics; Hellenists priests, bishops of the present day: Is it possible that such ministers and members are obeying; keeping God' commandments and watching and praying for God's glorious appearing, while they join these scoffers in their unholy and ungodly remarks? This is not any easy talk at all!. But painful and shameful talk: Are we ashamed? I weep as I write.

Athanasius-John T. Nkomo

If Christ Jesus does come, where must they appear? And what a dreadful account they will meet or represent in the tremendous hours! It is the lot of our God's servants to suffer opposition and reproach from their contemporaries. Now, as in the time of our Lord Christ Jesus, the Saviour of the whole world, men build the sepulchers and sound the praises of the dead prophets while they persecute the living messengers of the most high God the Creator. However, with all early century reformers were despised and hated by the secular world and unbelieving creatures; but they profoundly influenced and their hard works were a blessing to the world. Under their preaching, thousands of sinners were saved.

Backsliders were reclaimed and multitudes were led to study the Scriptures and to find in them a beauty and glory before unknown the call to prepare for Christ' returns spread from state to state and from nation to nation: We also need to get prepared for our lives for what is ahead.

The prophecy of the first angels message, brought to view in Revelation. In both Europe; Africa; and Asia men of faithful and prayerful deeply moved as their attention was called to the prophecies, and tracing down the inspired record, they saw convincing evidence that the end of all things was at hand as Jesus had said at very early centuries. The Spirit of God urged his faithful servants to freely give the warnings. Far and wide spread the message of the everlasting gospel. "Fear God and give glory to God; for the hour of His judgment is come." [Rev 14: 7].

Yes; there were missionaries had penetrated; were sent the glad tidings of Christ' speedy return. However, some of these missionaries in some different land were found isolated bodies of Christians who solely by the study of the Scriptures had arrived at the belief that the Saviour's was near. Some were malicious lies. They were fugitive-escaping their treason crime. In some portions of Europe where the laws were so oppressive as to forbid the preaching of the gospel! Little children were impelled to declare and many listened to the solemn warning. Missionaries who fled to Africa and India, some of them were secular, and uncircumcised in hearts.

Their fruit were not eatable. As Jesus said; you will know them by their fruits. We said about this in early beginning chapters extensively length.

To William Miller and his co-laborers it was given to preach the message of God in America and the light kindled by their labours shone to distant lands. Miller was made big difference. The testimony the Scriptures pointing to the coming of Christ in 1843, awakened wide-spread interest!. Many were convinced and the arguments from the prophetic periods were correct, and sacrificing their pride of opinion, they joyfully received the truth. Some church ministers laid aside their sectarians views and feelings, left their salaries and their churches and united in proclaiming the coming of Christ Jesus. There were but few ministers, however, who would accept this message; therefore it was largely committed to humble laymen…

Everywhere was heard the searching for true testimony warning Enmity sinful nature both secular world and church members, to flee from the wrath to come. It was like the day of John the Baptist, the fore-runner of Chris' the preachers laid the ax at the root tree, and urged all to bring forth good or eatable fruit meet for authentic repentance! Their stirring appeals were in great marked contrast to the assurance of peace and safety that were heard from popular platform pontiff priests; and wherever the message was given or proclaimed, it moved the multitude people. Like John the Baptist, warned the Pharisees who came to him: "But when John saw many of the Pharisees and Sadducees coming to his baptism; he said to them: "Brood of vipers!" Who warned you to flee from the wrath to come?" Therefore bear good fruits worthy of repentance!" and do not think to say to yourselves; "We have Abraham as our father: "For I say to you that God is able to raises up children for Abraham from these stone!" [Matt 3: 7-9]. Furthermore John says [v. 10] "And even now the ax is laid to the root of the trees: Therefore every tree which does not bear good fruit is cut down and thrown into the fire!" See also John 8: 33] Jesus in person, charging- condemned the Pharisees-Jews: Yet they openly claimed as Abraham's seeds. Jesus totally denied them to condemnation of hell! Enmity-Satan is their father. He is a murderer from the beginning like them since then they have been killing many innocent blood till day!.

The simple direct testimony of the Scriptures set homes by the power of the Holy Spirit, brought a weight of self-conscience-conviction which few were able wholly to resists. Professors of religious/religion were able from their false security based into their scholasticism! They saw their own backslidings and unbelief their selfish-pride. Many sought the Lord God with repentance and humiliation. The affections that had so long cling to earthly things they now fixed upon the Christ solid rock house up in heaven. This is the perfect place all ought to end if they only believe in Christ Jesus the world's saviour!

The Spirit of the Mighty God rested upon them and with hearts softened-humbleness, and subdued they joined to sound the out-cries; "Fear God and keep His commandment, and give glory to Him; for the hour of his judgment is come!"

Enmity-sinners and Satan inquired with weeping eyes; "What must I do to be saved?" Those whose lives in corruption had been marked with dishonesty were anxious-obnoxious to make restitution. All who found peace in Christ Jesus longed to see others share the blessings. The hearts of parents were truly turned to their children, and the hearts of their parents were felt. The barriers of self-pride and reserve were swept away! Heartfelt confessions were made, and the members of the household were fully obligated serving for salvation of those who were nearest and dearest friends-relatives. Often was heard the sound of earnest intercession. Everywhere were souls in deep anguish, pleading with God for their Enmity sinful forgiveness. Yes! This is what we today modern age ought to seek before the eyes of God pleading with God for our Enmity sinful forgiveness!

Many wrestled all night in prayer for the assurance that their own Enmity sinful were pardoned, or for the conversion of their relatives or neighbors. That earnest, determined faith gained its object.

Had the people of God continued to be thus importunate in prayer, pressing their petitions at the mercy seat, they would be in possession of a far richer experience than they now have, even including us today would be the same. Perhaps much better: Today there is too little prayer, too little real conviction of Enmity sinful; and the lack of living faithful leaves many destitute of the grace so richly provided by our most gracious living God in Christ Jesus the world saviour! Our comforts cause us to ignore God who's the provider of all providence resources.

The Lord then held up the spirit of opposition in check while His faithful servants explained the reasons of their faith. Sometimes the instrument was feeble; but the Spirit of God gave power to his truth. The presence of holy angels was felt in these congregations gathering, and many were daily added to the believers. As the evidence of Christ's soon coming were repeated, vast crowds eagerly listened in breathless silence to the solemn words. Heaven and earth seemed to approach each other. The power of God would be well felt upon old, young adults and middle-age and even young children would feel/sense God's presence. Men and women sought their homes with praises upon their lips, and the glad sound rang out upon the still night air. None who attended those gathering can ever forget those scenes of deepest interest.

The proclamation of a definite time for Christ's coming called forth great opposition from many of different ministers in the pulpits down to the most less, heaven daring sinner. No man knows the day nor the hour!. Was heard alike from the hypocritical ministers and the bold scoffers! They closed their ears to the clear and harmonious explanation of the text by those who were pointing to the close of the prophetic periods and the signs which Christ Jesus had foretold. The Bible shows no evidence. Neither did Noah know when God would pour rains on earth. God only knew in his own authority. Neither did Sodom knew nor Nineveh, nor Egypt! So they did not wish to hear no more about Christ's coming to judge the world in ultimate righteousness till this day there aren't many who wish to hear. But Christ' affirmative warning stands still! "I am coming, in my hand with my reward." They had been unfaithful believers; so us today we are very unfaithful believers! Our works would not bear the inspection of the heart searching God, and we fear to meet our Lord God in Christ Jesus. So much compromise with the secular world theories: Like the ancient Israelites at the time of Christ's they were not well prepared to welcome the Christ the highly anointed Messiah! Enmity Satan and his agents exulted and flung the taunt in the face of Christ and holy angels that his professed people has so little love for Christ that they did not desire his appearance. Enmity Satanic blinded them. Like us even today, because we are the seeds of the past still resisting against God as our fathers did. We are no better than our forefathers at all! As our forefathers deceived themselves; so we are deceiving ourselves!

Unfaithful watchmen hindered the progress of the work of God. As the people were roused, and began to inquire the way of salvation, these religious leaders stepped in between them and the truth, seeking to quiet their fears by malicious falsely interpreting and rational definition the word of God. In this work, Enmity Satan and unconsecrated ministers united, crying-screaming; "Peace, Peace!" when God had not spoken peace to them at all: Like the

Pharisees in Christ's day many refused to enter the kingdom of God themselves, and those who were entering in; they hindered. The blood of these souls will be required at their hand from the righteous blood of Abel to Zechariah the prophet whom they cold blood murdered. [Matt 23].

Wherever the message of truth was proclaimed, the most humbled and devoted in the churches were the first to receive it. Those who studied the Bible for themselves could not but see the unscriptural character of the pontiff popular platform views of prophecy, and wherever the people were not deceived by the efforts of the clergy to misstate and pervert the faith, wherever they would search the word of God for themselves. Like today' Christian fiction ebook written by popular platform authors. It is unbiblical book! Christian fiction ebook is written by the secular world authors who worship the devil! They are anti-Christ authors! Their conscience and motives for writing Christian fiction ebook it is basically for money acceleration for self-serving and prestigious-popularity. They are anti-Christ authors!

In the ancient days some consented to be silent in regard to their hope; but others felt loyalty to God forbade them thus to hide the truths which he had committed to their trust. Not a few were cut off from the fellowship of the church for no other reason than expressing the true belief in the coming of Christ Jesus. It was very precious to those who bore the trial of their faith were the words of the prophet, "your brethren that hated you, that cast you out for my name's sake, said, "Let the Lord be glorified. But he shall appear to your joy, and they shall be ashamed!" [Is. 66: 5].

The prophets of God were watching with the deepest interest the result of the warning. When the churches as a body of Christ, rejected the message, the prophets turned away from them in sad like the angels in heaven because the people rejected truth from God it was their sadness. Yet there were in the church many who had not yet been tested in regard to the Advent truth. Many were deceived by husbands; wives; parents; even children and their close friends and were made to believe it a sinful nature even to listen to such heresies as were taught by the prophets: Angels were bidden to keep faithful watch over these lost souls: For another light was to shine upon them from the throne of God.

Like today; with unspeakable desire those who had received the message watched for the coming of their Lord Christ Jesus. The time when they expected to meet him was at hand. They approached this hour with a calm solemnity. They rested in sweet communion with God, an earnest of the peace that was to be theirs in the bright hereafter. None who experienced this hope and trust can forget those precious hours of waiting. Worldly business was for the most part laid aside for few weeks. Believers carefully examined every thought and emotion of their hearts, conscience; motives as if upon their death-beds and in a few hours to close their eyes-ears upon earthly scenes.

There was no making of ascension robes, but all felt the need of internal evidence that they were prepared to meet the Lord Christ Jesus their white robes were purity of soul, characters cleansed from Enmity sinful by the atoning blood of Christ Jesus. God invented man to prove Himself: God' Mighty hand covered a mistake in the reckoning of the human prophetic periods: The man did not discover his own mistake-error, nor was it discovered by a human intellectual of their opponents-Enmity sinful nature. God shows man's errors from time to time; but man insists resisting against God. The later said; "Your reckoning of the prophetic periods is correct. Some great event is about to take place; but it is not what other preachers did such as William Miller predicted, it is the conversion of the world, and not the second advent of Christ Jesus." This argument is not new but old and rather complex, according to human scope limit. Human being scope is very limited! He strives daily, but he possesses no exclusive resolution. The time of expectation passed; so they thought; and Christ Jesus did not show up at the precise predicted time for the deliverance of his saints. Those who with sincere faith; hope and love had looked for their Lord Christ Jesus experienced a bitter disappointment. Yet, the Lord had accomplished his purpose: He had tested the hearts; conscience; motives of those who professed to be waiting for his appearing. There were among them many who had been actuated by no higher motive than fear or conscience: Their profession of faith had not affected their hearts or their lives. When the expected event failed to take place, these people declared that they were not disappointed; they had never believed that Christ Jesus would come:

They were among the first to ridicule the sorrow of the true believers. But Christ Jesus and all heavenly hosts looked with great love and sympathy upon the tried and faithful yet disappointed ones. Could the vial separating the visible from the invisible world have been swept back, angels and prophets would have been seen drawing near to these steadfast lost souls and shielding them from the shafts of Enmity Satan-sinful.

"For a thousand years in Your sight are like yesterday when it is past!"   And like a watch in the night: You carry them away like a flood." [Psalm 90: 4-5]. Furthermore psalmist declares: "Who knows the power of Your anger? For as the fear of You, so is Your wrath: "So teach us to number our days: That we may gain a heart of wisdom." [vs. 11-12] **A prayer of Moses the man of God:**

God calls all to forsake worldly things and decide our lives fully to God's full service. Only then as we do so can we experience really peace of hearts and number of our days; that we may gain a heart of wisdom. In every age, it is a call we all must always heed! Not to do so is to imperil our own lost souls-resulting our own death:

The church leaders and the people that rejected to receive or to believe the first prophets message light from God: That message was sent in full mercy to arouse them to see their true condition of worldliness and backsliding, and to see a preparation to meet their Lord Christ Jesus. God has ever required his peoples to remain separate from the secular world that they might not be allured from their allegiance to him. God delivered the Israelites from Egypt bondage because God would not have them corrupted by the idolatry with which they were exposed, there surrounded. The people of this world are the people of darkness but which is centered upon themselves and the treasures of earth. Blinded by the Enmity sinful nature the little god of this secular world, they have no just perception of the glory and majestic of the true-living God! While they merely enjoy God's great providence, they natural forget the claims of the great giver. Such have chosen to walk in darkness, and they are led by the prince of the power of darkness: Enmity Lucifer-Satanic drives them away from God. They do not love and enjoy divine things, because they do not discern their value or holiness-loveliness. They have alienated themselves from the light of true living God, and their understanding becomes so grotesque so confused in regard to that which is rightful, true, and holy, and that the things of the Spirit of God to them are foolishness. They chose their own death!

It was all about to separate the church of Christ Jesus from the corrupting influence of secular world like today that the first prophecy message was proclaimed. But with the vast multitudes, even of professed Christians, the ties which bound them to earth were stronger than the attractions heaven-ward. Therefore, they chose to heed to the voice of the secular world wisdom; tradition-cultural-intellectual, and turned away from the heart, conscience, motives searching message of truth from God their maker! Like today church leaders compromise with the secular world theories and passion. Saint Peter wrote as he was inspired by the Holy Spirit: He described the manner in which the message of God in Christ Jesus and his coming would be received: "There shall come in the last day's scoffers, walking after their own lusts;

and saying; "Where is the promise of Christ' coming? For since the fathers fell asleep, all things continue as they were from the beginning [Bereshith] of the creation." For this they willingly are ignorant of that by the word of God the heavens were of old, and the earth standing out of the water and in the water; whereby the world that then was, being overflowed with water, perished; but the heavens and the earth which are now, by the same word are kept in store, reserved unto fire against the day of judgment and perdition of ungodly men." [2 Pet 3: 3-7]… Well plausibly explained by Saint Peter who walked with Christ Jesus.

Jesus Christ is indeed, inevitable! You ignore him at your own wicked risky! Those who perished during Noah's day had an opportunity to escape: So, those who perished during Sodom and Gomorrah had an opportunity to escape: Those who perished during Moses day in Egypt, had an opportunity to escape: Nineveh had an opportunity escape, God spared them all inhabitants!. All were efficiently urged to find asylum in the ark; mountains; and caves; but the multitudes refused; resisted; disobeyed to heed the warning so they all perished! How and why it should not be the same thing with us today; when we still persisting stubborn resisting, disobedience; rejecting to hear the warnings?

So when the first prophets message was proclaimed, all who heard were invited to receive it, and share the blessing to follow its acceptance, like Noah, Lot, and Nineveh; Moses; but many others scorned and rejected the call. One turned to his farm, another to his merchandise, and they cared for none of these things from the word of God who desires to save them. We must make it clear that we are not teaching anything new. But we believe that we have God's obligation to remind all on earth that God will destroy the world as he did in the past! It is written in the Scriptures: That Jesus Christ is inevitable!. When the Spirit of God ceases to impress the truth upon the hearts of men, all hearings is in vain, and all preaching-teachings also is in vain! Will you agree? If we are wrong: The Scriptures is wrong! But God lives in truths forever!.

When the churches spurned the counsel of God by rejecting the prophet's message from the Lord God; God also rejected them:

The first prophecy was followed by the second prophecy proclaiming; "Babylon is totally fallen that great city because they made all nations drink of the wine of the wrath of their own fornication." [Rev 14: 8]… This message was understood by the prophet to an announcement of the moral fall of the church in consequence of their rejection of the first message. The proclamation, of "Babylon is fallen," was given in many decades past and as the result, about 50 thousand withdrew from these churches. Babylon is any ancient idol worshipers.

The phrase Babylon, derived from Babel Tower, and signifying confusion or grotesque is applied in Scripture to the various forms of malicious false or apostate religion like today' modern age; there are many diversity of man's made denominations with their contradicting doctrines. Babel Tower, the ancient people initial had one form of language. They desired to make a great name for themselves: They wanted to reach up into heaven. So they built Babel Tower. God stopped them with confusion scattering them around the globe [Gen 11]…

But the message announcing the fall of Babylon must also apply to some man's made religious body that was once pure, and has now become corrupted like today so many churches are corrupted. It cannot be the pontiff church is here meant; for that church has been in a fall condition for many centuries before the pontiff Vatican had fallen. But how appropriate the figure as applied to the Protestant churches; all professing to derive their doctrines from the Bible: Yet divided into almost innumerable sects. The unity for which Christ prayed does not exist. Instead of One Lord: One Spirit: One baptism: One faith, there are numberless Enmity conflicting hostiles creeds and theories. Man's made religious faith appears so confused and discordant that the world know not what to believe as truth: God is not all in this; it is the work of Lucifer-Satan who opposes all that is called of God, Enmity it is precisely the work of evil doers Satan!

Babylon is represented as a woman a figure which is used in the Scriptures as the symbol of a church; but a corrupted church [Rev 17]... A virtuous woman represents a pure church, a vile woman an apostate church! On other hand very heinous Enmity sinful. Babylon is said to be a harlot and the prophet beheld her drunken with the blood of many saints and martyrs. Babylon thus described represents ancient pagan Rome, that apostate church which so cruelly persecuted the faithful of the Lord Christ Jesus. Babylon also is the harlot is the mother of daughters who also imitate their mother example of harlotry corrupting practicing. Thus are represented those churches that cling to the contradicting doctrines and traditions of Rome and follow their worldly practices: And whose fall is announced in the second prophecy message. They were given ample opportunity to repentance.

The conclusion relation of the church to Christ is represented under the figure of marriage: The Lord Christ had joined his people to himself by a solemn covenant: He promised to be their true God, and them pledging themselves to be his, and his alone. As Saint Paul says addressing the church: "I have espoused you to one husband that I may present you as a chaste virgin to Christ Jesus:" [2 Corinth 11: 2] from him and she sought after vanity, and allowed the love of world things to separate her from God, she forfeited the privileges included in this peculiar and sacred relation." See James 4: 4].

Today' professional religion has become popular with the secular world' compromise: Rulers; politicians; lawyers; physicians; merchants, join the church to gain public confidence as worthy Christians as means of financial security and the respect and prestigious of society or community, and advancing their own world-gain interests. Whom they deceive? Their own deceit: Thus they seek to cover all their unrighteousness transactions under a skillful profession of Christianity. The various religious bodies, re-enforced by the wealth material things and influence of these baptized worldlings, make a still higher bid for popularity platform and esteemed-patronage. Splendid churches-compromise embellished in the most extravagant manner today, are erected on popular Christian fiction ebook avenues! The worshipers array themselves in costly and fashionable attire! A high salary is paid for a highly talented young minister to entertain and attract the young adults.

His sermons must not touch offensive-popular Enmity sinful but be made smooth and pleasing for fashionable ears appropriate to their works and evil doers!. Thus fashionable Enmity sinful nature are enrolled on the church records and fashionable Enmity sinful concealed under a pretense of malicious-grotesque godliness!. God looks down upon these apostate bodies, and declares them daughters of a harlot Babylon! To secure the favor and support of the great men of earth, they have broken their solemn vows of allegiance and fidelity to the King of kings the Lord Christ Jesus the world saviour! Is this a pleasant thing to talk about? Would you real wish to hear this talk? It pains at heart! Truth is hard to accept: But truth leads you to eternal life! Will you agree? Repentance is the call for all!

The great Enmity sinful charged against Babylon is that Babylon made all nations drink the wine of wrath of her fornication and harlotry! It is still spreading all over the world even today! Drunken world! This cup of intoxication which Babylon spread presents to the world; represents the malicious false doctrines which Babylon has accepted as the result of her **unlawful connection with the great ones of the earth!**

Compromising within the secular corrupts their faith and in

their turn they exert a corrupting influence upon the nations spreading by teaching doctrines that are opposed to the truth statements of the word of the true living God in heaven! Become prominent among these malicious-grotesque profligates falsehood doctrines which is that of the temporal millennium; more and more plus a more thousand years of spiritual peace and prosperity in which the world is to be converted, before the Second Advent of the Christ Jesus the ultimate righteous Judge to coming. This siren song has lulled thousands of souls to sleep over the abyss of eternal ruin on earth! Secular world; wake up! Jesus Christ is calling upon all too authentic repentance! "Come to Me, all you who labor and are heavy laden, and I will give you rest!"

"Take my yoke upon you," Jesus said: "And learn from Me, for I am gentle and lowly in heart, and you will find rest of your souls! "For My yoke is easy and My burden is light!" [Matt 11: 28-30] True freedom and peace is found in Christ Jesus the world savor! Listen to Christ' compelling call upon all! Repentance is contemporary required to all! Enmity sinful nature can then be radical eradicated! Otherwise; without Christ it is impossible!

The doctrine of the natural immortality of the soul has opened the way for the awful device-crafting of Enmity sinful-Satan the man of sinful and perdition through modern spiritualism; and besides the secular world pontiff corruptions; purgatory; prayers for the dead! Invocation of saints, etc.; which have sprung from this source, it has led many nations on earth; Protestants to deny the resurrection and the righteousness judgments; and has given rise to the revolting heretics of eternal torment and the dangerous psychological delusion of the whole entire universal. Today unceasing bloodsheds everywhere around the globe! This awfully dreadful profanes is well recorded and sealed within the Lord God' Treasure Store above in heaven: See [Deut 32:34-35] "Vengeance is Mine, and recompense:" [v. 35].

And even more dangerous and more widely held than these are the assumptions that the perfect law of God was abolished at the cross, and that the first day of the week is now a holy day: Instead, and totally ignoring Sabbath Day commandment. When also faithful preachers, teachers, and theologians expounded the word of God, there arise men of high talented- with high potentials learning, ministers, laymen professing to understand the Scriptures; who denounce sound doctrine as heresy, and thus turn away inquisitive after truths:

Were it not that the world is hopelessly intoxicated with the wine of Babylon-fornicators, multitudes-harlots would be convicted and converted by the plain explanation-cutting truth of the word of God in Christ. The Enmity sinful of the world's impenitence malicious lies at the door of the church: God warned Cain: **"If you do well, will you not be accepted?" But Enmity, heinous sinful is at your door! "You must overcome it!" God said to Cain**. [Gen 4: 6-7]. Cain did not heed God: As result, he killed his brother Abel in cold blood. Since then, there has ever been bloodsheds on ground till this day no ceasing!. Enmity persists: Early God had judged the Serpent: Eve: Adam, and God imposed Enmity between the Serpent and the Woman including all their offspring up coming generations after generations hostilities, conflicts ever compelling evil intent in men hearts continually!. [Gen 3: 14-19]. **Can we really excuse ourselves?**

Since then, God has ever been sending prophets, judges; kings, finally himself in the form of human flesh, in Christ Jesus, afterwards his disciples, apostles and the reformers. Still Enmity persists!. A state of mutual union, faith and love had been provided among those who from every denomination in secular world Christendom received the doctrine; and had the churches in general accepted the same truth; the same blessing results would have followed: But Babylon, like today' modern world; scornfully rejected the last means which God in heaven had in reserve for their restoration, and then with greater eagerness, the church, like Cain, turned away to seek the secular world compromise, like Cain who sought to kill Abel his brother, and it turned out to be the most heinous Enmity sinful nature ever to exist upon the whole entire earth!

Those who faithfully proclaimed the first God's message had no purpose or a slight psychological subconscious objection; or even expectation of causing psychological phenomenal delusion-division in the churches or even of forming separate organizations etc.: None! "In my hard task labor; says one prominent reformer Martin Luther: "I never had the desire or thought to establish any separate interest from that of existing church or to benefit one at the expense of another." I thought to benefit all! Supposing that all Christians would rejoice in the prospect of Christ Jesus' coming and that those who could not see as I did would not love any the less those who should embrace this doctrine. I did not conceive there would ever be any necessity for separate meetings. My whole object was a desire to convert souls to God, to notify the world of a coming judgment, and induce my fellow men to make that preparation of heart which enable them to meet their God in peace. The great majority of those who were converted under my labors united with the various existing churches.

When individuals came to me to inquire respecting their duty, I always told them to go where they would feel at home, and I never favored anyone denomination in my advice to such." Luther said:

In the days of Martin Luther, the Church Reformation, the gentle Germany Princes Protesting pointed out more clearly; "There is no other Sovereign Church can be found above Christ Jesus who have come down from heaven with the word of the living God! There is none! Who are purified it if not through Christ Jesus!" God's word could no longer regard the pontiff constituting the church of Christ Jesus, the corner-stone, the pillar and foundation ground of the truth, and the true message from God Head Father in heaven. He is all and for all!

Since the rejection of the first prophet message and a sad change has taken place in the church! As truth spurned Enmity sinful took over its place and cherished its own deep roots on ground surface. Love for God and faith in his word have ever grown cold: Indeed, the church has ever since grieved the Holy Spirit of the Lord God and it has been in a great measure withdrawn. The words of the prophet Ezekiel are truly fearfully applicable: "Son of man, these men have set up their idols in their hearts and put the stumbling-block of their heinous Enmity sinful before their faces. Should I be inquired of at all by them?" [Ezek 14: 3-4]. The Lord will answer him that comes according to the multitude of his idols." [v. 4]. Men may not have to bow down to idols of a cave stone or wood by man's hand, but all who love the things of the secular world and take pleasure in unrighteousness have set up idols in their own personal hearts. Your own-self conscience and motives matters: The majority who claim to be Christians are serving other gods besides the true-living God: 1. 2 billion claimed world Christians it is a large number to consider: If all are fully earnest-authentically Christians in the sight of God, there would be a better world to live upon today!. I said this before:

Pride and luxury it is a major issue cherished character; idols are set up in the sanctuary and their holy places are all awfully polluted; like Aaron's two sons who profaned God's Holy Altar. Nadab and Abihu: God killed them both at the spot for profaning God' Holy Altar [Num 3: 4].

God set up many examples for ungodly to observe. Early ancient days; the Lord God showed to his chosen people concerning Israel's leaders of his people cause them to commit Enmity sinful and corruptions, those who led of them are all destroyed! See [Is. 9: 16]... The prophets some; prophesy falsely and the priests bear rule by their means, and my people love to have it so; and what will you do in the end thereof?" [Jer. 5: 31]. Far from the least of them even unto the greatest of them, everyone else is given to covetousness, and from the prophet even unto the priest every one dealt falsely. [Jer. 6: 13]. The ancient Judaism church once so highly favored of the Lord God in the days of Moses, David, and Solomon; became any astonishment and a reproach through deliberate intent neglect to improve the blessings granted to them like today modern era, so much has been deliberately intent neglected. The same thing of Enmity sinful of pride, unbelief, hostiles; conflicts disobedient; disagreements and divisions lead us to our own ruin. How many today will notice? There aren't many: 1.2 billion world Christians what is their function?

But these are true biblical-scriptures do not only apply to ancient Judaism Israel only: The character or behavior and condition of many nominally Christian churches are here at present existing portrayed. 1. 2 billion Christians it is a large number to consider. Though in possession of far more great blessings than were granted to the ancient Jews, they are following in the steps of that people in the past; and the greater the light and privileges bestowed, the greater the guilty-measure of those who permit or allow them to pass unimproved! Like Balaam. The big picture which the apostle Paul had drawn of the ancient people and modern people of God in the last days is a sad and absurd but faithful delineation of the popular churches of our time. Having a form of godliness but denying the power of God thereof lovers of world pleasures more than lovers of God their maker and sustainer. Lovers of their own-selves covetous; boasters; proud, [2 Tim 3: 2-7] such are a few specifications from the dark catalogue which God has given.

And in view of the frequent and startling revelations of treason crime, even among those that ministers in holy things who dare affirm that there is one sin enumerated by the apostle which is not concealed under a profession of Christianity. Why we ever fight? But what mutual fellowship hath righteousness with unrighteousness? And what concord hath Christ with Belial?" And what agreement hath the temple of God with idols? For you are the temple of the living God; as God hath be their God, and they shall be My people. Wherefore come out from among them and be ye separate, said the Lord, and touch unto you, and ye shall be My sons and daughters, said the Lord Almighty." [2 Corinth 6: 14-18]. What else shall we say or tell? Will you agree? They look in vain for the image of Christ Jesus in the church. As the churches depart more and more widely from the truth, and ally themselves more closely with the secular world, the time will come when those who fear and honor God can no longer remain in connection with them. Like Paul was a Judaism Pharisee, he was transformed to Christ. Those who believed not the truth, but had pleasure in unrighteousness, will be left to receive strong psychological delusion, and to believe malicious lies." [2 Thess. 2: 11-12]. **Enmity stands against them to devour their souls. "Come out of her my people!"**

"You search the scriptures diligently because in them you think you have eternal life; and these are the very words which testify all about me!. But you are not willing to come to me that you may have eternal life." **I do not receive honor from men." But I know you, that you do not have the love of God in you!" Jesus said.** [John 5: 39-42]. Also see [Is. 8: 20: 34: 16, &. Luke. 24: 27]

"Do not think that I shall accuse you to the Father," Jesus said: "There is one who accuses you; Moses in whom you trust!" [v. 45].

There is always weeping with the nightmares!. But we have the promise that the morning comes when weeping nightmares shall be no more! To those who discover the great truth through man' made tradition-cultural church there will be many a disappointment before the great day breaks of the Second Advent Christ' returns upon all!. When the early centuries passed away unmarked by the church of Christ, those who looked in faith for his personal appearing were for a time in doubt and perplexity! But notwithstanding their disappointments, many people continued to search the Scriptures diligently, examining anew the evidence of their faith, and carefully studying the ancient prophecies to obtain further light! The Bible testimony in support of their position seemed clear and conclusive. Signs which could not be mistaken pointed to the coming of Christ as most near: The believers could not explain their disappointment, yet they felt assured that God had led them in their past experiences: Therefore, their faith became greatly strengthened by the direct and forcible application of those true scriptures which set forth a tarrying times: The Holy Spirit of God discerned them because they truly, authentically, and intrinsically sought for God's truths! God showed them. As early centuries the Spirit of God had moved to various reformers to devise the prophetic chart which was generally regarded by the fulfillment Christ' prediction of the command given by early prophecies to accurate records the vision and makes it clear or plain upon the Scroll. No one, however, then saw the tarrying time which was brought to view in the same prophecy.

After the disappointment, the full meaning of this true biblical scripture became apparent: Thus speaks the prophet: The book of Ezekiel prophecy is a strong comfort source of believers: "And the word of the Lord came unto me saying; "son of man what is that proverb that you have in the land of Israel saying?" "The days are prolonged and every vision failed?" Tell them therefore, "Thus says the Lord God: "The days are at hand, and the effect of every vision." "I will speak, and the word that I shall speak shall come to pass, it shall be no more prolonged!" They of the house of Israel say; the vision shat he sees is for many days to come and he prophesied of the times that are far off!"

"Therefore say unto them; "Thus says the Lord God: "There shall none of My words be prolonged anymore! But the word which I have spoken shall be done!" [Ezek 12: 21-25: 27-28].

The faithful waiting ones rejoiced at hearing God's assurance that only God knows the end from the beginning had looked down through the ages, and foreseeing their disappointment, had given them words of courage and hopefully. Had it not for such diligent searching for the right holy scriptures showing that they were in the right path their faith would have failed in that trying hour. Search the scriptures right with earnest open mind before the sight of your God. He will show you the right path. Jesus Christ told compelling parable in [Matt 25], ten virgin's females, it is well illustrated by the incidents an Eastern marriage: Five wise females and five foolish females. The five wise females preserved their oil; while the other five foolish females did not. Then shall be the kingdom of heaven," Jesus said: "Be likened unto ten virgins who took their lamps, and went forth to meet the bridegroom." While the bridegroom tarried, they all slumbered and slept!" The wide-spread movement under the proclamation of the first message answered to the going forth of the virgins, while the passing of the time of expectation, the disappointment, and delay were represented by the tarrying of the bridegroom. After the definite time had passed, the true believers were still united in the belief that the end of all things was at hand; but it soon became evident that they were losing, to some extent their zeal and devotion, and were falling into the state denoted in the parable told by Christ, the slumbering of the virgins during the tarrying time. The five foolish females lost their bridegroom. In other word; they failed to enter into the kingdom of heaven prepared for them. That is the big picture to see. Will you agree?

About this time, some profligates-grotesque malicious fanaticism began to appear: Some who strongly deceitful professed to be zealous to Christ

Jesus in the message rejected the word of God as the one infallible guide; claiming to be led by the Holy Spirit; gave themselves up to the control of their own feelings, impressions, and imaginations. There were some who manifested a blind and bigoted zeal, denouncing all who would not sanction their course or doctrine. Their fanatical ideas and exercises met with no sympathy; empathy from the great body of the early reformers; yet they served to bring reproach upon the cause of truth. It is same alike today there are many malicious profligates-grotesque fanaticism in our time.

Satan-Enmity sinful is seeking by this means to oppose and destroy the good work of God as he did in the past. Satan still loose today roaring lion for his prey: "Resist the proud fanatic; but give grace to the humble!." Says St. Peter: Casting all your care upon Him; for He cares for you!" [1 Pet 5: 6-9]. The people have been greatly stirred the reformers movement, thousands of Enmity sinful men and women had been converted and faithful men were giving themselves to the work of God's truth proclamation. Even in the tarrying time. Same idea today; we stand on Christ' solid rock in proclaiming this truth that Jesus Christ is inevitable!. We are very aware that the prince of Enmity Satan-evil doers is losing his subjects and in order to bring reproach upon the cause of God, he sought to deceive those who are confined into the scholasticism tool shaping young adults and drive them to extremes grotesque! The Lord God deplore them! Enmity, God will eradicate as he imposed it from the beginning!. It stands for God's righteousness judgments!

Then Enmity Satan or Lucifer with his evil angel agents will stand-ready to seize upon every profligate corruption, every failure unbecoming act, and hold it up before the righteous judgment in the most exaggerated light to tender his prey and their faith odious: Thus the greater the number whom he could crowd in to make a profession of the truth while his power controlled their hearts, the greater advantage would he gain by calling attention to them as representatives of whole body of believers on earth. Enmity Satan or Lucifer is skillful an accuser-opponent of all that is called of God and the brethren, and it is his spirit which inspires men and women to watch for the corruption and every defect of the Lord God's true believers, and to hold them up to notice while their good deeds are passed by without a mention. He is always active when God is at work for the salvation of lost souls. Satan is available to destroy what God builds. His skillful is just to destroy but unable to rebuild. God keeps ongoing rebuilding what Satan breaks. When the sons of God come to present themselves before the Lord, Satan also comes among them showing himself as worthy to the sons of God, yet he is there for their prey. He shows them good things to attract them. In every revival he is ready to bring in those who are unsanctified in heart and unbalanced in mind. He can devour very easily.

When they have accepted some points of truth, and gained-confidence, a place with believers, he works through them to introduce his corrupt theories like fiction ebook with faking facts that will deceive the vulnerable unwary. No man is proved to be a true Christian because he is found in company with the sons of God, even in the house of worship and around the table of the Lord God: Satan, Enmity sinful is frequently there present with his skillful of deceit upon the most solemn occasions, in the form of those whom he can use as his agents, as he did to the old Serpent in Eden. Eve was unaware that it was Lucifer in the form of a serpent her faithful-mutual friend. Satan possesses all these sophisticated devices to trap his prey. He is in spirit invisible-power. He knows you so well; while you know nothing about him. So he easily traps you! Lucifer, once a perfect angel in heaven: Now the great deceiver will profess anything in order to gain adherents. He possesses sophisticated wisdom beyond human scope. He will never approach you without knowing all your desperate needs: Then he comes to you with crafting-cunning words. You will indeed, believe him: You will believe him without a slight subconscious doubt or objection.

For example: When you think about having a beautiful young woman: He will show you one who is most beautiful so that you can easily tempt to rap her: Perhaps money; Lucifer will show you the best bank to break. Satan has all tricks to trap men and women into terrible danger! Beware! You ought to know better. But should Enmity Satan to be converted, should he, if it were possible? Enter heaven and associate with the holy angels? He would not be changed at all! While the true worshipers would be bowed in pure adoration before the Lord God their maker, he would be plotting mischief against God's truth: And the people devise means to ensnare souls, considering the most successful method of sowing evil seed-tares. He is subject to death once and for all when Christ Jesus returns. His days are numbered and very short! Satan is vividly aware for that reason he is so eager to devour or detour every godly man on earth!. This is a genuine warning to all! Will you agree? What is your motive? What is your conscience? Where it stands? Good or Evil? **Do not deceive yourself! Take initiative step toward Christ Jesus your Saviour: [Matt 11: 28-30].**

St. Martin Luther's Church Germany

Antiquity

The city has existed since before Roman times, when it was captured and fortified by the Romans under Drusus in 14 BCE. From that time, a small troop of infantry and cavalry were garrisoned in Augusta Vangionum; this gave the settlement its Romanized but originally Celtic name Borbetomagus: The garrison developed into a small town with the regular Roman street plan, a forum, and temples for the main gods Jupiter, Juno, Minerva (whose temple was the site of the later cathedral), and Mars.

Lucifer, Satan, Enmity sinful; strives to contests every inch of ground on earth where there are true godly people advancing their right journey toward the heavenly eternal life. Lucifer envy to possess what he formerly lost that he should also be reinstated as before:

Is there any possibility? There is no Scripture's evidence to confirm: In all the church history, no reformation has been carried forward without encountering serious catastrophic and obstacles that Lucifer did not get involved. Thus it was in Paul's day. Where the apostle would raise up a church, there Lucifer would be present to interfere; there would be some who professed malicious Christ's doctrine to receive the faith: But who brought in heresies that if received, would eventually crowd out the love of truth. Martin Luther and all his associates suffered great perplexity and distress from the course of malicious fanatical movement designed by the pontiff Rome who also claimed that God had spoken directly through them and who therefore set their own feeble ideas and human opinions above the testimony of the Scriptures as it is on this day of our modern age. Many people who were lacking in strong faith and experience but who had considerable self-confidence and self-sufficiency and who loved to hear and tell some new things, were spontaneously beguiled by the pretensions of the new teachings, and they joined the malicious lies agents of Satan with immediate effect in their work of tearing apart what God had built moved Luther to build up. Satan; the adversary the devil; the man of Enmity sinful and perdition has great power upon the human minds and hearts control of some present day of our modern age. You will know them by their fruits: Jesus early warned: "Beware!" And how that manner of spirit they are of? The Scriptures has the answers: "By their nasty-soar fruits you shall know them." There are many in spirits. The spirit that does not cause us to live soberly, righteously, and godly in this present world is not the spirit of Christ Jesus but it is the spirit of Lucifer-Satan. I am more and more convinced that Satan-evil spirit has much to do in all these wild movements on earth today! I truly believe in scriptures that teaches me truth. Because I see its practical evidence as I live on this horrible world! It afflicts me daily. It makes me very uncomfortable! I am surrounded by evil everywhere I go!. Evil beats me daily! Oh what a terrible world on which I dwell? I truly plea upon my Lord God Christ Jesus to rescue me:

Many among us who pretend to be wholly sanctified, are following the traditions of men' teachings, and apparently are as ignorant of God's truth as others who make no such pretensions, and are not half so modest! The spirit of Enmity Lucifer will lead us into the untruth and the Spirit of God will lead us into truth! But say you; a man may be in error and think he has the truth. What then? We answer; "The Spirit and Word agree. If a man judges himself by the word of God and finds a perfect harmony through the whole word, then he/she must believe he has the truth; but if he/she finds the spirit by which he is led does not harmonize or agree with the whole tenor of God's perfect law or scripture, then let him walk carefully, lest he be caught up in the snare of Lucifer-evil doers. I have often obtained more evidence of inward piety from a kindling eye a wet cheek, and a chocked utterance than from all the noise in the secular world Christendom.

The early century's reformers charged their enemies all the evils of malicious profligacy fanaticism upon the very ones who were laboring most authentically against it. Fanatics they circulated unfavorable reports that had not the slightest semblance of truth like today's daily news: These people were actuated by prejudice and Enmity hatred-hostiles. Their peace was ever disturbed by the proclamation of Christ at their doors. They feared it might be true, yet hoped it was not, and this was the secret of their warfare against Lucifer-Enmity and adversaries. It still here with us even this very day!.

The fact that a few malicious fanatics worked their way into the pontiff monks is no more a reason to decide that the movement was not of God, than is the presence of fanatics and deceivers in the church in Paul's day and Luther day as well as our modern age, a sufficient cause for discarding or ridiculing their work.

Let the people of God arouse out of sleep, and begin in earnest the work of true repentance and reformation! Let them search the Scriptures to learn the truth as it is in Christ Jesus: Let them make an entire consecration to God: And evidence will not be wanting that Lucifer Satan-Enmity sinful is still active and vigilant! With all possible deception will he manifest his power: **Calling to his aid all the fallen angels of his realm.**

It was about the proclamation of the Second Advent great message of the day: Their hearts were filled with great love for one another sharing, and for the Lord Christ Jesus whom they were filled with great enthusiasm of high expectation for Christ to return soon as promise to see him appearing. The one faith, the blessed hope, lifted them above-high the control of any human influence, and proved a shield against the assaults of Enmity Satan.

The midnight outcry was a powerful message when it went to reach-out like a tidal flood-wave through the whole land! The very urgency of it resulted in decision for and against it: The result was a revealing of many hearts! Unfortunately, like today' age; many preferred the secular world more than they wanted Christ Jesus the World's Saviour! It is the same principle even in our current modern world today!

While the bridegroom tarried," Jesus said: "They all slumbered and slept deeply." And at midnight there was a cry-out made: "Behold, the bridegroom is coming; go out to meet with him!" Then all those virgins' females rose and trimmed their lamps." [Matt 25: 5-7]… Powerful and meaningful parable told by Jesus. Referring to His own returning unknown Second Advent!.

The proclamation of this time message was another step in the fulfillment of the parable of the marriage, whose application to the experience of Christ ultimate righteousness judgment. In the very word of the Holy Scriptures; "Behold!"

Yes! Like a tidal wave swept over the whole land! Will you agree? Enmity will persist: Believers once more found their position and hope and courage animated their hearts: The word was free from those extremes which are ever manifested when there is human excitement without the controlling influence of the word and Spirit of the Lord God. It is similar in current modern world today to these seasons of humiliation-terrorism, and returning unto the Lord God which among ancient Israel, early century's pontiff till this day Enmity persists, following messages of reproof from godly people. It bore the characteristics which mark of God in every age on earth! There was little ecstatic joy, but rather deep searching of heart, confession of Enmity sinful and forsaking of the secular world. Preparation to meet the Lord was the severe burden of agonizing spirits till this day! There was persevering prayer and unreserved consecration to God: One prominent preacher describing that work: "There is no great expression of joy that is, as it were, suppressed for future occasion; when all heavens and earth will rejoice together with joy unspeakable and full of glory! There is no shouting that, too, is reserved for the shout from heaven."

The singers are silent; they are waiting to join the angelic hosts, the choir from heaven. No arguments are used or needed; all seem convinced that they have the truth and of one no clashing of sentiments; all are of one heart and of one mind." The midnight outcry was not so much carried out by argument, disagreement, dispute, or disobedience thought the Bible proof was clear and conclusive. There went with it an impelling power that moved the souls. There was no doubt or psychological dilemmas, no inquisitive-mind of any subconscious objection. Upon the occasion of Christ's triumphal entry into Jerusalem, the people who were assembled from all parts of the regions to keep the feast, flocked to the Mount of Olives and as they joined the throng that were escorting Christ Jesus, they were all caught up by the inspiration of the hour; and they helped to swell the shouts: "Hosanna in the highest! Blessed is He who comes in the name of the Lord!" [Matt 21: 9]… In like manner did the secular world-unbelievers who also flocked to the shouts! Some from curiosity, some merely to ridicule-Pharisees feel the convincing powerful-force attending the message: "Behold!" Neither could the Pharisees stop!

Like showers of rain upon the dry-thirsty earth, the Spirit of grace descended upon the earnest seekers: Those who expected soon to stand face to face with the World's Saviour felt a solemn joy that was unutterable! The softening subduing powerful of the Holy Spirit melted the hearts, as wave after wave of the glory of the Lord God the maker of all goodness; swept over the faithful, believing ones: Carefully and solemnly those who received the true message came up to the time when they fully hoped to meet their Lord God and **Saviour Jesus Christ. Glory to God Almighty!**

Each day they felt it is their first responsibility-duty to secure the true evidence of their acceptance with the Lord God the Creator! Their hearts were so-closely united and they authentically and intrinsically consistently praying much with and for one another, and sharing all they had equally. They often met together in secluded places to commune with the Lord God who is their strength and sustainer, and the voice of intercession ascended to heaven from the appalling fields and groves where they firmly stood! The assurance to the Lord Saviour's approval was more necessary to them than their daily bread/food which ever demands dissatisfaction; and if a cloud darkened their minds/hearts; they did not rest until it was swept away from them!

As they usually felt the witness of pardoning grace, they longed to look to him whom their souls loved and caring. As always Enmity sinful kept penetrating in their midst; like today the process of Enmity still in its persistence: Again and again they were destined to disappointment: The time of Christ soon return expectation passed; and their Saviour did not show as it seems to be alike today no show for Christ to appear anywhere the globe!. With unwavering confidence like us today; they had looked forward for Christ to his coming and now they felt as did Mary Magdalene [John 20: 1-17], when she came to the tomb where Jesus laid and found it empty; she exclaimed with her shading-tears on her eyes weeping: "They have taken away my Lord and I do not know where they have laid him!" She told Peter and others. Yet, Jesus stood by, and she did not recognize him. Jesus indeed, is raised! [John 20: 13].

A feeling of awe, a fear-shadow that the message might be true had for a time served as a restraint upon the slow/unbelieving word of truth from the mouth of the Lord God Almighty. Today' fear of terror often times bring slow/unbelieving as tears are shade on eyes weeping for their loved lose. After the passing on the time, this did not at once disappear: They dared not triumph over the disappointment ones but as no tokens from God's wrath were seen: Like us today, they recovered from their fears and resumed their reproach and ridicule: Mary Magdalene eventually recognized her Lord whom she most loved. She stayed at the tomb weeping. Jesus Christ showed himself to her. "Mary Magdalene: I AM Here!" Touch me not!" Jesus said [v. 17] Christ utters a message to her: "Go and tell my brethren that "I am ascending to My Father and your Father; and to my God, and your God." Mary Magdalene came and told the disciples that she had seen the Lord, and that he had spoken these things to her." [v. 18].

A large class of nobles who professed to believe in the Lord's soon coming renounced their faith: Some who had been very-confident were so deeply wounded in their selfish-pride that they felt like fleeing from the secular world: Like Jonah compromise with Tyre; Jonah couldn't make it, but boldly go to Nineveh and proclaim God's truth as commanded to Jonah! Like us today; they complained of God, and choose their own death rather than life: We are ongoing same online! Those who had based their faith upon the human being opinions or of others and not upon the word of God; were now as ready to again exchange their views! Shifting like chaff blown away by the shifting winds.

The scoffers won the weak and cowardly to their prestigious ranks and all united in declaring that there could be no more fears or expectations of anything from now on: This is the general spirit overshadowing many young adults today confined into the modern scholasticism scientific. Technology let it take its advantages in shaping their minds and hearts as they embrace it to hearts. The time had passed like Noah's day: The Lord God had not come or sends heavy rains: And the Secular world might remain the same for thousands of years unknown! "Oh, Lord God! "For a thousand years in your sight: Are like yesterday when it is past!" And like a watch in the night." [Ps. 90: 4-5]. What shall/should we teach to the secular world today? While they insist refusing to receive God's truth:

The earnest, sincere believers had given up all for Christ, should we also today? And had shared Christ' presence as never before. They had as they believed, given their last warning to the secular world expecting soon to be received into a society of their divine master and the heavenly angels, they had, to great extent withdrawn from the unbelieving multitudes.

With intense desire or eagerness they had prayed saying: "Come Lord Jesus, and come quickly." But he had not come. And now to take up again the heavy burden of life's cares and perplexities and to endure the taunts and sneers of scoffing secular world, was and it still indeed a terrible trial of faith and upon all including today' generation and to come until Christ returns! This is the truth according to the Holy Scriptures evidence which the secular modern world reject to receive today!.

The pontiff pope tour the world today: He is not seen to get involved about the Lord Christ Jesus returns: He does not seen to get involved in warning the world about the ultimate righteousness judgment is to come upon all! Yet, it is the pontiff Vatican Rome's obligation to warn the world! Like Noah; like Jonah; like Moses; like the early century's reformers and today the pontiff is reluctant to warn the world too. Yet, he tour the world since then no warning to the world! And so the Canterbury Archbishop in England, is also silent!. Why they compromise with the secular world? Did the Lord Jesus Christ compromise with the secular world? Or did his disciples? No!

When the Lord Jesus Christ rode on a donkey triumphantly entry into Jerusalem: His disciples and other followers believed that he was about to ascend the throne of King David: And deliver Israel from the Roman Empire Oppressors! With high hopes and great happiness-shouts anticipations they vied with one another showing honor-respect to their King! Many people even unbelievers secular world did participate the greatest occasion for Christ triumphant entry toward Jerusalem, they spread their own-outer garments on ground as a carpet of honor in Christ' path; or strewed before Christ the leafy branches of the palms: It was absolute an extra-ordinary occasion ever seen and heard in Jerusalem, that ancient City which is completely polluted with the shading innocent blood. In their enthusiastic joy that united in the glad acclaim: "Hosanna to the Son of David!" Unfortunately the shouts and screams did upset the extremist Pharisees; Sadducees; and Sanhedrin. They got very disturbed-uncomfortable and angered by this honest outburst of rejoicing mobilized crowd of multitudes. These Pharisees wished Jesus to rebuke the shouting people with the disciples: Jesus response: "If these people stop shouting-screaming:" These stones and trees would immediately starting shouting and screaming more loudly than them!." [Luke 19: 40].

Indeed, the prophecy must be fulfilled! His disciples were accomplishing the purpose of God Almighty followed by early century's reformers: Yet they were doomed to awful bitter Enmity **But** a few days had passed ere they witnessed the Christ' Saviour's agonizing death: and laid him in the tomb. Their expectations had not been realized in a single particular day, and their hopes died out with Christ Jesus. Not until their Lord had come forth triumphant from the grave could they perceive that all had been foretold early by prophecy; and that Christ must needs have suffered and persecuted risen again from the dead." [Acts 17: 3]. In like manner was prophecy fulfilled in the first and second prophecy messages: They were given at the right time and accomplished the work which God designed to accomplish by them. The world had been looking on expecting that if the time passed and Christ did not show, the whole system of Second Advent would be given up. But the Spirit of God will ever prevails! But many people like today, under strong Enmity sinful nature temptation yield them Satan there were some who firmly stood on Christ' solid rock no compromise or shift with secular world.

They could detect not Enmity sinful-error in their reckoning of the prophetic periods. The most able persons of their opponents had not succeeded in overthrowing their position. True there had been a failure like today as to the expected event; but even this could not shake their faith in the secular world which God has made well perfected. It shall prevail forever! When Jonah had proclaimed in the city of Nineveh for 40 days from every corner of Nineveh city that within 40 days the city will be destroyed by God if the people resist to repentance God indeed would overthrow all the Nineveh's kingdom. Then the Lord God accepted the humiliation of the people in Nineveh and extended their period of probation; yet the message of Jonah was sent by God and Nineveh was tested according to God's will. The warning from God was received by the people of Nineveh; they truly repented. God spared all none perished.

God never forgets or forsake his true peoples: His Spirit still remains with those who did not rashly deny the truth which they had received; and denounce the truth which Jonah proclaimed. Paul who most suffered persecution by his former Pharisees; looking back through the ages; wrote words of encouragement and warning for the tried: Waiting ones of this crisis: "Cast not away therefore your confidence, which has great recompense of reward." [Heb 10: 35-39].

The people here addressed were in great danger including Paul himself; of making shipwreck of faith. They had done the will of God in following the guidance of holy Spirit and words: Yet they could not understand his purpose in their past experience; nor could they discern the pathway before them, and they were tempted to doubt whether God had indeed leading them or not: At this time the words were especially applicable: "Now the just shall live by faith." As the bright light of the midnight cry had shown upon their pathway; and they had seen the prophecies unsealed and the rapidly fulfilling signs telling that the coming of Christ was near: But now, bowed down by disappointed hopes; they could stand only by faith in God's truth word. The coffering secular world were saying as they do even today: "You have been deceived: Give up your faith and say that Christ is dead and is not alive." They did discourage faithful from the beginning. It was after the day that God initially preside righteous judgment upon the old serpent-Lucifer: Then God imposed Enmity upon them all: Serpent: Eve: Adam. Since then there has ever been intense discouragement from those who implement Enmity sinful nature. [Gen 3: 14-19] the process of righteous judgment stands upon all men on earth until Christ returns! This is the greatest warning of the prophecy. God will fulfill his word truth!

Lucifer in the form of Serpent-Satan original, Enmity its major is the cause of all troubles on earth will persist until Christ returns. If a man draws back; my soul shall have no pleasure in him!" I have no pleasure in seeing man dying in his Enmity sinful nature: Repent and be saved!" [Ezek 18: 31-32]. Why die? To renounce their faith now, and deny the true-power of the Holy Spirit which had attended the message; would be drawing back toward perdition, the man of sin Lucifer-Satan who constantly discourage all who are godly people. He is also in evil spirit invisible. You will know by the fruit he produces. Some were encouraged to steadfastness by the word from Scriptures: "Cast not away therefore your confidence." You have need of patience;" for yet a little while and he that shall come will come, and will not tarry."

Their only safe course was to cherish the truth-light which they had already received from God, hold it fast to his promise and continue to search the Bible and patiently wait and watch to receive further truth from God alone: No one else! It is good thing to heed and practice daily! Embrace it into your heart-deep. Praise God always:

Finally: The Bible teaches us about a Sanctuary that was built at the Command of the Lord God Himself: This was a marvelous; magnificent; well perfected architecture designed by the hand of God-structure: And every well detail of it has been special meaning for us today! But the way in which its service-purpose foretold future events in God's truth great plan for all nations on earth are especially striking! You will want to learn more fully the purpose of the greatest [Heavenly Sanctuary] and what it means in your own daily living life right now:

The Bible-Scriptures [Torah] which is above all had been both the [Fundamental Foundation and Central Pillar] of all faith on earth: There is no other Book supersede it since there was no other Book ever written until on the day at Mount Sinai: Where God Himself Stretched His Holy Hand and Wrote This Magnificent Great Book. [Exodus 20; 30-33] The Bible is the Bereshith of all! The Word: The Living Word: God Himself: No! One Else! God is the Only [Living Word!] His Word: Creates: And Sustains Life. [Genesis 1; 2; 3 John 1: Bereshith: The Beginning! **"I AM!" Exo. 3: 14].**

The Bible Book; the most Magnificent Central Foundation in all the Universal and the Ministry of the Lord Jesus Christ for all, Creation is under His feet! Jesus Christ is the way; life; and truth to heaven! He is the Greatest Shepherd. He knows his own sheep! No sheep that belongs to Christ that Satan can plug off! No! [John 10: 11; 14; 18]. Jesus Christ has all the power! Scriptures evidences are truth! Jesus Christ is all authority! He is the ultimate Judge! No! One Else! Therefore; Jesus Christ is inevitable! You ignore him at your own wicked risk:

In the early century's church; these had been very familiar words to all believers in the Lord Christ Jesus soon up coming. By the lips of many prophecies with joyfully repeated as the watchword of their faith daily! All felt that upon the events therein brought to view depended their brightest expectations and most cherished their hopes to hearts. These prophetic days had been showing future generations after generations according to Dan 8: 26-27]. God's timing is well unknown. No prophet specifically confirmed or indicated a precise date to when the end with finally come. It will definitely come according to God's authority and timing alone. God has no limit for anything.

This they understood would take place at the Second Advent of Christ Jesus no human being gets involved. But humans need to get involved in preparation for the event. Henceforth, the conclusion that Christ Jesus will return to the earth once and for all! Although there are some denomination predicting date and time, such as

Jehovah' Witness and Adventist churches they assumed 1844 was the year expected nothing took place. These churches are cultic. To accept this conclusion id renounce the former reckoning of the prophetic periods; and involve the whole question in confusion. It was a deliberate surrender of positions which had been reached through earnest prayerful study of Scriptures by minds enlightened by the Holy Spirit of God, and hearts burning with its living power; positions which had withstood the most searching criticism and the most bitter opposition of popular secular religionists and worldly-wisdom shaped men through scholasticism and which had stood firm against the combined forces of learning and eloquence speech, and the taunts and reviling alike of the honorable and the base etc. with many others! This is the work of Enmity Satan who is ever bringing divisions among the people who are godly. And all this sacrifice was made in order to maintain the theory that the earth is sanctuary. How it can be? This earth is awfully, polluted and defiled with human blood killings! Since then, from Abel righteous blood and Zechariah, there has never been a ceasing of shading blood on ground till this day! This ground on which we grow food to eat is badly polluted! Even the water it's full of blood which we drink. Not only that; chemical which man produces spills into waters daily like cargo-oil and all other chemicals fill the oceans killing all fishes and wild animals.

In their investigation they learned that the earthly sanctuary built by Moses in the Exodus wilderness at the command of God, according to the pattern shown him in the Mount Sinai; was a figure for the time then present; in which were offered both gifts and sacrifices; that its two holy places were patterns of things in the heavens; that [Christ Jesus the Great High Priest is Minister] of the really Sanctuary and of the true Tabernacle; which the Lord God Pitched; and not man; that Christ is not entered into the holy place made with human hands; which are the figures of the true heaven itself: Now to appear in the presence of God for us: See [Heb 9: 9; 23; 8: 2; 9: 24]. The sanctuary in heaven in which Jesus Christ

Ministers in our behalf; is the Great Original; of which the sanctuary built by Moses was a duplicate or a copy. God placed His Spirit upon the builder of the earthly sanctuary. The Lord Christ Jesus entered into the most highly Holy of Holy in heaven where he stands on the right hand of God Almighty.

The artistic skill displayed in its construction was a manifestation of divine wisdom. The walls had the appearance of massive gold, reflecting in every direction the light of the seven lamps of the golden candlestick. The table of show-bread and the altar of incense glittered like burnished gold. The gorgeous curtain which formed the ceiling, inwrought with figures of angels in blue and purple and scarlet, added to the beauty of the scene: And beyond the second vail was the holy Shekinah, the visible manifestation of God's glory before which none but the high priest could enter and live, no one else. The matchless splendor of the earthly tabernacle reflected to human vision the glories of that heavenly temple where Christ our fore-runner ministers for us **before the throne of God Almighty.**

The sanctuary on earth which Moses built at Mount Sinai according to God's instruction it had two apartments, the only and the most holy, where Aaron only could enter once a year live, so there are two holy place in the sanctuary in heaven as it shows on earth in the days of Moses at Mount Sinai. Aaron's two sons; Nadab and Abihu profaned the Holy of Holy Altar God killed them both at the spot. [Num 3: 4]. And the ark containing the perfect Law of God, and the Altar of incense and other instruments of service found in the sanctuary below, have also their counterpart in the sanctuary above in heaven. In holy vision John at Patmos Island-isolation saw this as he entered into heaven, and there he beheld the candlestick and the altar of incense, and as "the temple of God was opened, "he beheld also the ark of God's testimony." [Rev 4: 5; 8: 3; 11: 19].

Those who were truly seeking, like John at Patmos; he sought for truth at the times of Rome intense persecution; found indisputable proof of the existence of a sanctuary in heaven. Indeed; Moses built the earthly sanctuary but he not the architect of it, God is, Moses built a duplicate-copy sanctuary from heaven designed by God's holy hand! The Israelites defiled or polluted the human made sanctuary!. It is a signal for their own-self destruction as result of Aaron's two sons; who deliberately profaned the holy place of God at Mount Sinai: God immediately killed them both. It was a significant example setting for both ungodly and Israel to be fearful at God's presence! Like us today; do we really fear at God's presence? As results; there is ever shading blood on earth:

"That pattern was the true sanctuary which is in heaven." Said Saint Pau:

As John at Patmos Island testified that he saw it in heaven. In the temple in heaven, the dwelling-place of Mighty God!. Heaven: His Throne: The Earth: His Footstool! [Is. 66:1-3]. In the most holy place is God's perfect Law: The great rule of all Rightful; Justice; Merciful; by which all nations on earth are ruled; tested; judged; and sentenced executed; live or death.

The ark that enshrines the tables of the perfect law is covered with the mercy-seat before which the Lord Christ Jesus pleads his blood in the Enmity sinful behalf upon those who truly observed the perfect law according to Christ's depth-path; suffering Christ' like-meekness-lowly in hearts. Thus is presented the union of justice and merciful in the plan of human beings Enmity sinful redemption. Jesus Christ is indeed; inevitable! This union infinite wisdom alone could devise and infinite power accomplish it is a union that fills all heavens with great wonder and adoration splendor! The Cherubim of the earthly sanctuary looking reverently down upon the mercy-seat; represent the interest with which the heavenly host contemplates the work of redemption. This is the mystery of mercy into which angels desire to look. That God can be just while God Himself justifies the repenting Enmity sinful man and renews his reconciliation with the fallen evil nations; that Christ Jesus could suffer death to rise unnumbered multitudes from the abyss of awful ruin; and clothe them with the spotless garments of Christ' own righteousness; and to unite with multitudes of holy angels who have never fallen into Enmity sinful; and to dwell forever in the presence of God Almighty in heaven. This is the unique-true big picture to look. The Bible Evidences are truth: God's Word is Truth! John 17: 17.

There is no more sanctuary had existed on earth since from the early termination of Moses and Aaron at Mount Hor. Moses stripped Aaron's garments and put them on Eleazar his son, and there Aaron died." [Num 20: 27-28]. For many centuries until Christ prediction for it's final down fall temple. It is very complex issue to discuss so, let God be the Judge.

The manifestation of the earthly sanctuary consisted of two divisions: The other Levites priests ministered daily in the holy place; while once a year the high Priest Aaron performed a special work of atonement in the most Holy of Holy once a year, for the cleansing of the sanctuary. This is where his two sons got killed because they profaned the Altar of Holy God. Nadab and Abihu had profaned God's Most Holy Place!. [Exodus 3: 4].

Day by day the repentant Enmity sinful brought his offering to the door of the tabernacle; and pacing his/hers hand upon the victim's head confessing his Enmity sinful, thus in figure transferring them to the innocent sacrifice. We do not do that today: The animal was then slain and the blood or the flesh-life was carried by the priest into the holy place so forth. Thus the heinous Enmity sinful was in figure, transferred to the sanctuary. Such was the work that went forward throughout centuries. The continual transfer of Enmity sinful to the sanctuary rendered a further work of ministration necessary in order for their removal. Christ is the righteous blood final to remove all sinful man causes on daily basis. This is the crucial deal that the people reject today. The Book of Daniel Chapters: 9; 10; 11; 12: Confuses many scholars' today definitions and interpretations as well as translations. Jesus himself quoted several times from Daniel' prophecy:

On the tenth day of the seventh month the high pries entered the inner-part of most Holy place which he was forbidden on pain of death, to enter at any other day or time. It had to be at the precise time which determined. God commanded Daniel: "Go your way Daniel; the Books are closed!" The End is on a long way to go." [Dan 12: 9.] It is about future un-known. Jesus repeats these words [Acts 1: 7-8]. His disciples ponder a sensitive question: "Lord, will you at this time restore the kingdom to Israel?" [v. 6] Jesus response: "It is not for you to know times or seasons which the Father has put aside in His own Authority." See v 7]

During the early centuries; the great day of atonements two wee of the goats were brought to the door of the tabernacle and lots were cast upon them; one lot for the Lord and the other for the scapegoat. The goat upon which fell the lot the Lord was to be slain as a sin-offering for the people. We don't do that today: And the priest was to bring his blood within the wall, and sprinkle it upon the mercy-seat, and before the mercy-seat. [Lev 16: 8; 16]. In those days: Aaron the high priest lay both his hands upon the head of the live goat, and confess over him all the heinous Enmity sinful committed of the children of Israel during the Exodus wilderness; and all their offensive transgressions in all their Enmity sinful putting them upon the head of the goat and shall send him away by the hand of a fit man into the wilderness:

The whole ceremony was designed to improve the Israelites with holiness of God and his abhorrence of Enmity sinful nature. Furthermore; to show them that they could not come in contact with heinous Enmity sinful nature but to radical refrain from it without becoming polluted or defiled no more! Every man/woman was required to afflict his own soul while this work atonement was going forward. All business was laid aside, and the whole congregation of Israel' mobilize spent the day in solemn humiliation before the sight of God, with authentic-intrinsically prayer; fasting and deep searching of self-examination heart/mind; conscience and motives. Complete empty-exhaust before God. This is why Christ Jesus came to show by example: Meekness; lowly at heart; gentleness; humble; lifestyle; no luxury-comfort as it is today everywhere so called Christians lifestyle. Yet they compromise with secular world Christendom comforts well money spend. They deviate from Christ' lifestyle as it was in the early centuries.

Important truths concerning the atonement may well be learned from the typical service: A surrogate was accepted in the heinous Enmity sinful' stead; but heinous Enmity sinful was not canceled by the animal blood of the victim. A means was thus provided by which it was transferred to the sanctuary. By the offering of animal's blood the Enmity sinful acknowledged the authority of the perfect law; confessed his own guilty in transgression; and expressed his desire for pardon through faith in a redeemer to come; but he/she was not yet entirely released from the condemnation of the law. It was a mere process to attain pardon. God searches hearts not mere action. On the days of atonement the high priest, having taken an offering from the congregation, went into the most holy place with the blood of this general offering; and sprinkled it upon the mercy-seat, directly over the law; to make satisfaction for its claims.

Then in his character of mediator; he took the Enmity sinful upon himself; and bore them from the sanctuary. Placing his hands upon the head of the escape-goat, he confessed over him all these Enmity sinful, thus in figure transferring them from himself to the scape-goat. The goat then bore them away and they were regarded as forever separated from the people.

Such was the service performed to the example and shadow of heavenly things. And what was done in type in manifestation of the earthly is done in reality in the ministration of the heavenly. After Christ Jesus ascension; the saviour began his eternal holy wok as the world's high priest ever to exist.

"Christ is not entered into the holy places made with man's hands; which are in the presence of God for us!" Said Apostle Paul in holy inspiring spirit. The Lord Jesus Christ resides into permanently built by the Mighty God's hand forever-lasting places. No wearing needing for any repairs! Jesus Christ is the figure of the truth: But into heaven itself, now to appear in the presence of God for us. [Heb 9: 24]. Psalmist ponders: "Who may ascend into the hill of the Lord? Or who may stand in His holy place? "He who has clean hand and a pure heart:" Who has not lifted up his soul to an idol: Nor sworn deceitfully!" [Ps. 24: 3-4]. That is the place which God builds. No compromise with earthly things under what circumstances: **"The earth is the Lord's and all its fullness!." "For He has founded it upon the seas: And established it upon the waters!" [v 1-2].**

And as the typical cleansing of the earthly was accomplished by the removal of the most heinous Enmity sinful nature by which it had been polluted, so the actual cleansing of the heavenly is to be accomplished by the removal, or blotting out of the most Enmity sinful nature which are there recorded: The necessitates an examination of the books of record to determine who through repentance of Enmity sinful and faith in Christ Jesus, are entitled to the benefits of his atonement. The cleansing of the sanctuary therefore involves a work of investigative judgment. This work must be performed prior to the coming of the Lord Christ Jesus Second Advent to ultimately redeem the people of the whole world; for he comes; his reward is with him in his hand to give to every man according to his/hers works whether good or bad: [Rev 22: 12].

Thus those who followed in the advancing insightful-light of the prophetic word saw that instead of coming to the earth at the end, Christ then entered the most holy place of the heavenly sanctuary, into the presence of the Lord God, to perform the closing work of atonement; preparation to his Second Advent great event: It was seen, also, that while in offering pointed to Christ as a sacrifice, and the high priest represented Christ as most perfect mediator, the escape-goat typified Enmity Satan, the architect and father of every Enmity sinful man-perdition of the truly penitent will finally be revealed and placed hellish death: When the highly priest, by virtue of the blood of the Enmity sinful offering, removed the sinful from the sanctuary, he placed them upon the escape-goat.

When Christ Jesus by virtue of his only sanctuary at the close of his ministration, he will place them upon Enmity Satan, who in the execution of the judgment must bear the ultimate penalty! The escape-goat was sent away into a land not inhabited, never to come again into the world or congregation of Israel-church. So will Enmity Satan be forever banished from the presence of God and around the whole universal among the peoples, and he will be radical eradicated or blotted from his existence in the ultimate destruction of every Enmity sinful nature and sinner no more to be seen or heard once and for all!

The subject of the sanctuary is most crucial-key which unlocks many truths in the Bible or Scriptures which have been little well understood: The study of the Biblical sanctuary opens to view a complete system of truth, connected and harmonious as it reveals the work of the Lord Christ Jesus is now carrying on for our own behalf in heaven until he returns.

After the passing of the time of expectation, still many people believed the Christ coming to be very near they held that they had reached an important crisis, and that the work of Christ as man's intercessor before God, had ceased. Having given the warning of the judgment near, they felt that their work for the world was done, and they lost their burden of soul for the salvation of many sinners, while the bold and blasphemous scoffing of the ungodly seemed to them another evidences that the Spirit of God had been withdrawn from the rejecters of his mercy. All this confirmed them in the belief that probation had ended, or as they then expressed it: "The door of mercy was shut!"

But clearer insight-light came with the investigation of the sanctuary inquisitive minds: Now was seen the application of those words of Christ addressed to the church at this very time: "These things, addressed to the church at: said Christ that is holy, Christ that is true: He that has the key of David, he that opened and no man shut; and he shut and no man opens door; and no a shut door is brought to view." [Rev 3: 7-8].

At the termination of the prophetic days; Christ Jesus was granted his ministration from the holy to the most holy place: When in the ministration of the earthly sanctuary, the high priest on the day of atonement entered the most holy place, the door of the holy place was closed, and the door of the most holy was opened: So, when Christ passed from the holy to the most holy of the heavenly sanctuary, the door, or ministration, of the latter was opened. The Lord Christ Jesus had ended one part of his work as the world believer's intercessor, to enter upon another portion of the work; and Christ still presented his precious blood before the Father Head in behalf of Enmity sinful nature: "Behold!" Christ declared: "I have set before you an open door; and no man can shut it!" [Rev 3: 8].

Those who by faith follow Christ Jesus authentically, and intrinsically in the great work of the atonement, receive the benefits of Christ's mediation in view this work of ministration, are not benefited thereby: The ancient or modern Jews who rejected the insight light given at Christ Jesus' first coming advent, and refused to believe in him as the Son of God, highly exalted Messiah and the World's Saviour of the whole entire of nations on earth, could not receive pardon through him. When Christ Jesus at his ascension entered by his own precious blood into the heavenly sanctuary to shed upon his disciples the blessings of his mediation, the Jews were left in total darkness, to continue their useless sacrifices and offerings. God had no more considering interest in them for that reason; rejecting Christ it was to reject their own life which God had initially granted.

The ministration of types and shadows had ceased! It was their own condemnation by choice like the modern Gentiles today: That door by which men had formerly found access to God, was no longer open! The Jews had refused setting awful example to Gentiles they too refused following the Jews to seek in the only way whereby Christ could then be found; through the ministration in the sanctuary in heaven. Who agrees to this kind of teaching truths today? As in the past; they still refuse to believe to this truth. There aren't many: It is also by choice as the past. Enmity sinful remains upon all who refuse to believe.

Therefore they found no communion with God in Christ Jesus. To them and to modern world the door was shut! They had no knowledge of Christ like today as the true sacrifice and the only mediator before God: Hence they could not receive the benefits of Christ mediation! And so, neither the modern world today! The conditions of the unbelieving Jews illustrates; the condition of the careless and unbelieving among professed Christians who are willingly ignorant of the work of Christ' merciful high priest. It is by choice for their condemnation. In the typical service, when the high priest entered the most holy place, all Israelites were required to gather about the sanctuary and in the most solemn manner humble their soul-hearts before the Lord God; that they might receive the pardon of their heinous Enmity sinful nature; and not be cut off from the congregation. How much more essential in this anti-typical day of atonement that we today well understand the work of our Lord Christ Jesus as most highly Priest and know what duties are required of us today? Men cannot with impunity reject the warnings which God in merciful sends them. It is very old stain to escape out. Rust decays ruin the whole old motor-car. It can no longer be repaired but destroy it all, no more useful you need to purchase a new car after all. A message was sent from heaven to the world in Noah's day; Moses' day; Abraham' day, Jonah' day;

and their salvation depended upon the manner in which they treated that message: Because they rejected the warning, the Spirit of God was withdrawn from that heinous Enmity sinful peoples, and they all perished in the deep waters of the flood; but Nineveh, God spared the whole city of Nineveh because they believed Jonah's warnings is from God.

In the time of Abraham, merciful ceased to plead with the guilty inhabitants of Sodom and Gomorrah and all but Lot with his household; wife; and two daughters escaped except Lot's wife couldn't she look back she became a salt pillar. But the rest of Sodom were consumed by fire from heaven. [Gen 19]. So in the days of Christ Jesus: The Son of most high God foretold to unbelieving Jews of that generation: "Your house is left unto you desolate!" [Matt 23: 38]. Israel did not recognize the precise time of the Christ, the Messiah coming to live in flesh in their midst daily. They saw signs; they heard his voice, and powerful performance in their eyes daily. Still they rejected him. And so it our burdens and obligation today of rejecting the Christ, the Messiah. God's begotten only Son dwelt on earth in flesh!. It is the serious offensive of the past: "Woe to the world! Because of offenses! "For the offenses must come; but woe to that man by whom the offense comes:" [Matt 18: 7].

Looking down to the last days the same infinite power declares; concerning those who received not the love of the truth that they might be save. For this cause God shall send them strong psychological delusion, that they should believe a malicious lies; that they all might be damned who believed not the truth; but had pleasure in unrighteousness!" [2 Thess. 2: 10-12]. As they reject the teaching of Christ' word truth, God withdraws His Spirit, and leaves them to the deceptions which they love as they chose. But Christ still intercedes in man's behalf and light will be given to those who truly seek it.

Although this was not at first well understood by all those who had gone before, it was afterward made plain as the scriptures which define their position began to open before them all. God's way prevailed. The passing of the time was followed by a period of great trial and tribulations persecution to those who still held faith in Christ Jesus followed by his disciples' foot-step examples. Their only relief so far ascertaining their true position was concerned was the insight light which directed their minds/hearts to the sanctuary above in heaven where Christ dwells into most high holy place in the presence of God Almighty. As has been stated earlier they were all with one code for a short time in the belief that the door of merciful was shut. This position was soon abandoned. Some renounced their faith in their former reckoning of the prophetic periods, and ascribed to human or Enmity Satanic agencies the powerful influence of the Holy Spirit which had attended the movement. Another class firmly held that the Lord God had led them in their past experience; and as they waited and watched and prayed to know the will of God, they saw that their great high priest had entered upon another work of ministration, and following him by faith, they were led to understand also the closing work of the church, and were prepared to receive and give to the world the warning of the third message of John at Patmos Island [Rev 14]. Also see [Leviticus 16: 29-30] Says: "In the seventh month on the tenth day of the month, you shall afflict your souls for on that day shall the priest make an atonement for you: To cleanse you, that you may be clean from all your Enmity sinful nature before the sight of the Lord God."

The earthly tabernacle was a figure for the time then present." [Heb 9: 9]. The earthly priest and services were] the example and shadow of heavenly things, as Moses was admonished of God when he has about to make the tabernacle: "For, see, said He, that thou make all things according to the pattern showed to thee in Mount Sinai." [Heb 8: 5]. **References:** [Matt 27: 50-51; Heb 9: 23; Dan 8: 14, &. 8: 17; Acts 17: 31; &. 2 Corinth 5: 10].

Today' modern world miss-out one of the most solemn warnings ever given in Scriptures is to be found in the thirteenth and fourteenth of the Book of last Revelation: What is the mark of beast? Enmity Satanic within our midst daily experienced today everywhere around the globe!. **Giants old of the renowned [Nephilim were in the earth]** and still exist today!. [Gen 6: 4] They grip anything by force and violence. They possess powerful Athanasius-John T. Nkomo machine-guns. When it will be given? Who receive it? And most important; what must you do in order to avoid receiving it? Who sales them?

This is a subject of overwhelming importance for today modern world to cautiously observe! It contains truths you should know better and adopt or embrace to heart! We are living in a world with very near to the end of time! Unfortunately, no one knows the day when it comes but Christ strongly warned: "When you see the green leave regenerating on a tree; you ought to know that the spring is here!" Signs tell us about that, and thinking men recognize that an immense is rapidly approaching! Men daily strife in vain today!. Violence increases daily everywhere! The whole earth is polluted with human blood! Enmity sinful overwhelmingly shows all its fullness existence! It grieves God's heart continually! [Gen 6: 5-6].

When the Lord Jesus Christ entered the most holy place of the heavenly sanctuary to perform the closing work of the atonement, He committed to his holy angels the last message of mercy to be given to the world! Such is the final warning of the third angel of Rev 14.] Immediately following its plausible proclamation, the Son of Man is seen by the last prophet [John] in Patmos Island prison where Jesus finally appeared, coming in glory to reap the harvest of the earth!

As foretold in the Scriptures, the ministration of Christ Jesus in the most holy place in heaven began at the termination of the prophetic to this day: To this time apply the words of the Book of

Revelation: It is the last Book. The temple of God was opened in heaven and there was seen in his temple the ark of His Testament. [Rev 11: 19]. The ark of God's Testament is in the Second Apartment of the sanctuary. As Christ entered there to minister in the Enmity sinful behalf, the inner temple was opened, and the ark of God was brought to view. To those who by faith beheld the Saviour Christ Jesus in his great work of intercessions; God's majesty and powerful were revealed! All the train of his glory filled the temple light from the holy of holies was shed upon his waiting people on the earth. Yes! John saw it all as he claims: They had strong faith followed their High Priest Christ Jesus from the holy to the most holy place, and they saw him pleading his blood below, the same that was spoken by God himself amid the thunders of Mount Sinai, and written with his own holy finger on the tables of stones: Hand flam flew upon it as he wrote; while Moses fearful watches. **"I AM The Lord God Almighty." [Exodus 20]:**

Not one command has been annulled: Not a jot or title has been changed: While the Lord God gave to Moses a copy or a duplicate of God's preserved the [Great Original] in the sanctuary above in heaven well secured kept. Tracing down its holy precepts, the seekers for truth found in the very bosom of the Decalogue, the fourth commandment as it was first proclaimed: "Remember the Sabbath Day to keep it Holy!" Yes! Moses saw. Six [6] days you shall work or labour; and do all your work; but the Seventh [day] is "Sabbath of the Lord your God: In it you shall not do any work: "You, nor your son, nor your daughter, your man-servant, nor your maid-servant, nor your cattle, nor your stranger-visitor that is within your house or gates: For in six days the Lord your God made heaven and earth, the sea-oceans, and all that in them is, and I rested the Seventh day, wherefore the Lord God blessed the [Sabbath-Day] and hollowed it!" [Exodus 20: 8-11]. Perfect Law: Stands still this day: No change! Christ Jesus came down from heaven to fulfill this Law!. [Matt 5: 17]. See also [John 1: 17-18]: "For the law was given through Moses, but grace and truth came through Jesus Christ!" No one else!

No one or any man has seen God at any time! The only begotten Son Jesus Christ, who is in the bosom of the Father; Christ has declared to see God for he came from heaven." See [Exodus 33:20; &. 1 John 4: 9]. Bible references evidence are so obvious.

The unique truth Spirit of the true Living God impressed the hearts/minds of these truly intrinsically of Bible studies either in theological; seminary; or any true religion sought after God's truth: The conviction was urged and it still being urged upon all, that they had ignorantly transgressed the holy commandment by disregarding its truth; and the Creator: God Almighty! How dare can be? A mere human being challenges God? This a subject that compel Enmity sinful with severe impending consequences upon all nations on earth as is written: **Why do nations rage? And the people plot a vain thing? The kings** of the earth set themselves: And the rulers take counsel together: Against the Lord God: And against the only **His Anointed [Christ]** saying: "Let us break their bonds in pieces! And cast away their cords from us!" Can they? Or could they? [Ps. 2: 1-3] However, they are actually breaking their own human cords and cast their own deaths! See also [John 1: 41 &. Luke 19: 14; Mark 3: 6; 11:18]…

Like all other generations up to this-day! They began to examine the reasons for observing God's law instead of the day which God had sanctified: They could find no Scripture evidence. They had been honestly seeking to know and do God's will, and now as they saw themselves transgressors of God's law; sorrows therefore filled their hearts as it is today; sorrows fill our hearts! Enmity sinful remains upon all: They indeed, at once evinced their loyalty to God by keeping Sabbath-Sunday holy; still not completely well-done but some pollution remains till this day defiling God's perfect law. Many and earnest were the efforts made to overthrow their faith. Non could fail to see if the earthly sanctuary was a figure or pattern of the heavenly, the law deposited in the ark on earth was an exact transcript of the law in the heaven and that an acceptance of the truth concerning the heavenly sanctuary involved an acknowledgment of the claims God's law; and the obligation of the true worship sanctified day. Commandment [Exodus 20]…

Here was the secret of the bitter and determined opposition to the harmonious exposition of the Scriptures that brought to view the ministration of Christ Jesus in the heavenly sanctuary. Arguments and disagreements is the function of Enmity sinful nature which God is eagerly compelled to eradicate at the precise set up time by God alone!. How hard men tried to close the door which God had opened, and to open the door which he had closed! He that opened and no man shut, and shut and no man opens. It is impossible mission with a mere man! Yes! Christ Jesus has opened the door, or ministration of the most holy place, light was shining and still shining this day from that open door of the sanctuary in heaven and earth; the commandment was shown to be included in the law within the ark; what God had established, no man could or can overthrow! The compelling question to ponder is: "Who may ascend into the holy hill of the Lord God? Or who may stand in his holy place?" [Ps. 24: 3-4]. Those who have accepted the light concerning the mediation of Christ Jesus and the perpetuity of the perfect law of God, found that these were the truths brought to view in the message. The angel declares: "Here are they that keep the commandments of God, and the faith of the Lord Jesus Christ." Past: Present: Future: All are under Enmity sinful righteous judgment!. This statement is preceded by the a solemn and fearful warning: "If any man worship the beast; Enmity Satanic and idol image; and receive his mark in his forehead or in his hand; the same shall drink of the poison wine of the wrath cup of God which is poured out without mixture into the cup of God's Indignation." [Rev 14:9-10].

An interpretation to the symbolized was necessary to an understanding of this vitally essentially message. It is about you! And it is about me! Of course; it is about all human beings on earth! No exclusion but all!.

What was represented to John at Patmos by Christ in person; by the [Beast] the image; the mark: Again those who were seeking for the truth returned to the intense study of the prophecies. In the last Book of Revelation: Under the symbols of a great red dragon, a leopard-like beast and a beast with lamb like horns [Rev 12: 13] are brought to view to the earthly rulers governments; who are the secular world Christendom; who are especially ever engaging; disobedience; disagreements; waging cold war's; intent ignoring God's law; injustice; abusive of God's law; unfairness-dealing business; terrorism; instill malicious fears; trampling upon God's law; persecuting true born again Christians; ignoring vulnerable poor; world organization such as U.N. ever failing resolving world issues in unity: divisions in churches: Everyone else is very much aware about the appalling existing issues; but who dares to care? That is the beast reference from Revelation: World ever experience severe violence far than during of the Nephilim old the renowned giants. Past: [Gen 6: 4] Thistle seed remains in its multiplications. No changes taken place:

Every age and generation never lived to please God! Their wars are carried forward to the close of the precise time end! The people of true God symbolized by a holy woman and her children are greatly in the minority. In the last days only a remnant exists. John at Patmos Island speaks of them as those that keep the commandments of God hand full of people: Not many! And have the testimony of Christ Jesus [Rev 12: 17]. Echoed Jesus: "A narrow road is difficulty to find! But it leads to everlasting life: The wide-broad road easy to find! But it leads multitudes of people to everlasting destruction!" Yes! Jesus foretold all! He hides nothing:

Athanasius-John T. Nkomo

Through the great Enmity sinful powers controlled by Satanic; ancient Roman paganism, and imitating the Judaism Pharisees; Sadducees; Stoics; Hellenists; the early century's pontiff papacy; symbolized by the dragon and leopard like-vicious beast roaring; Enmity Satanic for many centuries destroying all God's faithful witnesses: Church Reformers under the dominion of Rome, they were tortured and slain setting them on fire alive for more than thousand years; but the papacy was at last overthrown-down and deprived of its strength, and forced to desist from persecution. [Rev 13: 3; 10]. This is a subject that compels all forces of evil acts we experience daily on earth today. This book does not affiliates or compromise with any form of man's made denomination on earth! But it backs/supports true biblical prophetic and revelation of the Lord Jesus Christ!

At that time John confined; isolation at Patmos, Greek Island in prison he beheld a new power coming up; represented by the awful beast with lamb like horns. A greedy and cruelty creature ready to kill: The appearance of this beast and the manner of its rise seem to indicate that the power which it represents is unlike those brought to view under the preceding symbols. The great kingdoms that have ruled the world obtained their dominion by conquest strengths and cruel revolution, and they were presented to the prophet Daniel as beasts of prey, rising when the four winds of the heaven strove upon the great sea." [Dan 7: 2]. But the beast with horns like a lamb is seen coming up out of the earth [Rev 13: 11] signifying that instead of overthrowing other powers to establish itself; the nation thus represented arose in territory previously unoccupied; and grew up gradually and peacefully. There and here is striking Enmity sinful figure of the rising and growth of many current modern world notorious and fundamentalist nations. And the lamb-like horns, emblems of innocence and malicious-crafting-cunning gentleness; well represent the character of many secular world governments; as expressed in its-full two fundamental principles: Republicans: Democrats: Conservatives:

Labour': Factions: The Christian Exiles: Nationalism: Shits: Judaism: Islamic: Long list; mention few: The Christian exiles who fled from Europe to the third world: Africa: Asia and USA: Sought Asylum from royal oppressions and priestly intolerance and they determined to establish a government upon the broad foundation of civil and human made religious liberty as a nation to eventually creating slavery dominion as well as world-wide segregation-racial discrimination-apartheid that brought appalling humiliation for decades while God watches with suspicion eye. It was the function of Enmity sinful nature! Today; modern nations reap what they sowed: Terrorism instills fears spread intensifying daily everywhere around the globe: So much violence killing in domestic affairs to each state government either in Europe, Africa, Asia, and America press reports persist daily!. This is the subject you reap what you sowed:

These principles are the secret of each state government power and prosperity-prestigious as a nation on earth: Many millions from other lands have sought their shores and UK; USA; France; Germany; Russia; China; Cuba; have risen to a place among the most powerful nations of the earth today: Now Iraq and Iran are emerging with their nuclear weapon threats for Middle-East. God Almighty is watching with suspicion eye upon all those who claim super-powers upon earth today.

But the stern tracing of the prophetic truth reveals a change in this peaceful/violence scene: The beast with lamb like horns speaks with the voice of a dragon, and exercises or practices all power of the first beast before him. The spirit of persecution manifested by Roman paganism and the imitate pontiff papacy is again to be revealed. The prophecy plain proclaims that this power will say to them that dwell on the earth, that they should make an image to the beast: [Rev 13: 14]. The image is made to the first or leopard-like beast which one is brought to view in the third angel' message. By this first beast is represented the pontiff Rome

Church, an ecclesiastical body clothed with civil secular power, having authority to punish all dissenters. The image to the beast represents another man' made religious body clothed with similar power.

The formation of this image is the function of that beast whose peaceful rise and mild professions render it so striking a symbol of the United States: Here is to be found an image of the pontiff papacy. Human compromise-affiliation: When the churches of our modern world land uniting upon such points of faith as are held by them in common ground, shall influence the State to enforce their decrees and sustain their scholasticism institutions tool to shape character; then will Protestant America have formed an image of the Roman hierarchy. Compromise and affiliation with secular Christendom is most current modern world dangers. Then true church will be assailed by persecution as were God's ancient people. Almost every century furnishes examples of what bigotry and malice can do under a plea of serving God by protecting the rights of Church and State. Protestant churches that have followed in the steps of pontiff Rome by forming alliance with world powers have manifested a similar desire to restrict liberty of conscience. In the 17th century thousands of non-conformist ministers suffered under the true rule of the Church of England headed at [Canterbury]: Persecution always follows religious favoritism on the part of secular governments.

The beast [Satan] with lamb-like horns commands all, both; small and great nobles; rich and vulnerable poor; free and bond-slave; to receive a mark in their right hand; or their foreheads; and that no man might buy or sell; save he that had the mark or the name of the beast; or the number of his name." [Rev 13: 17]. This is the mark concerning which the 3rd angel utters his warning: It is the mark of the first or the pontiff papacy; and is therefore to be sought among the distinguishing characteristics of that power. Secular world scholars dispute this biblical teaching as they strive for their crafting teaching in their scholasticism tool shaping all those who follow after them for world success. The prophet Daniel vividly proclaimed that Raman Church, symbolized by the little horn was to think to change times and laws [Dan 7: 25] while Apostle Paul affirms-styled it the "man of sin of the perdition." [2 Thess. 2: 3-4] who was to be or who exalt himself above God: He sits into churches looking like God!" Only by changing God true-law could the pontiff papacy exalt itself above as they severely persecuted the true reformers during the years of the early century's; whoever should understanding keep the law as thus changed would be giving supreme honor to that power by which the change is made. Such an act of obedience to pontiff papal laws would be a mark of allegiance to the pope in the place of God Almighty. The papacy has attempted to change the law of God for centuries. Yes! There is 1.2 billion world' Christendom under Rome pontiff controls. The commandments forbidding image worship has been dropped from the law and the commandment has been so changed as to authorize the observation of the first of commandments: "You shall not worship anything on earth or under the ocean or moon; image: "I AM The Lord God Almighty] who brought you out from Egypt."

But men urge as a reason for omitting the Second Commandment; that it is unnecessary being included in the first and that they are giving the law exactly as God invented it to be well understood. This cannot be the change foretold by the prophet. An intentional, deliberate change is brought to view: "He shall think to change times and laws." For this change the only authority claimed is that of the church. Here the pontiff papal power only sets itself above God. The claim so often put forth that Christ changed the law, is disproved by Christ's own words: "I did not come to change the prophecy or destroy, but I came to fulfill it all!"

Furthermore Jesus affirms: "For verily I say unto you: Till heaven and earth pass; one jot or one title shall in no means pass from the law, till all be fulfilled!" [Matt 5: 17-19]. Who else should you take account seriously; the pope or Christ? I would take Christ's words seriously rather than pope a mere human being. I am well made like anyone else. God made me from dust and so to dust I shall return including the pope. Christ is lives eternally. He never slept under grave and awaits for the resurrection. His flesh never decayed! While the pope's flesh decays for years in the grave-yard! All men die on same manner because God determines:

At Beth Israel Deacon Medical Center: I challenged my PC Dr. who attempted to expostulate my ability in Scriptures: "You are not a doctor!. You disobey me! You are very wrong!" He said: Yes! You might be right I'm not: But you are skilled by train with limit: You cannot prevent anything even for yourself: You die like anyone else: Precise, you do not even know when your death will come: God determines your death doesn't him? You cannot prevent a disease to attack you can you? You do not sustain life do you? You are dust like anyone else, aren't you? You do not last forever, do you? He remained speechless like a mute: He was consumed with his own anger, then he walked away: I stood there watching him as he went away. I'm not sure how he took my sincere message. God knows.

The true fact of God is creative power it is cited throughout the Scriptures as proof that God of Abraham; Isaac; Jacob; and Israel is most superior to all heathen deities. Medic scientific has no answers when it is about human being nature. They strive to achieve for something that is beyond their human scope! The driving force conscience and motives is that they want to make a name for themselves in the medical professional field. Like the Babel Ziggurat Tower Genesis 11. How on earth can a mere man claims that he is able prolong life; when he is unable to prolong his own life? Why physicians deceive themselves and others? Through the powers of earth summon their forces to compel all, both small and great, rich and vulnerable poor, slave and free; receive the same mark of the beast, yet the people of true God do not receive it.

John at Patmos Island isolated prison; saw them that had gotten the victory over the [Beast] Enmity Satanic sinful and all over his wicked images; and over his mark, and over the number of his name stand on the sea of glass, having the harps of God Almighty. [Rev 15: 2] and singing the son of Moses led by Miriam his sister for all Israelites glorifying God Most High. [Exodus 15]: "I will sing to the Lord!" For He has triumphed gloriously! The horse and its rider; He has thrown into the sea!" The Lord is my strength and song!" [v1-2]. Also see [Is. 12: 1-6]. The blessed Israelites saw the greatest powerful work of God which the Lord had done upon the Egyptian nation in Egypt, and now at the Red Seas: So the Israelites feared the Lord God and they all believed the Lord God's truth including Moses.

And the Lord God went before them by day in pillar of cloud, and by night in pillar of fire to give light, so as to go by day and night. Yes! They saw God as their victorious triumphed. It shall be far worse victorious triumphs when Christ returns! And the world with Christ absolutely! Jesus Christ is inevitable! You ignore him at your own wicked risk:

Such were the tremendous momentous truths that had opened before those who received the 3rd angel's message. As they reviewed their experience from the first persecution of Enmity Satanic: The light from the heavenly sanctuary illuminated the past atrocities; the present; and the future! And they knew that the Lord God Almighty had perfectly led them by his unerring providence. Now with new great courage and firmer faith; they joined in giving the warning of 3rd angel! What had happened and said in the past; it also applies in our modern time today because we are the ancestors of past inheritance. And our God the Creator remains to be same forever! He never changes. We are the branches made in the law of God Almighty. The Lord God' commands by the same prophet; binds up the testimony, seal the law among God's people. [Is. 8: 16] The seal of God is found in the commandments. This only of all the ten, brings to view both name and the title of the true Lawgiver God alone! God's Law proclaims its own: "I am the Law of the Sabbath!"

To the law and to the testimony: While conflicting-Enmity doctrines and human theories to which all human rational and opinions, doctrines invented into their scholasticism theories are to be brought out! Says prophet Isaiah: "If they speak not according to this word, it is because there is no light in them!" [Is. 8: 20]. Again the command is given: "Cry aloud, spare not, lift up thy voice like a trumpet and show my people their transgression, and the house of Jacob their Enmity sinful nature!" It is not the wicked world! But those whom the Lord designates as "My people," that are to be reproved for their transgressions!" [Is. 58: 1-2]. The man himself is the cause of Enmity sinful! He is the trouble maker of his own! He destroys his-own-self because of his own Enmity sinful of which he is unaware! Here he is brought to view a class or status who thinks himself righteous, and appears to manifest great achievement interest in the service of God or Civic service: But the stern and solemn rebuke of the searcher of heart proves him to be trampling upon the divine precepts! The Lord Christ Jesus labels him as "hypocrites!" [Matt 23]. The prophet again; thus points out the ordinance which has been forsaken: "Thou shall raise up the foundation of many generations: And thou shall be called: "The repairer of the breach, the restorer of paths to dwell in!" If you turn away thy foot from the divine law, from doing thy pleasure on my holy day:" A delight the holy of the Lord honorable, and shall honor Him:" It is all applying for modern generation age. The past are dead and we live in their place. Above all we are their inheritance. Not so much differences. We carry on or walk on their footsteps-marks. Enmity sinful nature remains with all! Since the Church Reformation, there have been in every generation and age witnesses for God to uphold the standard of the past. Though often in the midst of reproach and persecution, a constant testimony has been borne to this truth:

Today, we live with great events! Also we live with great unresolved events! We are living in the most solemn period of this world's great history! The destiny of earth's teeming multitudes **[lost]** is about to be decided! Our own future destruction well-being and also the salvation of other lost souls depend upon the course which we now pursue: Popularity; power; great names; self-sufficiency; and great top discovery like the ancient Babel Ziggurat [Gen 11]:

We truly, desperately need to be guided by the Holy Spirit that can give of truth. Every born again follower of the Lord Christ Jesus should earnestly, intrinsically inquire or ask: "Lord Christ Jesus, what would you want me to do?" We need to humble ourselves before the Lord God our maker; and our sustainer, with fasting and earnest prayerful, and to mediate much upon Christ' words; especially upon the scenes of the righteous judgment mercy-seat. We should now seek a deep and living experience in the things of true living God in Christ Jesus:

We have not a moment to lose. Events of vital importance are taking place around us: We are on Enmity Satan's enchanted ground: Sleep not, sentinels of God; the foe is lurking near, ready at any moment, should you become lax and drowsy, to spring upon you and make you his prey!.

See the prodigal son who returns to his good-loving father empty handed: He had recklessly squandered all precious treasures given to him by his wonderful-loving father. Magnificent parable told by our Lord Christ Jesus: It relates God our maker and sustainer of life whose abundant providences we recklessly squander! [Luke 15: 17-22]. An extended invitation/appeal to all by Christ himself: "Come to me all you who labor and are heavy laden, and I will give you rest!. Take my yoke upon you and learn from me. For I am gentle and lowly in heart, and you will find rest of your souls!" [Matt 11: 28-30].

There are many Christians who are deceived as to their true condition before God. They congratulate among themselves upon the wrong acts which they do not commit, and forget to enumerate the good and noble deeds which God requires of them, but which they have neglected to perform. It is not good enough that they are green trees in the garden of God. They are to answer to God's expectation by bearing good-quality fruits which men can eat and God Himself as the owner of the garden. He indeed holds them accountable for their failure to accomplish all the good work which they could have done through his great merciful-seat, strengthening them to work. How you will face God on the last day of your righteous judgment when Christ returns? Something you need to grasp before Christ returns.

Every individual person, in the Books of heaven they are registered as cumberers of the ground. Yet the case of even this class is not utterly hopeless. With those who have slighted God's merciful and abuse His grace, the heart of long-suffering love yet pleads to God.

Wherefore he said: "Awake thou that sleep and arise from the dead!" And Christ shall give you light. See then that walk circumspectly redeeming the time, because the days are evil." [Eph. 5: 14-16]. Jesus Christ is inevitable! You ignore him at your own wicked risk. Enmity sinful will then cease. [Rev 22: 12-13; &. 2 Corinth 5: 10]

Chapter 8

Glossary
Enmity Big Unresolved Theme!

Other theories define Adam as: "Error; a falsity; the belief in "Original Sin," Sickness, and death; Evil; the opposite of good; of God and His creation, a curse; a belief in intelligent matter, finiteness and mortality; "Dust to dust;" Red sandstone; nothingness; the first god of mythology; not God's man; who represents the one God and is His own image and likeness; the opposite of Spirit and His creations; that which is not the image and likeness of good, but a material belief, opposed to the one Mind, or Spirit; a so-called finite mind, producing other minds, thus making "gods many and lords many" [1 Corinth 8: 5]; a product of nothing as the mimicry of something; an unreality as opposed to the great reality of spiritual existence and creation; a so-called man, whose origin, substance, and mind are found to be the antipode of God, or Spirit; an inverted image of Spirit, the image and likeness of what God has not created, namely, matter, sinful, sickness, and death, the opposer of Truth!" termed error; Life's counterfeit, which ultimate's in death; the opposite of Love; called "Hate;" the usurper of Spirit's creation, called self-creative matter-idol arts; immortality's opposite, mortality; that of which wisdom saith "Thou shall surely die!" [Gen 3: 19].

The name Adam represents the false supposition that Life is not eternal, but has beginning and end; that the infinite the finite intelligence passes into non-intelligence, and that Soul dwells in material sense; that immortal Mind results in matter, and matter in mortal mind; that the one God and Creator entered what He created, and then disappeared in the atheism of matter. God claims

Living God; not dead: "I AM, the God of: "Abraham; Isaac; and Jacob." [Exo. 3: 15]. He is not in the atheism matter: But living God made all the matters that exist. [Isaiah 66: 1-3. See John 1: 2; 4; 10]. How then you do not understand?

EVE: A beginning; mortality; that which does not last forever; a finite belief concerning life, substance, and intelligence in matter; error; the belief that the human race originated materially instead of spiritually; that man started first from dust, second from a man's rib "Adam" [Gen 2: 21-23:], and third from an egg or embryo. "Having eyes, do you not see? Having ears, do you not hear?" [Mark 8: 18] "How is it you do not understand?" Jesus asks his disciples several times. [v 21]. Spiritual discernment, not material but supreme mental!

God, Head-Father: Eternal Life; the One Mind; the Divine Principle, commonly called 'God!" The knowing of all things: Unlimited-Being everlasting Life! The Creator!

God: The Great "I AM!" the all-knowing; all-seeing; all-acting; all-wise; all-loving; and eternal; Principal; Mind; Soul; Spirit; Life; Truth; Love; all substance intelligence! **"I AM WHO I AM:"** "Before Abraham was:

"I AM!" Jesus said: [John 8: 58]. Echoes [Exo. 3: 14-15]. **One God! Powerful!** Controls the whole universal!

Gods: Mythology; a belief that life, substance, and intelligence are both mental and material; a supposition of sentient physicality; the belief that infinite Mind is in finite forms; the various theories that hold mind to be a material sense, existing in brain, nerve, matter; erring and mortal; the serpents of error, Enmity which say, "Ye shall be as gods!" [Gen 3: 5]. Malicious-crafting-cunning words: That can-never happen God is one, infinite and perfect, and cannot become finite and imperfect!.

Good: God; Spirit; omnipotence; omniscience; omnipresence; omni-action! **"I AM Who I AM!"** [Exo. 3: 14-15].

Indeed; God is one God, infinite and most perfect, and cannot become finite and imperfect. Never!

Enmity: What its meaning?

Heart: Conscience: Motives: Mortal: Feelings: Guilty: Affections: Joys: And Sorrows: Crafting: Cunning: Malicious: Hateful: Hostility: Disobedience: Rebellions: Grotesque: Gossip: Bitterness: [Love]? Verses-hateful: [John 3: 16]. Heart-Store.

Heaven: Harmony; the reign of God's Spirit; Government by Divine Principle; spirituality; bliss; the atmosphere of all Souls. But hell; mortal belief; error; eternal death; suffering and self-destruction; self-imposed agony; effect of Origin Enmity Sinful; that which "worketh abomination of desolation or maketh a malicious lie" The father of lies; original Enmity sinful self-imposed: [Gen 3: 15]. "From the beginning he is a murderer," Jesus said: [John 8: 44], he is the father of lies!" Enmity Satan, Devil." In other word: "He is the seed of lie." No truth can be found in him, lies, it is his nature! [Zerah-seed] original Hebrew word:

Lord: In the Hebrew-Phrase: This term is sometimes employed as a title, which has the inferior sense of master, language-differences-translations: Master or ruler. In the Greek Language [the word kurios almost] always has this lower sense, unless specially coupled with the name God. It's higher significant is Supreme Ruler. Well, God Rules too!

Lord God: Jehovah: This phrase or double term is not used or appear in the First Book of Genesis, the record of spiritual creation. Word utters. It is introduced in the Second Book of Exodus and following Third Book of Leviticus, when spiritual sense of God and of infinity is disappearing from the recorder's thought, when the true sense statements of the Scriptures become clouded through a physical sense of God as finite and corporeal. Some argue from this follow idolatry and mythology; belief in many gods, or material intelligences; as the opposite of the one Spirit, or intelligence, named [Elohim, or God] Hebrew word: Language translation causes grotesque arguments. Enmity sinful. One God only Rules the whole Universal. No other God: [Isaiah 45: 4-5]. **"Am God of Israel. And Israel My Elect" "There is no God beside Me!" [v 5].**

Matter: Mythology; mortality; another name for mortal mind; illusion; intelligence, substance, and life in non-intelligence and mortality; life resulting in natural death, and death in life; sensation in the sensation less; mind originating in matter; the opposite of truth; the opposite of Spirit; the opposite of God; that of which immortal mind takes no cognizance; that which mortal mind sees, feels, hears, tastes, and smells only in belief.

Man: The only thing God used hands to mold dust and shape man in His own-image and likeness: Well-perfected: Guaranteed eternal life: The compound idea of infinite Spirit; the spiritual image and likeness of God; the full representation of Mind-Soul living being. Belief deceitful: Intentional or unintentional or deliberate intent, disobeying God: Choice-matter; self-destruction; brought upon his own death: Including all his following offspring after him; generation to generations. Enmity self-imposed: Genesis 1: 1-30] God declared 7 times: "It is very good!" [Gen 3: 14-19] God pronounces: Imposing Enmity upon man: Judgment then, still on its process until Christ Jesus returns; because man still live in Enmity sinful nature as it was from the beginning!.

Serpent: Hebrew word: [nacash] Greek word: [ophis]: Enmity

Subtlety; malicious lie and origin of lies [father of it] the opposite of Truth, named error; the first statement of mythology and idolatry; the belief in more than one God; animal magnetism; the first malicious lie of limitation; infinity; the first claim that there is an opposite of Spirit, or good, termed matter, or evil, the first psychological delusion that error exists as fact, the first claim or original that Enmity sinful, sickness, and deaths are the realities of life a so-called "part of life," Its malicious lie because death was not there to begin with. Man was meant to life eternal life because God is eternal so He creates eternal life. Jesus Christ is best example. Christ replaces Adam. So, Jesus Christ existence is eternal in the place of Adam!.

The first audible claim that God was not omnipotent and that there was another power, named evil or Satan-Lucifer which was as real and eternal as God, good. Then, how/what had happened in heaven, that most perfect environment? [2 Thess 2: 3-4].

Finally:

Death: Other definition for death; an illusion, the lie of life in matter; the unreal and untrue; the opposite of Life.

Matter has no life; hence it has no real existence. Mind is immortal. The flesh, warring against Spirit, that which frets itself from one belief only to be fettered by another, until every belief of life where Life is not yield to eternal Life. Any material evidence of death is false, for it contradicts the Spiritual facts of being. God absolute Eternity!

Devil: Evil; a lie; error; neither corporeality nor mind; the opposite of Truth; a belief in Enmity sinful, sickness, and death; animal magnetism or hypnotism; the lust of the flesh, which saith: "I am life and intelligence in matter. There is more than one mind for I am mind, a wicked mind, self-made or created by a tribal god and put into the opposite of mind, termed matter, thence to reproduce a mortal universe, including man, not after the image and likeness of Spirit, but after its own image." Self-destruction by choice; opposing God the maker of all Life:

Dust: Nothingness; the absence of substance, life, or intelligence. Dust ground where man is taken. He returns to dust forever: Affects all men no exclusion. Death! [Gen 3: 19]. Enmity,

God Imposed upon man as deserved!.

Truth: God designed the human machine to run on himself! God is the fuel of our spirits; were designed to burn continually; without ceasing! God only determines to stop burning of our spirits-death it is absolute!

"In the sweat of your face you shall eat bread: Till you return to the ground: For out of it you were taken: "For you are dust: And to dust you shall return!" God Judged, sentences execution that stands continually till this day!. [Gen 3: 19]

Athanasius-John T. Nkomo

Chapter 9

The Pope, World's Religion Figure

How Then Can't he Heal Any Sickness Or Raises up Dead Like Saint Peter?
[Acts 3: 2-8 &. Acts 9: 36-42]

1. Peter and John: Born lame man healed [Acts 3: 2-8]

2. At Lydda; Aeneas bedridden for eight years healed [Acts 9:32]

3. At Joppa Tabitha Dorcas dead woman was raised [Acts 9: 36]

Then Peter said: "Silver and gold I do not have, but what I do have I give you: "In the name of Jesus Christ of Nazareth, "rise up and walk!"

And he took him by the right hand and lifted him up, and immediately his feet and ankle bones received strength. So he, leaping up, stood and walked and entered into the temple with them, walking, leaping, and praising God!." And all the people saw him walking and praising God. [v 9].

At Lydda, same thing Peter healed Aeneas who was paralyzed eight years: There he found a certain man called Aeneas who had been bedridden for eight [8] years and awful paralyzed. "And Peter said to him; "Aeneas Jesus the Christ heals you!" Arise and make your bed." Then he arose immediately. So all who dwell at Lydda and Sharon saw him and believed to the Lord. [Acts 9: 32-34]. Ref

1 Chro. 5: 16; 27: 29: 7. Acts 11: 21; 15: 19].

At Joppa; Saint Peter works great mysteries again:

There was a certain woman in the name of Tabitha which is translated as "Dorcas." This woman was full of all doing good [Ethic] works and charitable deeds and very generosity to the vulnerable widows poor which she performed daily. She sowed tunics and garments gave them to vulnerable widows and doing all necessary for them always.

Time passed by doing great good works in the eyes of God. She became sick eventually to her death. That time, Peter was still at Lydda not far from Joppa. The good news of miraculous healings that Peter performed in Christ' name spread to all neighborhood region fast like wild fire!. The people at Joppa sent two men to Peter imploring him not to delay in coming to them. Peter went with them. There Tabitha Dorcas lays dead at the sight while all the vulnerable widows sadly wept, when Peter arrived. Those vulnerable widows brought to Peter the evidence of Tabitha Dorcas performance during her life among them, showing Peter the tunics and garments she made for them Practical works Dorcas performed which all widows benefited, provided by Dorcas. Tears and sorrows filled their eyes and hearts. Tabitha Dorcas had made for them. What great memory they missed. Their genuine mourns deeply moved Peter as Christ Jesus had at Lazarus tomb where Jesus wept. [John 11: 35].

But Peter put them all out, and knelt down and prayed: And turning to the body he said: "Tabitha, arise!" And she opened her eyes, and when she saw Peter, she sat up.

Then he gave her his hand and lifted her up, and when he had called the saints and widows, he presented her alive. And it became known throughout all Joppa, and many people believed on the Lord God and praising. [Acts 9: 36-42]. See John 11:45.

The Vatican pontiff Pope is great world figure and

popularity. Is the pontiff real holy man like Peter?

He tours around the world in great extend prestigious as world religion figure representing 1.2 billion world Christians so well claimed that he leads as modern world shepherd exist leader.

The compelling question to ask: How then he is unable to heal the sick and raise up the dead like Saint Peter? How many sicken people did the pope heal, and how many did he raise from dead? Wherever he tours on earth as a most popular pontiff pope!.

If the pope is real God representative as he so well claims, why can't he heal those vulnerable sicken and dead people as Saint Peter did and all others who truly represented Christ Jesus in Holy Spirit? Why our religious leaders are not able to do that when they claim to have God's power as those in the past; like Prophet Elijah, Elisha, and other apostles; Saint Paul did miraculous mysteries in the name of the Lord Jesus Christ.

Evidence clearly proves that saint Peter and Paul were truly God's chosen men to perform God's works of their appointed days. They truly observed all God's perfect Law according to Christ like!. Peter then could perform miracles in the name of Christ Jesus the Savior of the World: Because the Holy Spirit was upon him as result he miraculously performed heavenly mysteries as Christ Jesus did. Nothing could hinder him because the Spirit of God was upon him. Is it offensive question to ask?

Does it surprises the world seeing the popular pope touring the world surrounded with sicken and dead people but he is unable to heal and restore life in the name of Christ Jesus, whom he so well claim to follow after his steps. 1. 2 billion world Christians whom he visits, but are spiritual dead!. The pope should set up that example as the world religion figure, restore life in the name of the Lord Christ Jesus. He would draw multitudes of people who are saved both physical and spiritually. This is what Saint Peter and others did during the early century's. Jesus Christ is alive! As they

[Thessalonians-Pharisees] rejected and disbelief the teachings of His word; God withdraws His Spirit and leaves them to the deceptions which they love. [2 Thess. 2: 10-12]. Although this was not well understood by those who truly preached the gospel it was afterward made plain as the Scriptures which defined their true position began to open before them. It is exactly the same character even today for many claim to be world Christians figure extrinsically!. They cannot perform heavenly miraculous mysteries like Saint Peter!.

The passing of the time was followed by a period of great trial to those who still held the true faith in Christ Jesus; rather than faking tradition denomination teachings. It has not worked in the past, neither has it worked in the present day!. Enmity it is inescapable in the midst and hearts of many anti-Christ!. Those who live by faith follow Christ Jesus in the great work of the atonement receive the benefits of His mediation in their behalf; but those who disbelief and reject the light that brings to view this work of ministration, are not benefited thereby. The Pharisees Jews who rejected the given light by Christ Jesus, and refused to believe in Christ as Messiah expected of the world, could not receive pardon through Christ neither. So is 1.2 billion world Christians so claimed cannot receive pardon through Christ neither!. Otherwise the world on which we live today, would be a better world to live!.

So in the days of Christ: The Son of God will unveil to the unbelieving Pharisees Jews as well as Gentiles secular world of that generation: "Your house is left unto you desolate." [Matt 23: 38]. Looking down to the last days, the same infinite power declares concerning those who received not the love of the truth that they might be saved." Jesus Christ is inevitable!. Men cannot afford with impunity reject or ignore the true living God; the warnings which God in merciful gives us. Jesus Christ greatest Man was sent from heaven to the world! The people whom he came to show full merciful through his own sacrificial yet men dare not to receive him with heartfelt-embrace open arms. The same issue today! Our only relief so far as ascertaining our true position is concerned, is the light which directs our minds/hearts to the sanctuary above extrinsically. There is no other way so, Jesus well claims: "I am the way, the truth, and life! No one comes to the Father except through Me!" [John 14: 6]. Guarantees!

No way to heaven for hypocrites!. [Matt 23].

The position was soon abandoned: Some renounced their faith in their former reckoning of the prophetic periods, and ascribed to human tradition or satanic agencies the powerful Enmity sinful influence opposing the Holy Spirit; he is sitting in temple exalting himself he looks like God: [2 Thess. 2: 3-4]. Beware! Enmity Satanic roars like lion-prey. His hunger for vulnerable poor deer, he eagerly pants for it!. Yes! Satan pants for you:

The pontiff Rome cannot restore life or heals the sick. His popularity is showing himself on world tourism. 1.2 billion world' Christians: "Let the dead bury their own dead!" Jesus said, [Matt 8: 22]. "Follow Me!" Said Christ Jesus:

One of the most solemn of God's warnings ever written in Scripture and given to the people upon earth is to be found in the Exodus 20: Rev. 13 and 14 chapters: What is the Mark of the Beast or Enmity? The perfect Law: When will it be given? God opened His Mouth: He Spoke Plainly: The whole Mount Sinai was shaken!. The Israelites hearts mechanism melted with fear!. And God wrote His Perfect Law by His powerful Hand!. Who will receive it? And most important; what must you and me do in order to avoid receiving it? "God's perfect Law," it is not human tradition faking laws: This is a subject of overwhelming importance!. It contains practical truth-facts you and I should know. We are living very near the end of time yet; no one knows when it comes; and thinking men recognize that an immense crisis is rapidly approaching!. Jesus Christ is indeed, inevitable! If individuals and humanity are to progress; Jesus Christ is inescapable!. You ignore him at your own wicked risk. What we see and hear today? It is a sinking world! Like Titanic Ship sank into "Deep Indian Ocean." All aboard perished! No survivors!

When Jesus Christ entered into the most Holy place of heaven stands on the right hand of Mighty God Heavenly Sanctuary to perform the closing work of the atonement: He committed to His holy angels the **[Last Message of Merciful]** to be given to the whole entire world!. Such is the final overwhelming warnings of the 3rd angel in [Rev. 14-backs up vigorously Exodus 20 of Mount Sinai; where God's infinite forceful word was uttered. Enmity ought to be ultimately eradicated radical! Jesus Christ is the Man set up for performing heavenly miraculous mysteries once and for all! Why should you believe it when you are actually a secular world Christendom: It is given to those who were chosen from the foundation of the world. They believe truth as God's angels remind them.

In the Book of Exodus under the symbol of a great red dragon, a leopard like beast and a beast with lamb like horns [Rev 12: 13] are brought to view those on earthly secular governments which are especially engaged in trampling upon God's perfect Law persecuting saints and deceiving common vulnerable peoples as subjects under their feet. They are satanic agents on earth. And the Vatican pontiff imitates the character in compromise. Through the great powers controlled by Rome paganism and the pontiff papacy, symbolized by the dragon and leopard like beast, Enmity Satan for centuries destroyed God's faithful saints and witnesses on earth till this day!. 1.2 billion follow after him while they see him as God's representative exalting himself in popularity world tourism. Yet he is unable to heals the sicken and restore life, like saint Peter and Paul who truly observed God's Law were able to heal the sicken and restore life, in the name of Christ Jesus!. They did not compromise with earthly things. [Rev 13: 11]. Signifying that instead of overthrowing other powers to establish itself. The nation thus represented arose in territory previously unoccupied and grew up gradually and peacefully.

Here is a striking figure of the rise and growth of our own nation. And the lamb like horns, emblems of innocence and gentleness, well represent the character of our government, as expressed in its two fundamental principles: Republican; Democrat; and Protestantism!. The Christian exiles who first fled to America, sought an asylum from royal oppression pontiff priestly intolerance, and they determined to establish a government upon the broad foundation of civil and religious liberty-symbol New York City. Torch up-lifted on man' made island. It shows shallow unfulfilled in practice. The principles are the secret of our power and prosperity as a nation: Yet it never last-long life in the eyes of God!.

To the perfect law and to the testimony: While Enmity conflicting human tradition doctrines and theories contradicting God's truth abound the law of God is the one unerring standard to which all opinions, doctrines, and theories are to be brought. Yet the prophet, says: "If they speak not according to this word, it is because there is no light in them." [Is. 8: 20]. Again the command is given; "Cry aloud, spare not, lift up thy voice like a trumpet, and show my people their awful transgression, and the house of Jacob their Enmity sinful." It is not the wicked world, but those whom the Lord designates as "My people," that are to be reproved for their transgressions. On the other hand; the world is not wicked but those who dwell-therein are wicked defiling the world!. These words apply and show in the Christian ages as is shown by the context: "The Lord God which gathered the outcasts of Israel said: "Yet will I gather others to him, beside those that are gathered unto him." [Is. 56: 8]…

Here again is foreshadowed the gathering in of the outcasts Gentiles by the gospel. And upon those who then honor the pontiff, and the state secular world faking laws!. Therefore, the pontiff fails to heal the sick and raise up the dead like Saint Peter and Paul did during the early centuries. They did this in the name of Jesus Christ whom the pontiff Rome extrinsically claims the leader of 1.2 billion dead Christians as past Pharisees!. The modern Protestant Church shifts to this truth in compromise with secular world material wealth accumulation. God still command by the same prophet: "Bind up the testimony! "Seal the Law among my peoples!." [Is. 8: 16] The seal of God's Law is found Mount Sinai in the fourth Commandment [Exodus 20]. This only of all the "Ten Commandments" bring to view both the name and the title of the "Lawgiver!." Indeed: It obviously declares God's Sovereignty: The Creator of Heaven: The Earth: And the Oceans: And all human kind dwelling therein. Thus shows His perfect claim to reverence and worship Him in Spirit and Truth above all others! No one else:

"But the hour is coming; and now is; when the true worshipers will worship the Father in Spirit and truth;" Jesus said: "For the Father is seeking such to worship Him: "God is Spirit, and those who worship Him must worship Him in Spirit and truth!" [John 4: 23-24]. Jesus Christ affirms the Mount Sinai proclamation. [Exodus 20: 2-4]. "I am the Lord your God!"] "I brought you out of the land of Egypt!" God's claims to reverence and worship above all others! Aside from this precept, there is nothing in the Decalogue to show by whose authority the Law is given!. "I AM Your God who brought you out of the land of Egypt." No one else! Jesus Christ fulfilled this truth on earth in flesh voice utterance. Yet filled in Spirit. [Is. 61: 1]. "The Spirit of the Lord is upon Me!" Jesus said: "Because the Lord has anointed Me!. To preach good tidings to the poor!." He has sent Me to heal the brokenhearted; to proclaim liberty to the captive and the opening of the prison to those who are bound!." Enmity sinful! Set them free! Jesus declared: See Luke 4: 18-19]. Words are fulfilled: The true disciples of the Lord Jesus Christ are called upon to restore it in the fulfillment of the Lord Jesus Christ the center of all life on earth to exalting His holy name until Christ returns. The fourth commandment of Exodus, to its rightful position as the Original Creator of all forms of life in heaven and on earth. He is the [Central Factor's Memorial] and the sign of His rightful authority. Jesus Christ is inevitable!

The Holy Bible is a Great Treasure House of all precious truth! How deeply thankful we can be that such powerful word from the mouth of the living God information is before us, to read and preserve, register it to heart forever. The word gives us eternal life. Nourishing our souls and feel no more hunger that God's word feeds us from his mouth. [Matt 4: 4]. "It is written." Jesus said: To refute such arguments it was needful only to cite the teachings of the Bible and the history of the Lord God dealings with His peoples in all ages: God works through those who hear and obey His voice-word, those who will, if need be, speak unpalatable truths, those who do not fear God to reprove popular Enmity sinful.

The reason why God does not often chose men of highly learning or educated and with high position-prestigious is, that they trust too much to their creeds, theories, and theological systems, and feel no need to be taught of God one who possesses all wisdom. Only those who have a personal connection with the source of God's wisdom are able to fully understand or explain the Holy Scriptures. God gives them the Holy Spirit of wisdom and ability to heal the sick and raise up the dead. Men who have much less education, such as Peter, a fisherman; with little of the learning of the human schools are called to proclaim the truth, not because they are unlearned, but because they are not too much self-righteous; self-sufficient to be taught of God who possesses all knowledge and all wisdom; and the creator of all wisdoms in heaven and on earth. They learn far much better in the heavenly school of Christ Jesus; meekness; and their humility and obedience make them greater; heal the sicken and raises up the dead. Human scholasticism tool, shapes shallow-negative, assumptions and meaningless-purpose that never last. "You will know them by their fruits," Jesus said:

In committing to them a knowledge of His truth, God confers upon them an honor, in comparison with which earthly honor and human greatness sink like titanic ship into insignificance measure of the world. They never last!. When the Thessalonians church received erroneous views concerning the Second coming of Christ, the Apostle Saint Paul counseled them to be more carefully test their hopes and anticipations by the word of God. Saint Paul cited them to prophecies revealing the events to take place before Christ should come, and showed that they had no ground to expect Christ soon in their day: [2 Thess. 2: 3-4]. Beware modern world because we are current experiencing same arguments of deceitful. Thousand years is like yesterday in the eyes of God. See Ps. 90].

There was a certain man from Ramathaim, a Zuphite from the hill country of Ephraim, whose name was Elkanah. He had two wives one was called Hannah and other Peninnah: Peninnah had children, but Hannah had no children. There was great rival among them. So, Hannah lived a miserable life. Longing to have Athanasius-John T. Nkomo **a male child she wept bitterly praying unto God's temple where Eli ministered as priest. [1 Sam 1: 10-18]**

And she made a vow, saying; "O Lord Almighty, if you will only look upon your servant's misery and remember me, and not forget your servant but give her a son, then I will give him to the Lord for all the days of his life, and no razor will ever be used on his head." [v 11].

Hannah, the mother of Samuel Elkanah's wife: God granted her petition. God indeed, gave her a son: She named him Samuel saying; **"Because I asked to God for him." [v.20].** After she had weaned him, she brought him to God as promised to serve God all his life. And the boy Samuel ministered to God all his life as prophet, priest, and Judge in the house of Israel for all his life. God was with him throughout of his life. "Samuel, Samuel; God called him three times. Then Samuel said; "Speak Lord for your servant is listening." He was just a little boy when God called him.

Samuel, the first Judge; prophet; and priest ordained by God himself to rule this great nation, Israel. He ruled for 40 years!. All neighborhood kings could dare not invade Israel because they feared God who protected them. They heard all the signs which God did to Pharaoh in Egypt; Og, king of Amorites/Moabites and Red Seas opened its mouth to dry land and let Israel walk through while Pharaoh's chariots and horsemen; God wiped them all, and saw them floating by the sea-shore. Their stomach melted like ice. "When we heard all what your God has done at the Red Seas, and to all kings; our hearts melted." Rahab said; she is a harlot. [Josh 2: 8-12]. The history of Israel is phenomenal-psychological striking illustration of the ancient riches of corruptions and most provocative in the sight of God Almighty; intensively reproaching God the maker of all goodness and sustainer of all life; it was in the days of Moses in Egypt and in Exodus wilderness for a period of 40 years long in wilderness wanders. Almost all of the elder peoples who left Egypt were not clean at all in hearts but bitterness-sours which they carried through. As result they all perished in the wilderness with all their pollutions. Meanwhile, God raised up the young generation born in the wilderness to reach unto the Promised Land. Thus the old generation needed to be cleaned, but they resisted against God.

Those who persist in this notorious error will at last fix future for the coming of Christ Jesus. God could not allow them to enter unto the land with their polluted hearts. Thus they too will be led to rest in a false undeceived until it is too late, like today modern world's error. In the great disappointment their faith was severely tested but not beyond their scope was that at Red Seas. As always God knew what would fall or come upon them. In like manner, it was not the will of God that coming of Christ should be so long delayed and people should remain so many years in this world of sinful and sorrow. There shall never be any rest until man fully repents. But unbelief separated them from God like us today, are fully separated from God. In the merciful to the world, Christ Jesus delayed his coming, that sinners may have an opportunity to hear the word and come to full repentance of warnings and find in him shelter before the wrath of God shall be poured out on earth. The whole entire earth ought to heed the word of final warnings. When Hiram King of [Sidon or Tyre] heard Solomon's message, he was very greatly pleased and said, "Praise be to the Lord today for he has given David a wise son to rule over this great nation Israel." [1 Kings 5: 7] At the same time Solomon had first dealt with his enemies; within the David's family: He was old man and well advance in age; so he was ever cold no matter how many covers they put on him he couldn't keep warm himself. So, they found Abishag, the Shunammite girl; she was a beautiful, and brought her to the king.

Solomon's Enemies Dealt:

1. Joab, the son of Zeruiah; he killed Abner the son of Ner and Amasa.

2. Shemei, the son of Gera the Benjamite, because he curse King David as he got old

3. Adonijah, he asked Abishag the Shunammite to be his wife. Solomon saw Adonijah to be great threat and rival to overthrow him from the throne which he inherited from his father, King David.

4. Joab for conspiring with Adonijah though not with Absalom, he

fled to the tent of the Lord and took hold of the horns of the altar. King Solomon ordered Benaiah son of Jehoiada, "Go, strike him down!" So, Benaiah did as told.

"Let Abishag the Shunammite be given in marriage to your brother Adonijah." Bathsheba said to her son Solomon. Appeasing on behalf of Adonijah: Solomon answered his mother: "Why do you request Abishag the Shunammite for Adonijah? You might as well request the kingdom for him, after all he is my older brother; yes for him and for Abiathar the priest and Joab son of Zeruiah!"

Then Solomon swore by the Lord: "May God deal with me, be it ever so severely if Adonijah does not pay with his life for this request! And now; as surely as the Lord lives, he who has established me securely on the throne of my father David and has founded a dynasty for me as he promised; Adonijah shall be put to death today!" [1 Kings 2: 21-25].

The kingdom was now firmly established in Solomon's hands. Eli the priest with his two son; Hophni and Phinehas were now all dead according to God's prediction. It was after many years past for Eli failing to discipline his two sons who were wicked in the eyes of God.   [v.34]. God's word was fulfilled. See verses 27-33] at the time Israel, had no human king to run on their daily affairs, until Samuel was in his advance age, then they came to ask Samuel for a human king. One God's family choice with severe grief's: They became great nation on earth till this day.

And what is our duty in view of this? Shall we conclude that the truth ought not to be presented, since its effect is so often to arouse men to evade resist its claims? Is God wrong? No; we have no more reason for withholding the testimony of God's word truth because it exists and excites opposition than had Christ Jesus, his disciples, the apostles and reformer Martin Luther.

Martin Luther; declared himself to have been urged on, compelled by the Holy Spirit of God, to battle against the evils of his time; and in the same manner must we still carry on forward the work of reform until Christ returns. Let God in Christ be the righteous Judge.

To the righteous servants of God at this time is the command addressed: "Lift up your voice like a trumpet, and show my people their transgression and the house of Jacob their Enmity sinful." Yes! The true followers of Christ Jesus do not wait for truth to become popular. Being convinced of their duty, they deliberately accept the cross and thus remove the greatest obstacle to the reception of truth, the only argument which its advocates have been able to refute in past; present; and future.

It is weak, inefficient world-servers that think it praiseworthy to have no principle in religious things. We need to choose the right because it is right, and leave consequences with God. To men of principle, faith and daring, is the world indebted for its great corruptions reformed! Jesus Christ is inevitable!

By such men must the work of reform for this day of time be carried forward!

Christ Jesus the most wise and Powerful of God: "For the message of the cross is foolishness to those who are perishing, but to us who are being saved it is the power of God. For it is written:

"I will destroy the wisdom of the wise; the intelligence of the intelligent I will frustrate." Where is the wise man? Where is the scholar? Where is the philosophy of this age? Has not God made foolish the wisdom of the world? For since in the wisdom of God the world through its wisdom did not know him, God was pleased through the foolishness of what was preached to save those who believed:" [Is. 29: 14-15; 1 Corinth 2: 19-21; Matt 15: 8-9].

Thus said the Lord God: "Listen unto Me; you that know righteousness, the people in whose heart is my law; fear ye not the reproach of men, neither be ye afraid of their reviling's. For the moth shall eat them up like a garment, and the worm shall eat them like wool; but My righteousness shall be forever; and My salvation from generation to generation!" [Is. 51: 7-8]. The Bible is God's word unique truth! God's word prevails forever! It sustains life on earth and in heaven. All men's wisdom is sinking sand! Will not last! All men die and return to dust where God took the man Adam: The character-instinct and tendency of modern man rival/revivals has awakened no little anxiety-obnoxious in thoughtful minds among all denominations; scientific; technology and religious including all secular world governments: Many of the rival/revivals which have occurred during the last 10th, centuries have given no evidence of the work of the Spirit of God! The real true light which flames up for a time, soon dies out, leaving the darkness denser than ever before! Jesus Christ will indeed bring the ultimate world's illuminating light once and for all! He is inevitable! For the Spirit of the Lord God is upon him forever! He is the Master-mind and Lord of all redemptions!

Popular revivals are too often carried by appeals to the imagination, by exciting the emotions, by pandering to the love for what is new and startling nerves. Converts thus gained have no desire to listen or hear to Bible truths: any more interests in the testimony of prophets and apostles, real-true written Christian books than has the novel-reader. Unless a religious service has something of sensational-entertainment characteristic; and it has no attractions for them either! A message which appeals to unimpassioned reason awakens no response to our young adults today: They are like ice on their cold shoulders and hearts. The plain warnings of God's word, relating directly to their eternal interests fall as upon the ears of the dead: So Christ affirms: "Let the dead bury their own dead!." [Matt 8: 22]. "Can a dead man think or reason?" John Pipe said. One who speaks truth he is their enemy and offender. The converts are renewed in heart or changed in character. They do not renounce their selfish-pride, love, conscience, and motive, of the world. Their seeds are naturally fixed up forever. "You will know them by their fruits!" A skunk cannot change its own stings-shape! Neither the leopard can change its own spotted color. So God destroys the wisdom of the wise. They are no more willing to deny self-spotted color like leopard, to take up the cross, and follow Christ Jesus, the meek and lowly gentle heart than before their conversion. Enmity sinful overwhelming dominates upon them. In a genuine revival when the Spirit of God convicts the conscience, the earnest, anxious inquiry will be heard: "What must I do to be saved?" Then God puts a new different seed at his will. And this is not merely for a day. With every truly converted soul the relation to God and to eternal things will be the great topic of life. "You become a new creation in Christ Jesus. New seed God puts in, changes individual life to become new. Yes! God is able in Christ Jesus. Nothing is difficulty for God.

But where in the popular churches of to-day! Is the deep conviction of Enmity sinful? Where is the spirit of consecration to God? The spirit that controls the world rules in the church today! Human religion has become the sport of infidels and skeptics because so many who bear its name are ignorant-obnoxious grotesque of its principles. So, much in appropriate operational perspective!.

The power of godliness has well-nigh departed from the churches to-day! Heart union with Christ Jesus is very rare thing now! The majority of church-members know no tie but that which joins them to an organized body of professed Christians. Often times we rephrase the tem: Love of pleasure and thirst for excitement are everywhere prevalent. At times it sounds meaningless. The Lord Christ Jesus would not affiliate with world excitement and pleasure!. But he became a man of sorrows. Yet he came to his own. Picnics church theatricals, church fairs, fine houses, personal display, have banished thoughts of God. Lands and goods and worldly occupations engross the mind, and things of eternal interest receive hardly a passing notice. To-day attitudes snares God's true and embrace world's atrocities. Yes, pleasure-lovers may have their names upon the church-records today, they may stand high as worldly-wise men; but they have no connection with Christ Jesus of lowly Calvary. It is our challenge today modern age; but who cares or notice? Neither did they care about John's warning; "prepare the way for the Lord." Neither did they care about Noah; "Let us build the ark." Finally Christ came, neither did they care: The challenge, and warning stand among us today, neither have we cared. Those who care, they receive eternal salvation.

Paul describes a class who are "Lovers of pleasures more than lovers of God: concerning about them Paul said: "From such turn away." Be not deceived by them, do not imitate their practices." [2 Tim 3: 4-5]. Notwithstanding the wide-spread declension of faith and piety in the churches, the Lord still has honest faithful believers among them and before Christ' judgments shall be visited upon the earth, many ministers and lay-members will separate from these bodies, and gladly receive the special truths for this time. The enemy Enmity sinful of souls desires to hinder this work, and before the time shall come for such a movement, he will arouse what appears to be great religious interest in the churches.

They will exult that God is working marvelously for them, when the work is that of another spirit. Under a religious guise, Enmity Satan will spread his influence over the land. He hopes to deceive many by leading them to think that God is still with the churches. Satan is well skilled to deceive many as it is his nature from the beginning. He possesses world wisdom to craft-cunning purpose. He intends to achieve it with great world's power which never last. Many will follow after him as they did before till this day. The whole entire secular world governments are under Satan control. These secular world governments are Satan agents. You know them by their fruits. But Satan cannot over-come God Almighty. He is wounded under Christ Jesus feet!

The excitement manifested is well adapted to mislead the unaware young adults: Yet none need be deceived. In the light of God Almighty; word it is not difficulty to determine the nature of these religious movements. The history of God's dealings with his people in the past testifies that His Spirit is not poured out upon those who neglect or oppose God's warnings sent them by true prophets. King Solomon first dealt with his enemies in order to establish his government according to God's prediction early before Solomon succeeded his father David to the throne.

And by the rule which Christ Jesus himself has given; "You shall know them by their fruits." It is evident that these movements are not the work of the Spirit of God Almighty. So they never last!.

Nicodemus! Jesus said: "Unless a man be born again, he cannot see the kingdom of God!. Nicodemus, a Pharisee, a council of the Jews needs a new seed to become a new creation that Christ Jesus could give! [John 3: 3] For to set the mind on the flesh is death; but to set the mind on the Spirit is life and peace. For the mind that is set on the flesh is hostile to God, for it does not submit to God's law; indeed, it cannot! Those who are in the flesh can never please God Neither!

[Rom 8: 6-8]. Nicodemus, a Pharisee fully understood what the Lord Christ Jesus described him. He got save. Do you want to get saved? Be wise like Nicodemus. He chose right. [John 3: 16].

The doctrine of sanctification or perfect holiness, which fills a prominent place in some of human made religious movements of to-day, is among the causes that have rendered modern secular world rival revivals so ineffectual. True sanctification is a Bible doctrine which God himself speaks. The disciples and apostles in particular, saint Paul a former Pharisee zealous declared to the Thessalonians church; "This is the will of God, even your sanctification." [1 Thess. 4: 3] and again Paul prayed the very God of peace sanctify you wholly, and I pray God your whole spirit and soul and body be preserved blameless unto the coming of our Lord Christ Jesus." [1 Thess. 5: 23]. So it was in the days of Samuel, he prayed for the whole Israel to be sanctified. [1 Sam 8-12].

But the sanctification now so widely advocated is not that brought to view in the Holy Scriptures. It is false in theory, and dangerous in its practical results. This modern generation like the past; is ever opposing, and rejecting God Almighty. Enmity sinful will persist until Christ returns. Modern scholasticism, tool shapes both behaviors either positive or negative-operational condition. Nowadays!. Its advocates teach that the law of God is a grievous yoke and that by faith in Christ, men are released from all obligation to keep God's Commandments. The Bible sanctification is a conformity to the will of God, attained by rendering obedience to his perfect law through faith in the Lord Jesus Christ!.

The Lord Jesus Christ prayed for the disciples and those who believe through their teaching: "Sanctify them by your truth! Your word is truth!" [John 17: 17]. There is no genuine sanctification except through obedience to the truth! God's word that sanctify souls is truth!. "You have done foolishly!" [1 Sam 13: 13] Samuel said to Saul. Saul disobeyed God' Command. "Thy Law is the truth." [Ps. 119: 142.] The law of God is the only standard of moral perfection. The law was exemplified in the life of Christ Jesus. He well affirmed: "I have kept my Father's Commandments." [John 15: 10].

Spurious sanctification carries with it a boastful, self-righteous spirit which is foreign to God's sight: Meekness and humility are the fruits of God's true Spirit. Daniel the prophet was is an example of true sanctification. His long life was filled up with noble service for the Lord God. It is only when the law of God is set aside, and men have no standard of right, no means to detect Enmity sinful, that erring mortals can claim perfect holiness! But let none deceive themselves with the belief that God will accept and bless them while they are willfully violating one of God's requirements of his perfect law. There are severe impending consequences on the Last Day!.

The commission of a known Enmity sinful silences the witnessing voice of God's Spirit, and separates the souls from God: Jesus Christ will honor those only who honor Him. Whosoever committed sin transgressed also the law: For Enmity sinful is the transgression of the law. Whosoever abide in him cannot commit Enmity sinful: Whosoever commits Enmity sin transgress the law hath not seen Him!. **Neither known Him:"** [1 John 3: 4-6].

During the early centuries church there were those who joined the church like today are many who confine into churches; government; civic center leaders law makers; businessmen; scientists; claim so fully upon love [John 3: 4-6], yet John does not hesitate to reveal the true characteristic of that class who claim to be fully sanctified while at the same time living in transgression of the perfect law of God Almighty: And they contend that they are justified to be forgiven their Enmity sinful nature!. "He that said Lord, Lord I know Him and keeps not His Commandments is a liar!" And the truth is not in him."

[1 John 2: 4]. Affirming Christ' word: "Not all who call me Lord, Lord!." You will know them by their fruits:"

Sanctification is believed by many to be instantaneously accomplished. "Only believe," say they, and the blessing is yours." No further effort on the part of the receiver is supposed to be required. But the Scriptures teach that sanctification is progressive process. Christian will feel the promptings of Enmity sinful, but he will keep up a constant warfare against the Enmity sinful nature until Christ returns. Here is where Christ Jesus help is desperate needed!. With Christ' help you can do all!.

Satan asked for Peter to sift him like wheat! Christ Jesus prayed for him [Luke. 22: 31-32]. Peter was restored and strengthened in Spirit! Judas Iscariot, was not restored!. Neither were the Pharisees; Scribes, and Sadducees, Sanhedrin, Priest as well Pilate and Herod!. They were joiners on high rank church it is the same thing even today era!.

Human beings weakness becomes to divine strength and faith exclaims: "Thanks be to God, who gives us the victory through our Lord Jesus Christ!" It was for Saint Peter's victory and all others who followed after him like Saint Paul!. [1 Corinth 15: 57]. Saint Paul exhorts other brethren, "Who work out your own salvation with fear and trembling,' [Phil 2: 12] and concerning himself, he affirms: "I press on toward the mark for the prize of the high calling of God in Christ Jesus!" [Phil 3: 14]. "For me to live is Christ! And to die is gain."

The successive steps in the attaining of Scriptures sanctification are set before us in the words of Peter: "Giving all diligence, add to your own faith, virtue; and to virtue knowledge; and to knowledge temperance; and to temperance; patience; and to patience; godliness; and to godliness, brotherly-sister-kindness; and to brotherly kindness; charity." It is progressive process. As Christ strengthens your faith: Satan is after you to sift you like wheat!. You need Christ to pray for your strength as you progress in faith. "Abide in me," Jesus said: Wherefore the rather brethren, give diligence to make your calling and election sure; for if you do these things, you shall never fall!" [2 Pet 1: 5-7, 10].

This is a daily hard work continuing as long as life shall last according to your numbered days. God determines your last day. Jesus Christ is inevitable!

Spurious sanctification carried with it a boastful, self-righteous spirit which is Enmity sinful to the Spirit of God in Scriptures: Meekness; lowly- humility are the fruits of Holy Spirit. His long life was filled up with noble service for the Master. Jesus Christ meekness-lowly-gentleness human beings ever fail to attain! How then a mere man dares to claim to be sanctified before Christ' guarantees: It is all in his power for such guarantee. Hypocrites how dare you? You ought to tremble before Christ Jesus the ultimate righteous Judge!.

He was a man greatly beloved: Heavenly and granted such honors as have rarely been vouchsafed to mortals. Yet his purity of characteristic and unwavering fidelity were equaled only by his humility and contrition. Examine where he was born into animal stable and laid on a manger. His life style had no pillow to lay on his head yet slept under the shadow of a tree. Always he was on street and mountains proclaiming truth of Gospel. Jesus Christ came down from heaven!. And he lives in heaven even today forever! Yes! He is! [Isaiah 61: 1-3].

Instead of claiming to be pure and holy; this honored man, the Christ, the Messiah Most High Priest ever lived on earth identified himself with really Enmity sinful of Israel whom he came to save, as he pleaded before God on the cross: "Father forgive them; for they do not know what they are doing:" He was placed on undeserving devastating awful earthly agony. Enmity Satan darkness was upon him. Why and how God could allow?

Human beings or peoples: We do not present our supplications before Him for our righteousness, but for His great merciful. We have sinned; we have done wickedly from the beginning: And for our Enmity sinful, and for the transgression of our forefathers from Adam; we the peoples are became a reproach!. Can we really save ourselves? Enmity sinful is ever upon us: Who can save us? Jesus Christ is the answer. He is the way, the truth, and life, no one else, except through Christ Jesus. [John 14: 6].

Those who are truly seeking to be perfect Christian characteristic will never indulge the thought that they are sinless or self-righteous. The more their minds remain or dwell upon the character of Christ, and the nearer they approach to his divine image, the more clearly will they discern its spotless perfection and the more deeply will they feel their own weakness and own defects.

Anyone who claims to be without **Enmity sinful**, give evidence that anyone is very far from the Holy Spirit. He is on the side of Lucifer Enmity who maliciously claims to be God. It is because he has no true knowledge of Christ that he can look upon himself as reflecting his image. He is a brutal liar! The greater the distance between him and his saviour, the more righteous he appears in his **own eyes.**

Notwithstanding these high spiritual principle inspiring declarations, how many professed Christians are enfeebling their powers in the pursuit of self-gain or the worship of fashion; how many are debasing their godlike manhood by gluttony, by wine drinking, by forbidden pleasure! And the church instead of rebuking, too often encourages the evil by appealing to appetite to desire for gain or love of pleasure; to replenish her treasury which love for Christ too feeble to supply!

Were Christ Jesus to enter the churches of to-day and behold the wicked-feasting and unholy traffic there conducted in the name man's made religion, would Christ not forceful-drive them out those desecrators, as he banished the money-changers from the ancient temple? Yes! He would: And that will be done on the Last Day when he returns! Had he encountered those who take the precious name of Christ Jesus upon lips defiled by tobacco, those whose breath and person are contaminated by its foul odor, and who pollute the air of heaven and force all about them to inhale the poison, had the apostle come in contact with a practice so opposed to the purity of the gospel, would he not have denounced it as "earthly sensual devilish?" Slaves of tobacco, fornicators claiming the blessing of entire sanctification, talk of their hope of heaven; but God's word plainly declares that; "there shall in no wise enter into it anything that defiled!." Hypocrites get it right before Christ returns!. [Rev. 21: 27]. Jesus Christ is inevitable! If an individual and humanity are to progress; Jesus Christ is inescapable! **You ignore him at your own wicked risk:**

The sanctification set forth in the Holy Scriptures embraces the entire well-being Spirit; soul; and body inseparable!

Whole spirit and soul and body is well-being preserved blameless until unto the coming of the Lord Christ Jesus the ultimate righteous Judge of the world! [Rom 12: 1] "I beseech you therefore," says Paul: "Brethren, by the mercies of God that you present your bodies a living sacrifice; holy, acceptable unto God!" So all true Christians are required to preserve all their moral-powers in the best possible condition for the Lord's service: [Abstain from flesh lust which war against the soul:" Said saint Peter. [1 Pet 2: 11]. The word of God will make but a feeble impression upon those whose faculties are benumbed by any Enmity sinful gratification. The heart cannot preserve consecration to God while the animal appetites and passions are indulged at the expense of health and life. "Let us cleanse ourselves from all filthiness of the flesh and spirit, perfecting holiness in the fear of God." [2 Corinth 7: 1].

And with the fruits of the Spirit: "Love; Joy; Peace; Long-suffering; Gentleness; Goodness; Faith; Meekness:" Saint Paul classes temperance, [Gal 5: 22-23]. You and I ought to know to embrace to heart until our Lord Christ Jesus returns.

He is the living God: "I am the God of Abraham; the God of Isaac; and the God of Jacob." Unmatched! Yes! Jesus Christ is inevitable! Those who are in the flesh will never, and never please God neither!

LEAD ME LORD

1. Lead me Lord from the dark to the light!.

You are eternal light Lord: Lead me to your light Lord. I am ever in darkness. Lord lead me, and guide me to your light that I may see the way. Lead me Lord, please Lord lead me!.

2. I am weak, but you are strong and wise. Hold my hand and lead me Lord: I will not fall. Lead me Lord: Lead me: I am a little child. I need you Lord: Lead me. If not you Lord who else?

Lead Lord through me will follow.

3. In your hand I'm well secured: Lead me Lord.

Feed me by your Spirit I will hunger no more.

You fed Israel with manner bread for forty year in the wilderness, they lacked nothing. You led them through-the way into Canaan flowing with milk and honey!.

4. You gave them water to drink; Lead me Lord.

I am weak but you are strong, wise-knowing all and merciful lead me Lord. I am under your guard like eagle spies for its nest where offspring lay. Lead me Lord by mighty-power and deliver me from evil one I will be safe in your mighty hand.

He whose body is the temple of the Lord God Holy Spirit will not be enslaved by a pernicious habit or even to grotesque! His powers belongs to Christ Jesus who has bought him with the most precious blood on the Cross! His property is the Lord God's. How could he be guiltless in squandering this entrusted capital? Professed Christians yearly expend an immense sum upon useless and pernicious indulgences, while souls are perishing for the word of life. God is robbed in tithes and offerings, while they offer upon the altar of destroying lust more than they give to relieve the vulnerable poor or for the support of the gospel of God the sustainer of all sources. They would neither give thanks to Almighty God!

If all who profess to be followers of God through Christ Jesus were truly sanctified, every channel of needless expense would be turned into the Lord God's perfect treasury, and Christians would set an example of temperance, self-denial, self-sacrifice, Christ like life-style. He completely emptied himself to nothing; yet he owns all as he came to his own. Yet he never lived under want. He did lack nothing!

Then they would be the light of the world; only those who are truly in Christ Jesus. The world today is given up to self-indulgence! The lust of the flesh, the lust of the eye, and the selfish-pride of life control the masses of the multitudes people's conscience and motives to pursue negative crafting-cunning for self-gain. Men are totally lost in the sight of God. Above all, God abundance riches generosity continues with His supplies unceasing to the wicked world! Thus reinforcing Enmity sinful impending severe consequences until Christ Jesus returns!. While men remain blind they become puffed! And yet God watches immensely with suspicious eye!. His righteous wrath stands upon those who provoke His long-suffering anger. Jesus Christ had long enough pleaded to God: "Father forgive them for they do not know what they are doing."

But for how long? While the Enmity sinful still on its persistence on earth.

But Christ's followers have a holier calling: "Come out from among them and be you separate:" Christ said; and touch not the unclean things of this wicked world; and I will receive you, and you will be a Father unto you, and you shall be my sons and daughters;" said the Lord God Almighty. [2 Corinth 6: 17-18].

It is the privilege and duty of every Christian to maintain a close union with the Lord Christ Jesus, and to have a rich experience in the things of God. Then his life will be fruitful in good-shape and good works. When we read the lives of men who have been eminent for their integrity piety, we often regard, admire their experiences and attainments as beyond our own reach like:

John Wycliffe; Martin Luther; John Huss; Jerome; early centuries; and our current modern men like: Mahatma Gandhi; Dr. Martin Luther King, Jr. and Nelson Mandela.

But this is not the case: Jesus said: "Herein is my Father glorified, that you bear much fruit." As the branch cannot bear fruit of itself, except it abides in the vine, no more can you, except you abide in me." Jesus said. "Choose Life." [Deut. 30: 11-21].

"He that abideth in Me, and I in him, the same bringeth forth much fruit." [John 15: 8]. The prophets and apostles did not perfect Christian character by a miracle. They used the means which God had placed within their reach and all who will put forth a like effort will secure a life result.

"We do not cease to pray for you," says Paul "and to desire that you might be filled with the knowledge of His will in all wisdom and spiritual understanding; that you might walk worthy of the Lord unto all pleasing, being fruitful in every good work and increasing in the knowledge of God; strengthened with all mighty, according to His glorious power, unto all patience and long suffering with joyfulness." Such are the fruits of God's Spirit sanctification. [Colo. 1: 9-11]. Choose Life! We admire those men who achieved so much in the name of the Lord Jesus Christ. In setting aside the claims of the law of God, the church has lost sight of God's blessings of His gospel. Holy Scriptures conversion and sanctification, a radical change of heart and transformation of character, is the great need of the church members of to-day modern world. Revivals in which men become members of the church without real conviction of Enmity sinful, without repentance, and without acknowledging the claims of the law of God, are a cause of weakness to the church members and an occasion of stumbling to the world!.

What subject is more important than that of Judgment Day?

How urgent it is that we learn all we can about this great day ever to be experienced is so soon to come upon us all. Who dares to take account in seriously consideration? The Holy Scriptures teaches us so much about it: When it will convene, how it will be conducted, who will take part, the books of record, the statute book, and our Advocate: Who will decide?

The investigative judgment; one of the most solemn events in all history a matter that affects all of us!. No matter how you overlook the issue. Jesus Christ is inevitable! I am mindful that it is about me and you and the rest of the world's inhabitants. The Angels of God have accurately kept a faithful record of the lives of all on earth, and they are all to be judged adequately according to their deeds. In view of this Judgment, Saint Peter exhorted the people of Israel: "Repent all of you therefore, and be converted that your Enmity sinful may be blotted out, when the times of refreshing shall come from the presence of the Lord God and He shall send Jesus Christ," whom the heaven must receive until the times of restitution of all things, which God had spoken by the mouth of all His holy prophets since the world began." [Acts 3: 19-21]. Choose Life!. [Deut. 30: 11-21].

"Whosoever therefore shall confess Me before men; him will I confess also before My Father who is in heaven. But whosoever shall deny Me before men; him will I deny before My Father who is in heaven!" Jesus said [Matt 10: 32-33].

The life of all those who have truly believed on the Lord Jesus Christ pass in solemn review before the Lord God Head Father in Heaven the maker of all life in heaven and on earth. [Bereshith: the beginning] with those who first lived upon the earth, our advocate examines the cases of each individual's successive generation, and closes with the living who chose life. Every individual's name is mentioned; every case closely investigated: Names are accepted; names are rejected: From age to age; from generation to generation; all who have truly repented of Enmity sinful, and by faith claimed the precious blood of Christ Jesus as their atoning sacrifice, have had pardon written against their names in the Books of Life in Heaven; and in the closing work of Judgment their Enmity sinful nature are blotted out for ever; and they themselves are accounted worthy of eternal life with the Lord God everlasting life!. Oh! What a glorious day! To experience! Joy forever!. I long for that day: Who doesn't? The deepest interest manifested among men and women in the decisions of earthly tribunals but faintly represents the interest evinced in the heavenly Courts when the names entered in the Book of Life come up in view before the Judge of all the earth. Jesus Christ the ultimate righteous World's Judge. He is inevitable! If individuals and humanity are to progress; Jesus Christ is inescapable! You ignore him at your own wicked risk.

Those who are owned and approved or recognized of God in Christ Jesus are not often times therefore, recognized and honored or respected by the secular-ungodly world. The very names that are taken upon the lips of Jesus as belonging to His own chosen sons and daughters, joint-heirs with the Lord God King of all glories; honored among the heavenly angels; are often those that are spoken with contempt and mockery; snaring; by the world ungodly. Steadfast souls whom Christ Jesus delights to honor-faithful like little child; are for His sake defamed; imprisoned; mobbed; hunted; and slain. True God's people must live by faith! They must look over into the great beyond; and choose life; divine honors and the recompense of the reward above every earthly gain of preferment.

The hard as it sounds; but it is the most precious-valuable thing for eternal gain. Faithful counts. Not easy at all! Christ Jesus went through toughest!. Beyond human scope: But triumphant in Spirit. He is the perfect model to follow!. While probation continues, they must expect that the world will know them not, "because it knew Him not." Great and small, high and low, rich and poor, are to be judged out of those things which were written in the Books of Life;

according to their works. All will stand before Jesus Christ Judgment Seat. Something to grasps to the heart!. You cannot afford to ignore. Includes: The Past: Present: and Future:

The divine intercessor presents the plea that all who from among the fallen sons and daughters of men have overcome through faith in Christ' blood, be forgiven their transgressions that they be restored to their Eden, and crowned as joint-heirs with holy angels in heaven to the 'First dominion." [Micah 4: 8]. Satan in his efforts to deceive and tempt all mankind had thought to frustrate the divine plan in man's creation; but Jesus Christ now ask that this plan be carried into effect as if man had never fallen before. He asks for His people not only pardon and justification, full and complete, but a share in His glory and a seat upon His throne. They are those whom he careful selected for such high throne status. While Christ Jesus is pleading for the subjects of His grace, Satan accuses them before God as transgressors earthly prosecutor. The great malicious deceiver has sought to lead them into skepticism, to cause them to lose confidence in God, to separate them from His love, and to break God's law. Now he points to their defective characters which he manipulated to them to their unlikeness to Christ which has dishonored their redeemer, to all the Enmity sinful which he has tempted them to commit, and because of these he claims them as his subtle subjects. Satan, it is his device skillful to deceive, and manipulate godly people. He possesses sharp crafting-cunning words to blind the world!. The Lord Jesus Christ does not excuse their Enmity sinful, but shows their penitence and faith, and claiming for them forgiveness, He lifts up to show His wounded hands, feet, and head before the Father and the holy angels; saying: "I know them by name. I have graven them on the palms of my hands." Jesus showed Thomas his wounded hands, so that Thomas should not doubt but believe that Christ is risen! Yes! Satan envies the holy angels in heaven. "The sacrifices of God are a broken spirit; a broken and contrite heart. Oh God, you will not despise." [Ps. 51: 17]. And to the accuser of His people: "The Lord rebuke you oh Satan; even the Lord that has chosen Jerusalem rebuke you." Is not this a brand plucked of the fire?" [Zech. 3: 2]. Satan, envy; he wants to make sure that all godly people fail like him. But the Lord Christ Jesus will place his own signet upon his faithful people; that he may present them to his Father. "I know them by name."

This is the outcry that God Almighty heard from above in heaven: He came down Himself to see the appalling outcries: He then Rescued His vulnerable people and wiped their tears from their red eyes forever-lasting!. Jesus Christ is inevitable! If any individuals and humanity are to progress; Jesus Christ is inescapable! You ignore Him at your own wicked risk.

Quoted from: Dr. Martin Luther King, Jr: **"Let justice run down like waters! And righteousness like mighty stream!"** [Amos 5: 24]…

As the features of the countenance are reproduced with marvelous exactness in the camera of the artist, so is the characteristic faithfully delineated in the books above in heaven. If Christians **[1.2 billion]** so well claimed on earth were as solicitous to stand faultless in the heavenly records as they are to be represented without a blemish in the big picture, how different would their life-style history appear. Could the vail which separates the visible from the invisible world be swept back, and the children of men behold an angel recording every word Athanasius-John T. Nkomo and detailed deeds to meet them again in the judgment, how many words that are daily uttered would remain unspoken; how many deeds would remain undone. When all the details of life appear in the well recorded books that never contain a false or deceitful entry, many will find too late that the record testifies against them. God's records are perfect-honesty and truth!. All their hidden grotesque-selfishness stands revealed! There is the perfect record of all unfulfilled duties/piety to their fellow-men; of forgetfulness of the Lord Christ Jesus' claims:

"I was hungry you gave me no food; I was thirsty and you gave no drink; I was a stranger and you did not take me in; I was naked and you did not clothe me; sick and in prison and you did not visit me!" "Depart from me, you cursed into ever-lasting fire prepared for the devil and his angels:" [Matt 25: 41-44].

There they will see how often were given to Enmity-Satan the time, thought and strength that belonged to Jesus Christ the World' Savor! Sad is the record which angels bear to heaven. It is about you and me!. "Choose Life Now!" Familiar phrases but meaningful to grasp and embrace to heart and live forever! Unfortunately, it's tough to practice; but it is necessary to practice!

Intelligent beings, professed followers of Jesus Christ, are absorbed in the acquirement of worldly possessions or the enjoyment of earthly pleasures; all are God's providence for your benefit in order to glorify God your maker and sustainer of your life. God demands pure thanksgiving, nothing else!. Show God your broken and contrite heart; that pleases Him. Money, time, strength, prestigious; are sacrificed for display and self-indulgence; but few are the moments devoted to prayer; to the searching of true-Scriptures; to humiliation of soul and honesty confession of Enmity sinful nature [Ps. 51].

"Have mercy upon me Oh God! According to your lovingkindness:

According to the multitudes of your tender mercies: Blot out my transgressions: Against You: You only, have I sinned! And done this evil in your sight: That you may well be justified when you speak: And blameless when you Judge." [V 1, 2, 3, 4, 5].

What it means to you? Satan or Evil invents unnumbered schemes and devices to occupy our minds and hearts that they may not dwell upon the very work with which we ought to be best acquainted. Evil causes us to shift from truth. Psalm 51: Full story told from [2 Sam 11-12] constitutes a famous King David who committed the most heinous Enmity sinful in the sight of God. God forgave David. See Uriah and Bathsheba; the mother of King Solomon.

The arch-deceiver Satan; hates the great truths that bring to view an atoning sacrifice; broken and contrite hearts and an all-powerful mediator! Satan or Lucifer; he knows that with him everything now depends on his diverting minds from Christ Jesus and all Christ' truths!. This is the world on which we all live on!. It is fully surrounded by evil every-where!.

Those who would share the benefits of the Lord Christ Jesus, the saviour, and mediator should permit nothing to interfere with their piety duties to perfect holiness in the fear of God the maker of all goodness!. The hours heretofore given to pleasure, to display, or to gain-seeking, should now be devoted to an earnest, prayerful study of the word of truth; God's truth in Christ Jesus the World's Savor!. The subject of the sanctuary and the investigative judgment should be clearly well understood by the people of God. All need knowledge for themselves of the position and work of their great high priest. Otherwise it will be impossible for them to exercise the faith essential at this time, or to occupy the position which God designs them to fill-up.

Fearless; we are to bear testimony of the great truths which God in Christ has committed to all who claim to follow Christ! 1. 2 billion claimed Christians need to work for Christ tirelessly. Christ is the fuel of our spirits were designed to burn continually! The sanctuary in heaven is the very center of Christ Jesus' perfect work in behalf of all men. What you believe? Choose Life and Live! [Deut. 30: 19-20].

It concerns all souls living upon the earth no exclusion! It opens to all our views the plan of redemption, bringing us all down to the very close of time and revealing the triumphant issue of the contest between righteousness and Enmity sinful. It is of the utmost importance that all who have received the illuminating light, both old and young, should thoroughly investigate subjects and be able to give an answer to everyone that asked them a reason of the hope that is them faithfully. Jesus Christ is the fuel of our spirits that burns to energize our strength continually. You will see and experience the result that is deep beyond human scope. It is the mysteries that God invents:

"As the wind blows where it wishes; and you hear the sound of it, but cannot tell where it comes from and where it goes; So is the mysteries of God." [John 3: 8]. How can these things be? Are you the intelligent being, and do not know these things? How? And so is your sound voice on your lips; in your mother's womb you have no voice until she gives birth; and when you die, your voice disappears and no more sound but silence: Where it goes, and where it came from?"

The intercession of Christ Jesus in man's behalf in the sanctuary above in heaven is as essential to the plan of salvation as was His death upon the cross. By his death Christ began that work which after his resurrection Jesus triumph ascended to complete in heaven. By faith; we can only enter within the vail; without faith otherwise none can enter whither the forerunner is for us entered. There the light from the cross of Calvary is reflected. By faith, we may gain a clearer insight into the mysteries of redemption. Otherwise; it is impossible!

The salvation of man is accomplished at an infinite expense to heaven; the sacrifice made is equal to the broadest demands of the broken law of God. Jesus Christ has opened the door to the Father's high throne, and through his mediation the genuine sincere desire of all who respond with honesty-heartfelt to his full invitation, "Come to me all you who labour and are heavy laden, and I will give you rest." [Matt 11: 28] of all who come to Him in true faith may be presented before the Father; the Mighty God ever-lasting: It is place we all long to be: But it is for those who well deserve for it. Jesus Christ knows them all by names. He that covered his Enmity sinful nature shall not prosper; but whoso confess Enmity sinful and forsake them shall have mercy."

[Pro. 28: 13]: If those who hide and excuse their faults could not see how Satan exults over them, how he taunts Christ and holy saints and angels with them, they would make haste to confess their Enmity sinful nature and to put them away. They resist intensively. Satan is continually seeking to deceive the followers of Christ Jesus with his fatal sophistry that their defective traits of character render it impossible for them to overcome! You truly need Christ to shield you. Christ stands to pleads on your behalf, his wounded hands, legs and his bruised body; and he declares to all who would follow him; "My grace is sufficient for you." Take my yoke upon you, and learn from me; for I am meek and lowly at heart, and you shall find rest for your souls." [Matt 11: 29-30].

Let none, then, regard their defects as incurable. Jesus Christ is inevitable! Jesus Christ is inescapable! Jesus Christ will give faith and grace to overcome them! Choose Life!. All those who would have their names retained in the book of life in heaven, should now, in the few remaining days of their probation, afflict their souls before God by sorrow for Enmity sinful, and true repentance. There must be deep faithful searching of broken heart. The light frivolous spirit indulged by the majority of professed 1.2 billion Christians must be put away. There is earnest warfare before all who would subdue the evil tendencies that strive for the mastery-evil activity. Solemn are the scenes connected with the closing work of the atonement. Momentous are the interest therein involved.

The judgment is now passing in the sanctuary above in heaven. Forty years has this work been in progress. Soon, none known how soon, it will pass to the cases of the living. In the awful presence of

God our lives are to come up in review. At this time above all others it behooves every soul to heed the saviour's admonition: "Watch and pray for you know not when the time is to come." "Watch, therefore, you weaken lest coming suddenly He finds you sleeping." [Mark 13: 33, 35-36]. How perilous is the condition of those who, growing weary of their watch, turn to the attraction of the world. Torn apart marriage because they had grown weary of their watch, turn to the attraction of the world harlots. While the man of business is absorbed in the pursuit of gain, while the pleasure-lover is seeking indulgence, while the daughter of fashion is arranging her adornments, it may be in that hour the Judge of all the earth will pronounce the sentence:

Aramaic: "Mene, Mene, Tekel Upharsin. "You have been **weighed in the balance and found wanting: Your kingdom has been divided and given to the Medes and Persians."** [Dan 5: 26-28].

Then Belshazzar gave the command; and they clothed Daniel with purple and put a chain of gold around his neck.

Every soul that has name of Christ Jesus has a case pending at the heavenly tribunal. It is Court week with us and the decision passed upon each case will be final. Jesus Christ is the solemn Righteous ultimate Judge; once and for all!

In Egypt: Jacob is old and knows his death is near: Called all his 12 sons: And said: "Gather together, that I may tell you what shall befall you in the Last days:" [Gen. 49].

Starting with **Reuben his firstborn,** Simeon, and Levi, charging them for their crime acts. **Reuben slept with Bilhah** his father's concubine; [wife] And Israel heard about it. Reuben defiled his father's bed! [Gen 35: 22]. But Simeon and Levi, Dinah's brothers [Leah' daughter] killed all males; Including Hamor and Shechem his son who raped Dinah!. They were in Pain because all males had been circumcised in three days. [Gen 34: 25].

"Simeon and Levi are brothers: Instruments of cruelty in their dwelling Place." Jacob said as he prayed for them: "Let not my soul enters their Council: Let not my honor be united to their assembly: For in their anger they slew a man: And in their self-will they hamstrung an ox: Cursed be their anger, for it is fierce! And their wrath, for it is cruel! I will divide them in Jacob and scatter them in Israel." [Gen. 49: 5-7]. Did Jacob utter these words from his own mouth or from God's mouth to prophesy? When Jacob had finished his prayer, commanding his sons, he drew his feet up into the bed and died. [v. 33].

None can neglect or defer this work but at the most fearful peril to our Souls: It rests with us all to cooperate with Christ Jesus who came down From heaven with greatest work of conforming and transforming Characters to the divine perfect model-ever! We all have obligation to carry on this great work to the entire world until Christ Jesus returns!.

It is mysterious, unaccountable to excuse it; is to defend it. Could it be excused could a cause be shown for its existence, it would cease to be Enmity sinful nature: Our only definition and interpretation of Enmity Sinful is that given in the whole entire World! It is the transgression of the Perfect Law of God Almighty the Creator!

Pontiff Papacy: Aleander: Scandals Speech

Tetzel: Scandals Escape High Treason Crime

Pontiff pomp failures: But Martin Luther stood on God's side, Triumphant!. God sustained his strength throughout the Church Reformations campaign: Why the nations outrage? He who sits in the heavens shall laugh: The Lord God shall hold them in derision. Then He shall speak to them in His wrath: And distress them in His deep displeasure! Yet I have set My King on My holy hill of Zion." See [Ps. 2: 4-6].

Jesus Christ is inevitable! If individuals and humanity are to progress; Jesus Christ is inescapable! You ignore him at your own wicked risk: Future event and greatest righteous judgment that Jesus Christ will ultimately presides once and for all! Only for true born again Christian look forward to this great event: Jesus Christ knows all his true sheep by names! Will you be available? Great Last Day!.

Jacob's sons with Leah: [Gen 29: 31-35].

1. Reuben

2. Simeon [plus one sister Dinah]

3. Levi

4. Judah

5. Isachar

6. Zebulum: Leah bore 6 sons for Jacob sons. While Rachel bore 2 sons for Jacob. Among the two sisters, was a tense rival.

Jacob son with Zilpah Leah' maidservant:

1. Gad

2. Asher: They were born after Mandrake exchange between Rachel and Leah: There was any awful rival among them, yet they are sisters with one man Jacob their husband given to him by Laban their father who is Rebekah's brother; Isaac' wife. [Gen 30: 15] So Leah' total sons are eight [8] in a roll number:

Jacob's sons with Rachel:

1. Joseph

2. Benjamin: She immediately died after giving birth: They were on a journey to Hebron: They buried her under a tree. Rachel had no children for a while because God made her a barren. She quarrels with Jacob for not giving her children. "Am I in God's position who closed your womb?" Jacob was angry with Rachel for such demand

request.

So she gave Jacob Bilhah her maidservant to be his concubine wife:

Jacob's son with Bilhah Rachel maidservant:

1. Dan

2. Naphtali Reuben slept with Bilhah his father's concubine wife. Israel heard about it. [Gen 30: 3].

Rachel had 4 sons for Jacob plus 8 from Leah became 12 tribes of Israel as a nation well known today.

In the long course, Jacob's 12 sons multiplied filling the world as God promised to Abraham early years past before Isaac was yet not born. The children of Israel did not have a human king for many years; but God did run their daily affairs perfectly well since God had rescued them from Pharaoh wicked hand for 450 years; living under slavery-bond in Egypt!. God had also foretold Abraham that "your offspring will be alien, and afflicted, but that nation which afflicts them; I will judge!." [Gen 15: 13-16]. God knew everything about the people of Israel what shall befall before them from generation to generation up to this time of modern days. This nation is God special chosen people from Abraham who walked with God. He was blameless and righteous man in the eyes of God Almighty. Abraham believed all things that God had told him that will take at its place at God's precise timing.

Potential kings were born like: Saul; David; and Solomon and many others following after them. Years later, the Israelites rejected God to run their daily affairs as their King, but preferred to have a human king like all other nations around them who had human kings. No resistance from God even though they rejected him as king. God allowed them to have a human king as they wish rather than God who is perfect to run their daily affairs. So God chose

Saul, the first human king of Israel. "You want it, you have it!" That's what it means "Saul" in Hebrew language, translated into English. As result, Saul was no good king for the Israelites neither he was good in the eyes of God. But God gave them what they asked for; "You have him!." To many minds the origin of Enmity sinful and the reason for its existence are a source of great Perplexity and griefs. In their interest in these questions, the truths plainly revealed in God's Word and essential to salvation are neglected in the house of Israel from the past up to the present day of our modern age, the progress to success according to their God is seemingly exponentially neglected to stable its stagnation. And the fact that the Scriptures furnish no explanation is seized upon as an excuse for rejecting the words of Holy God Writ. Tradition and misinterpretation and definition have both obscured the teaching of the true-God in the Bible concerning the character of the Holy God, the nature of His Government, and the principles of His dealing with Enmity sinful nature. "You have him as ask!." [1 Sam 16: 14-16].

Saul the first king of Israel; God ultimately resolved to reject Saul plainly because of his obstinate disobedience; therefore, God removed His Spirit from Saul and imposed Enmity upon him as he deserves it: Then God chose David as the next king of Israel. A man who truly sought after God's heart [1 Sam 16: 7-13]…

It is impossible to fully explain the origin of Enmity sinful nature, or to give a reason for its existence, we truly do not know or fully understand how it exists!. God knows! Enmity; it is an intruder for whose existence no reason man can well understand can be given if not God alone. Heaven most perfect and holy place; how then could Lucifer fall to that most high treason crime! Yet, he was created to be the most perfect. We do not know how!. However, all human beings fall into this Enmity un-conditionally. No excuse: It became instinct and tendency un-conditionally. Enmity affects all! No escape!. The subject of Enmity sinful is complex. All men endeavor to resolve it, but it is impossible! [Is.

14: 12-16] Enmity Gen 3:15.

David prestigious: Kills a champion named Goliath, who was from Gath, came out of the Philistine camp. He was over nine feet tall. [1 Sam 17: 4-12]. See v. 45-51].

Abraham #: One Prestigious Ancient Patriarchy of the Jews: Isaac, his son Sarah his wife.

Met his wife at a well: Rebekah, Bethuel' daughter:

Bethuel the son of Milcah the wife of Nahor; Abraham' brother:

Abraham had loyalty servant named Eliezer of Damascus: Really and truly faithful servant: Met Rebekah at a well for Isaac' wife. He prayed to the Mighty God for the possibility! God heard the prayer of Eliezer of Damascus [Gen 29]. Rebekah came with her father' flocks to the well to water them after day long of thirsty. All the patriarchies met their wives at a well. What a mystery history to teach all the earth!. All was set up by God Almighty for reason. [v.24].

Isaac and Rebekah bore two sons: Esau: Jacob: [Gen 25].

Jacob saw a well: There he met Rachel: Laban' daughter. Laban and

Rebekah is brother-sister: Bethuel children: Rachel came to the well to water her father' flocks: Jacob helps her to water the flocks. [Gen 30: see Gen 29]. Jacob escaped from Esau his elder brother. He had a long journey from Isaac his father escaping to Laban his mother' brother. It was Rebekah' idea that her son should leave their household for certain time till Esau' anger cools down. Esau planned to kill Jacob his brother like Cain did to Abel. God protected Jacob from the hand of Esau. See [Mal. 1: 1-8]

"Jacob I loved." God said. Laban had two daughters: Leah and Rachel. Jacob loved Rachel more than Leah. Jacob married them both: These two women with their maidservants; are the product of

Israel nation. The most prestigious God's chosen people on earth; from one single man Jacob filled the earth!.

So the two sisters had severe rival. Mandrake: [Gen 30].

Reuel: Is he the same person named Jethro?

Jethro: Zipporah' father: [Exodus 2: 18 and Exodus 18: 18]

Moses escapes from Egypt to the Medians country: There at a well met Zipporah Jethro daughter who came to water her father' flocks. Zipporah Moses' wife bore two sons for him. Moses helps Reuel' daughter to water their flocks [v. 18].

Moses had killed an Egyptian in defense for his brethren who were enslaved. So, Pharaoh sought to kill Moses. Therefore, Moses escaped from the face of Pharaoh King of Egypt who oppressed the Jewish people for 450 years as slaves. Moses was born as a slave, but Pharaoh' daughter rescued him from the Nile Rivers where he was found floating to un-known. God had plan for him. So Moses was well protected by the hand of the Mighty God for a crucial mission that was to come after he had raised him up with great wisdom and courage. Moses was raised up in Pharaoh's Palace. True Love compels all! The ancient Patriarchies in the hand of God Almighty! Nothing could overcome them. No such obstacle could hinder them because God' mighty hand was upon them. No!. Not one! "If God is on our side; who can be against us?" Nobody!. "I am your shield Abraham: Do not be afraid!" God said.

Finally: Jesus Christ our Lord sits at Jacob' well [John 4:]

There Christ met the Samaritan woman who came to draw water. Like all ancient Patriarchies met their wives at a well. "Give me a drink:" Jesus asked the woman: The response was negative: "We Samaritans have no deals Jews and Samaritans: How dare you to ask a drink from a Samaritan Woman:" Oh, she did not know to whom she was speaking. Yet he is the giver of living water. [John 4: 24].

1. Love and Truth:

2. Worship and Truth:

3. Spirit and Truth:

4. **[Agape]:** What is the meaning of the phrase?

God is Spirit." Jesus said: And those who worship Him must worship Him in spirit and truth." [v. 24]. Sums up all ancient patriarchies love for their wives whom they met at well from Abraham; Isaac; Jacob; Moses: Hear is truth meaning words:

1. When I survey the wondrous cross on which the Prince of Glory died, my richest gain I count but loss and contempt on all my pride. Forbid it, Lord that I should boast, save in the death of Christ, my God; all the vain things charm me most I sacrifice them to his blood.

2. See from his head, his hand, his feet, sorrow and love flow mingled down; did ever such love and sorrow meets, or thorns compose so-rich a crown?

3. His dying crimson, like a robe, spreads over his body on the tree, then am I dead to the entire globe, and the entire globe is dead to me.

4. Were a present far too small; love so amazing, so divine, demands my soul, my life, my all. [Agape] Christ Jesus: True Love: True Spirit: Worship in spirit and truth: God is Spirit: Worshiped in Spirit and Truth: And that's what God seek from all on earth.

Jesus Christ is inevitable! If individuals and humanity are to progress; Jesus Christ is inescapable! You ignore him at your own wicked risk. [Mal. 1: 1-8].

God desires from all men on earth he created to perform the service of true love; homage that springs from an intelligent appreciation of God's characteristic like Christ Jesus depth! God takes no pleasure in a forced allegiance, and to all he grants freedom of free-will, that they may render to God voluntary service of their free-will. But; and unfortunately; over this happy state there came a change: Enmity drawn upon man through his free-will which brings to his own death: Wrong choice!. "Thine heart was lifted up because of thy beauty, thou has corrupted thy wisdom and freedom-through thy free-will by reason of your brightness." [Ezek. 28:17]. Choice by free-will matters! Also, with severe pending consequences!. Choose Life!. [Deut. 30: 21].

God created Lucifer noble and beautiful, and had exalted him to high honor among the angelic host in heaven: Yet God had not placed him beyond the possibility of Enmity- Evil. It was in Satan's power, did he choose to do so, to pervert these gifts. He might have remained in favor with God his maker, beloved and honored by all heavenly angelic throng, presiding in his exalted position with generous un-selfish-care, exercising his noble power to bless others and to glorify God his eternal maker. The world' at large today following Lucifer self-exalting they all fall into eternal death!. [Isaiah 14: 12-15]. God imposed Enmity upon him extremely hush punishment. Enmity cannot be resolved by men today! This is the most serious and severe case today that many cannot fully understand its meaning. Enmity shall persist until Christ returns! All men on earth are under the judgment of Enmity which remains until Christ returns!. No matter how you overlook the issue; God will fulfill His eternal Powerful Words. Lucifer; little, by little, he began to seek his own honor, influences, and to employ his evil power to attract attention and win praise to himself from other heavenly angelic: He also gradually led the other angels over whom he ruled to do him service, instead of devoting all their powers to the service of their God who created them with perfect hearts, mind; and soul to glorify God their maker: This course perverted his own imagination, and perverted those who yielded implicitly to his authority. Lucifer desire to have support and sympathy to consolidate his Enmity cause upon all men on earth.

The heavenly Council admonished Lucifer to change his course. The Son of God presented before him the greatness, the goodness, and the justice of Creator and the sacred, unchanging nature of God's Perfect Law.

God himself had established the order of heaven. The Son of God warned and entreated him not to venture thus to dishonor his maker, and bring ruin upon himself-Enmity. [Gen 3: 15]. But instead of yielding; Lucifer-Satan represented to those who loved him that he had been wrongly judged, that his dignity-integrity was not respected, and that his liberty was to be abridged: [Malicious-Lies] He begins spreading around the globe seeking for support and sympathy. Don't all men on earth pursue for support and sympathy? Yes! All ask for a help!. Don't we? Working with mysterious secrecy, and for a time concealing his real purpose under an appearance of reverence for the Lord God, he endeavored to excite dissatisfaction concerning the laws that governed heavenly beings, intimating that they imposed an unnecessary Enmity restraint. He deserved to have it as he required it by his free-will choice; exalting himself as God. Since the heavenly natures were holy; perfect; he urged that the angels should obey the dictates of their own free-will. He was wrong!. See [Ezek. 28: 17] and Isaiah 14: 12-15] summed up [Gen 3: 15].

That Jesus Christ should regard him as needing to be corrected, and should presume to take the position of a superior, aroused in him a spirit of resistance, and he charged the Son of God with a design to humble him before the angels. With all his devices and techniques: Lucifer failed!. But accurse fell upon him forever!. He was reduced to zero!

By his own malicious misrepresentation of the words of Christ Jesus, by prevarication and direct malicious-falsehood; Satan secured the sympathy from Eve, and Adam under his control, and they united with him in revolt, disobedience, breaking God's Heavenly Perfect Law and Authority. Therefore, they received

Enmity as they deserved including all their offspring generation to generations up to this day. Enmity persists and unresolved!. Is there any other better Biblical explanation? Yes! Only when Christ returns will bring all the perfect answers, and resolution. No one else! What we all experience today? Restless!. See [Gen 3: 19].

"In the sweat of your face, you shall eat bread: Till you return to the ground!. For out of it you were taken: For dust you are: And to dust you shall return!" God said. Who can escape from death? Enmity is absolute.

To the last, Satan refused to acknowledge his own course to be deserving of censure: Since then he has been resisting; disagreement; disputing; hostility; antagonism; animosity; hatred; envy; and slaughtering godly people everywhere he goes! The discord which his own course had caused in heaven, Satan or Evil, charged upon the law and heavenly Government of the Mighty God!. All evil he declared to be the result of the divine administration. Furthermore; he claimed that it was his own object to improve upon the statute of the Lord God Almighty!. Therefore; and indeed he insists: "It was necessary that he should demonstrate the nature of God's claims, and show the working out of his proposed changes in the divine law." Is he real able to overcome God his maker and take charge in order to change in the divine law? Like today men claim to change the world atmosphere: Lucifer or Satan, with his own work must condemn him! Same thing with modern men with their own work must condemn them! Satan had claimed from the beginning [Bereshith] Genesis 3: 5; 6; 7; 9; 10-15] #: one champion malicious lies that he was not in rebellion. The whole universe must see the deceiver unmasked when Christ returns. When the consequence of his disaffection became apparent, and it was decreed that with all his sympathizers he must be forever banished from the abode of bliss, the arch-deceiver threw the blame wholly upon Christ Jesus who shall be his ultimate righteous Judge. Nowadays; is not about luxury but is about Lamentations and tears.

With one accord, Satan and his hosts declared that had they not been reproved, the rebellion would never have occurred!. Thus making Christ responsible for their wicked corrupted course! Thus grotesque; profligacy; stubborn; obstinacy; and defiant in their Enmity disloyalty seeking vanity to overthrow the Mighty God Government which they will never! Yet it was their own eternal destruction. Like today modern world. Yet blasphemously claiming to be themselves sufficiently the innocent victims of oppressive power, the arch-rebel and all his sympathizers were at last banished from heaven to eternal hell. The rebellion in heaven was prompted by the same spirit which inspires rebellion on earth today. Satan or Lucifer has constantly continued with men and women the same policy which he pursued with angels. His spirit now reigns in the people of disobedience. There is a constant hatred; hostility; and bitterness defiling many of reproof, and a disposition to rebel against it continually today, as we all experience daily at home; at work; everywhere around the glove is filled with violence and instilling fear to all public transports; airports; trains; ship-harbor as well as domestic fear and suspicious upon neighbor. No trust to anyone!

Enmity, it is a negative phrase. But it exists in our midst eternally. When God sends to wrong-doers a message of warning or correction; Satan leads them to justify themselves, and to seek the sympathy and support from others. Instead of changing or correcting their wrong doings, they manifest great indignation against the reproved, as if he were the sole cause of difficulty. Satan twists everything in their minds and hearts: They even boast; "we are doing great!" From the day of righteous Abel to our own modern day; such is the spirit which has been displayed toward those who dare to condemn Enmity sinful nature. They refuse to recognize its existence and acknowledge like Cain who expostulates in the eyes of God: "Am I my brother's keeper!"

[Genesis 4.] Hatred; Cain killed his brother in cold blood! Since then killing never ceased!

Satan the killer; had excited sympathy in his favor by representing that God has dealt unjustly with him in bestowing supreme honor upon Christ: Like Cain represented that God had dealt unjustly with him in bestowing supreme honor upon Abel his young brother. Jealous and envy made Cain to kill Abel. Same thing even today in own modern world: Before God had sentenced Lucifer to banishment from heaven, his course was with convincing clearness shown to be vividly wrong, and he was granted an opportunity perhaps to confess or repentance of his awful sinful, and submit to God's authority as just and righteous. Selfish-pride; he omits! So, many ungodly people who omit to repent:

Lucifer chose to carry on his points at all hazards. To sustain his charge of God's injustice toward him, he resorted to misrepresentation, even of the words and acts so highly honored, and all his acts were so clothed with mystery, that it was difficulty to disclose to the angels the true nature of his work. Until fully developed, Enmity sinful would not appear the evil thing it was. This is what most of modern men practice in their developed religious. Heretofore it had had no place in the universe of God, and holy beings had no conception of its nature and malignity. Neither it has universe of God, and holy beings, has no conception of its nature and malignity even today in our own modern world!. God never gets involved at all! They could discern the terrible consequences that would result from setting aside the divine perfect law. Satan had at first, concealed his work under a specious profession of loyalty to God. He claimed to be seeking to promote the honor of God, the stability of Heaven Government and the good of all the inhabitants of Heaven. Another of his malicious lies. When he urged that changes be made in the order and laws of God's Government, it was under the pretense that these were necessary in order to preserve harmony in Heaven. How could he, after all he chose to break God's law.

Here for a time, Satan had the advantage; and he exulted in his arrogated Superiority and supremacy with respect, to the angels of heaven, and even to God Himself! While Satan can employ fraud and sophistry to accomplish his objects, God cannot lie; while Lucifer in the serpent form, can choose a tortuous course, turning, twisting, to conceal himself, God moves only in a direct, straight-forward line. Satan had disguised himself in a cloak of malicious falsehood, and for a time it was impossible to tear off the covering, so that the hideous deformity of his character could be well seen. He must be left to reveal himself in his cruel artful manner; wicked works. We see him in action even today to many. He had sought to falsify the word of God, and had misrepresented God's plan of Government lawsuit before the great angels claiming that God was not just in laying laws and rules upon the inhabitants of heaven; that in requiring submission and obedience from God his creator. He was seeking merely the exaltation of himself. Like our modern politicians, during elections, they entice voters to vote for them; they are seeking merely the exaltation for themselves. After they have gained power, they will never remember or think who voted for them.

For the good of the entire universe through ceaseless ages, Satan must more fully develop his principles like our own modern political leaders and religious; that charge against the divine holiness authority might be seen in their true light by all created beings, that the justice and mercy of God and the immutability of his law might forever be placed beyond all questions. Nothing new which we see things and constantly experience it year after year. It is our own accumulating fire upon our own destruction! Jesus Christ is inevitable! The righteous judgment is upon all!. Satan's rebellion was to be a lesson to the universe through all coming ages. But not all who dare to notice. Let the dead bury their own dead! It would testify that with the existence of God's truth, and Government and His Perfect Law is bound up the well-being of all the creatures he has made with powerful word. With his powerful word will judge all righteously. Jesus Christ the ultimate Judge is inevitable!

Satan, he was not immediately dethroned when he first ventured to indulge the spirit of discontent and insubordination, nor even when he began to present his malicious false claim and lying representation before the loyal angels. Long was he retained in heavens: Still he does visit heaven at certain occasion: See Job 1. Again and again he was offered to afflict Job on condition of repentance and submission: God challenged Satan with Job was very successful. He failed to reduce Job. No! Satan couldn't! Job was entirely in God's hand. As he did to Abraham: "I am your shield: Don't be afraid!"

Such efforts as God alone could make were made to convince him of his Wicked' error, and restore him to the path of rectitude. How often Satan tries to sift Peter like wheat. But Christ' hand protected him, so Satan could not sift Peter. Peter was safe in the hand of Jesus Christ. He was in good shape! He was in the presence of Christ, the mighty God! God would preserves the order of the heavens, and Lucifer been willing to return to his allegiance, humble and obedience, he would have been re-established perhaps in his office as covering cherub. We truly do not know God's mind and ways how he operates in heavenly matters. But God is just and mercy. To the very close of the testimony in Heaven, the great usurper continued to justify himself. When it was announced that with all his sympathizers he must be expelled or cast out from the heavenly abodes of bliss, then the rebel leader boldly avowed his contempt for the Creator's Law. He reiterated his claim that angels needed no control, but should be left to follow their own free-will, which would ever guide them right. Perhaps he said something like that: He denounced the divine statutes as a restriction of their liberty, and declared that it was his purpose to secure the abolition of law; that freed from this restraint the hosts of heaven might enter upon a more exalted, more glorious state of existence. But as he stubbornly justified his course, and maintained that he had no need of repentance, it became necessary for the Lord God of heaven to vindicate his justice and the honor of his throne; and Satan and all who sympathized with him were all cast out!. God's justice is fair for all. You reap what you sowed. To be sure God is well justified when he speaks word.

Chapter 10

Old David Second King of Israel After Saul
[Cold Body]

When King David was old and well advanced in years, he could not keep warm even when they put covers over him. So his servants said to him, "Let us look for a young virgin to attend the king and take care of him. She can lie beside him so that our lord the king may keep warm." Then they searched throughout Israel for a beautiful young girl and found Abishag, a Shunammite, and brought her to the king. The young girl was very beautiful; she took care of the king and waited on him, but king had no intimate relations with her. [1 Kings 1: 1-4].

Adonijah, whose mother was Haggith, exalted himself and said; "I will be king!" So he got chariots and horses ready, with fifty [50] men to run ahead of him: [But his father David had never interfered] with him by asking; "Why do you behave as you do?" He was also very handsome and was born next after Absalom. [v 5-6]….Adonijah spontaneously believed to be the next king as right heir, since he is now the oldest son. Amon and Absalom are dead.

Adonijah conferred with Joab son of Zeruiah and with Abiathar the priest, and they gave him their support. But Zadok the priest, Benaiah son of Jehoiada, Nathan the prophet, Shemei and Rei and David's special guard did not join Adonijah. Adonijah then sacrificed sheep, cattle, and fattened calves at the Stone of zoheleth near En Rogel. Invited all his brothers, the king's sons, and all the men of Judah who were royal officials, but he did not invite Nathan the prophet or Benaiah or the special guard or his brother Solomon.

Adonijah put on himself to undeserved position. As result of his own death. Adonijah lusts for Abishag which worsened his undeserved position to upset more Solomon the newly appointed king of Israel. Bathsheba the mother of Solomon, Uriah's wife whom King David murdered in cold blood appease for Adonijah. Bathsheba said: "Let Abishag the Shunammite be given to Adonijah your brother as wife." Solomon in response to his mother said: "Ask for him the kingdom also for he is my older brother, for him and for Abiathar the priest and for Joab the son of Zeruiah." Solomon said to his appeasing mother, Bathsheba. [1 Kings 2: 22]. Solomon's anger-wrath expostulating his mother then solemn swore by the Lord saying: "May God do so to me and more also: If Adonijah has not spoken this word against his own life!"

Now therefore, as the Lord lives, who has confirmed me and set me on the throne, and of David my father, and who has established a house for me as he promised, Adonijah shall surely be put to death today!"

Adonijah had been early warned by Solomon that if Adonijah behave well he shall live; but if he miss-behave, then his life shall be lived-short. "Go to your house." Solomon said. Adonijah' eagerness to become king of Israel brought him his own death. His rival between Solomon and Adonijah was overwhelming unfitting because David his father had not chosen him king. Solomon was to be the king for Israel after him as promised.

So Benaiah the son of Jehoiada was well instructed to slaughter Adonijah by the sword on the very day that Solomon solemn swore to struck him; following all others who in the past offended king David because he was an old man. Solomon carried on what David his father told him to do, before his death at his well advanced old age. [1 Kings 2-3].

Solomon then made treaty with Pharaoh king of Egypt, and married his daughter, then brought her to the city of David until he finished building his own house and the temple of the Lord God: Afterwards; God appeared to Solomon in a dream: "Ask! What shall I give you?" God said to Solomon. [1 Kings 3: 6]… Solomon asked God for wisdom to discern the people of Israel. That request, well pleased God; in addition God gave him more than what he had not asked.

See Solomon the wise King [1 Kings 3: 16-18]:

Two harlots [argued bitterly] came to the king stood before him. One of them said, "My lord, this woman and I live in the same house. I had a baby while she was there with me: The third day after my child was born; this woman also had a baby. We were alone; but the two of us."

Then the king said: "Bring the sword." So they brought the sword for the king. He then gave an order: "Cut the living child and give half to one and half to the other." The woman whose son was alive was filled with compassion for her son and said to the king, "Please my lord, and give her the living baby! Don't kill him!"

But the other said: "Neither I nor you shall have him. Cut him in two." Then the king gave his ruling: "Give the living baby to the first woman. "Do not kill him; she is his mother!" That remarkable ruling was God's revelation rather than Solomon whom God gave him abundant wisdom. [V 27]. Yes! God is all wise knowing all!

The Ancient &. Modern World

Remains Same One World

The same spirit that prompted rebellion in heavens still inspires rebellion on earth today! Satan has continued with men and women of the past; and presents the same policy which he pursued with the heaven angels. His evil spirit now reigns in the modern world as it was in the past of disobedience! [Enmity]… Like him they seek to break down the restraints of the perfect law of God Almighty, and promise men and women false-full liberty through transgression of its precepts. Reproof of Enmity sinful still arouses the spirit of hatred; hostility; disobedience; disagreement; antagonism; animosity; jealous; envy; and resistance. But the Eternal One God Himself proclaims His Own Eternal Character. The Lord God; Merciful and Gracious; Long-suffering and abundant in all Goodness and Truth; keeping mercy for thousands and thousands; forgiving iniquity [Enmity sinful] and transgression and evil and that will by no means clear the guilty. [Exodus 34: 6-7]

In the banishment of Satan from heaven; God denounced Satan and imposed; sentenced His justice and maintained the honor of his throne! But when man has sinned through yielding to the deception of this apostate spirit; God gave him any evidence of His love-caring by giving up His only Begotten Son to die on the Cross for the Fallen Race on earth! Nothing can change that. Only God who is able can:

In the atonement the characteristic of the Mighty God stands revealed. The mighty argument of the cross demonstrates to the whole universe that God was in no wise responsible for the course of Enmity sinful that the Arch-Angel Lucifer had chosen: That it was no arbitrary withdrawal of divine grace; no deficiency in the divine Government-Authority which inspired Lucifer in the spirit of rebellion or revolt. [Gen 3: 14-15].

In the contest between Christ and Lucifer; during the Saviour's earthly ministry; the character of the great deceiver [Satan] was unmasked by Christ among those who are Satan's agents. Nothing could so effectually have uprooted or eradicate Satan from the minds; hearts and affections of the heavenly angel and the whole loyal universe as did his cruel warfare upon Christ the world's redeemer. The daring blasphemy of his demands that Christ should worship and bow down in homage before him, his presumptuous boldness in bearing Him to the mountain summit and the pinnacle of the temple, the malicious intent betrayed in urging Christ to cast Himself down from the dizzy height; to change stone into bread; the unsleeping malice that hunted Christ from place to place; inspiring the hearts of priests and the people generally to reject God's love and at the last to raise the outcry: "Crucify Him! Crucify Him!" All this excited the amazement and indignation of the whole universe today! Yet; Christ insists: **"It is written!"** [Matt. 4:4, 10]

It was Satan that prompted the world's rejecting of Christ Jesus resulting modern world scholasticism; governments; and other civil world leaders. Satan the prince of all evil exerted all his power and cunning-crafting to destroy the Christ on Cross; for he saw that the World's Saviour's merciful and love, Christ' compassion and pitying tenderness, were representing to the world the perfect character of the Lord God Almighty. Indeed; it is God Head Father Perfect Plan to redeem the whole entire world and restore Bereshith Eden Garden. God raised the Lord Jesus Christ on the Third Day:

Satan contested every claim put forth by the Son of God and employed men and women as his agents thru scholasticism and government institution around the whole world: To fill the Lord Jesus Christ the World's Saviour's life with suffering and sorrows including all who follow after Him. The sophistry and falsehood by which he had sought to hinder the excellence work of Christ Jesus; the hatred manifested through the ungodly of disobedience; disagreement; his cruel accusations against Christ whose life is one of unexampled goodness; all sprang from deep-seated revenge. Today, everywhere around the world we see this severe apostate in actions.

The pent-up fires on Calvary against the Son of God while all heaven gazed upon the scene in silence horror; God's heart grieved almost caused Him to separate from His Son: Jesus Christ would plead:

"Eli, Eli, lama Sabachthani? "My God, My God, why have you forsaken Me?" [Matt 27: 46]. [Aramaic language]

When the great sacrifice had been consummated; Christ ascended on high; refusing the adoration of angels until He had presented the request; **"I will that they also whom thou have given me, be with me where I am, [John 17: 24]** Then with inexpressible love and power came forth the answer from the Head Father God's Throne: "Let all the angels of God worship Him!" [Heb. 1: 6]. Not a stain rested upon Christ Jesus. His humiliation ended; His sacrifice completed; there was given unto Him a name that is above every name in heaven and on earth: "Jesus Christ is Lord!"

Now the guilty of Satan Enmity stood forth without excuse! His malicious cunning lying charges against the divine character and government appeared in their true light. He had claimed that the transgression of God's perfect law would bring liberty and exaltation; but it was seen to result in bondage and degradation. Satan proved to be failure throughout his false claims. He has accused God's Son of seeking merely the exaltation of himself in requiring submission and obedience from Christ and all his followers after him: And had declared that while the creator exacted self-denial from all others; He Himself practiced no self-denial and made no sacrifice. Satan's language crafting influence many ungodly men and women on earth today!.

Now it was seen that for the salvation of a fallen and Enmity sinful race; the ruler of the universe [Satan] had made the greatest sacrifice which God could make. It was seen also that while Lucifer had opened the door for the entrance of sin Enmity, by his desire for self-honor and supremacy; Christ had in order to destroy every sin Enmity; humbled Himself and become obedience unto undeserved death: Worship God in Spirit-Truth."

God had manifested His abhorrence of the principles of rebellion. All heavens saw his justice revealed; both in the condemnation of Satan and in the redemption of man. Lucifer had denounced God's perfect law to be of such a character that its penalty could not be remitted and therefore every transgressor must be forever debarred from the God's favor. He had claimed that the Enmity sinful race were placed beyond redemption, and were therefore his rightful prey.

But the death of Christ was an argument in man's behalf that could not be turned aside. He suffered the penalty of the law. God was just in permitting His wrath to fall upon Christ who was equal with God Himself; and man was set free to accept the righteousness of Christ, and by a life of penitence and humiliation to triumph as the Christ Jesus the Son of God had triumphed over the power of Satan Enmity sinful nature. And that is part of the process to go thru Christ' depth: **"I am the way; life; and truth:"** [John 14: 6].

But it was not merely to accomplish the redemption of man that Jesus Christ came to the earth to suffer and to die. He came to magnify the perfect law, and to make it honorable. Not alone that the inhabitants of this earth would might regard the law as it should be regarded: But it was to demonstrate to all the worlds of the universe that God's perfect law is unchangeable! Could its claims have been set aside, then the Son of God Christ Jesus need not have yielded up his life to atone for its transgression. The death of Christ proves it immutable. And the sacrifice to which infinite love impelled the Father Head God Almighty and the Son; that sinners might be redeemed; demonstrates to the entire universe what nothing less than this plan of atonement could have suffered to do that justice and mercy are the foundation of the law and authority of God Almighty! The cross of Calvary while it affirms the perfect law immutable proclaims to the universe that the wages of sin is death! In the Christ Jesus, the Saviour's expiring cry; "It is finished!" The death-knell of Satan was rung! The greatest ever proclaimed which had been so long in progress was then decided and the final eradication of evil-Enmity was made certain. Therefore it will persist until Christ Jesus the ultimate Righteous Judge Returns: **"And behold! I am coming quickly, and My reward is with Me**

to give to everyone according to his work." [Rev. 22: 12].

God's perfect law stands fully vindicated! He is just and yet the justifier of all who believe in Christ Jesus! Nothing less than this plan of atonement could convince the whole entire universe of God's full justice! In the final execution of the judgment it will be seen that no cause for Enmity sinful exists! When the Judge of all the earth, the really truth authority demand of Satan; "Why has thou rebelled against Me and robbed Me of the subjects of My kingdom?" The original of Enmity of evil can render no excuse! Every mouth will be stopped to silence; and all the hosts of rebellion will be speechless like mute before the greatest tribunal! The Perfect Law of God which Lucifer with his evil earthly agents has reproached as the yoke of bondage; will be honored as the law of liberty!. A tested and proved new creation will never again be turned down from allegiance to Him whose character has been fully manifested before them as fathomless love and infinite wisdom...

"I will put Enmity between you and the woman: And between your seed [offspring] and her seed [offspring] it shall bruise thy head; and you shall bruise his heel." [Gen 3: 15].

The divine sentence pronounced against Satan in the form of the Old Serpent after the fall of Man [Adam] was also a prophecy, embracing all the ages to the close of time, and foreshadowing the great conflict to engage all the races of men who should live upon the earth. So God impose Enmity.

This Enmity is not naturally entertained. When man transgressed the divine perfect law; his nature became evil and he was in harmony and not at variance, with Satan. Magnificent eternal history to read: All ought to read!   Enmity [Gen 3: 15].

ENMITY: Whole Summery Conclusion
By the definition:

Feeling condition of: Ill-will:

1. Hatred
2. Hostility; grotesque; and profligacy
3. Disobedience and resistance
4. Disagreement and disbeliefs
5. Antagonism
6. Animosity
7. Envy and Jealous
8. Bitterness springing up and defiling many nations on earth.

Long list; but mention few. It is incomplete definition.

"I will put Enmity between you and the woman: And between your seed and her seed." [Future] God imposed, Christians literary read this biblical phrase with different human perspectives and often times miss-leading themselves. But the Lord Christ Jesus, by his wondrous grace, will change the hearts and lives of all who earnestly cry out to him for strength and help. To the most humble repentant believing souls, nothing is with-held that he needs in order to keep close to his precious the Lord Christ Jesus the Saviour of the whole World!

God indeed, imposed Enmity! "I will put Enmity!" This Enmity is not actually naturally entertained. When Man [Adam] transgressed the Divine Perfect Law; his nature became Enmity sinful original evil, yet to begin with he was in harmony; and not at variance with Lucifer in the form of the Serpent. There exists naturally no Enmity between sinful man and the originator of Enmity sinful. Both became sinful through apostasy. The apostate is never at rest since then, except as he obtains sympathy and support thru inducing vulnerable men to follow his sinful example thru-crafting and cunning.

For this reason, fallen heavenly angels and wicked men unite in desperate companionship. Had not God specially interposed, Lucifer or Satan or Evil and man would have entered into an alliance against God in Heaven: And instead of cherishing Enmity against Satan, the whole world with human kind family would have been united in opposing God. Choice matters today around the whole globe.

Lucifer in the form of the Serpent; tempted Man [Adam &. Eve] to sinful as he had caused himself to sinful to choose to rebel against God Almighty his maker!. That he might thus secure cooperation in his warfare against God in Heaven. He too tempted the Christ: He failed!. Christ the author of the Scriptures: "It is written!" Be-gone Satan!." There was no dissension between himself and the fallen angels and man as regards their hatred of Christ Jesus: While on all other points there is discord they were firmly united in opposing the authority of God the ruler of the whole universe. Satan couldn't stand a chance to deceive the Christ.

But when Lucifer heard the impeding Enmity being announced descriptively against him should exist between himself and the woman; and between his seed [offspring] and her seed [offspring] Lucifer knew that his efforts to deprave vulnerable human beings nature would be interrupted and difficulty that by some means man was to be enabled to resist his forceful wicked power. So, as Enmity stands; the man resists to some extending within the help of the divine spirit entrusted upon him. However, the man ought to be aware the existence of Enmity.

The grace that Christ Jesus implants in the individual' soul creates the Enmity against Satan. Without this converting grace and renewing power, man would continue the captive of Satan a servant ever ready to do his biddings, or a slave of sin. But the new principle in the soul creates conflicts, hostiles, hatred, where hitherto had been peace. The power which Christ imparts enables man to resist the tyrant and usurper. Whoever is seen to abhor sinful instead of loving it, whoever resists and conquers or overcome those passions that have held sway within displays the operation of a principle wholly from above in heaven!. Jesus Christ protects his own: "I am your shield Abraham! Do not be afraid!" Honest and faithful promise from God Almighty. The antagonism that exists between the spirit of Christ Jesus and the spirit of Satan is most strikingly displayed in the modern world reception of Christ Jesus today! It was not so much because Christ appeared without worldly wealth-material things; pomp; or grandeur that the Jews and Gentiles are led to reject Christ Jesus! They see that he possessed divine powerful which would more than compensate for the lack of these outward advantages! Christ Jesus unmasked their hidden evil deeds plainly! The purity and holiness of Christ called forth against him the hatred; hostiles; and envy of the ungodly. His life style, meekness of self-denial and sinless devotion was a perpetual reproof to a proud sensual people like Pharisees; hypocrites and self-righteous external. It was shameful! It was this that evoked Enmity against the Son of God Almighty. Lucifer or Satan and evil agents joined with evil men. All the energies of apostasy conspired against the truth of Christ Jesus whom they could not defeat by reason and wisdom; holiness and powerful above all. This defeat by reason and wisdom of God process still lives among the true believers even today; they are unbeatable by the secular world' wisdom and reasoning.

The same Enmity is manifested toward Christ Jesus' true followers as was manifested toward their Lord and Master the Saviour of the world! Whoever sees the repulsive character of Enmity sinful, and in strength from above in heaven, resists temptation thru-Scriptures, will assuredly arouse the wrath of Satan and his subjects. Most of the secular scholasticism is controlled by Satan who looks like God who invents and describes to them the textbooks for the young adults. They are anti-Christ textbooks written by the most intelligent secular scholars. Title: Christian fiction ebook. It is a secular world modern bible textbook.

Hatred of the pure principles of truth and reproach and persecution of its advocates will exist as long as Enmity sinful and individual sinners remain or exist. The followers of Christ and the agents of Satan cannot harmonize. The offense of the cross has not ceased. Its powerful stands challenging the secular world today!. All that will live godly in Christ Jesus shall suffer persecution and with scoffers surroundings. [2Tim 3: 12]

Satan or Lucifer or Enmity sinful agents are constantly working under his direction to establish his authority on earth and build up his kingdom in opposing all that is called of God to the authority of God Almighty. To this end they seek to deceive young adults in all scholasticism institutions, deceiving all Christ Jesus followers and allure them from their allegiance. Like their leader they misconstrue and pervert the Scriptures into their scholasticism so that their anti-Christ textbooks title Christian fiction ebook becomes popular and overcome the true holy Bible, and accomplish their object. All this is the genius work of Lucifer to consolidate his Enmity. But he will not win because he is sentenced to condemnation. His malicious cunning will not last forever. But Christ triumph and victorious stands against Lucifer Enmity sinful nature. Lucifer with his evil agents is very aware. As Satan endeavors to cast reproach upon God, so do his agents seek to malign God's true believers. The spirit which put Christ to death moves the wicked to destroy Christ Jesus followers. All this is fore-shadowed in that first prophecy, "I will put Enmity between you and the woman; and between your seed and her seed." [Gen 3: 15]. It is continually process until Christ returns. Yes! Enmity will persist. For God spoke and it was done! For the word of God is living and active. [Heb. 4: 12]. Jesus!

Such is the function that will be carried forward in the great Judgment Day between Christ and Lucifer to the end of time.

God rebuke Satan for the body of Moses and Joshua: Accusing them: The devil advocate stands against the saints. [Jude 1:5-25; Zech. 3: 2; Dan 10: 5; Ezek. 1: 26; Is. 49:2 Acts 10: 10; Job 1-2].

"Now Joshua was clothed with filthy garments, and standing before the Angels in heaven: "Take away the filthy garments from him;" God said: [Zech. 3: 3-5]. Lucifer malice advocates of persecution failed to execute Moses and Joshua.

Satan summons all his evil forces and throws his whole power into the combat. Why is it he meets with no greater resistance? Why there are so many Christians who follow after Christ are driven so sleepy and indifferent everywhere today? Because they do not realize their peril: There is but very little Enmity against Satan' agents such as scholasticism institutions; universities; colleges and elementary schools including numerous denominational churches. So much crafting and cunning!

There is little Enmity against Satan' agents and his works, because there is so great emphasizes of education; careers; success; comforts; prestigious; and ignorance concerning evil' power and malice-cunning and the vast extent of his warfare against Christ and his church. They claim as Christians in churches; they are cunning for self-gain and win public confidence that they are Christians. See them when it is about general presidential campaign. They show up their faces with their crafting and cunning sharp words. They are puffed! Yes! They are sharp and well knowledgeable about the public opinion. They well know how to manipulate your minds. They carry you away where you never know and make you feel puffed. Multitudes are deluded here. They do not know that their enemy is a mighty general who knows how to control the minds of evil angels or agents and that with well-matured plans and skillful movements-propaganda he is warring against Christ to prevent the salvation of your soul! Among professed Christians and even among church ministers of the gospel, there is heard scarcely a reference to Satan, except perhaps an incidental mention in the pulpit. It is not a health picture to look at our modern world!.

They overlook the evidences of his continual activity and success, they neglect the many warnings of his subtlety: They seem to ignore his very existence. While men and women are ignorant of his devices this vigilant foe is upon their track every moment. He is intruding his presence in every department of the household, in every street of our modern cities, in the churches in the councils, in the courts of justice, perplexing, deceiving, seducing everywhere ruining the souls and bodies of men and women, breaking up marriages; families; sowing hatred; emulation strife, sedition, murderer. And the Christian world seems to regard these things as though God has appointed them and they must exist. No! It pains God's heart. He is grieved in heart. [Gen 6: 6]. Ancient Israel and Gentiles were enticed into Enmity sinful when they ventured into forbidden association with the pagan-heathen Canaanites. In a similar manner are modern Israel and Gentiles led astray today. The god of this world has blinded the minds of them which believe not, lest the light of the glorious gospel of Christ who is the image of God, should shine unto them, [2 Corinth 4: 4]. All who are not decided followers of Christ Jesus are followers of Satan Enmity sinful.

In the unregenerate heart there is love of Enmity sinful and a disposition to cherish and excuse it. In the renewed heart there is hatred of Enmity sinful, and determined resistance against it. When Christians choose the society of the ungodly and unbelieving, they expose themselves to temptation. Satan conceals himself from view, and stealthily draws his bandage across their eyes. They cannot see that such company is calculated to do them severe harm, and while all the time assimilating to the world in character, words, and actions, they are becoming more and more blinded. Familiarity with sinful inevitably causes it to appear less repulsive. He who chooses to associate with the agents of Satan soon ceases to fear the Lord God their maker and their sustainer. God's long suffering bears their own impending consequences. It tempter often works most successfully through those who are least suspected of being under his control. The opinion prevails with many that all which appears like courtesy or refinement must, in some sense pertain to Christ.

Never was there a greater mistake. These qualities should grace the character of every Christian, for they would exert a powerful influence in favor of true gospel: But they must be consecrated to God or they are a power for evil. Many people who are affable and intelligent and who would not stoop to what is commonly regarded as an immoral act, are but polished instruments in the hands of Satan!. This argument is practical and truth in our modern world.

The insidious, deceptive characteristic of their influence and example renders them more dangerous enemies to the cause of Christ Jesus than are those who are unattractive; coarse; rough; and degraded!

By earnest prayer and dependence upon God, King Solomon obtained the highest wisdom which God could offer which exciter the wonder and admiration of the whole world that brought attention to the queen of Sheba. "Ask me; I will give it to you." God said to Solomon. But when he turned from the source of his strength and went forward relying upon himself; he fells a prey to terrible temptation perhaps; far worse than David his father. The marvelous powers bestowed on this wisest of kings, only rendered him a more efficient agent of the adversary of his soul. While Satan again is constantly seeking to deceive; to blind their minds to the fact; let Christians never forget that they wrestle not against flesh and blood, but against principalities; against powers; against the rulers of the darkness of this corrupted world! Against wicked spirits margin in high places, [Eph. 6: 12]…

The inspired warning is sounding down the centuries to our modern times. "Be sober, be vigilant, because adversary the devil, as a roaring lion, walking about, seeking whom he may devour." [1 Pet. 5: 8]. "Put on the whole armor of God that you may be able to stand against the wiles of the devil; Enmity sinful" [Eph. 6: 11]. God's truth: God is Spirit: Worship God in Spirit and Truth: This is what God seeks to all who claim to be Christian. [John 4: 23].

Athanasius-John T. Nkomo

From the days of Adam and Eve to our time, our great enemy Enmity has been exercising and practicing his power to oppress and destroy many nations on earth. He is now preparing for his last campaign against the church! All who seek to follow Jesus Christ will be brought into hostiles; conflicts; hatred, and with this relentless foe! The more nearly the Christian imitates the divine pattern, the more surely will he [Satan] make himself a mark for the attacks of Satan: All who are actively engaged in the cause of God, seeking to unveil the deceptions of the evil one and to present Christ before the people, will be able to join in the testimony of saint Paul; in which he speaks of serving the Lord with all humility of mind; with many tears and sorrows and temptations. Paul lived for it continually on chains for Christ. [Phil 1: 21-22] "For me to live is Christ! To die is gain!"

Satan assailed Christ with his fiercest and most subtle temptations; but he was repulsed in every conflict. Those battles were fought successful in our behalf; those victories make it possible for us to conquer or overcome! Christ Jesus will give us strength to all who seek after it. No man without his own consent can be overcome by Satan. Satan; the tempter has no power but weak in the eyes of our Lord Jesus Christ. He has no power to control the will or to force the soul to Enmity sinful. He may distress, but he cannot contaminate. He can cause agony, but not defilement. If God is on our side: Who can be against us? Be Still! The Lord God is on your side: "Choose Life!" [Deut. 30:]

The fact that Christ has conquered death; should inspire all his followers with courage; faithful; strength; to fight manfully the battle against Enmity sinful; Satan is weak creature!. Our God is our Strong Shield to Defend all who are true believers. **"Do not be afraid Abraham. I am your shield!". [Gen 15: 1].**

Athanasius-John T. Nkomo

GOD'S PERFECT LAW
Upon All
GOVERMENTS [Exodus 20]

The First Man Adam and Eve; at their creation, had a knowledge of God's Perfect Law; they were acquainted with its claims upon them; its precepts were all written upon their hearts! When they fell by transgression the law was not changed, but a substantial remedial system was truly established to bring them back to absolute and authentically obedience! The promise of a unique Saviour was given, and sacrificial offerings pointing forward to the death of the Lord Jesus Christ as the great Enmity sinful offerings was established. But had the perfect of God never been transgressed, there would have been no death, and no need of a World's Saviour the Christ; consequently there would have been no need of sacrifices neither: The man would live forever!

"But you must not eat from the tree of the knowledge of good and evil, for when you eat of it you will surely die!" [Gen 2: 16].

Indeed, Adam taught his wife Eve; and his children Cain and Abel and their descendants the perfect law of God, and it was handed down from father to son through successive generations up to this day of our modern age. But notwithstanding the gracious provision for man's redemption, there were and still are few accepted it and rendered obedience. By transgression the peoples in the world at large became so vile that it was necessary to cleanse it by the awfully Flood from its corruption. The perfect law was preserved by a single man Noah and his family, and Noah taught his descendants the Ten Commandments, the descendants of Abraham; Isaac; and Jacob through Moses written by the hand of God at Mount Sinai.

As men on earth again departed from God's perfect law; the Lord God chose one single man "Abraham, of whom God declared; **"Abraham obeyed My voice, and kept My charges; walked with Me; My Commandments; My statutes; and My Covenant Law." [Gen. 26: 5].**

To him was given the rite circumcision, which was a sign that those who received it were authentically devoted to the service of God, a pledge that they would remain separate from world's idolatry, and would truly obey the perfect law of God. The failure of Abraham descendants [the Israelites] to keep this pledge, as shown in their disposition to form alliances with the heathen or uncircumcised peoples and adopt their Enmity sinful practice, was the cause of their sojourn-wilderness and bondage in Egypt. This Enmity sinful its process isn't yet in its completion until Christ returns. But their involvement intercourse with idolaters, and their forced lust submission to the heathen Egyptians, the divine precepts became still further corrupted with the vile cruel teachings of heathenism as it is even today being practiced. Therefore when the Lord God brought them forth from Egypt, God Himself came down upon Mount Sinai, enshrouded in fully glory surrounded by His angels, and in awful majesty spoke His Perfect Law direct in the hearing of all the Israelites nation that God had rescued from Egyptians bondage!.

He did not even then trust his precepts to the memory of the peoples who were prone to forgetful His pure requirements, but wrote them upon tables of stones, handed them to Moses. God would remove from Israel all possibility of mingling heathen traditions with His holy precepts, or of confounding His requirements with human ordinances or customs. But God did not stop with giving them the precepts of the Decalogue.

The people had shown themselves so easily led astray that God would leave no door of temptation unguarded. Moses most meek servant of God was commanded or instructed to write, as God should bid him, judgments and laws giving minute instruction as what was required. These directions relating to the duty of the people to God even today, to one another, and to the stranger were only the principles of the Ten Commandments amplified and given in a specific manner, that none need err.

They were designed to guard the sacredness of the ten precepts engraved on the tables of stone. If man had kept the law of God, as given to the first Man, Adam and Eve after their fall, preserved by Noah, and also observed by Abraham, there would have been no necessity for the ordinance of circumcision. And there would have been no death neither. And if the descendants of Abraham had kept the covenant of which circumcision was a sign, they would never have been seduced into idolatry neither us even today, nor would it have been necessary for them and us to suffer a life of bondage in Egypt; including us today; they would have kept God's perfect law in mind including us today, and there would have been no necessity for it to be proclaimed from Mount Sinai or engraved upon the tables of stone. And had the people like us today practiced the principles of the Ten Commandments, there would have been no need of the additional directions given to Moses. Christ would have neither come down to die on awful cross.

The sacrificial system, committed to Adam and Eve was also perverted by their descendants. Superstition, idolatry, cruelty, and licentiousness corrupted the simple and significant service that God had appointed. Through long intercourse with heathen idolaters the people of Israel as well the Gentiles had mingled many heathen customs with their worship; therefore the Lord God gave them at Mount Sinai instruction concerning the sacrificial service. The process is the same. Though we do not sacrifice because Christ ultimately perfected the sacrificial once and for all!. But Enmity sinful remains within all human beings on earth until Christ returns. After the completion of the tabernacle, God communicated with Moses from the cloud of glory above the mercy seat, and gave him full directions concerning the system of offerings and the forms of worship to be maintained in the sanctuary. It must be done with holiness and perfection according to God's Holiness. The ceremonial law was thus given to Moses, and by him only written in a book. But the law of Ten Commandments [Exodus 20 spoken from Mount Sinai] had been written by God Himself on the tables of stones and was sacredly preserved in the ark holy place no one could enter or look at it where it was placed. You would be natural dead. It was covered by curtains of colorful.

There are many who try to blend these two systems, using the texts that speak of the ceremonial law to prove that the moral law has been abolished; but this is a perversion of the Scriptures!. The distinction between the two systems is broad and clear!.

The ceremonial system was and is made up of symbols pointing to Christ Jesus, to His sacrifice and His priesthood. This ritual law with its sacrifices and ordinances, was to be performed by the Hebrews until type met antitype in the death of Christ Jesus, the Lamb of God that taketh away the Enmity sinful of the whole entire world!. This is unique of the Lord God's mystery unknown or hidden to human perspectives.

Then all the sacrificial offerings were to cease. It is this law that Jesus Christ took out of the way, nailing it to his awful cross!. [Colo. 2: 14]: But concerning the law of Ten Commandments the psalmist declares: "Forever, Oh Lord God, Thy Word is settled in Heaven!" [Ps. 119: 89]. And Christ Himself says: "Think not that I am come to destroy the law; but I am come to fulfill it." I say unto you" making the assertion as emphatic as possible: "Till heaven and earth pass, one jot or one title shall in no wise pass from the law, till all be fulfilled." [Matt 5: 17-18]. Here Christ teaches, not merely what the claims of God's law had been, and were then, but that these claims should hold as long as the heavens and the earth remain. The Perfect Law of the Lord God stands for very serious issues upon the whole entire world when Christ Jesus returns. The compelling question is: Who notice seriously as it is being proclaimed? In the past few took notice: It is the same thing today, few take notice. The people are prone to forgetful about God commands since from the beginning. But the word stands still proclaims its own according to the Lord God.

The law of God is as immutable as His heavenly throne. It will maintain its claims upon mankind in all ages concerning the law proclaimed from Mount Sinai, Nehemiah says; "Thou came down also upon Mount Sinai and spoke with them from heaven, and gave them right judgments and true laws, good statutes and commandments." Neh. 9: 13]. And Apostle Paul declares: "The law is holy and the commandment holy, and just and good." [Rom 7: 12]. This can be no other than the Decalogue: For it is the law that says; "Thou shall not covert!" [v. 7]. While the Lord Christ Jesus the World's Saviour's death brought to an end the law of types and shadows: It did not in the least detract from the obligation of the moral law! On the contrary, the very fact that it was necessary for the Lord Christ Jesus to die in order to atone for the transgression of that perfect law; proves it to be immutable!.

Those who claim that the Lord Christ Jesus came to abrogate the perfect law of God and to do away with the Ancient Testament, speak of the Jewish or Judaism age as one of darkness, and represent the human made religion of the ancient Hebrews and modern world scholasticism rather than of the Holy God as consisting of mere forms and ceremonies etc. Of course; Christ condemned such mere forms and ceremonies which Judaism practiced till this day at our modern age. Indeed; this is an awfully error that cause Enmity to persist till Christ returns!. Obviously; it all make sense according to the Scriptures descriptive!.

All through the pages of the sacred history where the dealings of God Almighty with His special chosen people [Israel] are recorded: There are burning traces of the **"Great I AM."** Never has God Almighty given to the sons of men more open manifestations of His power and glory than when He alone was acknowledged as Israel's ruler; and gave the law to His special chosen peoples "Israel." Here was a scepter swayed by no mere human hand: And the stately going forth of Israel's invisible powerful King, who's the knowing of all; were unspeakably grand and awfully!.

In all these revelations of the true divine presence the glory of God Almighty was completely manifested through the Lord Christ Jesus: Complete Image of God Almighty visibly seen with their naked eyes: Heard his voice through their ears from his holy mouth uttering truths!. It is the same manner today: Modern men hearing Christ' voice through Scriptures and its proclamation!.

Not alone at the Saviour's advent: But through all the ages after the Fall of Man [Adam] and the promise of redemption, God's true image was visibly in Christ Jesus: Reconciling the entire world unto Himself. [2 Corinth 5: 19]. Jesus Christ was and still is; the foundation and center of the ultimate sacrificial system in both the patriarchal and all the Jewish age.

Since the Enmity was imposed of our first parents [Adam-Eve] there has been no direct communication between God and man: No more! Till the Lord Jesus Christ returns!. The Scriptures is the only means of order to communicate with Christ Jesus and through faith: **"Look! Your house is left to you desolate! For I tell you: You will not see Me again until you say: "Blessed is he who comes in the name of the Lord!"** [Matt. 23: 38-39]. Yes! Christ meant it so well: No mere man can hear the voice of Christ' boom into the ears!. No more! Till Christ returns!.

The Head Father God has given the entire world into the hands of the Lord Christ Jesus the ultimate righteous Judge: That through His mediatorial perfect law works He may redeem all mankind in the whole entire universe and vindicate the ultimate perfect authority and pure holiness of the law of the Lord God Almighty!. The Government and Perfect Law: All the communion between heaven and the fallen and corrupted peoples of the whole entire world has been cleanse through the Lord Christ Jesus!. It was and still is the Son of God that gave to our first parents [Adam-Eve] the promise of redemption!. It was Christ who revealed Himself to the patriarchs: Adam: Noah: Abraham: Isaac: Jacob: and Moses: They understood the true "Gospel" from his uttering mouth: **"I tell you the truth: "Before Abraham was, "I AM!"** The Lord Jesus Christ declared [John 8: 58].

They looked for salvation through human beings surrogate and surety! They couldn't find it: Neither us today can!. These holy men of ancient days held communion with the Lord God direct who was to come to our wicked world in human flesh form and some of them talked with Christ and heavenly angels face to face. Christ Jesus was not only the leader of the Israelites or Hebrews in the wilderness: The angels in whom was the name of "I AM!" and veiled the cloudy pillar, went before the host but it was Christ who gave the Perfect Law to His special chosen peoples the "Israelites:"

Jesus Christ is the One through whom God Head Father has at all times revealed Himself to men. But for all there is but one God only: No one to compare: The Head Father of whom are all things and we in Him no one else: And one Lord Christ Jesus by whom are all things and we by Him! [1 Corinth 8: 6]. "This is he "Moses" that was in the temple or tabernacle in the wilderness with the Angel which spoke to him in Mount Sinai and with our forefathers: Who received the Lively Oracles to give unto us today! [Acts 7: 38]. This Angel was the Angel of the Lord God's presence [Is. 63: 9]: The Angel in whom was the name of the **"Great I AM!"** [Exodus 3: 14]. Also see 23: 20-23. God's presence continually in the cloudy guarding Israeli His special chosen peoples. Making sure that they fully understood as they heard His powerful voice booming into their ears uttering!. But no form only the voice in cloudy could be heard atmosphere!

Again: Jesus Christ is called: "He is the Word of God!" He is so called so because God gave Christ His revelation to man in all ages through Christ Jesus: No one else! [John 1: 1-3]. It was His Spirit that inspired the ancient prophets. [1 Pet. 1: 10-11]. He was revealed to them as the Angel of the Lord God Almighty: The Captain of the Lord God of host! **"Michael the-Archangel:"** Amid the awful glory of Mount Sinai, Jesus Christ clearly declared in the hearing of all the peoples the ten precepts of His Father Head Perfect Law. The only Mighty Eternally God! [**Bereshith**] **"I AM WHO I AM!"** [Exo. 3: 14] Hebrew Original word: Beginning!."

It was God Himself who handed the Perfect Law to Moses at Mount Sinai: Written on stones by God's Holy hand: It was Christ Jesus as God spoke to His special chosen people Israel through the prophets. The disciple Saint Peter writing to the newly founded Christian Church says this: "That the prophets prophesied of the grace that should come unto you: Searching what, or what manner of time the Spirit of Christ which was in them did signify, when it testified beforehand the suffering of Christ Jesus and the glory that should follow." [1 Pet. 1: 10-11]. It is the voice of Christ Jesus that speaks to us even today through the Old and New Testament. The testimony of the Lord Christ Jesus is the spirit of prophecy." [Rev. 19: 10]. During His earthly dwelling; Jesus Christ' teachings while personally among men and women Christ directed the minds of the people to the Old Testament. And so did the disciples and apostles followed after Him. Today, we use both, Old and New Testament for Scripture references. These books are inseparable! They both utter the Sacred Word of the Lord God!. The Perfect Law remains the same! "For the Word of God is living and active!" It charges: It Judges: It teaches: It corrects: Nothing is hidden: [Heb. 4: 12] "today, if you hear his voice do not harden your hearts!" [V. 7] Jesus Christ teachings: He said to the Jews as well as to the Gentiles: "You search the Scriptures, for in them you think you have eternal life: And these are they which testify of Me." [John 5:

39]. The ancient Judaism as well as the modern religious still strives to fully understand the meaning. So much human's rational perspectives: Enmity blinds the past and the present. At this time the book of Old Testament was the only Original part of the Holy Bible [Torah] in its existence. It still remains to be the same till this day modern age and future generations until Christ returns! "Do not think that I shall accuse you:" Jesus said: "Moses in whom you trust will accuse you!" [John 5: 45]. In addition Jesus said: "For if you believe Moses, you would believe Me: For he wrote all about Me." [V. 46].

The ceremonial law was given by the Lord Christ Jesus. Even after it was no longer to be observed; Paul presented it before the Jews in its true position and value; showing its place in the plan of redemption and its relation to the work of Christ Jesus: And the great apostle pronounces this law glorious worthy of its divine Originator. The solemn service of the sanctuary typified the grand truths that were to be revealed through successive generations. The cloud of incense ascending with the prayers of Israel represents His righteousness that alone can make the Enmity sinner's prayer acceptable to God; the bleeding victim on the altar of sacrifice testified of a unique Redeemer to come "the Christ" and from the Holy of Holies the visible token of the divine presence shone forth!.

Thus through age after age of darkness and apostasy faith was kept alive in the hearts of men and women until the time came for the advent of the promised Messiah, the Christ! Yes! Christ came! Christ Jesus was and is the light of his people; the Light of the whole entire World! Before He came to earth in the form of humanity! The first gleam of light that pierced the gloom in which Enmity sinful had wrapped the world from Christ Jesus! And from Him has come every ray of heaven's most brightness that has fallen upon the inhabitants of the earth: In the plan of redemption Christ indeed is the **"Bereshith"** the First and the Last! Since the

Christ, the Saviour of the whole entire world shed his blood for the remission of Enmity sinful nature, and ascended to heaven "to appear in the presence of God for all" [Heb 9: 24], the light has been streaming from the cross of Calvary and from the holy places of the sanctuary above!. But clearer light granted all should not cause us to despise that which in earlier centuries was received through the types pointing to the coming Christ. The gospel of Christ sheds light upon the Jews and Gentiles economy and gives significance to the ceremonial law.

As new truths are revealed and that which has been well known from the beginning **"Bereshith"** is brought into clearer light, the character and purpose of God are made manifest in His dealings with his special chosen people Israel. Every additional ray of light that we receive gives us a clearer understanding of the plan of redemption which is the working out of the divine will in the salvation of man. We all see new beauty and force in the inspired word, and we study its pages with a deeper and more absorbing interest. The opinion is held **[Segregation or Apartheid]** by many that God placed a separating wall between the Jews or Hebrew and Gentile-outside world; that His care and love withdrawn to a great extent from the rest of mankind-race were centered upon Israel only. But God did not design or invent that his created people in his image and likeness, should build up a wall of partition between themselves and their fellow neighbor and nations or men. No! God didn't! The heart of Infinite Love was reaching and still reaching out toward all inhabitants of the earth; color or creed but all belongs! For "Thou oh Lord created them all!" It was for Thy pleasure!" Though they had rejected Him, so the Jews rejected him: He was constantly to reveal Himself to them all and make them partakers of His true-Love and Grace! His blessing was granted to chosen people, either Jews or Gentiles that they might bless others. Abraham a Gentile, God chose him among Gentiles to be a blessing for others: And so was Noah with his family!.

God called Abraham, and prospered and honored him and the patriarch's fidelity was a light to the nations in all the countries of his sojourn. Segregation or Apartheid that many people practice is evil in the eyes of God the Creator of all mankind; for He created them all for His pleasure! Abraham did not shut himself away from the people around him. He maintained friendly relations with all the neighborhood kings of the surrounding nations, by some of whom he was treated with great respect; and his integrity and unselfishness, his valor and benevolence; were representing the character of God. "Pharaoh and Abimelech" kings of ungodly.

In Mesopotamia, in Canaan, in Egypt, and even to the inhabitants of Sodom and Gomorrah; the God of heaven was revealed through Abraham as His representative. No such wall was built to block out the way of relations with other surrounding neighbor nations.

So to the people of Egypt and of all the nations connected with that powerful kingdom; God manifested Himself through Joseph. Why then did the Lord God choose to exalt Joseph the young son of Jacob so highly among the Egyptians? He probably might have provided some other way for the accomplishment of His purposes toward the children of Jacob: But God desired to make Joseph a light and He placed him in the palace of king Pharaoh; that the heavenly illumination might extend far and near neighbors. God was with Joseph with his wisdom and justice, by the purity and benevolence of his daily life, by his devotion to the interests of the people and that people a nation of evil and idolaters: Joseph was representative of God in Christ. In their benefactor to whom all Egypt including Canaanites turned with gratitude and praise; that heathen nation of Egypt were to behold the God's love of their Creator and Redeemer; and sustainer of their lives. So in Moses floating on Rivers Nile; also God placed a light beside the throne of the earth's greatest kingdom; that all who would might learn of the true and living God in heaven and on earth among all His peoples: And all this light was given to the Egyptians before the hand of God Almighty was stretched out over them in judgments. The awful judgments upon the Egyptians came after decades because they did not recognize and acknowledge God His existence among them!. The consequences proved to be very severe! The prophecy was fulfilled. [Gen 15: 13-14].

In the deliverance of Israel from Egypt knowledge of the powerful of God was heard and spread fast far and wide. The warlike people of the stronghold of Jericho: Sihon: Og king of the Moabites; Ammonites at Jordan Eastern River trembled as their stomach melted. "As soon as we had heard these things;" said Rahab, a Canaanite harlot: "Our hearts did melt, neither did there remain any more courage in a man; because of you!" For the Lord your God; He is God in heaven above all; and in earth beneath." [Josh 2: 11]. Centuries later the Exodus the priests of the Philistines reminded their people of the terrible plagues of Egypt and warned them against resisting the God of Israel! Yes! Rahab recognized the Lord God of Israel to be powerful and she acknowledged with fearful heart. As result; God spared her life including all her parents and siblings stayed with the Israelite's camp safe.

God called Israel and blessed and exalted them, not that by obedience to His law they alone might receive His favor and become the exclusive recipients of His holy blessings, but in order to reveal Himself through them to all the inhabitants of the earth big and small the same. It was for the accomplishment of this very purpose that He commanded them to keep themselves distinct from the idolatrous nations around them. Is God wrong? Idolatry and all the Enmity sinful that followed in its train were abhorrent to God and He commanded His people not to mingle with other nations, to "do after their evil works" and forget God. He forbade their marriage with idolaters, lest their hearts too should be led away from Him. It was just as necessary then as it is now that God's special chosen people should be pure; "unspotted from the world things." They must keep themselves free from its spirit, because it is opposed to truth and righteousness.

But God did not intend that His special chosen people, in self-righteous exclusiveness should shut themselves away from reaching out to the world, so that they could have no influence upon it. No! They were meant to spread the light with its illumination to all who are in the darkness to come to the light. "You are the light of the world!." Jesus said. Like their Master, the followers of Christ Jesus in every age were to be the light of the world: "I am the light of the world!" Jesus said: "A city that is set on an hill cannot be hidden: Neither do men light a candle and put it under a bushel; but on a candle-stick and it gives light unto all that are in the house." That is in the world. And he adds: "Let your light so shine before men that they may see your good works and glorify your Father who is in heaven." [Matt. 5: 14-16].

This is just what Enoch and Noah, Abraham, Joseph, and Moses did: It is my duty and your duty to carry on this light to others. It is just what God designed that His people Israel should do including you and me today, it is the same duty needs to be carried on. We ought to remind ourselves that Christ is the light of the whole entire world! His commands still stand for us to carry it on to others. Darkness cannot drive out darkness: Only light can do that!. It was their own evil heart of unbelief controlled by Satan: And it is our own evil heart of unbelief controlled by Satan that leads us to hide our light instead of shedding it upon surrounding peoples; it is same bigoted spirit that caused them and still same cause for us today either to follow the iniquitous practices of the heathen or to shut ourselves away in proud exclusiveness as if God's love and care were over them alone as we see it even today on our own modern age.

It was necessary then as it is now that God's special chosen peoples should be pure unspotted from the corrupted world. Like them; we must keep ourselves free from its spirit because it is opposed to truth and righteousness of the Lord our God! But God did not intend that His people, in self-righteous exclusiveness, should shut themselves away from the world, so that they could have no influence upon it.

As the Bible presents two laws, one changeless and eternal, the other provisional and temporary, so there are two covenants. The covenant of grace was first made with man in Eden, when after the fall there was given a divine promise that the seed or offspring of the woman [Eve] should bruise the serpent's head. [Enmity] To all men this covenant offered pardon and the assisting of God for future obedience through faith in Christ. It also promised them and us eternal life on condition of fidelity to God's perfect law. Thus the patriarchs received the hope of salvation including their offspring.

This same covenant was renewed to Abraham in the promise: "In your seed [offspring] shall all the nations of the earth be blessed because you have obeyed My voice." [Gen. 22: 18]. This promise pointed to Christ also. So Abraham understood it [see Gala. 3: 8, 16-29] completed description; and he trusted in Christ for the forgiveness of sins. It was this faith that was accounted unto him for righteousness.

The covenant with Abraham also maintained the authority of God' law!. The Lord God appeared unto Abraham and said: "I am the Almighty God; walk before Me, and be thou perfect!" [Gen. 17: 1], The testimony of God concerning his faithful servant was that; "Abraham obeyed My voice and kept My charge: My commandments: My statutes; and My laws." [Gen 26: 5]. The Lord God indeed, declared to Abraham; "I will establish My covenant between Me and you and your seed after you in their generations, for an everlasting covenant, to be a God unto you and to your seed after you." [Gen 17: 7].

Though this covenant was made with Adam and to Abraham, it could not be ratified until the awful death of Christ! It had existed by the promise of God since the first intimation of redemption had been given; it had been accepted by faith; yet when ratified by Christ, it is called a new covenant. The law of God was the basis of this covenant which was simply an arrangement for bringing men again into harmony with the divine will, placing them where they could obey God's law.

Another compact called in Scriptures the 'Old" covenant was formed between God and Israel at Mount Sinai and was then ratified by the blood of a sacrifice. The Abraham's covenant was ratified by the blood of Christ Jesus, and it is called the "Second," or "New," covenant, because the blood by which it was sealed was shed after the blood of the first covenant. That the new covenant was valid in the days of Abraham is evident from the fact that it was then confirmed both by the promise and by the oath of God, the 'two immutable things in which it was impossible for God to lie or to break." [Heb 6: 18]. But if the Abraham' covenant contained the promise of redemption, why was another covenant formed at Mount Sinai? In their bondage the people of Israel had to a great extent lost their knowledge of God and of the principle of the Abraham covenant. In delivering them from Egypt, God sought to reveal to them His power and His mercy, that they might be led to love and trust Him as their true God who cares for them. He brought them down to the Red Seas where pursued by the cruel Egyptians to tear them apart for good, escape seemed impossible for them that they might realize their utter helplessness; their need of divine power-aid; and then God wrought deliverance for them. Thus they were filled with love and gratitude to God their strong deliverer and with confidence in His powerful to rescue them from Pharaoh's wicked horsemen. He had bound them to Himself as their mighty deliver from temporal bondage.

But there was a still greater truth to be impressed upon their minds. Living in the midst of idolatry and corruption, they had no true conception of the holiness of God of the exceeding sinfulness of their own hearts; their utter inability; in themselves, to render obedience to God's perfect law and their need of a true strong saviour. All this they must be taught. God brought them to Mount Sinai: He manifested His glory: He gave them His perfect law: with the promise of great blessings on condition of obedience: "If you will obey My voice indeed, and keep My covenant, then you shall be unto Me a kingdom of priests, and a holy nation." God meant it so well! [Exodus 19: 5-6]. Did they fully obey God?

The people of Israel didn't even realize about the Enmity sinfulness of their own hearts: Neither us even nowadays, realize about the Enmity sinfulness of our own hearts: And that with Christ it is impossible for us to keep God's perfect law: And they too readily entered into covenant with God: Unthinkable: Feeling that we are able to establish our own righteousness: Like our forefathers did we are doing same thing like them: "All that the Lord God had said will we do, and be obedient." But in vain in the eyes of our God [Exodus 24: 7]. We, like our forefathers have witnessed the proclamation of the law in awful majesty and have trembled with terror before the Mount Sinai, and yet only a few weeks passed before we broke our covenant with our God, and bowed down to worship a graven image [Money] and self-gain prestigious and power. We cannot hope for the favor of God through a covenant which we have broken and now, seeing our Enmity sinfulness and our need of pardon, we are brought to feel our need of the Saviour revealed in the Abraham' covenant and shadowed forth in the sacrificial offerings. What can we give back to God?

Now they were prepared to appreciate the blessings of the new covenant. The terms of the "Old Covenant" were "Obey and live:" If a man do, he shall even live in them" [Ezek. 20: 11] Leviticus

18: 5] but "cursed be he that confirmed not all the word of this law to do them." [Deut. 27: 26]. The new covenant was abolished upon better promises, the promise of forgiveness of sins and of the grace of God to renew the heart and bring it into harmony with the principles of God's law. This shall be the covenant that I will make with the house of Israel: After those days said the Lord, I will put my law in their inward parts and write it in their hearts." I will forgive their sins and will remember their sins no more!" [Jer. 31: 33-34].

The same law that engraved upon the tables of stones is written by the Holy hand of God and by the Holy Spirit upon tables of the heart. Instead of going about to establish our own righteousness we accept the righteousness of Christ Jesus! His [Christ] blood atones for our Enmity sinfulness. His obedience is accepted for us. Then the heart renewed by the Holy Spirit will bring forth the fruits of the Spirit." Through the grace of our Lord Christ Jesus we shall live in obedience to the law of God written upon our hearts.

Having the Spirit of Christ, we shall walk even as He walked. Through the prophet he declared of Himself; "I delight to do your will, oh My God: Yea, Thy law is within My heart." [Ps. 40: 8]. And when among men, Jesus said: "The Father has not left Me alone; for I do always those things that pleases Him." [John 8:29] The apostle Paul clearly presents the relation between faith and the law under the new covenant: He says: "Being justified by faith, we have peace with God through our Lord Christ Jesus. Do we then make void the law through faith? God forbid: Yea, we establish the law!" For what the law could not do, in that it was weak through the flesh" it could not justify man because in his Enmity sinful nature he could not keep the law; God sending his own Son in the likeness of sinful flesh, and for sin, condemned sin in the flesh: That the righteousness of the law might be fulfilled is us; who walk not after the flesh, but after the Spirit." [Rom 5: 1; 3: 31; 8:3, 4]. God's work is the same in all time, although there are different degrees of development and different manifestations of His power, to meet the wants of men in the different ages. Beginning with the first gospel promise and coming down through the patriarchal and Jewish ages, and even unfolding of the purposes of God in the plan of redemption.

Jesus Christ typified in the rites and ceremonies of the Jewish law is the very same that is revealed in the gospel. The clouds that enveloped His divine form have rolled back; the mist and shades have disappeared; and Jesus Christ, the world's grand redeemer stands revealed! He who proclaimed the law from Mount Sinai and delivered to Moses' hand the precepts of the ritual law, is the same that spoken the Sermon on the Mount. The great principles of love to God which He set forth as the foundation of the law and the prophets are only a reiteration of what He had spoken through Moses to the Israelite peoples: "Hear! 0 Israel: The Lord our God is One Lord: And you shall love the Lord your God with all your heart; and with all your soul; and with all your strength." [Deut 6: 4-5]. "You shall love your neighbor as yourself." [Lev. 19: 18]. The teacher is the same in both dispensations. God's claims are the same from the Bereshith! For all proceed from God alone no one else! With who is no variableness neither shadow of turning!. [James 1: 17].

Jesus Christ is inevitable! If an individuals and humanity are to progress; Jesus Christ is inescapable! You ignore him at your own wicked risk…

God did not create the earth to be empty! But God created the earth to be filled with people to glorify Him and honor. Because created all in His own image and likeness for His pleasure and honor. His eyes delight in them when He looks to all His creation that created in His image and likeness. God gets grieved when His creatures disobey Him. [Gen 6: 6].

Then God said: "Let us make man in our image in our likeness and let them rule over the fish of the sea and the birds of the air over the livestock over all the earth and over the creations that move along the ground." [Gen 1: 26-27].

Phinehas: Son of Eleazar, son of Aaron, the priest took a spear or javelin in his hand, and followed the Israelite into the tent: He drove or thrust the spear through both of the Israelite and into the woman's body: Then the plague against the Israelite stopped, but those who died in the plague numbered 24,000.

The Lord God said to Moses: "Phinehas son of Eleazar, the son of Aaron the priest, has turned my anger away from the Israelite for he was zealous as I am for my honor among them, so that in my zeal I did not put an end to them." Therefore, tell him I am making my covenant of peace with him. He and his descendants will have a covenant of everlasting priesthood because he was zealous for the honor of his God and made atonement for the Israelite!" [Num 25: 7-13]. Zealous and honor for the Lord God: God the creator deserves all the credits for his own creations. All the praises, honor and glories worship ought to be to God alone! His name ought to be hollowed and honor. All nations on earth ought to bow down their heads before God the maker and sustainer of all life above in heaven and on earth beneath! That is the purpose that God owns all creatures! No other gods. Human beings cannot afford to disobey God who is above all! Enmity stands upon all men because man disobeyed God his maker! Decalogue; the Perfect Covenant-Law of God's Sacred Word eternally that the man dares to break! God provided a remade to cure all! Jesus Christ the perfect Lamb. All men ought to lift upon Christ Jesus for everlasting salvation. Jesus Christ is inevitable! If individuals and humanity are to progress; Jesus Christ is inescapable! You ignore him at your own wicked risk.

Athanasius-John T. Nkomo

Chapter 11

The Lord Jesus Christ Conquers All Enmity!
"I am the Resurrection!" [John 11: 25]

Satan or Lucifer could have power: He would blot out all and destroy everyone who claims to be Christian on the face of the whole entire earth! If Satan could, he would destroy and blot out everyone else on the face of the earth too. Nothing that should exists; absolutely he would wipe out all that claims to be godly on earth: With countless fallen heavenly angels to do his abiding, and a mind in advanced of our own: We are no match for his power that drives his motive and conscience for crafting and cunning.

"Surely God is good to Israel, to those who are pure in heart:" But as for me, my feet had almost slipped; I had nearly lost my foothold. For I envied the arrogant when I saw the prosperity of the wicked! They have no struggles; their bodies are healthy and strong. They are free from the burdens common to man; they are not plagued by human ills. Therefore pride is their necklace; they clothe themselves with violence.

From their callous hearts comes Enmity; the evil conceits of their minds know no limits. They scoff, and speak with malice; in their arrogance they threaten oppression. Their mouths lay claim to heaven, and their tongues take possession of the earth. Therefore their people turn to them and drink up waters in abundance.

They say: "How can God know?" Does the Most High have knowledge?" This is what the wicked are like: Always carefree, they increase in wealth. Their wealthy never last forever: They all belong to Dust where they were all taken. [Ps. 73: 1-12].

But in Jesus Christ there is the powerful needed: Our danger is in not recognizing the strength and number of Satan's agents and thus thinking ourselves safe: We do not flee to Christ Jesus the strongest solid rocky, moment by moment, for the help we desperately need! My personal care doctor threatened me with his oppressive attitude and said: **"You are not a doctor! You are wrong! You disobey me!"** Wicked pride speech took up himself a position of a little god: In my response to him, I said: You are a mere human being made out of dust! You eat food from dust and you return to dust where you were taken! And you die! You return to dust for good! You are trained by a mere man who is also made out of dust. Both of you are limited!. You do not sustain life! God sustains all life; including yours! Neither you know when your destination takes its place!. It surprises you! You cannot prevent any disease or symptom that threatens your life!. You get sick any time and you die any time!. Your days are numbered. And you do not know how! Do you really know? The name "Bethel Israel stands for God:" The doctor was mute and speechless. He was consumed with his own anger as he became mute: Now I changed to another PC at BIDMC. I never had a desire that he should be my pc no more. Arrogance speech!. Some doctors who work there do not know what it means "Bethel Israel:" They neither have a clue! Those men who named the Hospital Bethel Israel: Who were they and where they came from? The history of its name; some or most of them do not know the meaning that it stands for God!.

Satan, the existing evidence of evil on earth and the agency of Satan evil spirits are true facts well established in both the Old and New Testament: It is very old evidence! From Bereshith [Genesis] [Beginning] days of Adam; Noah; Moses; Christ Jesus; Disciples; Church Reformation and through all the succeeding ages up to John at Patmos [Revelation-Book] the final latest Gospel writer: Satan is well recognized as an active device machine personally agency, the originator of all evil activities!. The enemy of God and men who constantly opposes all that is of God: He is a roaring lion, but his power is very limited!. He fails to wipe everyone who claims to be Christian or godly men.

It is true that imagination and superstition have given their own coloring to these facts and have linked with legends and human [fiction] traditions of heathens; Judaism; Jewish; Christian; Gentile nations; but as revealed in the word of God they are of the utmost solemnity and importance! What we need to tell the world is: **Jesus Christ is Able to Conquer All Evil Activity!** In Christ; All are Safe! The connection of the visible with the invisible world, the ministration of angels of God, and the agency of evil angels or demons present psychic; are inseparably interwoven with human history!.

We are so often told or taught of the fall of the angels from their purity; of Lucifer their leader occasional he visits heaven; the instigator of rebellion, of their confederacy and human governments of their various orders of their great human scholasticism intelligence and subtlety of their malicious designs and shaping against the innocence and happiness of men. We are indeed, told of One Mightier than the fallen foe [Satan] One by whose authority Satan's power is very limited and well controlled!. And we are told and taught, also, of the punishment prepared for the originator of Enmity Lucifer!. Deceived Eve!. The existing evidences are obvious: Christian unresolved struggles remain the same since from the past; present; and future. All human tradition teaching on earth is unable to resolve the originator of Enmity: Not so, until Christ Jesus returns! During the time when Christ Jesus was still upon the earth, Enmity evil spirits manifested their power in a most striking manner! Christ faced the spirit evil and cast them out with violence resistance. They couldn't stand against the power of Christ but to yield! And why was this? Jesus Christ had come to enter upon the plan devised for man's redemption, and Satan therefore determined to assert his right to control the world as permitted with limits. He couldn't overcome Christ!

Satan had succeeded in establishing idolatry in every part of the earth except the land of some Palestine. To the only land that not fully yielded to the tempter's sway; Christ Jesus came to shed upon the people the light of heaven!. There weren't many to be found. Here two rival powers claimed supremacy. Jesus Christ was stretching out His mighty army of love inviting all who would to find pardon and peace: And while Satan was stretching out his arms of hostility and hatred Enmity: Who wins? And who decides? Jesus Christ! It is written!.

The hosts or agencies of darkness or Enmity well understood that if the mission of Christ should be successful, their darkness rule was soon to come to an end. Satan as the chief command, rage like a chained lion, and defiantly exhibited his power over the bodies as well as the souls of the weak minds of men. The idea is still on the process even to this day. The fact that men have been possessed with demons; psychic; is clearly stated in the Old and New Testament. The whole text is written concerning Jesus Christ and all are under his feet!.

The persons thus afflicted were, and are not merely suffering with disease from natural causes. Jesus Christ had perfect understands of that with which he was dealing, and he recognized the direct presence and agency of evil spirits existence evidence. A striking example of their number power, and malignity and also of the power and mercy of Christ, is given in the Scripture account of the healing of the demoniacs at **Gadara.** Powerful event they all saw. Those wretched maniacs, spurning all restraint, writhing, foaming, raging, were filling the air with their cries; doing violence to themselves and endangering all who should approach them. Jesus Christ, defying Enmity to hellish condemnation. Their bleeding and disfigured bodies and distracted minds presented a spectacle well pleasing to the prince of darkness. It is the same thing even this day. God's truth in Christ still prevailing in our eyes!. One of the demons controlling the sufferers declared his name: "My name is Legion; for we are many." [Mark 5: 9]. They were all trembling at the sight of Christ' presence! In the Roman army a legion consisted of from three to five thousand men. Satan's hosts or agencies also are marshaled into companies and the single company to which these demons belonged numbered no less than a legion!. Even today; legions are visibly seen in their existence; Christian fiction ebook a new modern version spread around the globe shaping the young adults minds.

At the command of Christ Jesus, the evil spirits Enmity departed from their victims, leaving them calmly sitting at the Saviour's feet, subdued, intelligent, sober-mind and gentle. But the demons or psychic were permitted to sweep a herd of swine into the deep sea; and to the dwellers of **Gadara** their loss outweighed the blessings which Christ Jesus had totally destroyed, and the divine healer was entreated to depart. But the great event was attained. Nothing could hinder Christ's mighty power.

This was the obvious result which Satan designed to secure. But he couldn't! By casting the blame upon Christ, he aroused the selfish fears of the people, and prevented them from listening to the voice of Christ' true words. Satan has constantly accusing Christians as the cause of loss, misfortune; economic, and suffering, instead of allowing the reproach to fall where it belongs, upon himself and his evil spirits agencies. But the purpose of Christ Jesus were not thwarted: He allowed the evil spirits to destroy the herd of swine as a rebuke to those Jews who by raising these unclean beasts for the sake of economic gain had transgressed the command of God perfect law. Had not Christ restrained the demons, they would have plunged into the deep sea, not only the swine, but also their keepers and owners. The preservation of both the keepers and the owners was due alone to Christ merciful interposition for their deliverance. Furthermore, this scene was permitted to take place that the disciples might witness the cruel power of Satan upon both men and the beasts.

And so, this is also the same witness message for today; all ought to heed. Jesus Christ is able to conquer all evil spirits.

The Lord Christ Jesus; the saviour desires all his followers to have a knowledge of the compelling foe whom they were to meet, that they might not be deceived and overcome by his devices. It was also Christ's will that the people of that region should behold his power to break the bondage of Satan and release his captives. And though Jesus Christ himself departed, the men so marvelously delivered, remained to declare the event of merciful of their Benefactor. They had the perfect obligation to carry on. Other instances of similar nature are recorded in the Scriptures. The daughter of the Syrophenician woman was grievously vexed with a devil, whose Jesus cast out by His powerful word; "Get out you devil!" [Mark 7: 26-30]. One possessed with a devil, blind and mute or dumb [Matt. 12: 22] a youth who had a dumb spirit that often times cast him into fire, and into the waters in order to destroy him," Mark 9: 17-27] the maniac who tormented by a spirit of an unclean devil, [Luke 4: 33-36], disturbed the Sabbath quiet of the Synagogue at Capernaum, were all healed by the powerful and the compassion of Christ Jesus on earth, the saviour of the world full of power and the conquer of death! No one else dares to claim for such truth of evidence!.

In nearly every instance, Jesus Christ addressed the demons as an intelligent entity, commanding him to come out of his victim and to torment him no more! Satan has to bow down at Christ' feet and yield at Christ' commands. The worshipers at Capernaum, beholding Christ Jesus' mighty power, were all amazed and spoke among themselves saying: "What a word is this so powerful! For with authority and power he commands the unclean spirits, and they come out!" Yes! They saw and they believed in Christ: Any sickness Christ healed by his powerful word from his mouth. No mere human physician can heal the disease that Chris healed. Even today no human physician is able. So much diseases and symptoms killing people; human physicians are not able to cure or prevent!. Neither do they prevent a disease that attacks them or know their numbered days to return to dust where they are taken. But very limited like anyone else. They are trained professions with limit.

Those possessed with devils are usually represented as being in a condition of great suffering, yet there were exceptions to this rule. For the sake of obtaining supper-natural power, some welcomed the Satan influence, like today modern era, physicians are Satan's affluence with their claims which are unfulfilling truth.

These of course have no conflict with the demons. Psychologist cannot cure. Of this class were those who possessed the spirit of divination, [e. g]; "Simon Magus, Elymas the Sorcerer or psychic, and the damsel who followed Saint Paul and Silas at Philippi. He wanted to purchase the divine power for self-gain. Jesus Christ with such great power to heal, did not charge any penny: Neither did Saint Paul or Peter. Simon Magus was made blind for desiring to purchase the divine power for self-gain after Paul had rebuked him. No modern physician would agree or believe to this truth record in the Scriptures.

None are in greater danger from the influence of evil spirits than are those who, notwithstanding the direct and ample testimony of the true Scriptures, deny the existence evidence and agency of the devil and his demon angels. So long as we are ignorant of their wiles, they have almost inconceivable advantage; many give heed to their suggestions while they suppose themselves to be following the dictates of their own wisdom. Like my previous pc who threatened oppression said to me: **"You are not a doctor! You are wrong! You disobey me!"** His influence to me failed!. He thought I would yield to his malicious influence making me to believe that pacemaker placed on my heart would prolong and sustains my life. It is man's made device machine, it operates by a battery. With high potential damage risk of: Breeding, and swallowing and many other unexpected risks. It isn't a safe device for everyone else. Precise, anything made by man isn't safe at all to be placed into the human body system: It wears off or defected!. It is made out with wires. It damages skin. They show you their confidence that it is safe and prolongs life with no guarantee. They want to make their names well prestigious for self-gain. On other hand, they are making themselves to be god. It is terrible offensive in the sight of God.

This is why, as we approach the close of time when Satan is to work with greater power to deceive and destroy, he spreads everywhere the belief that he does not exist. It is his policy to conceal himself and his manner of working; deceiving everyone with weak mind. Knowledge is important. The Bible possesses all the knowledge you need. It contains God's Sacred Word: God, the knowing of all! There isn't to compare with God! He is the Creator of all! All men on earth ought to take serious account about God their Creator!. Anything else is sinking sandy!

Satan, the originator of all Enmity activities: The better to disguise his real characteristics and purposes, he has caused himself to be so represented as to excite no stronger emotion than ridicule or contempt! He is well pleased to be painted as a ludicrous or loathsome object, misshapen, half animal and half human! He is well pleased to hear his name used in sport atlantes; Stoics; and mockeries by those who consider themselves as tool to shape scholasticism intelligent and well-informed ideals of self-gain. It is because he has masked himself with sheep mask with consummate skill that the question is so widely asked: "Does such a being really exist?" Yes! Evil exists in our midst!. Its attributions atmospheric are obvious! It is an evidence of his success that theories given through scholasticism-tool the malicious lie to the plainest testimony of the Scriptures are so generally received in the religious world; Christian fiction ebook. Supports sciences and psychic and same sex marriage and abortion activity!.

And it is because Satan can most readily control the minds of those who are unconscious of his influence that the word of the living God gives us so many examples of his malignant work, unveiling before us his secret forces; and thus placing us on our guard against his assaults!. Many young adults practice this activity unconscious of evil influence; because they read and taught from anti-Christ textbooks such as fiction ebook!. The power and malice of Satan and his agents [scholasticism] might justly alarm us, were it not that we may find shelter and deliverance in the superior power of Christ Jesus our most compassion redeemer. Jesus Christ went through before us all. He conquered evil including death!. Enmity; we carefully secure our houses with bolts and locks to protect our properties and our lives from evil men; but we seldom think of the evil ugly-angels or agency who are constantly seeking access to us, and against whose attacks we have no better method of defense. Fear surrounds us all!. If permitted, they can distract our minds, disorder, torment our bodies, like pacemaker device machine destroy our bodies; our possessions and our lives!. The Bible clearly warns all: "Be-aware!" It is written!

Their only delight is in misery and destruction! Fearful is the condition of those who resist the divine claims and yield to Satan's temptations until God gives them up the control of evil spirits: But those who follow Christ Jesus are ever safe under his wings and watchcare. Angels that excel in strength are sent from heaven to protect them as it was during Israel wilderness exodus. God watchcare those who love Him: Surely, God is good to Israel and those who truly love Him.

The wicked men cannot break through the guard which the Lord God Almighty has stationed authority about His true authentic believers the people of Israel. He truly cares! His mighty powerful hands are stretched upon Israel and all those who truly keep His commands. The Lord our God is One: Hear his voice and walk with Him!. Fear Him, and keep His Commandment. The fear of the Lord God is the beginning of knowledge: But fools despise wisdom and instruction. [Prov. 1: 7].

Chapter 12

The Lord Christ Jesus
Greatest than all things!
Even Death

"Before Abraham was; "I AM!" [John 8: 58]
Indeed, a greater than Jonah is here!"[Matt 12; 41]
Indeed, a greater than Solomon is here!" [Matt 12:42]
Jesus Christ affirmed truth.

1. "I am the bread of life!" [John 6: 35]
2. "I am the Light of the world!" [John 8: 12]
3. "I am the good shepherd!" [John 10: 11]
4. "I am the Resurrection and the life!" [John 11: 25]
5. "I am the way, the truth, and life!" [John 14: 6]
6. For if you believed Moses, you would believe Me: Therefore greater than Moses is here!" But if you do not believe Moses his writings, how will You believe my words and my teachings?" Moses writings Constitutes all about Me; "He wrote all about Me."

Jesus said to the Jews who had converted. Scriptures [Reference: Deut. 16: 1 &. John 5: 45-47].

7. But I have a greater teachings and witness than John; Jonah; Solomon, Moses; and Abraham; [John 5: 36-37].

There's no mere human being dares to imitate such profound divine claims on earth from any ages and generations in history! Everything that Christ claimed to be, was with divine approval and truth in the fulfillment of the Scriptures: It is all well recorded: Jesus Christ came down from heaven to illuminate and fulfill the Scriptures and prophecies. Indeed, Christ Jesus spoke plainly!

Jesus Christ is inevitable! If individuals and humanity are to progress; Jesus Christ is inescapable! You ignore him at your own wicked risky!. There's no other better message to proclaim that supersede Jesus Christ divine approval truth! There's none! But every other message proclaimed is human tradition sinking sand! No Christ' solid rock foundation!. No matter how you overlook the issue. Christ Jesus is the Greatest of all things on earth: As is written; "All things are under My Feet! "Heaven is my throne: The earth is my footstool!" [Is. 66: 1-3]. "Uphold my step in your paths that my footstep may not slip: I have called upon you, for you will hear me; 0 God: Incline your ear to me and hear my speech." [Ps. 17: 5-6]. "For since by man [Adam] came death; by Man [Christ] also came the resurrection of the dead: For as in Adam all die; even so in Christ Jesus all shall be made alive!" [1 Corinth 15: 20-23]. **Only believing matters for all. Will you agree? Truth!.**

Satan is very much determined to entrap anyone who seeks to become Christian and earnestly seeks following Christ. And Satan wants their children to entrap as well! Many people who earnestly sought for Christ are caught up every day not realizing how Satan operates! I am sharing my own experience: I was once trapped! I confessed before and I must confess again that I was trapped by a woman who was conceived by another man. One had abortion. The other gave birth to a baby boy she claimed that I am her husband. Likely to be true evidence because I knew her: But she was already conceived. I did not know.

Did Judah not sleep with Tamar his daughter in-laws: He did not know: [Gen 38: 13-20]: And so, Lot slept with his two daughters because they made their father drank with wine so that both could sleep with him without Lot knowing. [Gen 19: 32-37] I was not drank but I thought I was in love. It was a trap love.

Bekiwe Sigauke a profession harlot nature trapped many. She has been conceived by other men several times. Bekiwe siding with Ivy another harlot; and Kristine another harlot divorced her first husband John; she then deceived Marilyn my wife: This incident took place in my early youth life time before I was actually legal married to Marilyn Armstrong: Marilyn joined wrong part. It is not beautiful picture to look at: Christians ought to focus so-well!.

As the earnest godly people approach the perils of the last days; Satan also upholds earnest consultation with his evil agents as to the most successful plan of overthrowing through his sharp device crafting and cunning our faith. He sees that the popular church is already lulled to sleep by his deceptive power like he did in the past to Adam and Eve. By pleasing sophistry and lying wonders he can continue to hold us under his darkness control. Only the light of Christ can drive us out from darkness of evil.

Therefore, Satan directs his agents to lay their snares especially for those who are looking for the Christ Jesus' forgiveness for salvation and endeavoring to keep all the perfect law commands of the Lord God. Every Christian is very aware says the great deceiver Satan Enmity: "We must watch those who are calling the attention of the people to the true-living God in Christ Jesus." There are those who destroy innocent life in the name of God. They will lead many young adults to see the claims of the law of God and the same tight which reveals the truth about God reveals also about the ministration of Christ Jesus. They use every device possible to deceive many! Such as Christian fiction ebook: It's well designed to deceive many young adults confined in their scholasticism as a tool to shape them. They write this textbook as a major theme to students.

"Heaven is My Throne: And earth is My footstool!"

Where is the house that you will build Me?"

And where is the place of My rest?" For all those

Athanasius-John T. Nkomo

Things My hand has made; and all those things Exist:" God said, [Is. 66: 1-2].

The Holy Bible or the Holy Scriptures; stands to be the guide to all who wish or desire to become acquainted more close with the will of their maker or creator, [God]. No one else! God wrote His Word gave it to men the sure Word from His mouth and finally from Christ Jesus mouth in the form of human flesh came down from heaven to make known to all men on earth the things that must shortly come to pass! Those important matters that concern our salvation were not left involved in mystery!

The Word is not revealed in such a way as to perplex and mislead the honest; intrinsically seeker after truth: "The word of God is plain and clear to all who study it with true prayerful heart! Every honest soul will come to the light of truth! Light is sown for the righteous!" [Ps. 97: 11]. No single man can advance in holiness unless his heart is earnestly seeking for truth as in the past seekers found God plainly, clearly and walked with Him; as well as the disciples walked with Christ daily! Only one got lost by choice: Judas Iscariot. So as it is today some of us are lost.

When the true heart seeker study of the Scriptures is entered upon without a prayerful; intrinsically; humble; teachable spirit not like Cain; Judas and those modern scholasticism experts of Christian fiction ebook authors the plainest simplest as well as the most difficulty passages will be wrested from their true meaning! The ancient Pharisees selected such portion of Scriptures as best serve their Judaism purpose, interpret to suit their personal ego, and then present these to the vulnerable souls, while they deny them the privilege of prayerful in temple and understanding its sacred truths direct from God their maker. Unless the whole truth of Bible is given to the vulnerable souls just as it is written, reads it would be better for them not to have it at all. Our young adults in modern scholasticism desperately need such truths direct from the

Scriptures that connect them to God in Christ.

By the cry-out of "Liberality" from popular platform authors; men and women are blinded to the devices of their Christian fiction ebook adversaries, while they are all the time working steadily for the accomplishment of their objects. [Marketing] As they succeed in supplanting the word of truth faking by human tradition, intellectualism speculations; the true written Word of God is set aside and world market mainly [young adults] confined into their scholasticism are under the bondage of Enmity sinful nature while they claim to be merely free! In the past: "And even as they did not like to retain God in their knowledge, God gave them over to a debased mind, to do those things which are not fitting; said the Scriptures: "Being filled with all unrighteousness, sexual immorality, wickedness, covetousness, maliciousness, full of envy, murder, strife, deceit, evil-mindedness; they whisperers! Backbiters, haters of God, violent, proud, boasters, inventors of evil things, disobedient to parents; undiscerning; untrustworthy; unloving; unforgiving; unmerciful; unjust: Who, knowing the righteous judgment of God, that those who practice such things are deserved of death, not only do the same but also approve of those who practice them!" Therefore you are inexcusable!. O man whoever you are who judge, for in whatever you judge another you condemn yourself; for you who judge practice the same things." [Rom 1: 28-32-2: 1]. No escape for anyone who practices such! You better believe it! Enmity will persist until Christ returns!.

Another thing concerning modern man "Liberality:" Too many scientific research has become a curse, their finite minds are so fable and weak in the eyes of God their maker; yet they are unaware; that they lose their balance because they ever engage Enmity. There's nothing wrong with sciences discovery, since everything is God's providence for man privilege benefits. They fail to harmonize their views of sciences with Scriptures; the Word from God is the foundation of all. And they think that the Bible is to be tested into a tube by their human fable mind standard of "science falsely so called." Thus they error from the faith and are seduced by the devil and Enmity: Men have ever endeavored for years to be wiser than God their Creator: Human philosophy has attempted to search out and explain mysteries will never be revealed through the Scriptures the eternal foundation of all ages. Never! Psychological phenomenal out of touch!

If men would but search and understand what God has made known of Him and His Purposes; they would obtain such a view of the glory, majesty, and power of the Sovereign God the Creator of all secret mysteries. They would realize their own littleness-narrow and would be content with that which has been revealed for them and their future children. [Verse 22]: "Professing to be wise, they became fools!" Enmity; it is a masterpiece device of Satan's deceptions to keep the minds of men searching continually but no complete discovery or even see what God has hidden from their human intellectual. They are very limited as their lives is short lived. With their concentrated Enmity at minds, they will never agree to this truth as it was in the beginning professing to be wise, but they became fools!. [Gen 3: 15]. See verse 5. Enmity; God blinded them as Enmity is still persisting. **"The Spirit of the Lord is upon Me," Jesus Christ declared: "Because the Lord has anointed Me to proclaim Liberty to the captive!" [Is. 61: 1-2].** The ancient people did not receive the Spirit of true Liberty: Not that many: Neither will the modern men receive this Spirit of true Liberty that Christ brought down from heaven! Not that many! Enmity blinds all! See Luke 4:18-19].

Searching and conjecturing in regard to that which God has not made known, and which He does not intend that scientific mind shall neither understand God's abundant providences. It was Lucifer, the arch-angel who was cast out from heaven. He ever became dissatisfied because all the secrets of God Almighty, purposes were not confided to him and he entirely disregarded that which was revealed concerning his own wicked work in the lofty position assigned him. He was very limited! He couldn't be God as he claims nowadays on earth many churched sees him as God sitting in their churches everywhere around the world today. Not only in churches, Satan is found everywhere today and we know him by his seeds [zerah]. Satan by arousing the same discontent in the heavenly angels under his command, he caused their fall. Now he seeks to imbue the minds of men on earth with the same spirit and to lead them also to disregard the direct commands of true eternal God: Satan like modern scientists are ever restless with their research. Those who are unwilling to accept the plain, cutting truths of the Bible are continually seeking for pleasing fables that will quiet their consciences and motives. The less spiritual, self-denying and humiliating the doctrines presented, the greater the favor with which they are received.

These individual persons degrade the intellectual powers to serve their flesh desires. Too wise in their own conceit to search the word of God with contrition of soul and earnest prayer for divine guidance, they have no shield to defend from their psychological phenomenal delusion. Satan is absolute ready to supply the heart's desire and he palms off his deceptions in the place of truth. Enmity that God had imposed upon them is powerful force drives evil hostiles and hatred. It is self-death by choice like Judas and Cain. We need to remind ourselves that God is undefeated by men intellectuals. It was thus that the ancient Pharisees gained its power over the minds of men; and by rejecting of the truth which Christ brought for their salvation, because it involves a severe cross, false prophets are following the same path. This teaching is painful to accept but truth is undefeated its power prevails!. The Word of God is living and active! All who neglect the word of God to study convenience and policy that they may not be at variance with the world, Enmity will be left to receive damnable heresy for religious truth! No man on earth can afford to ignore God's Word of truth: To ignore God's truth, it is also to ignore your own death: Truth indeed, conquers all! And it says all:

Every conceivable form of Enmity; grotesque; profligate; will be accepted by those who willfully reject the truth from Christ Jesus mouth who came down from heaven. "Let no one deceive you by any means; for the day will not come unless the falling away comes first, and the man of sin is revealed, the son of perdition; [Satan] who opposes and exalts himself above all that is called God or that is worshiped, so that he sits as God in the temple of God, showing himself that he is God." [2 Thess. 2: 3-4]. Yes! He does: And you will never recognize him. He disguises his face into sheep's face yet he is a roaring lion!.

Satan has different deceptions prepared to trap everyone, to reach different expert minds; and some who look with honor and horror upon one deception will readily receive another so forth. Among the most successful scholasticism institutions particularly those who hold high ranks status as publishing press editor; agencies of the great deceiver are the delusive fiction doctrines and lying wonders of spiritualism: They are absolute sharp! They are church joiners to gain public confidence that they are faithful Christians. Far worse than the ancient Pharisees! They will never publish biblical truth written by unpopular authors. Like the days of Christ, the Pharisees would not agree with Christ teaching because they feared their secret of evil evidence would be exposed. Disguised as self-righteous as an angel of light, ancient Pharisees spread their nets where least suspected, like today's fiction ebook experts. Our modern scholasticism, tool it is too dangerous for our young adults who receive their teachings. They omit teaching God's eternal Word! Basically, their teachings definition of religion and inspiration contradicts truth.

If men confined in the scholasticism would study the word of God with earnest prayer that they might understand its teachings, they would not omit God, and be left in darkness to receive false doctrines. But as they reject the truth, they all fall a prey to these

Satan deceptions. Will they agree? Never!

Another severe dangerous heresy is the doctrine that denies the divinity of Christ Jesus who came down from heaven. Men who have no experimental knowledge of Jesus Christ, will yet assume an appearance of great wisdom, as though their judgments were beyond inquisitive and boldly declare that the Son of God had no existence prior to his first coming to this world. True Christians indeed, believe that Christ Jesus exists and lives in heaven this day. That Christ Jesus will return to ultimate judge the whole world! Will they agree? Never!

This position directly contradicts the plainest statements of our Lord Christ Jesus concerning him; yet it is received with favor by a larger upper class who claims to believe the Scriptures. With such peoples it is folly to argue; disagreement; dispute; Enmity causes: No arguments, however, conclusive; will convince those who reject the truth; the direct testimony of the Son of God Jesus Christ: "The natural man receives not the things of the Spirit of God; for they are foolishness unto him; neither can he know them because they are spiritually discerned." [1 Corinth 2: 14]. Those who persistently cling to such Enmity, give evidence of their own ignorance of God and of His Son, Christ Jesus: Like those who write fiction ebooks. They give evidence of their own ignorance of God and of His Son Christ Jesus. Will they agree? Never!

There still another subtle and mischievous Enmity that men penetrate is the fast spreading belief that Satan has no existence either; as a personal being; that the name is used in Scripture merely to represent men's evil thoughts and desires: However, there are numerous names for Satan named by numerous-world's diversity languages and traditions. The teachings so widely echoed from popular pulpits of denominations that second coming of Christ is his coming to each individual at death; is a device to divert the minds of men and women from Christ' personal coming in the clouds of heaven. Man has fully designed craft language in his mouth to deceive others. Enmity is the cause as it all fully said in the Scriptures. See [2 Thess. 2: 3-4]. Enmity, it all says: "Opposes God Spirit!" And that is the very dangerous act upon all.

"Therefore, I say to you;" Jesus said: "Every sin and blasphemy will be forgiven men; but the blasphemy against the Spirit will not be forgiven men!" Anyone who speaks a word against the Son of Man, it will be forgiven him: But whoever speaks against the Holy Spirit; will not be forgiven him; either in this age or in the age to come:" [future] modern world era!. This law stands. [Matt. 12: 31-32] most heinous act:

For years and decades, Satan has thus been saying: "Behold; he is in the secret chambers;" and many souls have been lost by accepting his deceptions. Again worldly wisdom in fiction ebooks teaches that prayer is not essential! Men of science claim that there can be no real answer of prayer; that this would be violation of law; a miracle, and that miracles have no existence. The whole universe; say they; is governed by fixed galaxy laws and God does nothing contrary to these laws. They argue with complete self-confidence fixed up at minds. They are unaware that Satan controls them. Thus they represent God as bound by His own laws; as if the operation of divine laws could exclusive exclude divine freedom. Such teaching is opposed to the testimony of the Scriptures. Will they agree? Never!

Blasphemy God's Holy Spirit: No man will be forgiven!. **God truly says it all! "Heaven is My Throne: And the earth is My footstool!" All those things; My hand has made!" And all those things exist!" [Gen 1: 1-31 &. Is. 66: 1-3].**

Were not miracles wrought by Christ and his disciples: [Matt. 12: 22-25] the same compassionate Christ lives today and Christ is as willing to heed to the prayer of true faith as when he walked visibly among all men on earth healing all diseases, including the dead being raised up. Why then men record such evidence if these miracles performed did not exist and experienced such things? The natural co-operates with the supernatural. It is a part of God's plan to grant us in every answer to the true prayer of faith that which Christ would not bestow, did we not thus ask?

Innumerable are the erroneous doctrines designed by men, and fanciful fanatic ideas that cunning are obtaining among the churches of the secular world Christendom. It is impossible to estimate the Enmity evil results of removing one of the landmarks fixed or locked up by the word of God. There are very few who venture to do this, stop with the rejection of a single truth. The majority continue to set aside one after another of its principles, until they become actual infidels!. Enmity, it is really deeply rooted to eradicate in man's heart and mind. Men cannot eradicate it if not Christ!.

And this is the object which Satan is very determined or eager to accomplish before Christ returns! He is very aware that his days are short for his eternal termination!. The more of his awareness; the more of his vigorous stumbling block! He is very hungry and thirsty to tear apart everything that God builds upon earth! Enmity is not politics talk! Enmity consists of spiritual talk that values all human life on earth daily. Enmity possesses no exclusion, but it involves all souls daily personal affairs everywhere on earth!. Big and small experiences the same thing. Weeping and lamentation daily no ceasing! It is like a stomach melting ice. Enmity is the most obnoxious phrase that disgust God Holy Spirit! It is unforgivable! Righteousness judgment stands against all on earth no escape!. [Gen 3: 15 &. Matt. 12: 31-32]. There is nothing that he desires more than destroy confidence in God and in God true word. Satan stands at the head of the great Enmity-hatred; hostility; disagreement of doubters and he works tirelessly to the utmost of his power to beguile souls into his wicked ranks. It is nowadays becoming obvious fashionable to doubt. There are many who seem to feel that it is a virtue to stand on the sinking sand side. But underneath an appearance of candor and humility, it will be found that such persons are actuated by self-confidence and selfish-pride.

It is a terrible thing to lose faith in God or in His word. Unbelief of strengthens as it is encouraged. There is a great danger in even once giving expression to doubt: a [zerah] seed is sown which produces a harvest of its kind. According to Satan will nourish the crop every moment! Those who allow themselves to talk of their doubts will find them constantly becoming more confirmed. God will never remove every occasion for doubt or deceit. He will never respond or work a miracle to remove unbelief when he has given sufficient evidence for true faith. Often times Jesus Christ would not show or perform a sign to Pharisees presence. They asked Christ to show them signs and they would believe him; Jesus strongly refused. Calling them the brood of "viper" how dare for them to ask for a sign, it will not be shown to them. [Matt. 12: 38-39].

The Lord God Almighty looks with deep displeasure upon the self-righteous and unbelieving people so called Scribes; Pharisees and Stoics who are ever doubting; opposing; and rejecting God's truth; and disturbing vulnerable souls and distrusting the assurance of Christ Jesus grace. They have become unproductive trees and their zerah spread their dark branches and bear bad fruits far and wide, shutting away the sunlight from other plants; they are like parasites trees ruining the other real good productive trees. Their root-hairs spoil the well call vented fields. Shutting away the sunlight from other plants, and causing them to droop and die under the chilling shadow! They are natural killers and they enjoy killing innocent souls! It is their nature to kill since they are evil zerah products. God uses the phrase [zerah] seed. Matt. 12: 33-35] well described by Jesus. The Scriptures evidence are obvious as distinctively described by the Lord Christ Jesus. Still the Pharisees could not merely fully understand what Christ meant to them.

Jesus Christ meant it so well for their benefits. Still even today Christ words stand as well distinctively described all modern men on earth. This kind of teaching rarely found or appears in any fiction ebooks!. Never! Fiction, by definition; it is an essay invented by intelligent man. Well trained journalist profession design fiction ebooks. Like industrial psychologist designs appealing commercial adverts on TV screens. It is none biblical view!. It omits and rejects every truth from the Scriptures!. And so it is another sophisticated device of Satan well designed device that draws many to his Enmity destruction. He goes on opposing all called God!. Jesus Christ is our only hope! No matter what!

These human tradition professions; journalists and industrial psychologists are highly skilled to manipulate every young adult minds with their genius crafting language reflected in fiction ebooks and commercial shows. Powerful to draw many to their overwhelming intellectual minds shaped by secular scholasticism. They will never consider the slightest view of God!. Yet, they claim to be Christians! It is the most astonishing factor that the secular scholasticism ever designed such device in order to manipulate large class in a particular society around the whole entire world today: However; the Scriptures well predicts it all. Therefore, we reap what our forefathers sowed. Enmity will absolute persist until Christ returns!. According to the Scriptures; I am well persuaded and convinced: It is the truth! There aren't many followers of Christ who know too little about the plots which Lucifer the original of Enmity and his agents are forming or inventing against them. But the Lord God who sits in the heavens will over-rule all these wicked devices for the accomplishment of His deep designs. God is not blind, deaf; or mute! He knows all taking place around the whole world from the beginning: After all; He is the Creator of all: So well claimed. The Lord God permits wicked peoples to be subjected to the fiery ordeal of temptations; humiliation; not because God takes any pleasures in their distress and afflictions; but because this process is vital essential to their final victory: See how he rescued Israel from Egypt: How he allowed His only Begotten Son to be hanged on Cross: Three days later it was tremendous great victory. Christ rising up from dead plainly.

God could not consistently with His own glory shield them from awfully temptations; for the very object of the trial is to prepare them to resist all Enmity the allurements of Enmity evil. Satan is well aware that the weakest soul who abides in Christ is more than a match for the hosts of his darkness, and that, should he reveal himself openly, he would be met and resisted. So he disguises his face making himself looks like God. You will not recognize him. Eve did not because he came to Eden Garden in the form of a serpent. Crafting to her good language!. She found out after her fall and shameful overshadowing on her face. It was too late. Therefore all men fell apart from God. And death prevails since then till this day. Satan therefore, seeks to draw away all believers if he can from their stronghold fortification, while his malice deceitful ambush with his forces ready to destroy all who venture upon his ground. It is his strategies point to attack and destroy what God builds. He is not able to build but he is very much able to destroy what is being built.

There's no man is safe for even a day or an hour without constant prayer: "Thy will be done on earth as it is in heaven." Jesus taught us great prayer to call upon God Almighty continually without ceasing. [Matt 6: 9-13]. Especially should we entreat the Lord God for wisdom to understand His eternal Word!. Lucifer is an expert in quoting Scriptures for his own weapon and device, placing his own crafting and cunning sharp words with clear interpretation upon each passage by which he hopes to cause us to stumble like Eve. We cannot match with his Scriptures expert in quoting. He lived in heaven from the beginning.

Furthermore; God predicted this to Abraham: "Know certainly that your descendants [children] will be strangers in a land that is not theirs; and will serve them; and they will afflict them four hundred years! And also the nation whom they serve I will judge; afterward they shall come out with great possessions!" [Gen 15: 13-14]. By this time that God spoke to Abraham, God had not yet given Abraham any child because his wife Sarah was barren: He was 75 years old.

We should study the Bible with humility of heart, never losing sight of our dependence upon God the sustainer of our lives. While we must constantly guard against the devices of Enmity, we should pray in faith continually. As Christ taught his disciples: "Lead us not into temptation:" But deliver us from the evil one: "For yours is the Kingdom, and the power, and the glory forever." [Verse 13].

India Says They Want One of the British Royal Crown Jewels Back to India!
N.Y. Times Reports: April 21St, 2016
Examine Scriptures fulfillments:
"Heaven is My Throne; and earth is My footstool!"
Where is the house that you will build Me?" And where is the place of My rest?" For all those things My hand has made; And all those things exists!." God said. [Is. 66: 1-2]

India rightful demands for their **Koh-i-Noor** diamond to be returned to India its origin; now in the British Royal Crown Jewels in London England U.K.

New Delhi, the Indian Government has begun a campaign for return of a historical **[105.6 carat]** diamond that was either a gift to Queen Victoria from the Maharajah of Punjab in [1849] or stolen by the British; depending on some widely divergent perspectives.

After some indecision, the Indian Culture Ministry said on Tuesday [April 20th, 2016] evening that it would make "all possible efforts" to arrange the return of the diamond, the **[Koh-i-Noor]** now residing in the Tower of London England, where it is a centerpiece of the British royal family's Crown Jewels. There are four state governments countries want this diamond in their possessions:

- Greece
- Great Britain
- India
- Pakistan

Who will final possesses the **[Koh-i-Noor Diamond?]** The Mountain Light: It shall be seen as its controversy still on process as it seems will be a life time controversy. Why anyway?

Interesting historical both: Prophetic and tradition. As with Elgin marbles, the Parthenon sculpture and other artifacts that Greece has long tried to reclaim from Great Britain Government, the ownership of the diamond has been a contentious issue for decades. The N.Y. Times reports:

For many Indians, the **[Koh-i-Noor]** or Mountain of Light is a symbol of British colonial subjugation; imperialism; exploitation, and three centuries of cruel British Imperialism exploitation suppression that began with the East India Company in early 17th century; culminated in the absorption of India as a colon after a major uprising in [1857] and ended up with the independence monitored by **Mahatma Gandhi**, and partition of India in [1947].

Whether it was a gift or stolen, or not, Great Britain Government insists saying that "the diamond came into its possession after the defeat of Punjab in the Anglo-Sikh Wars of the [1840's" and was moved to Britain in [1850]. The British people omit to admit the fact that it was stolen by force. Among them, they are divided in the matters.

As recently as [2010] the British Prime Minister Mr. David Cameron said: "The diamond would stay put." In other word they resist for its stay in the British country. But critic in India say; "the British version of the story has been sanitized." The diamond originated in the Golconda Mines on India soil, in what is now the state of Andhra Pradesh; not British soil. It passed through the hands of Mughal and Afghan rules before landing with Maharajah Ranjit Singh, the ruler of the Sikh kingdom in Punjab who died in [1839]. His death led to a struggle and in [1843] the installation of his 5-year old son. In the power vacuum the East India Company rapidly extended its control over the once powerful kingdom, annexing it in [1849] after its victory in Second Anglo-Sikh War," Anita Anand; a journalist and co-author of a forth-coming book on the **[Koh-i-Noor]** diamond, the Jewel was then surrendered, Anita said "as part of an agreement ending the war and it was signed by the boy king." [A 5-year old boy]: Could he real be capable to make exclusive-decisive decision without an adult counsel advising him? If so, who were they? Precise it must be presumed British Captain; so it is bound to be stolen by force one way or the other. "It was a cynical exploitation at a time of flux in the Sikh kingdom," Anita Anand said:

The controversy may even extend beyond India. In Pakistan, a lawyer filed a petition in the Lahore High Court in February arguing that the diamond belonged to territory that is now part of Pakistan, and that the Pakistan Government should seek its return with immediate effect. This issue was raised this week by a private group that was seeking a court order requiring the Indian Government to request the diamond's return.

The Indian solicitor general Ranjit Kumar, at first argued against the suit; saying that the gem was to seek its return. This ignited a firestorm on social media and did not appear to sit well with some of the Judges. Who then will eventually win for its full permanent residence? Truly the diamond belongs to India. It was absolute taken by force to Britain in the days of imperialism colonial British Empire: Like in South Africa; the British kidnapped Tchaka Zulu in [1870] to Britain, murdered him to cold blood, and exposed his skeleton to Museum for economic purposes. In 1994 President Nelson Mandela demanded for its re-patriarch to South Africa! The British people yield to Mandela's demands. And so were Mahatma Gandhi pair of his sandals: his silver cup; and his glass; were returned to India in 2001: One wealth Indian business man demanded for them for India Museum expedition.

[105. 6 Carat of Koh-i-Noor: Mountain of Light] Diamond Belongs to India: The more Pharaoh persisted defying God: The more God hardened Pharaoh's heart: **"But indeed for this purpose I have raised you up that I may show My power in you, and that My name may be well declared in all the earth!" [Exo. 9: 16]. God assured Pharaoh. See Exo. 14: 17-18] God repeats same phrases.**

Pharaoh recklessly; cruelty afflicted the Israelites for four hundred years under slavery bondages; no wages for their hard labours! God knew all their afflictions. Finally God personally came down to rescue them all once and for all! They cannot leave Egypt without their wages being fully paid: Therefore, the Lord God Almighty the owner of all surroundings earth gave great favor to the people in the sight of all Egyptians: Every man asked his fellow neighbor and every woman from her neighbor; articles of silver and articles of gold to give it to the Israelites. There were no resistance occurred but they freely gave all they had to the Israelites before their departure. Indeed; they left Egypt with great treasures than ever before. [Exo. 11: 2-3]. But God had unfavorable Enmity message for Pharaoh: See Gen 15: 13-14] God's word was fulfilled the righteous judgment was done upon him. The outcry is overwhelmingly heard all over the land of Egypt. They lost all their male firstborn from Pharaoh's son on his throne to every other man including beasts they all mysteriously died by the hand of the mighty God the maker of all living. [Exo. 11: 4-6]. Early king of Egypt urged the two Hebrews midwives named: Shiphrah and Puah to kill every male child born to the Israelite families. However, the midwives feared God they didn't kill the male child but saved them. When the king heard this he was bitter upon them. Therefore God dealt well with the midwives that he provided household for them. But Pharaoh still made further fierce command that every male child born must be thrown into Nile Rivers. With exception of Moses who was rescued by Pharaoh's daughter. [Exo. 11: 19-22, & 2: 5-9]. Familiar stories that connect people to God need teachings to lost souls.

One of the most fantastic deceptions of all time was started by Lucifer Enmity in the Eden Garden enticing Eve. Surprisingly enough, very few Christians recognize it for it is: And yet it he catches souls and holds them fast no let it go! With the earliest history of human being; Lucifer or Satan began his efforts to deceive all mankind on earth. He who had incited rebellion in heaven desired to bring the whole God's perfect creation to unite with him in his warfare against God. Like all those earliest empires, God vividly shows them how weak they were in his sight. For example, Pharaoh in Egypt persistently defying God while God shows him his weakness, but he would not yield to God!

It is the earliest example that God showed the world how powerful He is! Another powerful example God shows is about raising up Christ Jesus from the dead! No better examples God setting up more examples than these two: But mere weak man still resist: What more or how much more we need to see? Death!

Indeed; it is the work of Lucifer, the evil one in us. But evil kills all! Lucifer envy and jealousy were excited as he looked upon the beautiful home prepared for the happy holy pair [Adam and

Eve,] Eden Garden most beautiful residence to dwell forever! Like the beautiful **[Koh-i-Noor Diamond]** Royal Crown Jewels it was taken from the Indian soil!. The British envy for it. And so the African wealth was taken from Africa. The work of evil did exist during the earliest empires and it still exists even this day because Enmity lives in every man's heart. The work of evil, Lucifer; had he revealed himself in his real character, he would have been repulsed at once! For Adam and Eve had been warned against this dangerous foe; and so all of us today are warned against this dangerous foe, but he worked in the dark, concealing his purpose that he might more effectually accomplish his object. He approached Eve in the form of a serpent, Eve mutual friend, engaged mutual dialogue. Yet it was most crafting Enmity talks from Lucifer. Eve did not recognize the evil disguised within the serpent's face.

Today there is so much fear; suspicious, mistrust because you do not know to whom you talk in train or bus sitting next to you. Perhaps you might engage a conversation with terrorist cunning efforts: Even at church, you sit on same bench, no talks at all, yet you are in a church where you worship God in spirit. In church; to a stranger, no engaging talks!. But what did Adam and Eve after their sin, find to be the meaning of the words: "In the day that you shall eat of fruit; you shall surely die!" Did he find them to mean as Lucifer had led him to believe that he was to be ushered into more exalted state of existence? Then indeed there was great good to be gained by transgression, and Satan was proved to be a benefactor of all mankind on earth. But perhaps Adam did not so fully understand the divine sentence: God said that as a penalty for his rebellion man should return to the ground where he was taken: "For dust you are: And to dust you shall return!" [Gen 3: 19]. Who dares to fully get this powerful message today? There aren't many: Is there any better teachings than this? None: There are many Ahithophel's counselors who deceived Absalom to sleep with all his father's concubine wives. [2 Sam 15]

The fruit of the tree of life had the power to perpetuate life. Had man after his fall been allowed free access to that tree, he would have lived forever! And thus Enmity sinful would have been immortalized. But God knew while Adam perhaps didn't. Therefore, a flaming sword was placed to keep the way of the tree of life, and not one of them or his family has been allowed to touch it again. That barrier and partake of the life giving fruit. Therefore there is not an immortal sinner. Enmity will continue to cause us to toil daily until Christ returns. There aren't many accept this teachings. But there are many who scoff of this teaching. They aren't alive but dead. Jesus said it all well:

"Let the dead bury their own dead." Follow me, you live." [Matt 8: 22]. Only one followed Christ Jesus, the rest did not.

Thus the arch-fiend clothes with his own attributes the Creator and Benefactor of mankind. Cruelty is Enmity Lucifer or Satanic. God is love: And all that he created was pure, holy and beautiful-lovely, until Enmity was brought in by the first great rebel. Satan himself in many forms of appearance is the enemy who crafts, tempts man to sin, and then destroy him if he can, and when he has made sure of his victim, then he exults in the ruin he has wrought. If permitted, he would sweep the entire mankind into his wire net. Satan eagerness is to see all perish with him. Were it not for the interposition of divine powerful, not one of Adam sons and daughters would escape.

Yes! Satan or Enmity and his emissaries represent God as even worse than themselves, in order to excuse their own malignity and rebellion: The great deceiver endeavors to shift his own horrible cruelty of character upon our heavenly God, Father, Creator, Sustainer; that he may cause himself to appear as one greatly wronged because he will not submit to so unjust a governor. Like Pharaoh, and all early empires followed after him, whether godly or ungodly secular world: Satan presents before the world the liberty which they may enjoy under his mild sway in contrast with the bondage imposed by the stern decrees of the Lord God Almighty. Thus he succeeds in luring souls away from their allegiance to God their maker.

How repugnant to every emotion of love and mercy; and even to our sense of justice; is the doctrine that the ungodly wicked dead are tormented with fire and brimstone in an eternally burning with hell, that for the Enmity sinful of a brief earthly life they are to suffer torture as long as God shall live. Yet this kind of doctrine has been generally embodied in the creeds of secular world Christendom: Says a trained medical doctor or a trained doctor of divinity or a trained scientist: "The sight of hell-torments will exalt the happiness of saints forever. When they see others who are of the same nature and born under the same circumstances; plunged in such misery, and they so distinguished, it will make them sensible of how happy they are."

Another uses these words: "While the decree of reprobation is eternally executing on the vessels of wrath; the smoke of their torments will be eternally ascending in view of the vessels of mercy, who, instead of taking the part of these miserable objects, will say, Amen, Alleluia! Praise ye the Lord!" Snares! Scoffers!

Where in the pages of God eternally Word is such sentiments expressed? Those who present them may be learned and even honest men; but they are psychological deluded by the sophistry of Lucifer Enmity sinful. He leads them to misconstrue strong expressions of Scriptures, giving to the language the coloring of bitterness defiling many souls and malignity which pertains to himself, but not to our Sovereign Lord God the Creator.

What would be gained to God should we admit that God delights in witnessing unceasing torturing doctrines from the secular world; that God is regaled with the groans and shrieks and imprecations of the world suffering people and all creatures whom he holds in the flames of hell-fire. Can these horrid sounds be sweet music in the ear of God infinite Love? No! But it is the work of evil-Satan.

It is urged that the infliction of endless misery upon the wicked would show God's hatred of Enmity sinful as an evil which is ruinous to the peace and order of the universal. Oh, dreadful blasphemy! As if God's hatred of Enmity sinful is the reason why He perpetuates Enmity sinful: For according to the received theology, continued torture without hope of mercy maddens its wretched victims, and as they pour their outrage in curses and blasphemy, they are forever augmenting their load of guilty!. This is the big picture of our current modern world character. Let me urge you so! God indeed; is increasing hardening our Enmity sinful through ceaseless ages since God did it to Pharaoh in Egypt. The more we defy God; the more God harden our hearts. The Bible evidence; shows it all! For the word of God is living and active! It is beyond the power of the human mind and heart to estimate the evil which has been wrought by the heresy of eternal torment. The God of Abraham; Isaac; and Jacob of the Word: In Old and New Testament [Bible] full of Love and goodness, and abounding in compassion; is darkened by superstition and clothed with malice-terror; Christian fiction ebook invented by secular scholasticism. Its world break sale causes more blinds to the world!

When we consider in what false colors Satan has painted the character of God, can we wonder that our merciful God is feared; dreaded; and even hated? Thus how Pharaoh defied God: "Who is this God that I ought to listen and let the people go?" I do not know him." Pharaoh' blindness caused him to stumble and brought his own catastrophic. The appalling views of God which have spread over the world from the teachings of the pulpits have made thousands; years; millions; of skeptics and infidels. Current modern world God has hardened their obsessed hearts for money lover brings them catastrophic.

Many ancient and current modern Christians consider or assume that God as being of love, merciful, compassion, and they cannot believe or consider that God will consign his people or creatures to the fires of an eternally burning hell. Even they are fully aware that God wiped up the entire earth with flood; wiped up all Pharaoh Stronghold of Egypt; wiped up all Sodom by fire from heaven. And that is how the true Scripture evidence present God. He is God of all; and He judges with righteous love. Thus the Enmity sinful can live in selfish pleasure, disregarding the requirements of God, and yet expect to be finally received into his righteous favor. Such a doctrine, presuming upon God's mercy, but ignoring his justice, pleases the flesh heart, and emboldens the wicked in their iniquity. How dare you? Skunk stings who can stand for it? Neither can God stands for the things of Enmity sinful: To show how believers in the universal salvation wrest the Scriptures to sustain their soul-destroying dogmas, it is needful only to cite their own utterances!. Let us all face this truth: "You reap what you sowed!" God imposed compelling question to Cain: "If you do well; will you not be accepted?" Where is Abel your brother?" I do not know! Am I my brother's keeper?!" Cain had killed Abel his brother. Now he denies in the sight of God. [Gen. 4]. Since then, Cain's first murder shading blood on ground, never ceased till this day!. Cain sowed a seed that grows continually. So we all reap what we sowed. Death! No escape!.

Truth; it has been taught by great and good men; but the light on this subject had not come to them as it has come to us in our modern era. They were responsible only for the light which shone in their time; we are accountable for that which shines in our day. If we only turn from the testimony of God's word of truth and accept false doctrines because our forefathers taught them; we all fall under the condemnation. Jesus Christ came down from heaven taught great and good things; showing great signs and lived perfect meek life-style his words connected all on earth!. But who lives to Christ' standard today? There aren't many: It is indeed; beyond the power of the human beings.

There are many modern Christians who regard the threatening of the Bible teachings as designed merely to frighten men in passive obedience, and not to be literally fulfilled. Thus the Enmity sinful can live in its selfish pleasure; disregarding the requirements of God, and yet expect to be received into eternal heaven life. They imitate on the wrong picture since they read the fiction ebook designed by the secular scholasticism tradition. There are several Bibles written with variety of versions invented by men today. They are anti-Christ scholars who claim to know the Scriptures. They will resist against God's truth whom they also claim. Most of modern scholasticism received it from ancient Roman Empires and Greek Hellenists and philosophers. Even so; they will not agree when engaging sensitive issues of the truth concerning Scriptures. They will strongly utterly plausibly resist! Knowing that they are truly against God. They strongly maintain Enmity.

A great evangelist Bill Graham was asked this question: "What will be the fate of those who leave the world in sin, die in sin; perhaps, in a state of inebriation, die with the scarlet stain of terrible crime unwashed from their robes, or die as this young man died, having never made a profession or enjoyed an experience of religion whether of Jesus Christ or tradition or not etc.?" Bill Graham was mute and speechless to response plausible its distinctive explanation of its meaningful. He simply said: "Ask God." He was right. God possesses all answers in Christ Jesus.

In these thoughts we would think or be well understood to believe that the salvation of heaven depends upon nothing which we can do in this life: Neither upon a present change of heart nor upon present belief, or present profession of religion. It is all in the hands of God Almighty the maker and sustainer of all life. He is the exclusive decisive decider. No one else! God decides all decisions on his own power and righteousness authority. Thus does the professed man made religious minister of Christ reiterate the falsehood uttered by the serpent to Eve in Garden of Eden. It could not work till this day! Wrong decision: [Gen 3: 5-6].

If the souls of all men pass directly to heaven at the hour of dissolution, then we may well covet death rather than life: Many secular world Christendom have been led by this belief to put an end to their existence. 1.2 billion World Christians, if they are all God fearful-faithful why we live on a chaos world today?

When overwhelmed with troubles, perplexity, suspicious; fear and disappointments, it seems any easy thing to break the brittle thread of life, and soar away into the bliss of the eternal corrupted world. Who cause it? Or God?! No! Men on earth: All men are accountable in the eyes of God for committing unceasing Enmity sinful.

God has given in his word more than enough ample time with abundance evidences that he will one day righteously punish the transgressors of his perfect law. God had long given men of holy character: "The Lord God, merciful and gracious; long-suffering tolerance and patience; abundant in goodness and truth; keeping mercy; justice; for thousands; forgiving iniquity and transgressions and Enmity sinful, and that will by no means clear the guilty." [Exo. 34: 6-7]. The power and authority of the divine will be employed to put down rebellions; yet all the manifestations of retributive justice will be perfectly consistent with the character of God Almighty as a merciful, long-suffering benevolent being. God's quality inaccessible invisible powerful attribution visibly seen with our naked eyes atmosphere!. Their exclusion from heaven is voluntary; it is just. Like the waters of the flood, the fires of the great day declare God's verdict that the wicked are incurable!.

They have no disposition to submit to divine authority. Their will has been exercised in revolt; and when life is ended, it is too late to turn the current of their thoughts in the opposite direction;

too late to turn from transgression to obedience from resistance hatred hostiles to love: After grave no more prayer!. Prayer is available before the grave. Choose Life! Enmity sinful kills souls. When in answer to his prayer: Hezekiah's life was prolonged for more 15 years: The grateful king rendered to God Almighty a tribute of great praise for his great merciful. In his song he tells the reason why he thus rejoices: "The grave cannot praise thee; death cannot celebrate thee; they that go down into ground or into pit cannot hope for thy truth! The living; the living; he shall praise thee as I do this day! The father to the children shall make known thy truth!." [Is. 38: 18]. See Eccles. 9:5, 6.10].

Prestigious human tradition theological scholars invented various fiction ebooks in the modern scholasticism represents dead as in heaven, entered into bliss, and praising God with an immortal language or tongue: But Hezekiah could see no such glorious prospect in death! With his words agrees the testimony of Scriptures: "In death there is no more remembrance of Thee: In the grave who shall give you thanks? The dead praise not the Lord, neither any that go down into silence!" [Ps.6: 5, &.115: 17]. Silence lips: The sound voice disappears. Where did it go?

"Men and Brethren let me urge you," St. Peter said: "That the patriarch David that he is both dead and buried, and his sepulcher [grave] is with us to this day." For David is not ascended into the heavens: The fact that David remains in the grave silent until the resurrection day proves that the righteous do not go to heaven at death. It is only through the resurrection, and by virtue of the fact Christ Jesus has risen that David can at last sit at the right hand of God." [Acts 2: 29-34].

Furthermore; St. Paul plausibly explained: "If the dead rise not, then Christ is not raised: And if Christ be not raised; your faith is in vain: You are yet in your sins: Then they also which are fallen asleep in Christ are perished." [1 Corinth 15: 16-18]. If for thousands of years the righteous had gone directly to heaven at death; how then could they be said to have perished; even though there should never be a resurrection? When Christ is about to leave the disciples: Christ did not tell them that they would soon come to heaven or to him. He said: I go to prepare a place for you: And if I go and prepare a place for you, I will come again, and receive you unto myself." [John 14: 2-3]. In addition Paul said: "The Lord himself shall descend from heaven with a shout, with the voice of the archangels, and with the trump of God: And the dead in Christ shall rise first. Then we which are alive and remain shall be caught up together with them in the clouds, to meet the Lord Christ in the air, and so shall we ever be with the Lord Christ Jesus: And he adds further; "Comfort one another with these words." [1 Thess. 4: 16-18].

But if the dead are already enjoying the bliss of heaven or writhing in the flames of hell-fires; what need of a future righteous judgments? The teachings of God's truth word on these important points are neither obscure nor contradictory; they may be well understood by common minds whether less educated or more educated makes no difference!. Fiction ebooks present unbiblical theology, and are anti-Christ critics!. But what candid young adult minds can see either wisdom or justice in the current scholasticism man designed theology? Will the righteous, after the investigation of their cases at the Judgment receive the commendation; "Well done, good and faithful servant; enter into your everlasting joy of your Lord God!." When they have been dwelling in his presence, perhaps for long time? Are the wicked summoned from the place of torment to receive the sentence from the Judge of all the earth: "Depart from me you cursed into everlasting fire?" Oh solemn mockery! Shameful impeachment of the wisdom and justice of God!. This is the true biblical teachings that tingles hearts.

Nowhere in the Holy Bible is found the statement that the righteous go to their heaven reward or the wicked to their punishment at death. All the patriarch; prophets; and kings have left no such evidence of insurance. Even our Lord Christ Jesus did not: And all the disciples have given no hint of it! The Bible clearly teaches that the dead do not go immediately to heaven. Only Christ Jesus did with exception of Elijah and Enoch who were taken to heaven alive. They were not dead bodies. The rest are represented as sleeping until the resurrection day that God put aside with his own authority. This is something to grasp in your own deep heart. Read the Scriptures well with constant prayer. It is no easy task but you need discerning Spirit from God alone who searches after your heart. God's discerning Spirit call; it is a wide open door for all!. Choose Life God can give freely gift. Will you agree and take it?

They are deep sleep they are awakened by the trump of God to a glorious immortality. As they are called forth from their deep slumber, they begin to think just where they ceased. Will you agree? Faithful: Yes! You ought to agree that this is truth.

Chapter 13

There is a Channel that is
Regarded as Sacred Word

By many channels through which Enmity Satan binds individual souls. Voices speak appearance are made; and a bewitching power [Psychic] enters a human being on earth: My grandfather as expert; practiced such [psychic-witchcraft]. Many people consider it but fakery; but then they see a more strength than human power revealed and they are spontaneously led on to their death!. Satan can begin so simply but later there seems no escape by fully trapped into his wire net cage. And so he stares at your face with hatred for his own failure: He got what he does not deserve from you as innocent person and becomes like him in the eyes of God. You believed his malicious lies. Likewise; you are in his state of Satan Enmity.

The doctrine of natural immortality has prepared the way for modern spiritualism: If the dead are admitted to the presence of God and holy angels; and privileged with knowledge far exceeding what they before possessed; why should they not return to the earth to enlighten and instruct the living about heaven? How can those who believe in man's consciousness in death reject what comes to them as divine light communicated by glorified spirit? Christ Jesus said: "No one has ascended to heaven but He [Christ] who came down from heaven; that is the Son of Man who is in heaven." [John 3: 13]. Scriptures references: [Is. 9: 6; Luke 9: 56; &. Rom 5: 8].

Here is a channel regarded as sacred word through which Enmity Satan works for the accomplishment of his crafting purposes: The fallen demons; angels; evils; or souls who do his [Satan original] biding appear as messengers or agents from the spirit world. While professing to bring the living into communication [like my grandfather inter-medium of demons] with the dead: Satan exercises his bewitching [psychic] influence upon their minds!. Earthiest paganism: Looks like spiritual impact into the eyes of men to be practical truth evidence so men believe. Enmity, Satan has power even to bring before men the appearance of their departed friends. Like king Saul had communicated with Prophet Samuel: Saul's inquiries with the Canaanite witchcraft [medium] was deceived: Samuel had died for years: God had taken away His Holy Spirit from Saul and replaced upon him evil spirit: Saul the first king of Israel disobeyed God's holy commands. [1 Sam 28: 11-25] Saul consults medium: Saul believed: Reference: [1 Sam 28-29].

The counterfeit is perfect in human eyes and minds: The familiar look the words the tone, are reproduced with marvelous distinctness. Many earthiest people, even some Christians are comforted to believe this malice evil practicing of medium like my grandfather deceived many for his economy fortunes: Many were comforted with the assurance that their loved ones are well enjoying the bliss of heaven: And without suspicious of danger or agony; they give ear to seducing spirits and doctrines of devils, such as Christian fiction ebooks designed by modern journalists into their scholasticism. Christian fiction ebooks designed is a new form bible version for modern secular world opposing God!.

When the people have been led to believe that dead actually return to communicate with them: Satan Enmity causes those to appear who went into the grave unprepared. They claim to enormous happy in heaven! And even to occupy exalted positions there! And thus the error! Is widely taught that no difference is made between the righteous and the wicked: That what the young adults read in the fiction ebooks!. The fiction ebook is conformed and transformed into movie script misogyny and minstrel shows: **Manipulates many!**

The pretended visitants from the world of spirits sometimes utter cautions and warnings which prove to be correct to convince the victim. Then as confidence is gained; they present doctrines which directly undermine faith embrace to heart in the Scriptures. Yet it's all faking! With an appearance of deep interest in the well-being of their audiences, friends, relatives, co-workers etc., on the whole entire world: They insinuate the most dangerous to young adults who purchase textbook with full of Enmity errors! Title: Big "Spiritualism and Inspiration."

The fact: That they state some truths and are able at times to foretell future events: Gives to their statements an appearance of reliability and their false teachings are overwhelming accepted by the multitudes of young adults and all secular world as readily, and believed as implicitly as if they were the most God's sacred word truths of the Scriptures! Thus large sum of dollar accumulation accelerating into their bank accounts. That's what cause their strength motivation and conscience to drive out Enmity into the entire world community!. Enmity will persist until Christ returns! The perfect law of the Lord God Almighty is set aside: The Spirit of grace despised: The blood of Christ is counted an unholy thing: Yes! The devil is power upon all human beings on the whole earth today!. The spirits deny the divinity of the Lord Christ Jesus and place even the Creator on a level within themselves: Thus under a new bible version invented in scholasticism to disguise the great rebel Enmity still carries forward the existence of his warfare against God Almighty: Begun in heaven and for decades since from the beginning in Eden Garden [Gen 3: 15] the process continued upon the earth till today' modern era!

Everyone else endeavors to account for spiritual manifestations by attributing them wholly to fraud and sleight of hand on the part of the medium: After hearing the prediction from the woman's medium: King Saul immediately fell full length on ground and was dreadfully afraid because of the words of Samuel which the medium foretold Saul. [verse. 20]. But while it is true that the results of trickery have often been palmed off at genuine manifestations; there have been also marked exhibitions of supernatural power. The mysterious rapping with which modern secular world spiritualism began was not the result of human trickery or cunning; but the direct work of origin Enmity evil now monitored by human who thus introduced one of the most successful of soul destroying delusions. And there will be many people being ensnared through the belief that spiritualism is a merely human imposture; when brought face to face with manifestations which they cannot but regard as supernatural, they will be absolute deceived and will be led to accept them as the great power of God Almighty. Saul believed the medium foretell yet this is what God had commanded Saul to destroy in the land of the Amalek for this evil practice which Saul disobeyed God.

These Amalek people overlook the testimony of the Scriptures concerning the wonders wrought by Enmity-Satan like today modern men overlook the testimony of the Scriptures concerning the wonders wrought by Enmity-Satan and his agents. It was by Satanic aid that ancient Pharaoh; Judaism; early Vatican pontiff magicians were enabled to counterfeit the work of God till this day modern era! Enmity will still persist! The apostle John at Patmos prison describe the miracle working power that will be manifested in the last days, declares." "He does great wonders so that he makes fire come down from heaven upon the earth in the eyes of men and deceive them that dwell upon the earth by the means of those miracles which he had power to do." [Rev. 13: 13-14]. No mere impostures are here brought to view. Men are deceived by the miracles which Satan agents have power to do, not which they pretend to do.

The very name of witchcraft is now held in contempt [psychic]. The claim that men can hold intercourse with evil-Enmity spirit is regarded as a fable of the Dark Ages! But Spiritualism or Inspiration which numbers its converts by hundreds of thousands, year by millions which had made its way to great break world record sells into scientific circles; which has invaded churches and has found great favor in legislative bodies, and even in the tradition judicial courts of kings: This mammoth deception is but a revival in a new disguise of the witchcraft [psychic] condemned and prohibited of ancient evil practice!. Modern secular world is very aware!

Satan beguiles men now as he beguiled Eve in Eden by enticing exciting desire to obtain forbidden tree of knowledge of good and evil and death. "You shall be as gods," knowing good and evil." [Gen 3: 5] But the wisdom which Spiritualism imparts is that described by James which "descended not from above but it is earthly sensual, devilish." [James 3: 15]. Enmity, Satan, the prince of earthly darkness has a genius masterly mind, and he skillfully adapts his temptations to men of every variety of condition and culture; status and high ranks, such as king Saul and all others after him till this day modern era: The process is pretty much the same! No distinction or exclusion all fall this way!. Evil, Enmity works with all deceivableness of unrighteousness to gain control of the men; but he can also accomplish his object only as they voluntarily-willing yielding to his temptations like Balaam.

Those who place themselves in his power by indulging their evil traits of character, little realize where their course will end. What else the people need to be taught better than the truth word of God Almighty? Who else is able to sustain all living creatures on earth? The rains; the air; and the sun: Who else provides such necessity resource? The Satan the tempter accomplishes their ruin and then employs to ruin others! He has none resource to sustain life! Those genius journalism; well trained to invent Christian fiction ebook; to those who regard themselves as well educated and well refined: Satan addresses himself by exciting the imagination to lofty flights in forbidden fields, leading them to take so great selfish-pride or puffed in their well education superior talent-wisdom that in their hearts they despise the really Eternal God Almighty: They say to themselves: "I am great genius and I have achieved great successfully from most highly prestigious university." I am well known around the world for my great success!" Oh man: For how long you will last on earth? You are very limited! Your days are numbered: You are made from dust on ground: The most made lower creature to live short life! And to dust you shall return!. So where is your great success? [Gen 3: 19]. Self-deceit kills itself! Jesus Christ is inevitable! He is inescapable! You ignore him at your own wicked risk. Good teachings sounds to you as bad teachings!. So "Let the dead bury their own dead!" Jesus said: [Matt 8: 22]. You truly need Jesus Christ for your salvation!. Take it! Reject it! It is your choice:

To this great class the great deceiver presents Spiritualism and Inspiration Christian fiction ebook. In its more refined and intellectual well trained journalist aspects, and he thus succeeds in drawing many young adults into his snare! The text is great to read and manipulates minds.

Satan he who could appear clothed with the most brightness of the heavenly seraphs before Christ in the wilderness of temptation, comes to men in the most attractive manner as an angel of light: Jesus Christ was hungry! 40 days and 40 nights: No food to eat or water to drink!. Satan seizes the opportunity to appeal by Scriptures reason; by the presentation of elevating themes Enmity: "If you are the Son of God: Command that these stones become bread!" [Matt. 4: 3]. Yes indeed! Christ had that power to obtain bread from stones. But Christ did not do that!.

Satan delights the fancy with enrapturing scenes and he enlists the affections by his eloquent language portrayals of love and charity. To whom he did this? To Christ, his maker!. He dares to tempt!. Jesus Christ: The foundation of heaven and earth: Christ in the flesh form could not be defeated by food that which sustains much less life than the Spiritual eternal food from the mouth of God Almighty. That mighty being who could take the world's redeemer to an exceedingly high mountain, and bring before him all the kingdoms of the earth and the glory of them; will present his temptations to men in a manner to prevent the sense of all who are not shielded by heavenly divine eternal powerful!.

Many modern men whether Christians or none Christians: To the self-indulgent the pleasure loving; the sensual; the grosser forms of Spiritualism are adapted; and multitudes eagerly accept teachings that leave them at liberty to follow the inclinations of the flesh heart! Enmity, Satan studies every indication of the frailty of human nature he marks the Enmity sinful which each individual is inclined to commit, and then he takes care that opportunities shall not be wanting to gratify the tendency to evil: He tempts men to excess in that which is in itself lawful, causing them through intemperance to weaken physical, mental, and moral power. He has destroyed and is destroying thousands again through the indulgence of the passion; thus brutalizing the entire nature of man! The human history evidence is obvious:

When the people on earth are led to believe that desire is the highest law that liberty is license; and that man is accountable only to himself who can wonder that corruption and depravity teem on every hand? The reins of self-control are laid upon the neck of lust; the powers of mind and soul are made subject to the animal propensities; and Enmity sinful Satan exultingly sweeps into his wire net cage thousands who profess to be followers of Christ Jesus. Unfortunately none needs to be deceived by the lying claims of spiritualism. God has given the world sufficient light to enable them to discover the snare!

If there were no other evidence; it should be enough for the Christians that spirits make no difference between righteousness and wicked, between the noblest and purest of the Disciples of Christ and the most corrupt of the servants of Satan-Enmity. By representing the basest of men as in heaven; and highly exalted there Satan virtually declares to the world: No matter how wicked you are; no matter whether you believe or disbelieve God and the sacred word. Live as you please: Heaven is your home: Moreover the disciples as personated by these lying spirits are made to contradict what they wrote at the dictation of the Holy Spirit when on earth. They deny the divine origin of the Bible, and thus tear away the foundation of the Christian's hope and faith; and put out the light that reveals the way to heaven.

Yes indeed! Enmity sinful: Satan is absolute making the world believe that the Holy Bible is a mere Christian fiction book; or at least a book suited to the infancy of the race; but now to be lightly regarded or cast aside as obsolete: So men designed new Christian fiction ebook version to suit their human ego rather than the true Holy Bible God Sacred Word: It is indeed absurd to believe such! The Scriptures evidences are obvious! We all well know. And to take the place of the word of God he holds out spiritual manifestations. Those who claim to be genius journalists; are making up their own grave yards for their own eternal condemnation!. God Almighty is undefeated! Obviously they know that so well. History repeats itself.

Here is the channel wholly under his control; by this means he can make the world believe what he will. The book that is to judge him and his followers he puts into the shade; just where he wants it; the Jesus Christ the saviour of the world he makes to be more than a common man. And as the Roman guards that watched the tomb of Christ Jesus spread the lying report which the priests and Pharisees paid bribe to put into their mouths to disprove Christ's resurrection; so do the modern world believers in spiritual manifestations try to make it appear that there is nothing miraculous in the circumstances of our ground; they call attention to their own miracles declaring that these far exceed the works of Christ Jesus! God speaks to Isaiah to prophesy:

"When they shall say unto you Seek unto them that have familiar spirits; and unto wizard that peep and that mutter: Should not a people seek unto their God?" For the living to the dead? To the law and to the testimony!. If they speak not according to this word, it is because there is no light in them." [Is. 8: 19-20].

If the people on earth have been willing to receive the truth so plainly stated in the Scriptures that the dead know not anything; they would see in the claims and manifestations of Spiritualism the working of Enmity sinful Satan with power and signs and lying wonders. But rather than yield the liberty so agreeable to the flesh heart and renounce the Enmity sinful which they love the multitudes close their eyes to the light, and walk straight on; regardless of warnings while Enmity sinful Satan weaves his snares about them; and they become his vulnerable prey. Because they received not the love of the truth; that they might be saved!. Therefore God shall send them strong delusion that they should believe a malicious lies. [2 Thess. 2: 10-11]

Those who oppose the true teachings of Spiritualism are assailing not men alone, but Enmity sinful Satan and his agents. They have entered upon a contest against principalities and powers and wicked spirits in high places. Enmity sinful Satan will not give up one inch of ground except as he is driven back by the power of heavenly divine messengers. True Christians and true godly people should be able to meet him, as Christ did and the disciples; apostles and the early century's reformers with the words: "It is written." Enmity sinful Satan can genuinely quote the Scriptures now as in the days of Christ, and he will pervert its teachings to sustain his delusions. Remember he was once in heaven standing on right hand of God. So he is wise but brood of vipers! But the plain statements of the Bible will furnish weapons powerful in every conflict. Our Lord Christ Jesus did that: "It is written." The Word of God is written it cannot be removed or conquered.

David &. Ziba [2 Sam 16: 1-3]

Ziba supply the food and wine for David and all the people of Israel who fled from Jerusalem because Absalom David's son wants to take over the throne from his father:

Shimei cursed David [v 5] As David was escaping from Absalom, Shimei the family of Saul cursed David with all harsh words while all David's soldiers and servants and the rest of Israel heard him cursing David plainly.

"The Lord has repaid you for all the blood you shed in the household of Saul; he said: "In whose place you have reigned!" The Lord has handed the kingdom over to your son Absalom." Shimei said to David as he cursed him throwing stones on his face." [v 8].

Abishai the son of Zeruiah wished to kill Shimei with his sword, David would not let him to kill Shimei, Saul family. [v 11]. My son, who is of my own flesh is trying to take my life." David said to Abishai. "How much more, then, this Benjamite!" "Leave him alone, let him curse, for the Lord has told him to curse me." It may be that the Lord will see my distress and repay me with good for the cursing I am receiving today." David said.

Hushai and Ahithophel advice Absalom:

Hushai the Arkite who is great friend of David went to Absalom and greeted him saying: "Long live the king! Long live the king!" [v 17] Absalom asked Hushai: "Is this the love you show your friend?" Why didn't you go with your friend?" [David]: Hushai answered Absalom: 'No, the one chosen by the Lord, by these people, and by all the men of Israel that I will follow, and I will remain with him. Furthermore, whom should I serve? Should I not serve the son? Just as I served your father, so I will serve you." All sound good. [v 20]. Absalom said to Ahithophel: "Give us your advice, what should we do? Ahithophel answered: "Sleep with all your father's concubines' wives whom he left to take care of the palace. Then all Israel will hear that you have made yourself a stench in your father's nostrils, and the hand of everyone with you will be strengthened."

So they pitched a tent for Absalom on the roof and he slept with all his father's concubines wives plain as it was prophesied by Nathan early when David had slept with Bathsheba and killed Uriah and took Bathsheba to be his wife. [2 Sam 12: 11-12]. King David recall the occasion, the consequences bound to take place. He is a prophet who sought after God's heart. [See v. 13]. The Bible evidence concludes: "Now in those days the advice Ahithophel gave was like that of one who inquires of God: That was how both David and Absalom regarded all of Ahithophel's advice [v 23].

Absalom could not become a king of Israel because God did not appoint him. He died a terrible death on a tree trap! He hangs up! Both Ahithophel he too hanged up himself and died, [2 Sam 17: 23].

Absalom, he was riding his mule and as the mule went under the thick branches of a large oak tree, Absalom's head-long hairs got caught on the tree. He was left hanging in midair while the mule he was riding kept going on leaving him hanging on the oak tree. Joab said: "I am not going to wait like this for you? So he took sword in his hand and plunged it into Absalom' heart while Absalom was still alive on the oak tree." [2 Sam 18: 14-15] Absalom died there on the oak tree hanging up. It is all about evil activities! What should we do about it? Enmity brings us sad history all along from Genesis 3 to 50. Till this day!

Enmity is never old act, because it is constant process with no end until Christ returns! Quietly forces are working in our modern world today everywhere around the globe, to undermine the Christian faith. Yet but very few are aware of these Enmity developments: Liberties that so many people take for granted were not won in a few hours or few days. They took centuries to gain, and they can go very fast! A great danger is impending!

God's Word reveals it loud! The deadly Enmity nature of which will soon come with great devastating powerful force ever to be experienced on earth when Christ returns for the ultimate righteousness judgments: It will be far worse than Noah's day; far worse than Sodom; far worse than Egypt days! Enmity the ancient Rome is nowadays regarded by modern Protestants Church with far greater favour than in former years of the early century's reformers!

There is great increasing indifference concerning the doctrines that separate the reformed churches from the pontiff Rome papal hierarchy: The opinion is gaining ground that after all, we do not differ so wide upon vital essential puzzling mind issues today as has been in the early century, supposed, and that little concession on Protestants part will bring us into a better understanding with pontiff Rome. The time was when Protestants placed a high value upon the liberty of conscience which has been so deadly purchased. Too much compromise with deadly Enmity secular world scholasticism, so to speak! Early century, they taught the children, young adults to abhor popery and held that to remain at peace with Rome pontiff would be disloyalty to God. Nowadays, they teach children and young adults to abhor Christian fiction eBooks texts designed by well skilled journalists who are fully confined into modern scholasticism, tool to shape the young adults into their institution classes to be anti-Christ faith! But how widely different are the sentiments nowadays is expressed.

Enmity is expanded with opposing God's truth. The defenders

of scholasticism maligned: And the Protestants world is inclined to accept compromise the statement.

Many people around the world today urge that it is unjust to judge the church of today by the Enmity, the abominations of desolation and absurdities that marked the reign during David; Solomon; the centuries David's dynasty of ignorance and darkness: Yet today, far worse ignorance about the Enmity than ever before on our door posts: They excuse horrible cruelty as the result of the barbarism anti-Christ of our modern times and plead that civilization has changed our sentiments. Truly, it is not so because we are the seed of the past. [Zerah] God this phrase constantly making sure that we may fully understand the meaning: Not so until Christ returns! Enmity will indeed persist! **This is what the Lord God says to David:**

"Out of your own household I am going to bring calamity upon you: Before your very eyes I will take your wives and give them to one who is close to you, he will sleep with all your wives in broad daylight! You did it in secret but I will do this thing in broad public daylight before all Israel!" God spoke these words through Nathan, the prophet. [2 Sam 12: 11-12].

Earlier chapter; we stated that Absalom David's own son slept with all his father's concubines wives in a tent pitched on top of a roof. For the God spoke and it was done: Early Nathan had predicted as instructed by God. Therefore, the process was carried on through all David dynasties after his death. What we learn from the past? We are on same online in the fulfillment of Enmity until Christ returns. [Gen 3: 15] God imposed Enmity. No one can remove it only Christ, the ultimate righteousness judgments. All past men are dead but we live today with the same Enmity which all inherited from our forefathers. [Zerah] seed of Enmity is the same.

For the word of God is living and active: Sharpest than any double-edged sword, it penetrates even to dividing soul and spirit, joints and marrow: It judges the thoughts and attitudes of the heart; it discerns; and corrects! Nothing in all creation is hidden from God's eyes: Everything is naked and laid bare before the eyes of Him to whom we all must give account." [Heb 4: 12-13] Jesus Christ is inevitable! If individual and humanity are to progress; Jesus Christ is inescapable! You ignore him at your own wicked risk. Have these people forgotten the claim of infallibility for centuries put forth by this Enmity haughty powerful force? And also have we forgotten the claim of infallibility for the early century reformers put forth by this Enmity haughty powerful force? So far from relinquishing this claim the church in the 19th century has affirmed it with greater positive than ever before! As ancient Rome asserts that they have never erred, and never can they err, how they renounce the principles which governed their course in past pages? Like them we will not admit or confess errors: David did confess: "I have sinned against the Lord!" [v 13. God indeed forgave David. But with condition consequences that followed to his seed. What David did in secret, God exposed all things out on daylight where all people Israel saw. And so God will also expose all our secrets evils acts when Christ returns. If God did to David; why not for us? David and all others are gone into their graves and our graves will soon come no escape all will face his/her grave.

Decalogue: Enmity the Origin of all evils [Holy Writ]

Benevolence of God in all His dealings with Enmity evil!. Jesus Christ, the Father's wrought in the creation of all heavenly things: "It was the Prerogative of Christ Jesus alone to Wield." Tyrannical; Lucifer induced the Man [Adam] to sin. The daring blasphemy of Lucifer demand that Christ Jesus should pay him homage!. It is unforgivable blasphemy of most heinous sinful nature!. [Matt. 12: 31-32]. The sophistry and falsehood by which he had sought to hinder the perfect work of Christ Jesus; Enmity; hostiles, hatred and envy manifested through the generational of disobedience and disagreement upon his malicious cruelty accusation against Christ whose perfect life was one of exampled goodness all sprang from deep seated revenge! The death of Christ proves it immutable! And the sacrifice to which infinite love impelled the Father Head and the Son that sinners might be fully redeemed; demonstrates such view: **Deluge: [Latin-Deluvium]**

Dyluge: Early ad: Modified after the example of the words of popular formation. [Hatzf] of forms nearer to the Latin were deliver a great flood or over flowing of powerful violent water; a very severe destruction inundation. Often used hyperbolically e.g., of a very heavy falls of rains. Enmity falls: Every mouth will be stopped and all the hosts of rebellion will be speechless [mute]. The cross of Calvary, while it declares the perfect law, the most perfect Law of God; immutable proclaims to the whole universal that the wages of heinous sinful is death!"

In Christ Jesus the savior expiring outcry, "It is finished!" The death knell of Satan Enmity was rung: The great unresolved issues which had been so long progress was then decided: And the final radical eradicated of all evil acts was made certain: The Son of God passed through the portals of the tomb that through death Christ Jesus, might destroy Enmity! Satan who had a mere power of death that is the devil [Heb 2: 14] Lucifer desire for self-exaltation had led him to say: "I will exalt my throne above the stars,' he said: "of God, I will be like the most high God declares: "I will thee to ashes upon the earth and never shall thou be any more!" [Is. 14: 13-14; Ezek. 28: 18-19]. When the day comes that shall burn as oven; all the proud, yea, and all that do wickedly, shall be stubble: And the day that comes shall burn them up all! Says the Lord God of hosts!. That it shall neither leave them root nor branch!" [Mal 4: 1-2]: The whole world will have to become witness to the nature and results of sin. And its utter extermination which in the beginning would have brought fear to angels and dishonor to God; will now vindicate his love and establish God's honor before the whole universal of beings who delight to do God's will like Christ in whose heart is God's perfect law!

Never again there will be an evil Enmity again be manifest. God said by his powerful Word from his mouth. The law of God which Satan has reproached as the yoke of bondage will be honored as the law of everlasting liberty. No more faking human beings liberties. Enmity then will cease forever! Finally: "Woe to him who quarrels with his maker! To him who is but a potsherd among the potsherds on the ground:" [Isaiah 45: 9]… "Woe to the world because of offenses! "For offenses must come; but woe to that man by whom the offense comes!" Jesus said: [Matt 18: 7]. Also see [1 Corinth 11: 19-39]. Enmity; Deluge: Very destructive violence many people today, forgot: Mahatma Gandhi; Dr. Martin Luther King, Jr. And Nelson Mandela: Not so long ago they had gone with great achievements. These men were great reformers for our modern era.

Jonah v. Decalogue [Jonah 1-4]
Enmity &. Deluge [Gen 3: 15]

Jonah built walls in order to block the ways for the people of Nineveh City what God had set up for its salvation. The word came to Jonah: "Arise, go to Nineveh that great city, and cry out against it: For their wickedness [Enmity] has come before Me!" God commanded Jonah [v. 2]. "Yonah is the Hebrew word for [Dove or Pigeon] that's what Jonah means: Persistence in massive for its own nest. So Jonah deliberately ignored God's command with profligacy disagreement with God's mighty righteousness command. He fled to Tarshish from northeast to west. He couldn't make it! God is very serious with His command word. Nineveh city must be saved 150, 000 [150 thousand] inhabitants with many livestock need to be saved, [v. 3].

But the Lord God the creator of the dry land and the seas sent a great wind storms [Deluge] on the seas, and there was a severe-mighty tempest in which Jonah was in aboard was about to sink into the rough seas, causing all the crew was almost to perish [v. 4]. Jonah had gone down to the lowest deck part of the ship to hid, had laid down and he was in deep sleep! The Captain then came in search for him, found him in his deep sleep; "What do you mean you sleeper?" Arise, call on your God, perhaps your God will hear us, so that we may not perish!" So they cast lots and the lots fell on Jonah-guilty: They questioned him: "Tell us please! For whose cause is this trouble upon us? They knew that he ran away from God: "What is your occupation? And where do you come from? What is your nationality country? "I'm a Hebrew, and I fear God who made the dry land and seas," he responded while he is trembling with fear and miserable face; seeing all the loss of the ship merchandise which they threw into the waters [v. 9].

Jonah built walls rather than building bridges that connect the people of Nineveh to God. He in fact built walls for himself. Therefore the walls God broke them all so that the people of Nineveh could receive salvation from God direct. The command word of God must prevail. God had prepared a big fish to swallow Jonah: Did Jonah know? Neither the ship crew: But only God who had set up the perfect plan, it must proceed without fail! For the Lord God spoke and it was done! And Jonah was in the belly of the fish for three days and three nights; no food to eat or water to drink: Who then feed him during those three days and three nights no food to eat or water to drink. After intensive prayer, God spoke to the fish and vomited out Jonah onto dry land: The voice appealed Jonah: "Arise, go to Nineveh that great city cry out against it; for their wickedness Enmity sinful is before Me!"

This second time Jonah obeyed God's command. Powerful commanding word often wins evil for good cause of action. God did not intend to destroy the ship within its crew or Jonah, but intended to show them how ignorant, inability; inadequate; incompetent-hopeless, and weak human being is in His sight, as result, Jonah finally obeyed God and the whole crew believed in the Lord God and they sacrificed to God with thanksgiving. He is the Lord who controls the whole world. The earthiest crew was converted including all people of Nineveh city were all saved by God Almighty because they repented their Enmity sinful nature. God showed them His holy compassion and forgave them all! Glory to God Almighty! [See 4: 1-11]. "Is it right for you to be angry? [v 9] God asked Jonah. Also see [Gen 4: 6-8] "Why are you angry? God asked Cain. "If you do well, will you not be accepted?" And if you do not do well, Enmity sinful stands at your door [heart.] And its desire is for you, but you ought to overcome it yourself." Could Cain really overcome his own Enmity sinful? Can we? Can you? Oh what a challenge to face: No one can overcome sin on earth. Only Christ Jesus is able to overcome Enmity sinful nature in you. See [John 6: 44-58]. Jesus said: "No one can come to Me unless the Father who sent Me draws him: And I will raise him up at the last day!" [v 44]. "Does this offend you? He asked his disciples. It is also a question for us all even this day's generational modern era. It is written in the prophet; Jesus said: "And they shall all be taught by God. Therefore everyone who has heard and learned from the Father comes to Me:" [v 45.] Decalogue: The secular Oxford Dictionary omits Scriptures reference facts: [The Ten Commandments Exodus 20] collectively as the body of Law Key Rules all human beings on earth! John Wycliffe [1382] Rome Prol: 299 the number of the first maundementus of the Decalogue [1563]. Man musculus common place: The precepts of the Decalogue have been called the ten words: Both tables of the Decalogue are broken: Most of these still on question from variety of secular world scholars who invented Christian fiction eBooks. They are highly well respected journalists in the country well known as "Popular Platforms." They write anti-Christ fiction books.

Decalogue v. Deluge Enmity:

Ne-dop: So cruel harms 1393 church reformers; "scogan thou caused this," Deluge! There happen together with severe earthquakes, Deluge-violence; hostiles, destructive; cruelty harms everywhere upon the earth! This is no easy subject! Genesis chapter 3: 15; &. Chapter 4: 6-8. Cain the first cold blood murder took place since then there has never been cease shading blood on the ground till this day! Unless you are converted and become as a little child in the eyes of the mighty God, in Christ Jesus; [Matt 18: 3-6] there shall never be peace on earth until Jesus Christ returns!

All long; God never appoint great man in order to establish His purpose: Never! He often appoints simple lowly at heart like a little baby-child; Christ like whom He made Christ most humble-meek and lowly at heart setting up most challenging example upon all human nature! All the early century's church reformers were very simple men who upset down tables with great divine power up to this day of our modern era! They were not the sons of the governors; presidents; mayors; or prime ministers but very ordinary background on earth, God chose! They were shepherds and peasant farms! God raised them up for his special purposes!.

During our modern time we saw: Mahatma Gandhi in India purging the whole British Empire Conscience under Gandhi's feet! We saw Dr. Martin Luther King, Jr. purging the whole segregation conscience in U.S.A. And we saw Mr. Nelson Mandela in South Africa purging every part of appalling apartheid conscience once and for all! Deluge was severe upon them but God resolved the whole truth! Nowadays the most dominative aspect of general life is the journalism who are confined in the scholasticism similarity to the early century's Pharisees; Scribes; Priests; and Hellenist Cynics; pontiff are the generational seed of our forefathers Enmity that God had imposed upon them. Jesus Christ natural condemned them all "hypocrites," [Matt 23]. Many people today so called Christians religion-religious; spirituality and inspiration or spiritual, body and fattiness etc.; is drawing attraction to thousands of our young adults. 1.2 billion World Christian record is large number to consider. With new version bible Christian fiction eBook they embrace to heart as their best bible text to read.

Here they are very mistaken! This outward splendor pomp; and well popular platform journalists that only mocks the longing of the sin-sick lost souls, is an evidence of inward corruption today's modern era as it was in the past! It is the same thing even today: All constitutes the function of evil Enmity that brings Deluge upon all on earth today! Deluge; the religion of Christ needs not such attraction with empty lips to recommend it! In the shining light from the cross of Christ Jesus; truth of Christianity appears so pure, holy and lovely that externally decorations only hide its truth worthy! It is the most beautiful of holiness, meekness and lowly in heart, and quiet peace Spirit which is of deep value with the Lord God the Head Father of all well-beings! The most Brilliancy of eternal life-style ever shown on earth through the Lord Christ Jesus; it is not an index of pure, elevated human fiction thoughts-essays. Fiction kills and opposes all that is called God in our current modern world as it was during the early centuries; Judaism; Pontiff' killers of reformers heroes! The highest conceptions of all church reformation, the most delicate refinement of taste, often spring from minds, hearts wholly earthly and sensual!. They are often employed by Satan in scholasticism to shape young adults to lead men to necessities of the lost souls, to lost sight of today's and of future generational immortal life, to turn away from the true living Lord Jesus Christ, to become anti-Christ! 1.2 billion World Christian record it is a large to cause the world to live in peace! Deadly record today's generational **Enmity v. Deluge**: Jesus Christ is inevitable!

How long should we live under the yoke of Enmity? Fighting; blaming each other: Who cause it? Enmity sinful, who authentically confess against it? There aren't many today as it was in the past! A religion of external is very attractive to the un-renewed hearts and minds: The pomp reflected in fiction eBooks has a seductive, bewitching power by which many young adults are deceived. And they come to look upon the man's made denominational as the very gate of heaven, yet, it is the very gate of hell-death. So these young adults need to be warned expressively vigorously!

There are none proof against the influence, but those who have planted their zerah-seed firmly upon the foundation of truth and whose hearts minds are renewed by the Spirit of the Lord Christ Jesus. Thousands who have not an experienced knowledge of Christ will be swept into this deception. A form of godliness without the power is just what they desire! The well skilled journalist feels good at his liberty and popularity to Enmity v. Deluge which he invented successful to manipulate large number 1.2 billion World Christian record through his Christian fiction EBooks. Because the man's made religion church claims the right to pardon Enmity sinful nature. To him who loves self-indulgence, it is more pleasing to confess to a fellow mortal than to open the desperate lost soul to the Lord Christ Jesus who is able to pardon the Enmity sinful nature! It is more palatable to human nature to do penance than to renounce Enmity sinful nature which brings natural Deluge. It is much easier to mortify the flesh by sackcloth and nettles and galling chains than to crucify fleshly lusts which we early saw with David; followed by his own son Absalom and Amon with Tamar. Enmity v. Deluge is very heavy yoke to carry on your neck which the flesh heart is willing to bear or disobeying God your maker with clear conscience intent; deliberately refuse to bow down before the sight of your maker. See [Matt 11: 25-30].

Athanasius-John T. Nkomo

There is a striking similarity with our modern world current affairs today between the church of the early ancient Orthodox Judaism the time of our Lord Jesus Christ with his disciples followed by early century's pontiff Rome; till this day modern world era; no much difference. The outcry is very much the same, or perhaps much worse than ever before! Indeed, we could be the worse so far! The ancient Orthodox Judaism Pharisees secretly trampled upon every principle of the Decalogue-Law of God they were outwardly rigorous in the observance of its precepts, loading it down with exactions and traditional and burdensome upon the most vulnerable lost souls! The Lord Jesus Christ totally condemned them plainly to hellish! As the Jews, Gentiles professed to revere the law, so do the modern secular world today's modern era! Claim to revere the cross of our Lord Jesus Christ! They exalt the symbol of Christ suffering while in their practicing life-style practically, they deny Him whom they represent in their fiction textbooks. Those so called Christian tradition publishers embrace to heart fiction textbooks because it sells abundantly in the world's markets. Too much cash involved that's the key issue in business. They built unbroken walls to block good quality biblical Christian books that connect people to Christ Jesus!. While their anti-Christ books sells abundantly the more they are puffed! Their popular platforms hinder the quality books written by unpopular platform authors. "No market" they insist for the unpopular platform emerging authors who write books that build bridges to connect people to Christ Jesus around the world. These skilled journalists they extrinsically well claim while intrinsically they are anti-Christ. They totally fall-short in the eyes of God! Their popular books are obviously anti-Christ!

Another thing shows that they are anti-Christ is that they demand large sum of money to be upfront paid before they have done the actual work for publishing the book. At the end the author earns zero while they have filled Bank accounts milking the vulnerable author who spent decades to write a book.

Three publishers screwed me. I did not know how the publishing industry operates at the time. I believed their crafting-cunning language. One publisher demanded $999.95 upfront payment. In addition payment of $295.95 paying installment for 10 months: Another one demanded $800. Upfront payment: And then $600 payment JAVER for 5 years. And another one demanded $1,000 upfront payment with variety of options. These anti-Christ Christian tradition publishers place their names to every major website appealing to unpopular vulnerable authors to submit their potential manuscripts to them to publishing. But the truth about the teachings of Christ is buried beneath of their crafting and cunning language of senseless, falsehood. Empty lips! The words of Christ Jesus concerning the bigoted Jews applied still greater force to the publishing industry today in our modern world era. Well skilled journalists editors; they indeed bind heavy burdens and grievous to emerging vulnerable poor authors to be borne and lay them on them on their shoulders but they themselves will not dare to move or lift them with one of their fingers. As long as they earn abundant cashes. The vulnerable author pays all their expenses while they extrinsically doom the authors. There are numerous legitimate Christian publishing Companies in the country. But they have their own fixed marketing which no one can break. They too have built walls to block any. They are those who are particularly confined in the scholasticism institutions. See [Matt 23: 4].

Conscientious lost souls are kept in constant terror, fearing the wrath of an offended God, while the dignitaries of the church are living in luxuries; these skilled journalist editors and sensual pleasure is Satan, evil instigates the worship of money; the invocation minds and hearts of the people from God and Christ Jesus teachings, particularly young adults generational. In order to accomplish their ruin they endeavors to turn attention from Him through whom alone they can find salvation. [John 6: 44-58]. He will direct them to anyone that can be substituted for the one who has said, "Come to me all you!" [Matt 11: 28-30].

Christ Jesus is the most greatest to honor! He is coming back to judge the whole entire world once and for all! Jesus Christ is indeed, inevitable!

Unmatched the Word of God Almighty in Christ:

Jesus Christ words is unmatched non-science fiction; non-Christian fiction eBooks! Jesus Christ true living word from heavens full powers! Charges: Corrects: Teaches: Judges: Executes: Purges Enmity sinful nature of human kind on earth! Unmatched word of Christ connects the world to heavens! Unmatched words of Christ guarantees hope and trustworthy!

Unmatched Jesus Christ is coming back to judge the whole world once and for all! Unmatched Jesus Christ is King of kings; and Lord of lord. Unmatched Christ Jesus all knees shall bow down and confess that Jesus Christ is Lord! Unmatched Christ; He is the World's Savior! Eternally Glorious Lord: There's no-one else! No matter how the secular world overlook the issue. Unmatched Jesus Christ is inevitable! And he is inescapable!

Athanasius-John T. Nkomo

Unmatched Jesus Christ

Church Body

Religions

Enmity: Hostiles!

Religious Against God [Gen 3: 15-19]

Denominations

Disobedient

Man's made meaningless.

Conclusions:

Fear God!

Keep His Commandments! [Eccles. 12: 13].

For this is man's all."

    Languages: Hebrew: Aramaic: Latin: Greek: Syrian?

    For the mind that is set on the flesh is hostile to God; for it does not submit to God's Law; indeed, it cannot! Those who are in the flesh will never, never please God neither! [Rom 8: 6-8].

Decalogue [Exo. 20]

The Ten Commandments

"You shall love the lord your God

"With all your heart; with all your soul;

"And with all your strength:" This is the first and greatest!

And the second is like it: "You shall love your neighbor as yourself."

Athanasius-John T. Nkomo

On these two commandments hang all the Law and the Prophets."

Jesus Christ concluded: [Deut. 6: 4-6, &. Matt. 22: 37- 40].

When the standard of righteousness Law of the Lord our God is set aside, the way is open for the world's prince of evil [Satan] to establish his Enmity sinful nature rule on the whole entire earth, and strengthen Enmity in the presence of the Lord our God. It would be far more badly consistent for nations on earth to abolish their statutes, and permit the people to do, or behave as they please, than for the Rulers of the universe to annul God's righteous Law; and leave the world without a standard to condemn the wicked guilty criminals or justify the innocent obedient.

Would we know the result of making void the perfect Law of our Lord God? The experiment has been tried: It could not work at all! Terrible were the scenes enacted in France and the rest of Europe when Enmity, atheism powers-pagans became the controlling power in Europe; spread rapidly to Africa; Asia and Atlantic Oceans and elsewhere around the globe: It was then demonstrated to the world that to throw off the restraints which the Lord our God has imposed is to accept the perfect Law rather than to accept the rule of the cruelest of human tyrants nature!

Wherever the divine precepts are set aside stands still, Enmity sinful ceases to appear or exist sinful or righteousness desirable. Those who refuse to submit to the perfect Law of the Lord our God are natural hostiles and will never please God neither! They are wholly unfitting to rule or govern themselves on earth. Through their pernicious teaching, the spirit of insubordination is implanted in the hearts as zerah of their children and youth who are naturally impatient of control, and a lawless, no God fearing conscience, licentious state of society results as it is likely visibly seen nowadays activity in our modern civilized world with full of violence! Enmity controls everyone else mind today.

While scoffing at the credulity of those who obey the requirements of the Lord God's Law in Christ Jesus: The multitudes eagerly accept the psychological delusion and deluge of Enmity from Satan sinful nature! They give the rein to lust and practice the Enmity sinful nature which called down judgments upon all the pagans Rome and modern atheism!

Let the restraint imposed by the divine perfect Law be wholly removed and human appalling laws would soon be disregarded: Because our God forbids dishonest practices; coveting; lying; and defrauding men are ready to trample upon Christ Jesus statutes as a hindrance to their worldly corrupted prosperity; but the results of banishing these precepts would be such as they do not anticipate! If the laws were not binding, why should any fear to transgress? Properties would no longer be safe at all! Men and women would obtain their neighbor's possessions by wicked violence force, recklessly, and the strongest-giant Nephilim would become richest with no pity upon the vulnerable-weak-poor fellows. Life itself would not be respected, likely as it appears nowadays in our American society today gun shooting occurs everywhere nation-wide; gun shootings and uncontrolled guns are sold to wicked criminals and they shoot schools children, churches, clubs; and theaters gatherings. They shoot without pity because their hatred is deep!. Enmity; hostiles and hatred it is a growth zerah into hearts. The appalling current situation will not cease until Christ returns! It is old act!

Those who disregard **[Decalogue]** the Ten Commandments perfect Law of our God in Christ Jesus, the ultimate righteous Judge who is to come to earth; who saw the skunk rebellions, disobedience to reap-zerah of their forefathers disobedience and rebellions; they remain in Enmity, hostility, and hatred and bitterness backbiters-viper-brood at heart see **[Matt. 23]** will never please God neither! They are set on flesh! Spiritual death!

The marriage vow; "for poor; for richer' for sickness till death us depart" no longer stand firm as a sacred bulwark to protect the families and married life: [Matt. 19: 4, 5, 6, 7, 8, 9, 10, 11-12]… Jesus Christ plausibly explained in full length details context for us to fully understand and fear God's perfect Law. He who had the power, the giant like old Nephilim [Gen 6: 4] of the renowned would if he desires took his neighbor's daughter by violence force even his neighbor's wife; like Goliath a Philistine giant boasted and defied Israel, God's holy army: God handed Goliath to a youth David, killed him with a mere stone-sling.

The 5th Commandments would be set aside with the 4th. Jesus Christ explained it so well. Children and young adults would not shrink from taking the life of their parents, if by so doing they could obtain the desire of their corrupt hearts.

The civilized world on which we live in would become a horde of robbers and harlotries and assassins and peace rest and happiness would be banished from the whole entire world. However, that end will come into effect when Christ returns! Not now: Already the doctrine that men are released from obedience to God's Law requirements has weakened the force of moral obligation, and opened the flood gates of Enmity sinful nature upon the whole entire world. Lawlessness dissipation and corruptions are sweeping in upon every individual person today like an overwhelming deluge tide. In the most families, Satan is at his work. He banner violence-waves even in professed-so called Christian households.

There is envy; covet; obsession Enmity. Surmising, hypocrisy estrangement emulation, strife, betrayal of sacred trusts, indulgence of lust. The whole human system of religious principles and doctrines which should form the solid rock foundation and frame-work of perfect social life, seems to be a tottering mass ready to fall to ruin!. The vilest of criminals, when thrown into prison for their offenses, are often made the recipient of high gifts and attentions as if they had attained glorious an enviable distinction. The greatest publicity is given to their popular platform character and crimes are encouraged.

The press publish the revolting details of vice, thus initiating others into the practice of fraud, gun shooting; robbery profession and murder; and Satan gets exults and puffed in the success of his Enmity hellish schemes and agency. The infatuation of vice, the wanton taking of many life, the terrible increase of intemperance and Enmity sinful nature of every order and degree, should arouse all who fear our God to inquire what can be done to stay out the tide of evil. Courts of justice are corrupt; Rulers are actuated by desire for self-gain and love of sensual; prestigious; recognition; man praise and pleasure. Intemperance has clouded the faculties of many scholasticism so that Satan Enmity has almost complete control of every young adult mind; science fiction to adventures audible ebook text designed by well skilled journalist. Highly commercialized nation-wide.

No more fearing for God. This is what we see today in our modern civilized world current affairs. Jurists are perverted, bribed, deluded. Drunk-ness and revelry, passion, envy, dishonesty of every sort; using crafting language are represented among those who administer the laws. Justice stands afar off, for truth is fallen in the judicial courts, and equity cannot enter!.

The Darkness spiritual and Enmity that prevailed on earth for centuries under the supremacy of pagans Rome, slavery; colonialism; apartheid and man's made religious were the inevitable results of our forefathers zerah inheritance which remains in us, suppression of the Scriptures containing God's sacred word **Decalogue**: But where is to be found the cause of the wide spread infidelity, the rejection of the perfect Law of God in Christ Jesus, and the consequent corruption under the full blaze of gospel as it is today full proclaimed, light in an age of religious freedom. Whose freedom? While we shoot each other continually.

Enmity will persist till Jesus Christ returns! Incompetent man will not be able to resolve the issue of Enmity! Never! Will you agree never! Obstinacy that is the cause of Enmity; the flesh will never please God! [Rom 8: 6-8].

Do you call it or consider freedom of religious? Those who set the mind on the flesh will never, never please God no matter what cost! It is Enmity, hostiles, hatred, disobedient in God's eyes. Nowadays; that Satan can no longer keep the world under his control by withholding the Scriptures, he resorts to other means to accomplish the same object, Enmity sinful nature. We stated early that science fiction ebook textbook replace the Scriptures but it omits truth from God's sacred word. It is designed by well skilled journalist who is confined into scholasticism institution whose confidence and respect is well recognized with great respect in the whole community. He attends church service to consolidate public confidence and respect. He is well known for his genius achievements. He possesses sharp craft language. Humble appearance but all based on extrinsically. Jesus said: "You will know them by their fruit."

To destroy faith in God found in the Bible serves his purpose as well as to destroy the Bible itself: By introducing or inventing science fiction ebook text, the belief that God's perfect Law is not binding, Satan Enmity as effectually leads men and women, and young adults to transgress as if they were wholly ignorant of its precepts. Indeed, it is absolute Enmity, hostiles in the sight of God. They will never submit to God's perfect Law! This is very deep subject to deal with and to grasp to heart. Those who are in the flesh will never submit to God's Law! And now as in the past ages of generational to present, Satan has worked hard through the church, government, scholasticism to further or strengthen his skills through those who are well established, and well skilled journalists. As the religious organizations of the nowadays have refused to hear or listen to unpopular biblical truths plainly,

Enmity Theme brought to view in the truth of Scriptures affirmed by the Lord God in Christ Jesus who came down from heaven with complete perfect teachings. They have sown broadcast zerah the seeds of Enmity, hostility, hatred, violence and skepticism and miss-trust, fear and confidence loss.

They mostly clinging to the human tradition error of natural immortality and man's consciousness in death, they reject the only defense against the psychological delusions of spiritual death. Nor is this all! As the claims of the **Decalogue** on earth, popular teachers find that the observance of the Law is there enjoined; and as the only way to free ourselves from truth, God's duty which we are unwilling to perform fully, so we unthinkable declare that the Law of God is no longer binding or an relevant for our modern most civilized world generational. Yet we truly naturally ignore or intentional intent forget that we are also of the past zerah inheritance, the seeds planted from Bereshith of our forefathers remains with us generational forever! It is unresolved till Jesus Christ returns!. Something you and I ought to grip to heart deeply. Jesus Christ is inevitable! He is inescapable! You ignore him at your own wicked risk. He is again; inescapable! Are we not all made from dust? And to dust we all shall return! [Gen 3: 19]. No escape!.

The ancient days and moderns days both cast away the perfect Law of our Lord God altogether! The judgment result will be the same as the past when Christ Jesus returns. As the work of Satan strength persist and so God's perfect Law will be strengthened as much as doubled as it was with Pharaoh in Egypt. "Indeed, I will harden Pharaoh's heart as much so that I will be honored and glorified throughout all ages-generational!." God said: [Exo. 9: 16-18 &. 14: 17-18].

The reform still extends this rejection of the Lord God perfect Law to avoid the claims of the Lord Christ Jesus will become well-nigh universal. Upon those man's made religious leaders whose teachings have opened the door to infidelity into their modern scholasticism institutions, to negative spiritualism, and to contempt for God's holy perfect Law; rests a fearful responsibility for the Enmity sinful that exists in the Christendom world today! Let it be well clear to all that God will judge the world through Christ Jesus the ultimate righteous Judge!

Yet this very class of modern world put forth the claim that the fast-spreading corruption is largely attributable to the desecration of the so called "Christian Fiction ebook," and the true-original Bible is also one of the best written fiction book it greatly improved the morals of modern society around the world. They don't consider the Bible as God's sacred word. Combining the temperance reform with the journalism movement themselves as laboring to promote the highest interests of society and world community; and those who refuse or disagree to unite with them are denounced as the enemies heresy of temperance and reform.

But the true fact that a movement to establish error is connected with a work which is in itself good, is not an argument in favor of the corrupt error. We may disguise poison by mingling it with wholesome delicious food, but we do not thereby change its killing nature. Human when he sets up the mind on the flesh he becomes natural hostiles and hatred, he can never please God. On the contrary, it is rendered more dangerous, as it is more likely to be taken unaware or awareness intent. He is no longer on himself: It is the work of Enmity sinful, Satan's devices to combine with falsehood just enough truth to give it plausibility. Satan is ever opposing all that called of God the true maker of all living. Satan; Hebrew phrase it means: "Opposing." Original Opponent. Enmity, God imposed it in order to challenge Satan. "Go ahead." God said. Satan the leader of every opponent movement. Enmity its foundation it is unresolved. Not by mere man on earth: Only God who is able! The movement may advocate reforms which the people need, principles which are harmony with the Bible, yet while there is with these requirements which is contrary to God's perfect Law, Enmity therefore, will persist till Christ Jesus returns! If not so, why so much suffering which cause un-ceasing world's outcries?

The modern saints cannot unite with them. Nothing can justify them in setting aside the Decalogue: The Ten Commandments from God's Holy Mouth for the precepts of men. Throughout the centuries ancient and modern times; two or more, great errors; the immortality of the Enmity sinful souls and sacredness; Satan [opponents] will bring the people under his deceptions: While the former lays the foundation Spiritualism-Death; the latter creates a bond of sympathy with men made denominations, religious leaders; both Catholic and Protestantism will yet stretch their hands across the gulf to grasp or grip the hand of science fiction spiritualism: They will reach over the abyss to clasp hands with Enmity power, and under the influence of modern scholasticism of this threefold union, our country, and the world will follow in the steps of 1. 2 billion world's Christendom religious leaders in trampling on the righteous of conscience. Our Lord Christ Jesus truly warned in advice. It is bound to take place. In fact it's just beginning while we watch. Spiritualism is now changing its form, veiling some of its more objectionable and immoral features, and assuming a Christian guise. Generally, life is difficulty getting worse daily.

During the ancient Orthodox Judaism and early centuries Rome denounced Jesus Christ, his doctrine and the Bible; now they professes to accept both: The Bible is interpreted and defined in a manner that is attractive to the un-renewed heart; while its solemn and vital truths are made of no effect. The God of true love is presented; but His justice, His denunciations of Enmity sinful nature, the requirements of God's holy perfect Law are all kept out of sight. Pleasing, bewitching fables captivate the sense of those who do not make God's word the foundation of their true faith.

Today Christ Jesus is a verily rejected as before or perhaps worse as ever; but Satan has so much blinded the eyes of the people that the deception is not discerned.

As spiritualism assimilates more closely to the nominal Christianity of the day, it has greater power to deceive and ensnare. Satan himself is converted, after the modern order of things. He will appear in the character of a holy angel of light. Through the agency of spiritualism, miracles will be wrought, the sick will be healed, and many undeniable wonders will be performed. Satan will perform in order to convince people that he is God because he too can perform miracles. Pharaoh's wise men and magicians performed wonders in Egypt but Moses whose truth God message overcame Pharaoh's magician's false tricks. [Exo. 7: 11]. And as the spirits will profess faith in the Bible, and express regard for God and their work will be accepted as manifestation of divine power.

The line of distinction between professing Christians and the ungodly is now hardly distinguishable. Church members love what the world loves and loves and ready to join with them; thus Satan determines to unite them in one body and thus strengthen his evil cause by sweeping all into the ranks of science fiction spiritualism faking. Scientists who boast for success medical profession as of true miraculous as a certain mark of truth, will be readily deceived by this wonder-working power. They face their own death too like anyone else. They resolve nothing or prevent a death as they can't even prevent their own death. They are mere human beings taken from dust. And so to dust they shall return.

Early century pontiff, and reformers, having cast away the shield of truth, will also be deluded. Pontiff and Protestants, and world-wide will alike accept the form of godliness without the power, and they will see in this union a grand movement for the conversion of the world, and the ushering in of the long-expected millennium. Jesus Christ is inevitable!

Through science fiction faking ebook, spiritualism, Satan, Enmity appears as a benefactor of the race, healing the diseases of the people, surgeries, and professing to present a new and more exalted system of religious faith; but at the same time Satan works as a destroyer of all souls. Satan trembles because he is very much aware that he can't overthrow God's truth and powerful! The challenge imposed upon him is greater than he can bear. All who follow after him are potsherds on the ground. The whole earth and heavens; there is none who can dare to overcome God! After all; He is the Lord God the Creator of All! Can a clay overcome the potter? God shapes everything according to His will and power! Well declared: "Woe to him who quarrels with his maker; to him who is but a potsherd among the potsherds on the ground!" [Is. 45: 9]. Also see [v. 6-8].

Satan Enmity sharp craft language reinforce temptations are leading multitudes to ruin on the whole entire world-wide. His sharp craft language is the reflection of those who are anti-Christ who are well skilled and occupy high ranks into every prestigious scholasticism; religious leaders; government leaders; scientific leaders; and civic all work as Satan's agents. They are stiff-neck! They build walls to block everyone whose truth build bridges that connect all men to God!. Intemperance dethrones reasons, sensual indulgence, strife, and bloodshed follow! Indeed, Satan, Enmity delights in waging wars; for it excites the worst passion of the soul, and then sweeps into eternity its victims steeped in vice and blood. He is true God's opponent! It his nature object to incite the nations to wars against one another; for he can thus divert the minds and hearts of the people from the work of preparation to stand in the day that Christ Jesus returns to ultimate righteous judgments! Satan is very aware that he shall not have a chance to stand in the presence of the mighty God in Christ Jesus' Day! Yes! Satan works through the elements also to garner his harvest of unprepared lost souls.

Obviously; we see this in action in our America's society and elsewhere around the globe taking place daily; causing numerous outcries! He has studied the secrets of the laboratories of nature, and he uses all his power to control the elements as far as God allows him; like he did to Job. But it never worked! God allows him with limit. Satan is very weak in the eyes of God. For this reason, every true born again Christian possesses great and firm hope and trust in Christ Jesus the solid rocky! And all other ground is sinking sand! **Satan, Enmity:** When he was suffered to afflict and torture Job, how quickly flocks and herds, servants, houses, children, were swept away, one trouble succeeding another as in a moment! He really enjoyed seeing all that Job had all disappeared with immediate effect; he caused it because he envied Job's peace life-style; comfort and prosperity! Satan lacking what Job had been given by the mighty God the giver of all goodness. Job did not break God's perfect Law! **[Decalogue].**

It is God that shields Abraham; and all his creatures, and hedges them all from the power of Enmity hostiles, hatred, and the destroyer of every God's goodness on earth! Observe obedience in the eyes of God your maker: He shields you from all evil power. But the Christian world has shown contempt for the perfect Law of the Lord our God; and the Lord God does just what he has declared early from Bereshith: "I put Enmity between you and the woman!" [Gen 3: 15] that God would do every part of it in the fulfillment of the Lord Jesus Christ the ultimate righteous judgments. His rewards, and blessings on earth in his hands for those who are well prepared to stand before his presence. Yes! Jesus Christ is inevitable: He shall return! Christians why linger? God withdraws his blessings from the earth and remove his protecting care from those who are rebelling against his perfect Law, and teaching and forcing others to do the same like Satan. Satan Enmity, hostility; hatred has control of all whom God does not especially guard. His restraint order is removed. God will favor and prosper some in order to further his own designs and he will bring trouble upon those who lead men to believe that it is God who is afflicting them. No! God does not operate like that: He protects those who obey and keep his perfect Law to heart. See what he did to Abraham and Job. He will do to anyone what he did to Abraham and Job. Abraham and Job walked with God and blameless. These true biblical evidence. God shows no partiality. Do you or will you agree? Enmity is true with its full surrounding all atmosphere. It is impossible to resolve! It is instinct and tendency to every individual mind and heart. No escape. You are born with it. [Ps. 51: 3-5]. Enmity hangs on all!

Even now, Enmity is at work henceforth! In accidents and calamities by air; by land; by sea and in great conflagrations, in fierce tornadoes and terrific hailstorms, in tempests wind in which Jonah attempt to escape from the presence of God, floods, cyclones, tidal waves; and earthquakes; in every place around the globe you name it: Enmity is overwhelming surrounding all! Man broke God's perfect Law it is unforgivable! Judgment must prevail upon all men on earth! Is Satan really exercising his power? He sweeps away the ripening harvest, and famine and distress follow. Don't we experience these things daily? Who has the power to resolve Enmity? God imposed it: He has the power to resolve it. No one else! It all makes sense! Will you agree? You will not agree because it is written: "For the mind that is set on the flesh is Enmity; hostiles to God, for it does not submit to God's **Law; indeed, it cannot! Those who are in the flesh will never, never please neither!"** Enmity!

Enmity, hostiles is the key issue: And it remains unresolved till Christ Jesus returns! [Rom 8: 6-8]. The Bible has all the answers: But who dares to submit to God's Law? The subject is very old. Everyone else is trapped into his/hers own specific birdcage. "I'm safe here!" "Mind your business!" "It is my freedom!" "I choose what I like!" "It is my right!" So much to claim but so much less to be done to please God your maker: There are exceptionally few men mentioned in the Bible who pleased God and walked with God and blameless. There aren't many! Old and New Testament. The most well-known and popular men in the Old Bible are: Noah: Job: and Abraham. These men walked with God and blameless. Indeed, they submitted to God's perfect Law in its complete. They had their personal problems but God shielded them in protection. Nothing could hinder their human weakness. God assured Abraham: "Do not be afraid Abraham; I am your shield!" [Gen 15: 1]. God said. Will you agree? Yes! God is a shield to those who submit to His perfect Law. What else the author can tell you? It is not argument but excellent divine teachings comes to you. Look at yourself. What do you see on your face? Your conscience; does it pleases God and walk with God and blameless? Relationship with God, it is very personally. Check it out!

These personal relationship, visitations are to become more and more frequent and disastrous. Destructions will be upon the inhabitants of the world. The Enmity or the beast Satan of the field will groan, and the earth will languish. Stick and hang up to God in Christ Jesus your solid rocky. And then the great deliver will persuade men that those who serve God are causing these evils. The modern class that have provoked the displeasure of heavens will charge all their troubles upon the faithful few whom the Lord Jesus Christ has sent to them with perfect messages of warning and reproof. Believe them: It will be declared that the people and nations are offending God by violation of his perfect Law; that Enmity sinful nature has brought calamities which will not cease till Christ returns. God's perfect Law those who truly observe shall be strictly enforced, and that those who present the claims of the perfect Law Decalogue, thus destroying reverence law, are troubles of the nations, preventing its restoration to divine favor and temporal prosperity. Thus the accusation urged of ancient against the servant of God will be repeated, and upon grounds equally well established. And it came to pass when Ahab saw Elijah that Ahab said to him; Are you that who troubled Israel? And Elijah answered Ahab: "I have not troubled Israel, but you and your father's household in that you have forsaken the Decalogue, the Ten Commandments of the Lord God perfect Law; and you have followed Balaam and worshiped. See [1 Kings 18: 17-18]. Ahab remains speechless at hearing Elijah' truth from the mouth of God Almighty. That day; Elijah judged Ahab including all Balaam false-prophets. 450 were slaughtered by one single sword from Elijah' hand. Did Ahab know?

As the wrath of the peoples shall be excited by false charges, they will pursue a course toward God's true messengers very similar to that which apostate Israel pursued toward Elijah. God remains the same and no change. He is the God of yesterday and today is the day. [Mal. 3: 6]: "For I am the Lord, I do not change." [Heb. 13: 8]. God never changes! True messages will come from the Spirit that has sent them to warn the rejecters of God's perfect Law that they are in error; and that the man's made laws should be obeyed as the perfect Law of God. They will lament the great wickedness in the world, and second the testimony of man's made religious teachers, that the degraded state of morals is cause by the desecration of God's Law. Great will be the indignation excited against all who refuse to accept their true testimony. This book is well written from Scriptures references not from the author's thoughts!. It is not science fiction ebook. It is well researched and well scholarly written textbook. No faking Scriptures. It unveils every individual's daily living Conscience; unmatched selection from the Bible text.

Those who honor the Bible, they also honor God in Christ Jesus to heart. They will be denounced as the enemies of the law and order, as breaking down in the moral restraints of society, causing anarchy and corruption, and calling down the judgment of God upon the earth! This is nothing news! Their conscientious scruples will be pronounced obstinacy, stubbornness, profligate, and grotesque, and contempt of authority. Very unpleasant phrases, but it is obviously truth!

They will be accused of disaffection toward the religion and the government. Ministers and laymen who deny the obligation of the true divine Law will present from the pulpit the duty of yielding obedience to the civil authorities as ordained of God. In the legislative halls and courts of justice, commandments-keepers will be censured and misrepresented. A malicious false coloring will be given to their words; the worst possible construction will be put upon their motives! There are several man's made Protestant churches who have rejected the clear Scriptural arguments in defense of God's Law, and they long to stop the mouths of those whose faith they cannot overthrow by the Bible. Like Martin Luther who overthrow the pontiff Rome by the true Bible the word of God.

Though they blind their own eyes to the fact, they are now adopting a course which will lead them to the persecution of those who conscientiously refuse to do what the rest of the Christian world are doing, and acknowledge the claims of the pontiff Rome. Indeed, history repeats itself constantly. Enmity will persist! The dignitaries of Church and State will unite to bribe; persuade; or compel all modern classes to honor man's made laws rather than God's perfect Law. As long as the science fiction ebook continues gaining its sale strength, many people will be drawn to it unaware about the severe impending consequences that Enmity surrounds them in their midst!. There are many people who do not know or heard anything about this phrase; Enmity which is found in the Old Testament. In my research 100% never heard about this phrase before or understand its meaning by its definition. Showing them the Scriptures reference most of them were shocked!. [Gen 3: 15]. And yet they are Christians. Early; we stated that there is 1.2 billion world Christian record!. Yet most of them never heard this phrase Enmity. 100%. Our land and the rest of the world is in jeopardy! This book possesses great message to the whole entire world! Enmity it is the biggest unmatched audible selected Picture Theme to show the whole world! It is true: God placed Enmity between the Serpent and the Woman Eve: Because they both broke God's most perfect Law!. Since then Enmity stands in its full action till this day!. For the word of God is living and active!. It never ceases its function! [Heb 4: 12].

The time is absolute drawing on its legislators shall so abjure the principles of Protestantism as to give countenance to pontiff Rome apostasy. The people for whom God has so marvelously wrought, strengthening them to throw out the galling yoke of the early popery, will by a national act give vigor to the corrupt faith of Protestant and pontiff Rome, and thus arouse the tyranny which only waits for a touch to start again into awful cruelty and despotism. With rapid steps are we already approaching this period? When Protestant churches shall seek the support of the secular world power, thus following the example of that apostate church, for opposing which their ancestors-the reformers endured the fiercest persecution, then will there be a national apostasy which will end in national ruin!.

While Enmity still stands with its full strength? 1.2 billion World Christians record: Is that a small number or large number to consider? Yet 100% never heard or know anything about this phrase Enmity the Biggest Picture Theme: The world ought to hear and know!. Will you agree?

The suspected Mount Sinai where God handed Moses the Decalogue: Ten Commandments. See Exodus 20, 32, 33.]

The last few meters of the climb up

Oh Men of Modern

Secular World!

Oh Men of Modern Secular World! Earthiest! Pagan! You who afflict; conflict; kills; and oppose all that is called of God!. Christians who truly proclaim and write the word of God in Christ of truth; and build up bridges to connect the people around the whole entire world to magnify the Lord God in Christ Jesus who came down from heaven to gather together all peoples like mighty eagle gathers her wee chicks under her mighty wings but you are not willing!

The Lord God Almighty sent to you Christ Jesus to proclaim the most perfect words of truth from heaven Wisdom: Signs: Performed wonderful miracles: Still you rejected all the good things he taught and performed for your benefit!. Eventually, you killed him in cold blood including all those who followed after him!

And so upon you will come all the righteous blood that has been shed on earth, from the blood of righteous Abel to the blood of Zechariah son of Berechiah whom you murdered between the temple and the Altar; [Gen 4: 8; Matt. 23: 35-36].

You snakes viper! Backbiters! Malice! You brood of vipers! How will you escape being condemned to hell of fierce fire? Repent! And bear good fruits before Christ returns!. How often Christ have longed to gather your children together as the hen gathers her wee chicks under her wings. For Christ Jesus said:

"Look, your house is left to you desolate: For I tell you," Christ said: "You will not see Me no more until you say: "Blessed is he who comes in the name of the Lord!" [Matt. 23: 36-39].

Truth that magnifies the Lord God Almighty in Christ Jesus who came down from heaven to build bridges to connect all people around the world, and to promote his gospel through the word of truth from his holy mouth to the whole entire world!.

We truly believe that through the earnest written word; publication of truth Christian books: Christ Jesus and his words will be exalted, believers will be strengthened in their walk with Christ and the lost souls will be directed to the Lord Christ Jesus as the only way to eternal salvation!. [John 14: 6].

Enmity causes us to build walls that block/disconnect us and separate many Christians around the world! Those well skilled journalists who are confined into the scholasticism write Christian Science fiction ebooks to disconnect many people around the world today! They are anti-Christ authors! They build walls to separate or block many people around the world, like those walls of West Berlin which separated families and the rest of Europe continent since 1960's to 2000. The issue created the whole Europe's catastrophic.

In Christ there are bridges that connect the whole world to God Almighty when he returns!. He is the only of our hopes!. Jesus Christ is inevitable! If individuals and humanity are to progress; Jesus Christ is inescapable! You ignore him at your own wicked risk.

A Consistent Enmity within the family of Abraham starts early before Esau and Jacob were born: Struggles was resumed in their mother's womb: [Gen 25: 23].

Mal. 1: 2-3:

"Was not Esau Jacob' brother? Yet I have loved Jacob, but Esau I have hated." God said.

Gen 25: 23:

"Two nations are in your womb: Two peoples shall be separated from your body: One shall be stronger than the other: And the older shall server the younger." God said to Rebekah the wife of Isaac. Language translations:

- "I am weary."   [NKJV]
- "I am famished."   [NIV] Gen 25: 30. Esau birthright.

You have wearied the Lord with your words; "How have we wearied him?" You ask: By saying: "All who do evil [Enmity] are good in the eyes of the Lord God; and he is pleased with them," or where is the God of justice?" [Mal. 2: 17]: Parallel links with [Isaiah 5: 20].

"Woe to those who call evil good, and good evil; who put darkness for light, and light for darkness; who put bitter for sweet, and sweet for bitter!'

Early in Gen 25: 23: Enmity in the family of Isaac is foretold by the Lord God before the twins sons were born, God knows the zerah he planted into the womb of Rebekah, the wife of Isaac, the son of Abraham. It's all taking place in the family. The same phrase used with same meaning: "I am weary," "I am famished," meaning, "I am really about to die with hungry!" Hunger is the cause of weakness because the stomach is empty, no fuel burning the flesh or energy. For God designed both the fuel of burning spirit and the fuel of burning flesh. So Esau was desperate for food that satisfies the flesh rather than the food of the spirit that satisfies the spirit. The spiritual fuel that burns continually. Esau was lacking this fuel of the eternal Spirit. According to the Scriptures, God loved Jacob but hated Esau. Is God wrong? Jesus too was famished but he was filled with Spirit fuel.

Isaac loved Esau; but Rebekah loved Jacob: Are they wrong?

Husband and wife; Isaac and Rebekah. Both are the product of Esau and Jacob. Now who is the winner? God. He is the Creator of them all! He planted the zerah, seed and enables its growth to produce good fruits. According to the Scriptures: None of us can/will fully understand how God works. To every soul will come the searching test from the Lord when Christ returns. Shall I obey God rather than man? God's Law I shall obey! Will you agree?

The deceive hour is even now at hand: Are our feet planted on the solid rock of God in Christ Jesus? Are we all well prepared to stand firm in defense of the Decalogue, the Law the Ten Commandments of God and the faithful of Christ Jesus fully when he returns; destroyed their hopes and our hopes as if he had not foretold or warned them before-hand about the fearful of Decalogue, the Law. So in the prophecies, the future as it was opened to the disciple, Orthodox Judaism, early century pontiff Rome, and church reformers and all who live by the words of the Lord God in Christ Jesus even today of our modern era.

The events connected with the close probation and the work of preparation for the time of troubles like today's troubles around the world, are clearly brought to our eyes and ears for complete view. But multitudes have no more understanding of these important truths than if they had never been revealed or foretold beforehand. **The same wheel keeps on moving till Christ returns! While the peoples remain in their stiff-neck as ever!**

It was like that in the days of Noah; Sodom; Nineveh; and Egypt: Sihon and Og; two kings of the Amorites, God surprised them all!. [Josh 2: 10-11]. Will you agree?